15-6

A LONG WAY FROM
SILVER CREEK

A LONG WAY FROM
SILVER CREEK

A FAMILY MEMOIR

Margaret Gee

Published by Margaret Gee
PO Box 221, Double Bay NSW 1360, Australia
Tel: (02) 9365 3266 Fax: (02) 9365 3168
Email: margaretgee2@bigpond.com

First published 2000

National Library of Australia Cataloguing-in-Publication entry
Gee, Margaret
A long way from Silver Creek:
A family memoir

ISBN 1 875574 39 5

Design and print management:
Reno Design Group, Sydney R20055
Designer: Graham Rendoth
Printing: Griffin Press
Distribution: Gary Allen Pty Ltd, Sydney
Publishing manager: Sardine Waters
Fox illustration: Jon Hawley

Please note: Some of the names in this book have been changed
to protect the privacy of individuals.

DEDICATION

In loving memory of my parents Kath and Allan,
and for my brother Bruce and twin sister Christine

My deepest gratitude and respect to all
who served on HMAS Perth and for those brave souls,
the POWs on the Burma Railway

A donation from sales of this book will be given to
The Royal Victorian Institute for the Blind and Legacy

CONTENTS

FOREWORD

Writing a family memoir is like assembling a trillion piece jigsaw. All the characters, events and places you are trying to link seem to have been scattered to the four winds. It is at best a mercurial exercise, chasing the past and never quite catching up.

A Long Way From Silver Creek has been a challenging journey, assembling a mountain of letters, photographs, transcripts, and countless hours of phone calls, interviews and reminiscences. This book is not in any sense a formal autobiographical account of my family. It is probably best described as an impressionistic memoir. There are dozens of anecdotes gathered from family and friends who

Allan Gee.
(Drawing by
Ulf Kaiser)

knew my parents Allan and Kath, and their respective families. It also records my own memories of growing up on a farm at Wooragee, North Eastern Victoria near the historic gold mining town of Beechworth, in the heart of Kelly country.

Of particular interest to me was writing about my father's early life in picturesque Silver Creek, the Depression years, and his life in the Navy, especially his time in *HMAS Perth* which was tragically sunk in the Sunda Strait in March 1942 with enormous loss of life.

The surviving *Perth* men who were kind enough to share their anecdotes and official accounts made that critical part of the story possible. Sincere thanks to Gavin Campbell, Danny Riordan, Julius 'Judy' Patching AO OBE, Jim Nelson, Frank McGovern, George Jones, Charlie 'Jock' Lawrance, Al Parker, Ray Hegarty, and Allan 'Skeeter' Bishop OAM. Alan Lawrance, Jock's son has been exceptionally helpful and is dedicated to sustaining the spirit of *Perth*. 'Even though it is close to 60 years since *Perth* was sunk, she was such a proud ship that she is still very much alive in the minds of those who served in her.'

But what ultimately shaped my father's destiny were those dark days of his years on the infamous Burma Railway. Other prisoners of war who knew my father during that ordeal have been extremely generous with their time and their invaluable reminiscences. Special mention must be made of my father's close *Perth* and POW friends John 'Macca' McQuade, and Percy Partington. Sincere thanks are due to Captain Knocker White for sharing his story about the night *Perth* was sunk, and the inimitable Ray Parkin, an award winning author and outstanding maritime painter.

Heartfelt appreciation to *Perth* and *Rakuyo Maru* survivor and Burma Railway POW Bob Collins for his extensive recollections, including the truth about *Perth's* cat Redlead. Thanks to Bob I also now know what 'a bottle', 'a greenie', 'in the rattle', and 'under nourishment and stoppage of cheese' means. Thankyou Bob! I also owe a great debt of gratitude to Arthur 'Blood' Bancroft for sharing his remarkable personal story of survival.

Both my dear parents have now passed away. Researching and writing this memoir has in a heart-rending way revealed to me the hardship, my father in particular, endured during the Great Depression and the true extent of his experiences in the Second World War.

I believe my parents were extraordinary, ordinary people unwittingly thrown onto the world stage with the advent of war. Before my Mother died in my arms last year I promised her I would complete this book and tell their story. (Mum died from lung cancer. Don't smoke!). I am enormously grateful to my brother Bruce for spending hours faithfully recounting his version of events, and for my twin sister Christine's invaluable recollections.

My father's wartime experiences are a dominant part of this memoir, because it had such a dramatic effect on his life, and subsequently on our family.

There is also considerable detail about my Mother's family the Brewers, of Leneva. Her sisters Marge, Gwen, twin sister Mary and her last surviving brother Bert provided wonderful material and photographs.

Many family and friends from Wooragee, Beechworth and beyond came forward to share their memories. My cousin Lynette has been exceptionally helpful and supportive. Sincere thanks to both Lyn and her husband Cec Clark of 'Granite Ridge', Wooragee. My cousins Allan Brewer and Allan Gee both named after my father, and Meryl Brown provided many fascinating anecdotes. Thanks also to Marian Brewer, Wilma Gee, Robert Gee and his wife Carol. Vera and Lillian Gee were very helpful, as was my father's last surviving sibling Carmel Warwick.

An extra special thankyou to Alan French who provided invaluable information and history. Thanks also to Lorna French and 'Lucky'. Beechworth, Silver Creek, Stanley and Wooragee residents who generously assisted were Doris Turner, Ken Blake, Michael Sinclair, Alice Adams, Pos Shennan, Grace Irvine, Alec and Jeanette Webster, Geoff Crossman, Frank Blair, Amy Porritt, Neil Whitehead, June Powell, Nancy Dyball, Tess Gladstone, Stan Gladstone, Des Zwar,

Vivienne Harvey, Pat Devery and Judy Snell, Walter Methven, Reg Snell, Doug Malsem, Laurie Christesen, Nola Jarvis, Gwen Buckland of The Beechworth and District Progress Association and Jennifer Wilkinson at Finches Guesthouse. My thanks to the staff at the Burke Museum at Beechworth in particular Scott Jessup and Christine Dormer. Thanks also to John, Pam and Howard LeCouteur, Rex and Trish Forrest.

For marvellous anecdotes about the colourful characters in Beechworth I owe a great debt to our longtime family friend Reg Dixon who was a policeman in the town for 15 years. Thanks also to Reg's wife Maria and sons Alex and John. My gratitude to Rosalyn Shennan for extracts from her excellent book *Silver Threads and Golden Needles*. The late Roy C. Harvey's *Background to Beechworth* was also a vital reference work.

Thankyou to Bryce Courtenay who encouraged me to finish writing this book which I commenced in 1988. Although Bryce never met my father he always believed I had a good story up my sleeve. Max Grant suggested the book's title, and my friend Angela Rubin accompanied me on my trip to the site of the Burma Railway.

I would also like to thank Sandra Florance at the Bega Museum, Kate Boyce from the Moruya Historical Society, Alison Smythe of the Upper Murray Regional Library in Wodonga, the Albury Library, Lynne Daly and the Pictorial Section of the *Border Morning Mail* in Wodonga, Robert Wattson and Kerry-Anne Prideaux of The Woollahra Library, Bill Fogarty, Jillian Brankin, Adela Clayton, Mary John, Bronwyn Myrtle and Matthew Thomson from the Australian War Memorial, Karen Kentwell at the New Zealand High Commission in Canberra, Alan Condon, Sandy Thomas, Jon Hawley, Mrs Pat Packer, Jean Whitla, Kath Goddard, Crispin Hull, Mick and Dot McGuinness, Ulf Kaiser, Fiora Sacco, Doris Bracht, Keith Dunstan, Margaret Partington, Norma Collins, Mirla Bancroft, Betty Patching, Lesley Ann White,

Patricia McQuade, British war artist Jack Chalker, Burma Railway 'Guardian Angel' Rod Beattie, Barry and Maude Hedrick, Julie Wilson, Graham Rendoth of Reno Design and Reyna Matthes.

～

This book would never have been fully realised without the immense love and support of my loyal husband Dr Brent Waters. He also provided skilful editing and computing assistance.

～

Any omissions or errors will be amended in any future edition. Personal comments about individuals in the book were made in the utmost good faith. Our family has a deep affection for the people of Silver Creek, Beechworth, Wooragee and surrounding districts. Comments by friends of my father and former POWs have also been made with a genuine *esprit de corps*. For now, as my father was fond of saying, 'Let's get on with the job.'

PREFACE

A country girl

I consider myself lucky to have been born and bred a country kid, and will probably always think of myself as that, despite decades of living in Melbourne and Sydney. There's something about growing up in the bush which seeps into your skin and your psyche, and permeates your dreams forever.

Frequently my mind wanders back to those undulating, green valleys, lavender blue hills, and gurgling creeks in North Eastern Victoria. Wooragee, Silver Creek, Beechworth, Tarrawingee, Stanley, Chiltern, Milawa, Rutherglen, Wangaratta, Bright, Myrtleford, Yackandandah, Mount Beauty, Baranduda, Albury-Wodonga. These places and the people I knew there are an integral part of my landscape of memory. The natural beauty of these places is indeed a vision splendid.

Clumps of yellow wattle, and dense forests of pine, eucalyptus trees roped with purple sarsparilla, spotted egg and bacon bushes, and inhabited by magpies, currawongs, cockatoos, owls, parrots, galahs, possums, wombats, goannas, kangaroos and wallabies. In our creek there was a huge old tortoise with a ring in its back, and if you were lucky you'd catch a glimpse of a platypus darting under a rock, or the iridescent flash of a swooping kingfisher. Foxes and hares were not an uncommon sight and once dozens of koalas were released in the Woolshed area, and some took up residence on our property.

In winter there was the crunch of morning frost underfoot. 'Jack Frost's about,' my father would say. A robin redbreast perched on a fence, sometimes in falling snow, the paddocks, still and white except for the sheep and cattle sheltering under the trees. A soaring wedge-tailed eagle scanning for a rabbit, pink and grey flocks of galahs, and an echidna lumbering through the undergrowth. The bold colours

A LONG WAY FROM SILVER CREEK

of the bush in autumn, and masses of wildflowers in the spring.

In summer the baking sun and the hot breath of a North wind threatening to turn the whole place into an inferno. Swimming in the creek and sliding down mossy waterfalls, the screech of a million cicadas in the trees and a brown snake in the yellow grass are unforgettable images.

My parents Kath and Allan Gee owned a 238 acre farm at Wooragee a small farming area a few miles out of the historic town of Beechworth. It's bushranger country where gold fever struck in the 1850s and ripped up the surrounding landscape like a giant's plough.

It was a magnet for the thousands of miners and Chinese fortune hunters who descended on the area with their sluice boxes and gold pans. They came and left like an invading army, the brown earth picked clean of treasure, seams of rock smashed and creeks ransacked then abandoned. Some left with riches beyond their wildest dreams, but many got only dirt and despair for their trouble.

Nature is a great healer, and the scars in the valleys, creeks and escarpments which the miners plundered were soon blanketed again by blackberries and bush. But the memories and ghosts of that golden era have lingered, and the legends and folklore remain. It is now the foundation for a booming tourism industry which has saved the town from economic extinction.

Beechworth and the surrounding district is often referred to as Kelly country, the place where Ned, his brother Dan, and the rest of his gang robbed and terrorised the locals, culminating in a violent shootout with the police.

At the back of our place, the Woolshed down the Laserina, was where Joe Byrne shot Aaron Sherritt for dobbing them into the cops. And it was not too far away at Glenrowan where Ned was planning to blow up the train, that the police surrounded the pub and captured him at gunpoint. His legendary armour made by a local smithy saved his life, but he surrendered after surviving a hail of gunfire. Ned was imprisoned in the Beechworth gaol before being moved to Melbourne where he was tried and hanged in 1880, aged 21, but not before famously uttering, 'That's life.'

It was both a beautiful and dramatic environment in which to grow up, a place haunted by the hardship of the early pioneers, the frenzy of the gold-rush, and the notoriety of the bushrangers. A past of blood, sweat and tears, and heartache, but imbued with an indomitable spirit which rose above the deprivations of the Depression, and the ravages of both World Wars, and Vietnam.

I developed an acute awareness of the power of nature, a strong sense that for all the rich harvest of the seasons, at any moment a bushfire, flood, drought, insect plague or disease could destroy everything and reduce generations of hardwork to dust or ashes. There was a bittersweet resolve that nothing could be taken for granted, and in summer we always looked over our shoulder for a wisp of smoke on the horizon.

Country people feel an intrinsic part of their landscape, and are humbled by its awesome ability to make or break them. They tame it with their tractors, bulldozers, fences and fertilisers, but deep down they know their ultimate existence depends on a tenuous thread of hope and luck, and a bank manager who won't pull the plug if things get tough.

So much of country life is about sticking together as a family and community, not giving up and surviving against the odds. Helping out when a fire threatens to engulf your livelihood, staying up all night to get the hay in the shed before the storm arrives, and sheltering baby lambs before they freeze to death from an unexpected snowfall. It's how country people come through the scourge of a rabbit plague, milk fever, or just no rain.

You go down the creek to fix the water pump on a boiling day in December and a 'Joe Blake' takes you on, the bull gets bogged in the dam and nearly drowns, or just when you feel you're ahead the sheep price crashes, and you're stony broke. Talk of the romance of country life will bring a wry grin and a shake of the head to any cockie. But at the end of the day there's talk around the kitchen table, a hearty dinner, a yarn in the pub and a few laughs. That's what the bush is all about. In fact sometimes the worse it is the more country people seem to love it. Because for all the heartache there is a sense of freedom and of being part of an exquisitely beautiful bigger picture.

My father Allan always said you needed a big heart to live on the land. 'There's never any peace, and there's always more work to be done, but this is Paradise to me.' He loved our farm, 'Lyndale', which he shared with my mother for nearly 30 years because he was living his dream. A poor boy from Silver Creek, a small hamlet three miles out of Beechworth, where as a child he lived on rabbits, blackberries and homemade bacon, and walked miles to school with his shoes around his neck to make them last.

He survived one of the most formidable sea battles in Australian Naval history, the sinking of *HMAS Perth*, and the horror of the Burma Railway and the POW camps for three years. His saving grace was that he arrived home to marry his sweetheart Kath, my mother. He was mentally traumatised, broke and nearly blind but still clinging to his quest to go onto the land.

The farm was his rock solid symbol of freedom, control of his destiny for the first time in his difficult life, and the joy of the wide open spaces instead of the hell-holes of Java and Burma.

My father was passionate about birds, and had a sign on the main gate into our property, 'Gee's Place. Shooters will be shot on sight.'

God help anyone who was game enough to try to bag any of his wild ducks. In spite of his 'dead eyes' as he called them, he was never happier than when he was wrestling fence posts into the ground, stretching wire from one end of the property to the other, planting pine trees, fixing the dogs' fleas, drenching and crutching sheep, branding cattle, baling hay, checking the dams, painting and hammering and doing whatever was necessary to make the farm viable.

He didn't have a lazy bone in his body and neither did my mother. In every respect she was his right hand, and frequently his eyes. She had to do all of the driving, farm accounts, as well as caring, shopping, cooking and washing for all of us. She was also living with a man who was terribly traumatised by his wartime experiences, and although very loving, he was not always easy to be around. She loved him fiercely, and no matter how tough the day was they'd put the kettle on, have a cuppa, and for many years a cigarette, and talk things out.

My mother's own childhood growing up on a large property with eight siblings was a good apprenticeship for the myriad experiences of life at 'Lyndale' My twin sister Christine and I helped as much as we could, as did my older brother Bruce, before he went away to school in his teens.

I had an intense love of the bush and was forever rambling around the property, collecting wildflowers. Little billy buttons, blue pin-cushions, delicate green hoods, tiger, leopard and spider orchids, chocolate flowers, milk maids, golden everlastings and buttercups. I had an enormous butterfly collection expanded with a few dried lizards, praying mantises and stick insects, wasps, assorted moths, pine cones, chips of quartz and amethyst, feathers, birds' eggs, mounds of beetles and tufts of rabbit fur.

I was the Tom boy in the family, and relished going rabbiting with boys from the town, or being outside with my father, although that often meant assisting with tasks which would turn the stomach of the average city kid.

Dead pigs, ducks, chooks, rabbits, snakes, dogs, cats, sheep, flies, maggots, and blood. At times when I was a kid I felt as if I was swimming in it. If you harbour the illusion that farm life is comprised of rainbows, fluffy sheep dotted on hillsides, and home-made scones and strawberry jam read no further.

PART 1

Silver Creek

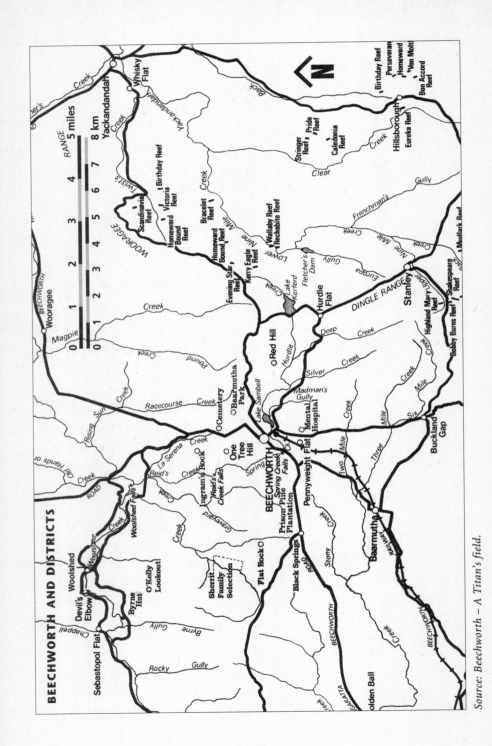

BEECHWORTH AND DISTRICTS

Source: Beechworth – A Titan's field.

20

1

A FIERCE
INDEPENDENCE

The Gee family

The name Gee originated from Gee Cross, a prosperous village near
Stockport, Cheshire. The Gee side of my family are descended from
James Gee, a transported convict born in Eckington, Derbyshire in
1817. At the age of 15 he was sentenced to seven years for house-
breaking, and allegedly stealing fowls. He sailed from Sheerness
aboard 'The Camden' on September 22, 1832 and arrived at the port of
Sydney on February 18, 1833. Described as 'a cutler's boy', he was 5ft
6in tall, with light brown hair, brown eyes, and a ruddy pock-pitted
complexion. He was sent to Carter's Barracks, a 'home of correction for
boys' where he trained as a blacksmith. The punishment meted out
there was either the treadmill or the lash. Already a perceptive and
ambitious boy, James' behaviour was described as 'very good'.

In 1834 James was granted a Ticket Of Leave and went to work for
John Hawdon at 'Kiora', a property in the Moruya district of New
South Wales. He was in charge of the horses on Hawdon's famous first
overland cattle drive to South Australia, an arduous journey of three
months herding 340 restless beasts.

James Gee settled on the south bank of the Moruya River about 1842 and left for
Bega about 1855. Vulcan Street was named for his smithy.
From: *Eurobodalla History of the Moruya District* by H.J. Gibbn

James was granted his pardon in 1839, and established a blacksmith's shop at Moruya. Blacksmiths were referred to as vulcaners, a name derived from Vulcan, the Roman God of fire and metal-working. On August 1, 1840 James Gee married Janet Robertson McKinnon, whose Highland family had arrived in Australia in 1835, from Glasgow, Scotland aboard the vessel 'Brilliant'.*

In 1855 James took up land in the first block of allotments sold at nearby Bega. James and Janet Gee's living children were George, William, John, Agnes, Nathaniel, Catherine, Hugh, and Thomas. Three other children died in infancy. James died of hepatitis in 1865 aged 48 years. His wife Janet died of 'general paralysis' at Tarraganda, Bega in 1912 aged 90.

James' third son John, a farmer of Dry River, Cobargo, married Georgina Smith Cowdroy of Wagonga, near Moruya, on May 30, 1876. Tragically Georgina lived only 25 years. Her great, great grandfather, William Cowdroy was the first proprietor of the 'Manchester Gazette'. Georgina's father Alfred Cowdroy, originally from Drogheda, County Louth, Ireland was the postmaster at Wagonga, for 20 years.

Georgina and John Gee had four children Alfred, John, Janet and the youngest Napier, born at Dry River, on March 13, 1882. Napier Cowdroy Gee was the father of my father Allan Gee. John Gee, my great grandfather, died in 1929 aged 81.

In 1988 I asked my father to record his life story. Because he was blind he dictated into a tape recorder. I was astonished when I first read the transcript. Parts of his story reminded me of 'A Fortunate Life', Albert Facey's book about the Depression years. I joked with my father that perhaps we should publish his memoir entitled, 'An Unfortunate Life'.

Dad died in Albury on August 17, 1992 from cancer. He was 72. To his words I have added those of other family members and friends.

DAD: I was born on October 10, 1919 at Beechworth in a house owned by Matron Dowling, who was the local midwife. I was the fifth of six children. There was Napier, Bramwell, Miriam, Carmel, Me and Lewis.

---

* During the course of the marriage James and Janet Gee accused each in court of attempting to poison the other with strychnine.

Many of the children of my vintage were born at her home which was more or less like a private hospital. The house is still there, as is the lovely old gum-tree out the front which is more than 150 years old. Her home was also the site of the town's first Council meetings.

I was born in Beechworth because my parents, who were Salvation Army Officers, happened to be stationed there at the time. My father said he heard a cry at my birth and his heart leapt for joy. If he had known the problems that I would create later on he may not have been that happy.

My mother Alice Haywood was born in 1884 at a place called Lal Lal near Ballarat in Victoria. Her family, were also pioneers. They knew how tough life could be, and were always prepared to work hard to try and lift themselves out of the mire.

UNCLE BRAMWELL [*Dad's brother*]: Mum's family were very intelligent people. I believe there were 14 Haywood kids including our mother Alice, but that only she and two others, Emma and Henry survived into adulthood. They were terribly poor and lived out of town. They were quite religious, but not in any sort of evangelical way. I remember I once met my old grandmother on my mother's side. She was a good old soul.

DAD: My father was born in 1882 in the Bega area where his family were some of the first settlers. His mother rode 50 miles by horse from somewhere up in the mountains of Bombala to where the midwife was. She died giving birth to him. He had two older brothers, John and Alf and an older sister, Janet. According to stories we were told, my grandfather married again to Annie Venus, and had a further nine children! (Annie Venus had wet-nursed my father, Napier Gee). His second wife's family had pretty big land holdings including two stations. Later on I heard their properties were acquired by a large consortium called 'King Ranch', which was an American owned business that bought up huge tracts of land in the district, especially in the 1850s-60s. In the mid-sixties my brother Lewis took Dad up to the area. They hoped to have a look at the old property, but there was a sign which said 'Keep Out'.

Napier and Alice Gee in a gig at Silver Creek

I was told that after my grandfather re-married his first family were more or less squeezed out by the stepmother. Luckily they were brought up by their maternal grandmother who apparently looked after them fairly well. To survive, my father and his siblings shot possums and kangaroos for skins. They were all great rifle shots. The only memory I have of Dad talking about those times is telling us how they played a lot of cricket, with a bat made out of sticks and the ball carved from a sucker off a gum-tree. I have a photograph of he and his two brothers at school.

Uncle John worked on the trams in Sydney. He came to visit us in Silver Creek in about 1934, and it was a happy time because Dad and his brother were obviously very close. Auntie Janet lived in a fancy house in Mosman in Sydney.

MERYL BROWN [*Auntie Miriam and Uncle Bert's daughter*]: Grandfather Gee's sister Janet from Sydney loved to punt. She adored going to the horse races. Auntie Janet was a delightful person, very gentle.

The Salvation Army Corps was opened in Beechworth on March 17, 1884, its first officer being Captain Phillips. A year later on September 28, 1885, the Barracks was opened. Since then the Salvation Army has continued to play its part in the life of our town, assisted always by the liberal support of its citizens.

A BACKGROUND TO BEECHWORTH BY ROY C. HARVEY [P 40]

DAD: I'm not exactly sure which year my father joined the Army, but it would have been 1907 or 1908, or even earlier. In those days it would have been considered worse than joining the Communist Party because the Salvos didn't enjoy the popularity they do today. My mother was born into a very conservative Church of England family. It must have been a great shock to the rest of her family when she converted to the Army, although her eldest brother Henry was in the Army and I believe he had encouraged her. I think my parents both joined the Army about the same time. They had a genuine calling to do what they described as 'the Lord's work'.

Under the colours: Army Comrades United for Service
Captain Napier Gee and Captain Alice Haywood, Kilkenny, SA

The announcement of a Hallelujah wedding caused quite a stir in the district, and people were anxious to watch proceedings. The bridal party, led by Lieut-Colonel Coin, walked on to the platform amidst many cheers. The Colonel started the meeting with the rousing song, 'Come Let Us Join Our Cheerful Songs.' Prayer followed. Brother L. Garnaut, Treasurer of the Corps spoke of the good work which had been accomplished during the term of Captain Haywood. Mrs Adjut. Drew spoke on behalf of the Lassie Officers in the South Australian Division. The bride and bridegroom then stood with the colours over them, whilst the Colonel performed the pleasing ceremony of the occasion, and amidst the prayer of the interested congregation pronounced them man and wife. The bridegroom was supported by Captain Mann, who next spoke on his behalf, and added to this talk a witty little incident. The meeting closed with prayers that God would richly bless and prosper the union. The bridal party proceeded to the marquee outside where refreshments were provided.

FROM *THE WAR CRY* FEBRUARY 8, 1913

ALLAN GEE [*Uncle Nape's son*]: Grandad rode around his flock in South Australia on an old motor-bike. He once told me, 'I pushed the darn thing more than I rode it.'

ALLAN BREWER [*Auntie Miriam and Uncle Bert's son*]: My mother was born at Moonta in South Australia on Christmas Day, 1917 and

Uncle Nape, christened Napier Haywood Gee, was born on January 21, 1914 nearby at Hawker. Grandfather and Nana Gee had met there and were preaching for the Salvation Army at the time. They later moved from South Australia to Silver Creek.

DAD: As children, we had religion taught to us from early morning until late at night. My parents never went dancing or sang anything except hymns, and there were always prayers before bedtime. They conducted what were called cottage meetings in either our house or other peoples' homes which was really a form of proselytizing.

The big dream of our parents was that all of us kids would somehow follow them into the Army, but only Bram (Bramwell) did. They were constantly telling us about how important it was for us to be saved. Somehow I never received any great enlightenment and never cracked at any of their cottage meetings.

This night August 19, 1911, I Captain Gee N.C. has reconsecrated myself to God, and the Salvation Army in the name of our Lord Jesus Christ, at the Army Penitent Farm, Riverton (South Australia). Heavy crosses, tears of pain. By thy grace I will follow thee.
INSCRIPTION IN THE FRONT OF MY FATHER'S BIBLE

I'll never forget the night when Bram became truly converted. It was during the time that Dad was working at the pine plantations at the back of Beechworth. Dad had had some of his workmates from there staying with us. After dinner his mates sneaked out the back for a couple of bottles of beer, as Mum and Dad were strict teetotallers. Suddenly Bram walked into the kitchen all dressed up. My parents said, 'Where are you going?' 'I'm going into the Army,' he answered and went off to a cottage meeting on this bitterly cold stormy night. He came home later and announced to my exultant parents that he had formally joined the Salvation Army. He was 15 or 16 years old.

Bram became a very active Salvationist, wore a uniform and worked at the Beechworth Tannery until he left to attend the Salvation Army training college. He became a Lieutenant and stuck with it for a while, but later he joined the Presbyterian church. At times he left the church to start up businesses. Bram could turn his hand at anything. A man called Chris Morley convinced him to attend Ormond College in Melbourne and become a fully fledged Reverend. Whichever parish he was in, he would end up being the bandmaster, and he was well known in musical circles. Somewhere along the way he and his wife Lillian, of Welsh parentage also owned a cake shop in Box Hill. They had a dog they adored called Rex.

LILLIAN GEE [*Bram's wife*]: Bram was a Presbyterian Minister for over 40 years. While he was a student at Ormond College, he preached at Campbellfield. He could play any musical instrument and sang beautifully. He was also the orchestra leader when we were based at Mildura. When Bram and I were first married we lived with his parents at Silver Creek. They were extremely hard working people. I sang at Allan and Kath's wedding in 1946. We transferred to Sydney and then we went to Henty, NSW for four and a half years. Bram had a kidney removed there and took a 12 month break. He was almost 83 years old when he died in 1999 — I miss him terribly.

DAD: Most of the religious people of those times were Salvation Army, Methodists or Baptists. They were extremely good people but often rather narrow in their views. Basically Mum and Dad thought that things would only get better when they got to 'the other side'. They said that there were no green valleys in life, just like the old Welsh mining people believed.

On Sunday the locals converged on the Silver Creek cricket ground to play cricket and collect water in kerosene tins from the beautiful deep well. My father sometimes reprimanded them for breaking the Sabbath. I think some people thought we were a bit strange.

When I was older I always tried to get out of going into the Salvation Army for the 11 o'clock worshipping and afternoon Sunday School. I preferred to stay home in the bush. Sometimes in springtime after church Dad would take us up into the glorious Mopoke Ranges and tell us stories of when he was a boy growing up in the Bega area. He told us how to shoot possums and about the aboriginals living in the area.

He said the aboriginals told him how foolish the whiteman was for killing everything in sight, rather than only what they needed for food. Dad was convinced the aboriginals had superior knowledge to the white farmers about nature. He also told us how many aboriginals died because the church people made them wear clothes. They weren't used to clothes, and wore them wet after it rained, so many died of pneumonia, and later from measles epidemics. He said some of the farmers wanted to remove the aboriginals from the land, and offered them what they called 'a free feed' which was flour laced with strychnine. Dad was appalled at this inhumanity.

AUNTIE CARMEL [*Dad's sister*]: Mum was a wonderful cook and a very practical person. Dad had a brilliant mind. In a different time he could have done anything. During the Depression we were never hungry and never cold. We always had plenty to eat because they had cows, chickens, and of course endless rabbits. They had the fires going all the time in the kitchen and in what was the dining room. They put hot bricks into the beds at night to keep us warm.

Both my parents encouraged us to read and to be individuals. They were very decent, hardworking people, and never had anything to be ashamed of. They brought us up the same. Most kids those days were out working at 14, not like today where they are so pampered.

MG: Auntie Carmel worked as a nurse and retired as Matron of the Port Fairy Hospital where she still lives today.

VERA GEE [*Uncle Napier's wife*]: Alice Gee was a small woman, but very hardworking. She was always a lady, and very polite, but she had a bad heart. Mr. Gee was a wonderful preacher with a big strong voice. He loved to tell our boys stories about when he got his first gun or how he trapped or shot rabbits, and they could never beat him at draughts. He was very widely read and could speak on any topic.

ALICE ADAMS [*A family friend*]: Mrs Gee was a gorgeous black-haired lady who wore glasses. She was a good communicator and nice to everyone. As a child, my mother Mrs Myra McGuigan and I used to get wood from them at Silver Creek. Mr Gee was a stout man and a thorough gentleman.

DAD: My earliest memory is of seeing my Uncle Alf frying eels in a pan, which probably dates from when I was about three years old. By that time we must have moved to Wangaratta on a Salvation Army posting.

Because they had six children the Army paid my parents some sort of a stipend. It wouldn't have been much because the Army was totally dependent on donations from their followers. The powers that be in the Army were very reassuring to my father that he was doing a good job and would be looked after. He was an Officer and my mother was an Adjutant. They were both very trusting people. Instead of staying with the Army for a full 20 years when they would have been entitled to a small pension, my father left after 17 years service for economic and health reasons, so they were denied the pension. They simply couldn't survive on this meagre income, and my mother was badly consumptive. That is, she suffered from tubercerlosis which at the time was highly infectious. Since most of their work involved visiting people, the Army deemed her to be a health risk. Perhaps this was the real reason for their leaving.

UNCLE BRAM: The Salvation Army should have been shot for what they did to Mum and Dad. In my view they were thrown out because they had too many kids. The Army just didn't want to pay them the allowance any more. So they sent them to more and more remote postings hoping Dad would leave voluntarily, which in the end he did. He was treated shamefully. The Army gave them no help whatsoever, but they both still loved the Army and talked about nothing else — how much they missed the work and the great sacrifices they made for us kids. It must have been immensely difficult for them to be thrown out in the cold cruel world on the brink of the Depression with six children to feed. But they were good people, free of bitterness, and they remained dedicated to the Army for the rest of their lives.

DAD: It was a very difficult time in my father's life because he was born in 1882 and left the Army in 1925, aged only 43 years. He must have felt as if he was on the scrap heap.

About that time we lived in a little house in Wangaratta directly behind the Roman Catholic Church, and my father was working as a fettler with the railways. I recall nursing my brother Lew (Lewis) just after he was brought home from the hospital. He was four and a half years younger than me. I also recall being at Wangaratta's Merriwa Park, in the old band rotunda, which is still there. I must have found a beer bottle somewhere and broken it, because I fell down the steps and landed on the broken glass. I ended up with three stitches in my arm which caused great consternation.

I can remember the day Mum brought Lewis home from the hospital. We were all sitting around the open fire in the little sitting room, all so excited about our new baby. The boys wanted Mum and Dad to call him Jack. I suppose that I was too young to have remembered Carmel and Allan as babies, but I can remember Lew so well, as I was seven years old. I used to take him for little walks in a sort of pram. Poor Hannah was just besotted with him from the start. She used to sing a funny little song about the big butter and egg man. Dad always called him Fumpta boy. I don't know why or how it sprang up. Anyway, he was our pet and we all loved him so much, spoilt him perhaps.
LETTER (EXTRACT) TO CLARA GEE (LEW'S WIFE) FROM DAD'S SISTER MIRIAM

When I was five years old we had a beautiful Ayrshire cow called Trixie. We had no land on which to run her, but she was very clever and used to swim the Ovens River into Merriwa Park. Trixie had a great eye for the pound keeper who was always trying to get her. I remember my mother yelling out, 'Open the gate, quick, they're after Trixie!' Trixie was galloping up this little side lane near the house with the pound keeper in hot pursuit. They never caught Trixie, even though the pound keeper vowed to get her. We took Trixie with us when we moved to Beechworth.

We milked Trixie for the family, and on Sundays we gave the Salvation Army officer in Wangaratta a jar of fresh cream. One day Trixie's milk had gone off and there wasn't any full cream, so my mother tried to whip up the creamy milk instead. This meant that they put a bit of sugar into the milk and whipped it up until it went all fluffy, which increased the volume by about three times. The Salvation Army officer said to my mother, 'We liked the whipped cream but we don't like it as much as the fresh cream.' I remember my mother smiling and saying that Trixie was not giving quite so much milk and we had to do the best we could.

After we moved to Beechworth Trixie was mated with the local bull from the Mental Hospital, which started a long line of cattle and provided us with plenty of milk and butter over the years. Her descendants are probably still roaming the paddocks of Beechworth to this day. We all loved Trixie.

I always associate Wangaratta with being literally penniless. I remember asking my father for a penny one day when he was talking to some men in the street. But he didn't have even one, and I think he was most embarrassed, even though at that time a lot of men didn't have a penny in their pockets.

I started school in Wangaratta, and I have a vague memory of scrounging school essentials out of a rubbish bin — old pencils and some paper — because my parents couldn't afford to buy me any. We always dreaded the start of the school year because there was never sufficient money to buy the books or clothes we needed.

I don't remember the move to Beechworth, however I do vividly recall the old stone house made from local granite in which we lived at Beechworth for a short time before moving to Silver Creek. One day my younger sister Carmel cut her finger, which bled profusely. I walked through the town into Ford Street calling out for my parents who were holding an open air prayer meeting. Mrs Crossman complimented me on what a Briton I was to walk a mile to get help.

The family moved two and half miles out of Beechworth in about 1925, when I was six years old. I remained in beautiful Silver Creek until I was 17 years old. I still remember putting all our furniture and other household effects into boxes and travelling in the dray to our new home.

My parents had very little money so they had borrowed the £5 deposit for nine acres of ground and an old weatherboard house. We bought the property off people called Pembertons, a very old Beechworth family. Silver Creek was very good land, but it was cursed with blackberries and rabbits, and it took many years to make the ground productive.

After the purchase two Pemberton men came out and told my father that the sale wasn't valid and they wanted the house back. With his fist in the air, he told them to get off the property. He was a gentleman but got wild when people tried to take advantage of him because of his Christian charity. But there was no lingering rancour, and I remember the Pemberton family with great affection.

Our old weatherboard house at Silver Creek consisted of two front rooms, with a verandah attached to the front and a lean-to at the back. About ten feet behind the house was the kitchen which had an adjoining room where Hannah, a girl my parents had taken in, slept. On the right hand side was the entrance to the stable.

The fire burned continuously for as long as I can remember. The kitchen had a double fireplace and was the warmest part of the house. I also remember a long table with a big bench on one side next to the wall, and a stool on the other side. There were two chairs at the head of the table where my mother sat so she could dish out the food. Dad sat on the chair next to her and Hannah sat at the other end. Grace was said before every meal. We kept a sow pig, so we always had a ton of bacon which Dad cured and salted himself. We put stringy bark poles across the kitchen to hang up sides of bacon and ham. There was always some beast or other soaking in brine on the verandah.

The stringy bark trees on the property were a great source of timber and bark. We used them to build our cow shed, sheds for the pigs, and two or three chook pens. The round timber was cut in the bush for rafters and rails. The bark was a marvellous insulator, and it made the buildings very warm in winter, and cool in summer. Well treated, it would last for 20 or 30 years. It was also the main roofing material for the early settlers.

Hannah, who was basically an orphan became a member of our family. She was known as Nanna Bailey for as long as I can remember. Mum and Dad had found her wandering around on the streets in Port Melbourne shortly after they were married. She was about 16 and completely homeless. They took her home and she stayed with us for the next 62 years. She helped raise the six of us kids. My mother became very dependent on Hannah, and soon gave any suitors the cold eye.

Hannah wasn't very fond of washing herself, and Mum used to complain that she stank. Mum let her do the washing up, but she didn't like Hannah to cook. If my mother was out, Hannah would always have a go at it, but she was never much good. She certainly wanted to learn, but my mother never gave her much encouragement.

The area we settled on had been more less the hub of mining operations during the gold-rush, so it was littered with mine holes every six or seven feet right up to the Mopoke Ranges. They varied in depth from 20 to 50 feet (32-80 metres). We could always tell the ones that had been used by the Chinamen because they were round as they tended to use baskets, instead of the buckets used by the Europeans.

The early history of Silver Creek, Beechworth

Silver Creek is situated on the main Beechworth to Stanley Road, approximately 270 km north-east of Melbourne. Gold was first discovered near the present-day town of Beechworth in February 1852, and the area became known as the Ovens Gold Fields. The town of Beechworth, then known as Mayday Hills began to develop.

A map by the surveyor William Bell dated December 1852, shows gold deposits along Silver Creek, the adjacent area being named Beesons Flat. Deposits were also shown along Spring Creek, Deep Creek and Three Mile Creek. In January 1853, gold was discovered at the neighbouring Madmans Gully, between Beechworth and Silver Creek. Soon after this discovery it was reported that over one hundred holes had been dug at Madman's Gully, and that the gold was found at a depth of eight or ten feet. By April that year Madman's Gully was proving a very rich ground, with almost five acres of new ground opened up in one week. There must have been many a digger who questioned the wisdom of trying his luck on the Ovens Gold Fields. The winters were bitterly cold, the gold often difficult to extract because of the abundance of water — many a claim was destroyed by floods in the winter months, and added to that the cost was generally higher than on the Ballarat, Castlemaine, and Sandhurst (Bendigo) goldfields.

One of the biggest rushes at Silver Creek took place in June 1856. Holes were sunk up to 50 feet in depth, and sluicing was carried on in the bed of the creek. Silver Creek was a frenzy of activity! It began to show signs of more permanent settlement. A hotel, the Australian Arms had been established on the main road from Beechworth to the Nine Mile (Stanley) and by 1857 there was also the Harp of Erin and the Crow Hotel.

Mining companies began to make an appearance at Silver Creek. Wages for labourers in the area in 1856 were between £6-7 per week, and many diggers preferred the labouring work, with its regular income, to the possibility of no income at all from their own efforts at gold seeking.

Some diggers returned to their original occupations as masons, blacksmiths or carpenters. People started to build houses in the area; although fairly rough dwellings of slabs or mud, they were an improvement on tents.

By the 1860s, some reef mining was taking place at Silver Creek and the vicinity. The mining population continued to decline over the next few years. By December 1864 there were reported to be 38 miners at Silver Creek, 20 at Madman's Gully and 35 at Chinamans Flat from a total of 1,797 for the Beechworth mining district. Over 1,000 of the latter figure were Chinese and they were still in the majority of the district mining population in March 1866 when there were a total of 991 Chinese and 847 Europeans. The Chinese were generally disliked by the European population. They were accused of stealing the 'washing stuff' from the European diggers and of damaging their water races. Several riots against the Chinese broke out and only police intervention prevented severe consequences.

The Chinese mainly worked on old ground, and almost never ventured into quartz mining. They worked extremely hard, and often obtained good yields of gold by going over old ground or 'tailings' that had been abandoned by the Europeans. They kept to themselves. There were few women among their number, and their strange customs, their opium smoking and Joss Houses helped to alienate them from the rest of the mining community.

While the presence of Chinese in the Beechworth mining community was eventually accepted, they remained the target for many taunts, especially by local children. Stone-throwing and pigtail pulling was not unusual and a favourite prank was to roll a tin full of bull ants into the tent where the Chinese were absorbed in a game of fan-tan.

Some of the Chinese returned eventually to their native land. Some remained and established market gardens, once the mining died out. Many died in the area as the large Chinese section in the Beechworth cemetery testifies. One of the last Chinese in the Silver Creek area was 'Blind Tommy' who lived in Dingle Road in the 1920s.

The Silver Creek State School opened its doors on February 1, 1882 with a nett enrolment of 73. Prior to the opening of the school it had been said that the teacher would have a lot of up-hill work as the 'boys of Silver Creek were unruly and unmanageable'. However, the local Truant Officer Mr Enoch Downs said that he had found the statement to have no truth in it, that he had met the children and talked to them and found 'that the germs of goodness had a resting place within their breasts, which only required careful and kindly treatment.' The post-War years saw few new families move into the area, and enrolment at the school dwindled. There were only thirteen children attending in 1925 and only six in 1927, and despite protestations from the parents, the school closed that Easter.

No church was ever built at Silver Creek. but the Independent (Congregational) Church established a Sabbath School there in 1862. Although the parents were happy to send their children off to Sunday School, they seemed reluctant to participate themselves in any Church matters. A Sunday School operated at Silver Creek for many more years and the church picnic became an annual event.

The end of the nineteenth century and the beginning of the twentieth century were times of change for Silver Creek. The main occupation of the population at this time was still mining or labouring, with a few exceptions. Several men were employed at the Lunatic Asylum and some (did) wood cutting and carting. The Silver Creek Post Office opened on June 1, 1906 in a small building on Tom Shennan's property. Tom's wife Emily was the postmistress for many years. Telephone services were introduced in 1912, the first local subscriber was Maurice Kavanagh, of the Crow Hotel. Silver Creek had a very keen and active cricket team. The date of its inception is unclear, but it was certainly in existence in the 1880s. The story of Silver Creek is about a survivor of the gold-rush days of the 1850s, when the population of Silver Creek and surrounding areas of Madman's Gully, Chinamans Flat and Deep Creek was measured in thousands. As the gold supplies were exhausted so the population dwindled, but somehow Silver Creek survived. The residents found employment at the Asylum, or worked as wood cutters, many still making a living from mining well into the present century. The population was such in 1882 that a school was opened there. The school is now long gone, the Post Office has gone, as has the Crow Hotel. They have been replaced by a very popular caravan park and a trout farm, which bring tourists to the area. There are only a handful of houses left, some occupied by descendants of the early pioneers of the district.

FROM *SILVER THREADS AND GOLDEN NEEDLES* BY M. ROSALYN SHENNAN

In the summer one of our favourite activities was to go down to Spring Creek, near Silver Creek, and look for gold. This was one of the major sluicing areas and tons of gold had been pulled out from there in the days of the diggings. Of course we always hoped we'd strike it rich. But the ground had been intensively worked over by Chinese gold diggers and every other miner in the world so we hardly found anything. The most we got was a pennyweight, which in those days was measured by the amount of fine alluvial gold you could fit on a threepence. At most we'd find five or ten shillings worth, but it was a lot of fun. In all my time at Silver Creek I never knew anyone who found much gold except for old Terry McMahon. He seemed to know exactly where it was.

There was also an Italian called Peter Begoni and his son who were always looking for gold. Peter was about 40 and had been in the First World War. They were very efficient but fairly secretive miners, although one day the old man excitedly showed me three ounces of gold that he had found. There was always talk that they were going to start crushing in the area again, but I think the exercise was a flop.

I crawled down dozens of mine holes scrounging for things, but there were only ever bottles and the old bones of animals that

Miners at Silver Creek in the early 1900s.
(From the permanent collection of the Burke Museum, Beechworth)

had been unfortunate enough to fall in. It was a hell of a job getting animals out of the holes, because after the miners had dug the shaft, they dug sideways as far as they could so the bottom of the shaft was even wider. It was strange but cattle generally didn't fall in, although horses dropped in all the time. The cattle seemed to have a sixth sense about where the mine holes were, especially if they were born and bred in the area. However if cattle did fall in, they lay down and waited until someone arrived, but the horses would panic. They'd bang their heads against the walls of the hole which caused all sorts of injuries. We had to dig down to the animal, rig up a winch and drag it out. This operation often took several days and our neighbours usually had to assist us. The holes were eventually filled in by the Mines Department around 1950. Much of the land in that area was still Crown land.

I can't imagine now how my mother coped with all the people she had to feed, with no refrigeration. All we had was a Coolgardie safe, and she had to bake bread and dish up food for between eight and twelve people. There were always extras. My parents seemed to pick up stray people like stray animals.

Because we couldn't afford woollen blankets, Mum made what in those days were called Wagga rugs out of hessian bags stuffed with old bits of material She decorated them with motifs and embroidery. We had flour mill bags on the floor which we called Kimpton carpets.

I will never forget the incredible courage and spirit of the people of those times. I never heard my parents complain about the harsh conditions they lived in and worked under. They always said 'our ship will come in'. They had tremendous faith in their religion and they believed that God would look after them.

They were radical thinkers in lots of ways and had a fierce independence about them. My children seem to have inherited this renegade streak. I'm a bit of a non-conformist myself so I've never judged the kids, although they have stretched my patience sometimes! I don't know who's better off, people who have ordinary lives and are satisfied to let things happen, or movers and shakers who are always challenging conventions.

Because rabbits were so plentiful we had them fried, boiled, steamed and baked. I've never eaten rabbit since the day I joined the Navy. And with our salt meat, homemade cheese, and fresh vegetables, we ate very well. But it was still pretty tough then, especially for women as they usually had one baby after another.

We had tons of fruit. We didn't have a bottling outfit but we cut up the fruit, put it on strings and dried it in the sun. We stored the dried apples and pears in jars, and Mum made pies all year round. There were many pear trees that had been left when the old homes around there had been dismantled. We had at least ten very fine pear trees and four mulberry trees on our property.

We were never short of potatoes or pumpkins because we stored them during the winter in a shed. We were never hungry. Unlike so many people in towns and cities during the Depression who were starving, I never experienced hunger until I was a prisoner of war. I vowed when I came home I would never be hungry again and couldn't bear to see food thrown out or wasted.

At the back of the house we had a wash-house and a bath in the corner. For boiling water, we had a fire burning under a 44 gallon drum with the top cut out and a rough chimney attached to it. All the water had to be drawn out of the well, or pulled up on sleds from the old water-race. These were water channels built by the old alluvial miners. Every Monday my mother was in the wash-house laundering mountains of clothes by hand. Hannah helped with the ironing and the iron had to be heated first on the stove.

It was a miracle how they coped with the sheer volume of work, and it must have been a battle to keep us kids clean, which we always were, before we went off to school. In spite of the most trying conditions, overall it was quite a happy time.

To make extra money Hannah walked into Beechworth where she washed and ironed clothes for a shilling an hour. She went in at least three times a week and spent her extra income on us kids, buying gifts for our birthdays and Christmas. She once gave me a pocket knife which I was thrilled with.

MERYL BROWN [*Auntie Miriam and Uncle Bert's daughter*]: I remember visiting the original old house at Silver Creek for Sunday lunch when I was a toddler of about 18 months. I can remember Grandpa swinging me high in the air. They had a large pantry in a corner of their big old kitchen. The house was eventually burned down by the man who bought it off Uncle Nape, when he discovered his cows were dying from licking the lead paint off the side of the house.

I was told that Grandpa and Nana had found Hannah wandering around the streets in Melbourne with a head injury, and a slight speech impediment. Her head shook all the time. Hannah was devoted to Nana Gee. She did a lot of the 'slog' in the house. Mum told me that Hannah would wake up in the morning, light the fire and take Nana in a cup of tea and a piece of toast in bed.

Nana worked incredibly hard and saved money so that my mother Miriam and Carmel could go away to study teaching and nursing. She made enormous sacrifices and always said, 'The Lord will provide.' (Uncle Nape also contributed significantly to pay for Auntie Carmel and Auntie Miriam's education.)

DAD: Education was partly subsidised for children who lived in the country. There was an allowance of threepence a day to help pay for the horses if you rode a horse or drove a buggy or gig to school. I'm not quite sure if the payment was for each child or per horse. We very seldom drove the buggy to school, perhaps once or twice a week. As we got older we picked up the pig feed in the buggy on the way home from school, but mostly we walked.

The best thing about school was not going there, but coming home. Our generation generally hated school because the teachers were very strict and often quite malicious. When I was in the second or third grade we had a headmaster of whom we were all terrified because he beat us mercilessly. He did the town a good turn when he left.

He was replaced by a pleasant man called Mr Weir who was very strict but fair. He had been a First World War digger and was extremely shell-shocked. Some of the older boys heard about this, and they taunted him by dropping heavy books behind him when his back was turned. You'd hear a loud bang in the class-room and poor Mr Weir would jump with fright. Little did I know that later in life, I would be a bit jumpy myself from my wartime experiences.

The teacher I had in fifth grade was very cruel to me. She regularly asked me in front of the class where my father worked, knowing full well he didn't have a steady job. Once she even snarled, 'Doesn't your father ever go to work!' Years later she lived near us on a farm in Wooragee, and whenever we drove past I used to give her 'two fingers' out the window. I hated the old cow.

We never had enough money to buy the right text books or pencils and our clothes were always hand-me-downs or made by Mum out of material from old dresses and leftover rags. Mum sewed the girl's dresses, and made us short pants and a sort of blouse which I loathed wearing. I always felt a bit embarrassed about our clothes, but Mum did her best.

I never really got over the humiliation I suffered at the hands of some of those teachers who put us down for being poor. They also made nasty remarks about my parents being in the Salvation Army as it didn't enjoy the popularity that it has today.

Another unpleasant school experience I had was in the eighth grade when a teacher stopped me getting my Merit Certificate because I was one mark short in arithmetic. At the time the Merit Certificate was more or less a passport for getting a decent job, so I was devastated. Later when I joined the Navy I passed the test they gave me quite easily, which overcame the problem of not having the Merit Certificate.

Overall our teachers didn't cultivate self-respect, or personal development. Most of the people I went to school with have very grim memories of that time apart from the fun we had on the way to and from school rabbiting and talking to the old miners. Lake Sambell was a great place for swimming, climbing trees, looking for birds' eggs, and sneaking into other people's orchards and pinching apples.

Prior to 1930 Beechworth had made many attempts to induce the Governments of the day to consider the possibilities of growing softwood timbers in the surrounding hills, where climate and rainfall were very suitable for this class of tree. It was not, however, until the Depression in the 1930s that a start was made on this work. Using gangs of unemployed, large tracts of the forest between Stanley and Yackandandah were cleared and planted with pines. All of this work was carried out by hand.

FROM *A BACKGROUND TO BEECHWORTH* BY ROY C. HARVEY [P 52]

It was always tough for Mum and Dad surviving those days, never knowing where the next bit of money was coming from. For a while before the Depression struck badly in 1929, Dad was travelling around the countryside in the sulky selling Griffiths tea. Later he sold insurance the same way. I remember his sulky well. He also tried selling Rawleigh's products. He was the first Rawleigh's dealer in the area, and he went to Myrtleford, Tallangatta and Yackandandah. But he stopped working for them after about four months because he said the company was too greedy.

Fortunately when the Depression hit my father found a job working three months on three months off at the Myrtleford and Stanley pine plantations. This was the work for the dole scheme of the day. We knew it as 'the susso'. Most of the people working at the pines had been thrown out of work, and were desperate for any job. There were people working there from all walks of life, some highly educated, some labourers all trying to make ends meet. During the school holidays when I was about ten I used to go and stay with him in tents on the banks of the creek with the other men. There were two men to a tent, and I was allowed to sleep between them on a mattress on the floor. We swam in the creeks, fished, caught rabbits and played with the other kids. It was a wonderful experience.

I realise now what a tough job it must have been for my father. He was about 50 then, and they had to climb at least a mile up this steep hill and cut down massive gum-trees so they could plant the young pines. They worked a 48 hour week. They had to leave the camp early to start work at 7.30am and they didn't knock off until 5.00pm. However the bosses on the whole seemed very generous, and I didn't see any signs of unkindness. Sometimes Dad couldn't even come home for the weekends, so when I was with him I would drive the gig seven or eight miles home, through Stanley and down into Silver Creek. Then I'd drive back the following weekend to fetch him.

Later on Dad helped harvest the huge plantations in the Beechworth area. It must have been very trying because he had a problem with his knee due to a fall from a horse years before which gave him terrible pain. Later he went to Melbourne where an x-ray revealed that part of the kneecap had broken off and was floating around. It wasn't until about 1935 that he could afford to have it operated on.

I'll never forget one Sunday night when my father was asked to hold a Christian service for the plantation workers. There were about one hundred men in the camp. It was very moving listening to him telling them about the meaning of the Lord's prayer in that beautiful setting beneath the gum-trees with all the stars out. Then they sang hymns, and I listened intently to their voices in the dark by the light of their fires. They had no wireless, so it was entertainment for them as well as being a religious occasion.

I also met a cook there who had previously worked for shearer's gangs. He told me that people always think cooks are dirty, so whenever he went to the toilet, which was just a pit in the ground, he came back and made a great display of washing his hands to prove that he really was clean when he prepared the men's meals.

One Saturday I asked the men what they were doing for the weekend. They told me they wanted beer and wanted it badly. They returned that night very drunk and the next morning were as sick as dogs. Me and other kids at the camp collected the empty beer bottles off the men that drank and sold them. I think we got threepence a dozen. Lew was a lot younger but he always tagged along. It was great fun to go in amongst the tents where the blokes would ask us about school.The poorer the men were the more generous and friendly they'd be to us kids. As an adult I could never tolerate people making nasty remarks about poor people, as I have such fond memories of those proud poor people I knew as a child.

My best friend at Silver Creek was a kid called Claude whose family were named Smith. I think he had some Maori or Aboriginal blood. I believe his father had died and the family left him to live with his lovely old grandfather. This dear old man gave my father a shotgun, which I later gave to my son Bruce. They were terribly poor, even poorer than we were. Claude spent half his life at our place. We had great times together roaming the hills rabbiting and working cattle and milking cows for local people. He knew every tree and rock in the bush, and was an amazing hunter.

Bess, our mare, was given to my father by a family called Paton who lived in the Tallangatta valley. They owned a lot of property and couldn't see the point in hanging on to this pitch black, stone blind mare. In fact they were going to shoot her, but Dad begged them to spare her life. Bess was part of our lives for 25 years, and died when I was a prisoner during the war. She was a wonderful horse. We all learned to ride on her like Indians. You didn't need a bridle or saddle because she was so sure-footed that she could easily be steered with your knees. We had to take care that she didn't fall down a mine hole, but she used to go down to the creek on her own. Despite being completely blind, we also drove her in a milk cart and later to school in an old buggy. We were very attached to her.

I vividly recall when a man brought a stallion over to Silver Creek to service Bess. Obviously he didn't believe blindness was hereditary. I heard Bess snorting and carrying on, but Mum and Dad immediately banished us kids inside the house. Miriam, Carmel and I sneaked out and hid in the gully and watched this stallion mounting Bess. Despite prolonged, loud whinnying going on, Bess never went into foal. I don't know what all the fuss was about because we'd seen dogs, goats, and cows mating. It was all part of growing up in the country. In fact by the time I was five I'd seen a bull serving a cow, a boar up a sow, and the rooster servicing quite a few chooks.

By the time I was seven or eight years old I was allowed to drive Bess into town in the spring cart with a load of wood that my mother had cut out in the lanes. We got four shillings a load, and sometimes Mum and I would do three trips a day. I remember once coming back to Mum with five shillings, proud as punch.

It wasn't that Dad was lazy, but he was often away doing whatever he could to bring in a quid. Mother was a very resourceful woman doing her bit at home to earn enough to feed and clothe us. She was a tower of strength in every way.

We became more productive when we selected another 25 acres and started to grow maize and potatoes. After a year or two we had spuds available for sale, although the price was often as low as £2 a ton. We also bought a draught horse, then a dray, and later a single furrow plough. Our first crop was four or five acres of oats which gave us hay for the winter to feed the horses and a bit left over for the cows.

We didn't buy bread until about 1935 because Mum baked our own from home-ground wheat flour. It was delicious and we smothered it with home-made butter. The bought stuff couldn't compare. We also made our own delectable wholemeal porridge.

There was great excitement at home when we got our hopes up of a huge inheritance from England. My mother's family, the Haywoods, were always talking about this Chancery money that was due to them (the Court of Chancery was the section of the English courts dealing with wills). A Mr Flyjack in England was hired to pry loose the money. Charles Dickens couldn't have written it better. One day a great sheaf of 30 or 40 documents arrived at the house. We were expecting to receive more than £38,000, which today would be like a million dollars. Mum and Dad told us kids to keep our mouths shut, but we told a few people and soon everyone in the town knew. In the end we missed out on the money by a weird twist of fate. The two vital documents needed to clinch the inheritance were lost in a house fire six or so months before the Chancery money was due to be allocated.

Our one windfall during the Depression was finding a pocket of alluvial gold in one of the old water races. It was worth over £30, not as much as our hoped for inheritance but still a goodly sum in those days.

Boots were always a great problem when we were kids. Money was very tight so most of the time we went to school barefoot whatever the weather. My mother bought worn out old boots for a shilling from travelling salesmen from Melbourne. We cut the tops off, patched them, and tried to make them look like ordinary boots.

I was aged about ten when I earned enough for my first new pair of boots called Bluchers. They were hob-nailed and cost four shillings.

I earned the money by picking blackberries and selling rabbits. My boots were so precious to me that I greased them with mutton fat to preserve them and put them under my pillow at night to keep them safe. I was so proud of them, and often wore them around my neck to protect them. I never wore them to or from school, only when I was at school.

I had very good feet and even when I was a prisoner of war I tried to look after them and scrounge some footwear. I brazenly stole a pair of boots from the Japs once when I was on the Burma Railway because I hated going barefoot. It reminded me too much of those hard early childhood days.

I loved coming home to Silver Creek from school and seeing the dogs running out to meet us. We always had at least five or six dogs, rabbit dogs and fox terriers. They'd charge the quarter mile length of our lane barking with joy. There was no time that I didn't have great affection for dogs and I always slept with a favourite fox terrier called Tiny in my bed. At bedtime Tiny would hear my mother coming down the hallway to kiss me goodnight and would jump off the bed and hide under a chair. She'd say, 'You haven't got that dog in there I hope?' Tiny would wait patiently until he heard her departing footsteps then hop in with me under the blankets. I'm sure Mum knew about Tiny but she went through the ritual. Her nickname for me was 'Reynard the Fox', because she said I was so quick that she could never outfox me.

There was an old lady in her 70s called Mrs Ross who had been born and bred at Silver Creek, and never left the area. I don't know what had happened to her husband, but she had a daughter who worked for many years at the Mental Hospital. When I was a lad of about nine or ten she had some cabbage plants for sale. I rode the horse about a mile down to her house and picked up the plants. 'Where's the shilling?' she said. I replied that I'd already given it to her, but apparently I hadn't. She started to scream at me, and I rushed out and jumped onto the horse. But she took a short cut through the bush, and beat me home. She started carrying on to Mum and Dad that I was a terrible boy and was trying to steal her cabbage plants. I remember my father gave her the shilling and I got a bit of a reprimand.

I can't ever remember being belted at home. I was probably given the occasional well-deserved slap but my parents weren't hitters. After being bashed by the Japs in the war, I came back determined never to hit anyone. I never hit my kids, although it was often warranted!

From the time that I was about ten I used to break in cattle. I received lots of bad scrapes until I got the hang of it. The moment I got on those steers they would go straight for the fence rail or the branch of a tree and you'd swear they were trying to kill you. They were incredibly cunning and determined to knock this young upstart into the dirt.

One Sunday I somehow managed to get out of going into Beechworth for the Salvation Army service. Feeling jubilant I asked some of my friends to our place to have a rodeo. We fixed up a rough corral and got hold of some pretty wild cattle. We let them go and jumped on them one at a time. It's a wonder we weren't killed. I remember my mother returning home from church and seeing my white shirt covered in blood. She admonished me for breaking the Sabbath, but I think she was basically thankful I was still alive.

Sundays were always different to the rest of the week. Being deeply religious, my parents never allowed work on Sundays apart from doing the basic chores of milking the cows and feeding the pigs and chooks. We were never allowed to swear — I made up for that later — and we had bible classes at home seven days a week. That was simply our way of life, but at least it gave us a great appreciation of music, and singing. I remember the wonderful hymns with great affection. Overall it probably didn't do us much good, but it didn't do any harm either.

UNCLE BRAM: I recall that the moral teaching from my parents was very strict. Often the weather was so bad, especially if it snowed, that we simply couldn't get into Beechworth for the church services. The roads were bad enough and after the rain there would be rivers of mud.

DAD: I remember this very gentle, wonderful woman called Mrs Withers. We called her husband Hugh 'the Adjutant', because that was his rank in the Salvation Army. They had a son called Danny who suffered from epilepsy.

The Withers were both Salvation Army Officers and like my parents had been kicked out with hardly any remuneration at all. They were nice people, but bone lazy and never used to get out of bed until about 10am. Mr Withers often sat on the front verandah picking his nose. Quite late most mornings they headed out to collect wood for the day. Old Hugh would be wheeling the empty barrow, and poor Mrs Withers used to carry the axe, and a bag on her back. Their son Danny trailed behind. On the way home it was Mrs Withers who carried the bagful of wood on her back.

Mrs Withers was a very talented writer, and sent stories away to different newspapers. Some of them were published. I remember reading one short story about a walk from Silver Creek into Beechworth describing all the things she saw, the different birds, plants and scenery.

They remained very religious. As I grew older old man Withers would tell me that I was the only child he knew who had not been saved, and that he hoped that in his own time God would give me the wisdom to give myself to the Lord. I went to Mrs Wither's funeral when I was about 50 and said, 'Adjutant, I really feel deep sympathy for you about your wife.' 'As far as I am concerned this is the day that we have lived and waited for,' he responded. 'My wife has risen and the day will come when I will rise with her.' I was struck by how very definite he was about his faith.

The tradition and popularity of brass bands

Brass bands played an important and interesting role in the community life of Australia during the latter half of the 19th century and the first half of the 20th century.

Many British migrants to Australia in the 19th century were mine workers or industrial workers and they brought with them the brass band tradition. Brass bands prospered in Australia to an extent rivalling their popularity in Victorian and Edwardian England. Many mining towns and country areas had their own brass band which played an important role in entertainment and ceremonial occasions.

The only reference to open air music in Beechworth was the occasion when the German Brass Band played at the laying of the foundation stone of the Ovens District Hospital in 1856. The next mention made of bands was Judge Cope's

Fife and Drum Band in the sixties. By the 70's bands were quite a feature of life in Beechworth. Heading the list was the Forester's Brass Band. During 1875 Luftons' Brass Band was formed. In addition to these there were the Rechabites' Fife and Drum Band and the Druids Fife and Drum Band. On entering the 1880s we hear of a Hartman's Brass Band. This was followed by Vandenberg's Brass Band formed somewhere around 1891 and conducted by M. George Farley. Its first public appearance was playing at the Railway Station as a welcome to the Boxing Day visitors.

At a public meeting in 1897 it was reformed into the Beechworth Town Band, with Mr Mulder as conductor. This was the first publicly subsidised band, and is the forerunner of the present day Town Band. Many will recall with pleasure the band recitals in Victoria Park during the early part of this century, the Saturday night playing when the shops were open, and the many fine processions that were headed by the Town Band.

SOURCE: THE BURKE MUSEUM, BEECHWORTH

DAD: Bands along with religion were constants in our life. Nape and Bram both played in the Town Band and I joined the school band when I was about nine or ten. I was never taught to read music properly because the tuition cost one shilling a week. It was always embarrassing for us when we couldn't come up with the money after the music lessons, so we were really self-taught. Nape was a bit of a plodder, by his own admission, and played the tenor horn, although Nape and Bram could read music.

When it came to music, Bram was brilliant. He was an extremely competent cornet and trumpet player and practised for five or six hours a day. On moonlit nights he'd go into town to play and the locals would swarm out to listen to him. When he joined the Tannery he even took the mouthpiece into work so that he could keep practising. I remember him playing his cornet till eleven or twelve most evenings. Bram later became the bandmaster of the Melbourne Tramways Board band and he played in the Salvation Army and the Fire Brigade bands. Nape also played in the Army Band and after the war, the Tramways Band.

My cornet playing was a wonderful gift because when I joined the Navy I became a ship's bugler in *HMAS Canberra* and *HMAS Perth*.

*Grandfather Gee and siblings at school at
Tarraganda, two miles from Bega, teacher
Miss Johnson*

Alfred Cowdroy, Bega (1871-1935)

*John Gee at Tathra
Xmas, 1928
(Died: Bega May 28,
1929, aged 81 years)*

Napier and Alice (Haywood) Gee

Alice (Haywood) Gee

Miss Alice Haywood

*Postcard Napier Gee
sent to Alice from
Kapunda, South Australia.
February 13, 1911*

*Mr Richard (Dick)
Cutting*

*Captain Napier Gee
preaching at Millicent,
South Australia, 1913*

*The Silver Creek State School, opened in
1882 and closed in 1927. (From the
permanent collection of the Burke Museum,
Beechworth)*

*Allan Gee outside
the house he was
born at – Dowling
Court, Beechworth
– named after
the midwife who
delivered him*

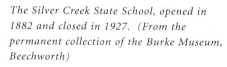

*The Gee Family.
Back row, L-R:
Napier, Carmel,
Miriam, Allan,
Bramwell. Front row:
Alice, Napier and
Lewis*

Chinese Burning Towers. Beechworth Cemetery (Photo: Vivienne Harvey)

The French's at 'Lyndale', Wooragee. George and Elizabeth (Rapsey) and family

Ned Kelly, the day prior to his execution

Ellen Kelly (Ned's mother) and son-in-law Edward Griffiths. (From the permanent collection of the Burke Museum, Beechworth)

*Allan Gee with
Mr and Mrs K.H.Zwar, Beechworth*

*The Phillips Family. Back row, L-R: Clara
(Brewer), Frederick (father), Frederick (son)
Julia (mother) Alice (Sister Christina). Front
row: Maud (Stasson), William (on father's knee)
Arthur, Bob (mother's arms) and Winifred*

*Zwar Brothers Annual Picnic, 1906, held
for the Tannery employees and their
families. (From the permanent collection
of the Burke Museum, Beechworth)*

*Silver Creek Post
Office, opened on
June 1, 1906 on Tom
Shennan's property*

Pop Brewer's
mother Cassandra
(Parr)

Kath Brewer and
Alan Condon
Albury Botanical
Gardens, 1943

The Brewer Family.
Back row. L-R: Frank, Artie, Gwen, Bert,
Marge, Reg. Front row: Mary, Arthur,
Clara, Kath and Ted

Reg and Kath
(Schneider) Brewer on
their wedding day.
August 26, 1950

Arthur Brewer
and Clara May
Phillip's Wedding.
April 29, 1912

Carmel (L) and Miriam Gee

Stanley Cricket Team, 1935

Hannah Bailey with Lew Gee's daughter Lynette at Silver Creek

Lieutenant Frank Brewer 8th Light Horse Brigade, 1940-45. Frank was killed in a car accident in 1964

Private Napier Gee, Alice Springs, 1942

Grandfather Gee as a teenager

*Gee Lane,
Silver Creek with
Mopoke Ranges in
the background*

*Grandfather
Gee's house at
Silver Creek*

Like all the early pioneering families, Mum and Dad knew how tough life could be and were prepared to work hard to try to improve our lives. I remember my dear Mother crying inconsolably because she had a bill of £38, 'Oh, I don't know how we will ever pay that bill.' On another occasion I was waiting in the spring cart for my parents while they visited the stonemason who had a little workshop in Beechworth. I overheard two men talking, 'Who are those people there?' said one. The other replied, 'Their name is Gee, they are very good people but they're terribly poor.' Later I told my Mother, and she looked very sad. I must have been about 12 years of age when I decided that I would always live within my means, and I always have. I've always tried to have a few bob up my sleeve. I think all my siblings had a similar attitude.

I don't remember exactly when Mr Richard 'Dick' Cutting arrived in our lives, but it was probably a couple of years after we arrived at Silver Creek. He was a tall, shambling man who couldn't read or write. He was one of the kindest men I have ever had the privilege of knowing. In every sense he was a gentle giant.

Mr Cutting proved to be a Godsend because he was a master of improvisation. He collected bits of tin and boards from the tip and

The Beechworth Town Band, c.1945.
Bram Gee is situated in the centre of the front row holding a trumpet.
(From the permanent collection of the Burke Museum, Beechworth)

added room after room to our house. As there were nine of us including Hannah, his inventive building completely transformed our home. We boys slept in a windowless sleep-out that Mr Cutting had built. It had a wooden floor, and about six different types of beds. Most of them came from the tip or somewhere. Whenever we were at the tip we had our eyes open for anything we thought Mr Cutting could use. We couldn't afford to pay him very much, but he got all his meals for nothing. He also became a suitor of Hannah's, but I think Mum discouraged him.

I can still see Mr Cutting walking up the road to our house with a couple of sheets of iron on his head. If he found an old piece of tin he was never satisfied until he had hammered it into some sort of design, which he would then paint. He also did odd jobs in the town and eventually married a lady in Beechworth who had a young child. They were very happy and had a couple of children of their own, and he completely transformed an old house that they bought. His descendants are now a very well respected family in Beechworth.

MG: Nancy Dyball, Mr Cutting's daughter remembers Hannah living in their house in Beechworth for a while. She said, 'I did hear that he was keen on Hannah but I can't confirm it. He married my mother quite late in life.' Sadly, Mr Cutting was killed in a hit and run accident in Melbourne at the age of 86.

DAD: One of the biggest bugbears for us children with increasing prosperity were the crops we grew on our newly acquired land. In those days they had to be cut with a scythe, and we all had to help out. Then we had to rake the hay and cart it into the shed. But the real curse of our life was cutting chaff at night using a hand operated cutter. Even Miriam and Carmel had to give a hand. It was a gruelling business and very hard on everyone.

One night Lew caught one of his forefingers when he was feeding the chaff cutter. He chopped about half an inch off the end and yelled blue murder. We were terrified because his arm was jammed in the mechanism, so we had to stop the blades and wind them back to extricate his hand. There was no doctor available so we just bound it up. I suppose because he was so young it healed up fine, but he always had a stubby finger, although eventually the nail grew back.

We cut chaff by hand until I was about 14. I remember later when my father bought a Morris car he would sometimes jack it up, and put a belt around one of the car's back wheels to drive the chaff cutter.

Another colourful friend of our family's was a man whose name I think was Simon Malsem. He moved in nearby with his son Norman, who was a big man and a great axeman. His grandson Fred became an Australian champion axeman. They were wonderful people. Simon had all these fantastic bush remedies. They were always telling us to chew eucalyptus leaves for colds, and compelled us to push pieces of fresh liver down the dog's throats which they said cured their worms and fleas.

I don't whether it was a lack of vegetables, but many people in those days suffered terribly from piles. Simon's miracle cure for piles was to put an old boot in a kerosene tin and burn it. When the boot became so hot that it started smoking the sufferer was told to sit over it for two or three hours until the piles dried out. I don't know whether it cured them or not, but they got burnt arses for their trouble. When I told our local doctor about Simon's piles cure, he said had never read anything like that in his medical journals.

The old people also believed that urinating on chilblains on their feet was a foolproof cure, and in the pine plantations the men urinated on their hands to treat their shocking blisters. There was nothing else then for minor cuts and abrasions except iodine. I also remember that many of us kids suffered with horrible boils on our backsides, probably due to a dietary deficiency. We held a pickle jar over the fire then stuck the bottle over the boil. The vacuum effect as the air cooled would draw out the pus. It was such a painful procedure that I only ever tried it once. In those days without penicillin and very few doctors available, these bush remedies were better than nothing.

We didn't get a decent wireless until about 1935, however we were determined not to miss out on the latest in home entertainment. Once when my parents went to a Salvation Army Congress in Melbourne they met up with my Uncle Henry, Mum's brother who was a Colonel in the Army. He sold them a wireless which only worked in fits and starts. In about 1932 I bought a crystal set for five shillings and rigged it up near my bed. It was fairly primitive, just the piece of crystal, the cat's whiskers and the earphones. On moonlight nights when there was no interference I could hear the programs coming in from Albury.

I would lie in bed till all hours listening intently. It was surprising what I could pick up. One night (October 24, 1934) after listening to the news and songs, an announcement came over that a plane was flying around trying to land in Albury. It was a Dutch airliner taking part in the London to Sydney to Melbourne Air Race which had become lost. I heard the urgent call on the radio for people to drive to the racecourse and shine their headlights to illuminate it as a landing strip. It was an emergency and the immediate response of the locals enabled the plane to touch down safely. Although disappointed about losing the race, the Captain of the plane was bonded with Albury from then on. A warm friendship between Albury and Holland ensued, and local dignitaries later made friendship trips to the Netherlands. At Albury airport there is a replica of the old Douglas DC2 plane involved called 'The Uiver' and a plaque to commemorate the event. It was incredibly exciting listening to this drama unfolding from my little bedroom at Silver Creek.

Another time around 1935 I was driving home to Silver Creek with my father in our old Morris car. The fog was so thick you could hardly see your hand in front of you. We heard a plane zooming around and soon realised it was in distress. We heard later that the plane called Southern Cloud (sister plane of the Southern Cross) had crashed. Many of the bushmen from our area went out looking for it as there was a reward offered of £100. It had gone down about 35 miles (56 km) from our place as the crow flies, but because of the inpenetrable bush it was not found until about 1960. (Remnants are on display at Cooma, NSW.)

The Boxing Day Sports Show was the highlight of the year in Beechworth as far as we were concerned. We loved the stalls, ice-cream, and spruikers flogging all manner of things including scissors which were as blunt as spades. There were also pushbike races and lots of horse events. My father was paid 15 shillings for the day to ride around the perimeter of the sports ground making sure people went through the entrance gate and didn't sneak in the back way for free. Needless to say we never paid.

The main interest for us were the showmen, especially Harry Johnson and his boxers. I have always admired great spruikers and I can still remember his patter. 'In a few moments Harry Johnson will present to you a troupe of fighters that can fight and wrestle and tackle any of your local number that are good enough, and tough enough to meet them in this marquee so hurry, hurry, hurry.' He and one of the boxers clanged a bell, and a big negro banged a drum. The locals poured in.

The troupe of fighters would emerge and stand stock still staring at the crowd with as much menace as they could muster. Harry Johnson would then announce to a gasp from the crowd, '£5 for the man who can knock out the heaviest man in the troupe.' The sort of person who came forward was usually a shearer from the backblocks who was probably alright having a stoush on a farm, but was useless against these professional fighters. The locals also thought they could handle themselves pretty well, but by the time they volunteered for the fight they'd be half cut from guzzling beer, and their Dutch courage soon evaporated. The boxers would give anyone game enough a good belting and throw them out of the ring. It was always the most popular event of the day.

My most unforgettable experience at the show occurred one year at the Wild West tent where there was a competition to catch a wild donkey. A prize of five shillings was offered to any boy who could catch a donkey which they let loose. Well this was no problem for me, because I'd been catching calves and horses all my life and breaking them in as well. I stood still, waited till the poor donkey bolted past, tackled it and brought it down in about two minutes. The bloke running the show was furious and told me to clear off, but he promised he'd pay me the next week. Nothing happened of course, so I asked him what had happened to my five bob. Quick smart he kicked me up the arse and told me again to get lost. My mother heard about my success from the townspeople and thought it was all a bit of fun.

In fact whenever she met anyone in town the next day she proclaimed, 'Allan caught the donkey last night.'

When I was a teenager we took up smoking as soon as we were able, encouraged by newsreels showing Americans puffing away. There was also one newspaper advertisement I liked which promoted Capstan cigarettes. It showed Good King Wencselas looking out on Christmas morning and saying, 'Good morning, give a cove a decent smoke.' My parents were vehemently opposed to smoking, but it didn't stop me from lighting up. To them smoking was an abomination because the body was the holy temple of the spirit, and to abuse it was evil. They described smoking as the Devil's fingers at work. How right they turned out to be.

Much to my parents' horror my brother Napier and Max Jarvis decided to grow tobacco during the tobacco boom as a get-rich-quick scheme. After months of soul searching Mum and Dad reluctantly gave their permission. I remember helping them to cart the leaf to their kiln. Like all these great schemes it turned out to be a monumental failure. Although they grew good quality tobacco and sold the first lot for £3/-/3, the American tobacco companies sabotaged them. They exerted enormous influence on Australia and cut the quantity of Australian tobacco they used in local cigarettes, so our stuff was soon worthless. What we had left was burnt under supervision, which was a bit of a pity, because we probably could have sold it to someone. Max and Napier remained great friends throughout their lives.

With the Great Depression in the wind, get-rich-quick schemes were all the rage. Jobs were scarcer, particularly in the country, and we struggled to be self-sufficient.

2

THE GREAT
DEPRESSION

'Our ship will come in'

Like many people of my generation I grew up with parents who were extremely careful with money. My father was habitually frugal, and when I encouraged him to blow some money and enjoy himself he would say, 'I came up too tough to do that.' He also detested food being wasted or thrown out, an understandable reaction after living through the Depression and acute deprivation as a prisoner of war. But as a human being he was not in the least bit mean-spirited, and his generosity to family and others in need was boundless.

DAD: Over the years my parents took in a number of boarders. Hannah had been the first, then Mr Cutting also became a fully-fledged family member. We loved the characters who stayed with us because they told great stories. The wireless was a late arrival in our house and a bit hit or miss, so we'd sit around on our haunches listening to these old-timers in awe. We suspected the truth of the stories but we didn't care, fact or fiction we'd listen utterly mesmerised.

During the Depression many men were on the move looking for work. We said they were 'on the track'. They rambled about and some camped in a shed on top of the old William Lawson mine in Silver

Creek, while others slept in the local school before it was pulled down. They had no family or homes and lived rough in the bush. Because of my parents Salvation Army beliefs, from the earliest days at Silver Creek anybody that was destitute finished up with us, or at least came in for a feed. Mum also made extra money by going around the district nursing some of these unfortunates.

Billy was one boarder whom I immediately picked as a great liar, but he was a superb raconteur. He told us tales about his trips around the world. He claimed to have climbed in the Himalayas, visited the Great Wall of China and crossed Mongolia into Russia. He then told us he went to France, and ended up in South America. We always asked how come he was able to do all these wonderful things and he'd say, 'I was doing secret service for the country and I cannot divulge any of the circumstances which caused me to be there.'

Around 1928 Mum saw an advertisement in the paper that an American woman needed someone to nurse her, so we took in a dear old soul called Mrs. Byrne who lived in the front room of the house for three years. In those days they didn't have nursing homes for the aged. Mrs Bryne had been left for dead by her own family and actually died in our house, because I can remember seeing the coffin in the bedroom. Mum was paid 30 shillings a week to look after her, which was a fortune for us.

The next person Mum nursed was a man called Fraser who was a member of the Exclusive Brethren sect. His family were well-to-do folk from Melbourne and they gave him five hundred pounds to set up a mission station in India. However he was obviously not a genuine man of the cloth because he invested all the money in a sugar mill and went broke. He then married an Indian lady, but much to the relief of his parents he returned to Australia without her.

Somehow Fraser ended up living with us, although we really didn't like him very much at first. Infuriatingly he used to clatter and bang around the house until 2am. Whenever he went to the lavatory he put a white cardboard sign on the door which said, 'Let'. We would throw stones at the toilet and he'd yell at us from the inside, which we all thought was hilarious. My mother thought it was funny too and mostly supported our childish pranks. At various times Fraser became quite obstreperous and my father had to straighten him out. Eventually we tamed him a bit, and he and Dad became very good friends.

In about 1933 Fraser bought a horse and cab from Nicholas Dowling for £10, who was the son of the woman who delivered me into the world. Fraser used to ride around the town and make quite a spectacle of himself. He insisted on giving us a lift into church on Sundays and the local yokels laughed at us for being pretentious.

One night when I was about 14, Fraser collapsed while sitting on the toilet. He called out and I ran to him but he died in my arms. I had never held anyone so completely limp. My mother laid him out on the bed. In those days you could rarely get a doctor on the same day, so my mother dressed him and put pins under his eyes. Fraser had once said that his wealthy family in Melbourne couldn't care less about him, and that my father was the only friend he had ever had. After he died his family had the nerve to come up to see if he had left them any money, and were aghast to discover he had left it to us.

Beechworth was special from the beginning because of the friendliness of the people there. We became very close to the Sergeant of Police, a man called Teddy Burke. He was a direct descendant of the explorer Robert O'Hara Burke of Burke and Wills fame, who coincidentally had also been a Police Superintendent at Beechworth. It was rumoured around town that Teddy had once had an affair with Dame Nellie Melba.

Teddy and his mate, an older man called Jim, had a contract to sell wood to the Mayday Hills Mental Hospital. They had two drays and two beautiful draft horses and did two trips a day, half a cord on each dray-load. They would travel through the lovely Mopoke Ranges to the Mental Hospital. We had a great time watching them load the wood. Sometimes they let us sit on top and hang on by the chain that kept it stacked. On Saturdays they lent us the drays and horses which we used to plant our crops. We had only been there a short time before they lost the wood contract.

Their next scheme was to dig for gold. They were quite a funny sight when they worked because Teddy walked about 200 yards in front of

Jim. We always referred to them as Burke and Wills. Luckily they got the wood contract back again about 12 months later.

Jim was a great guy and we loved him. He had a big sorrel horse and wore a slouch hat, brown jacket, black pants and riding boots. He also smoked and drank wine. The only time he ever rode his horse was on Sundays when he took a bottle of wine and visited his lady friend. We called her 'the guzzler' because she liked drinking so much. We sometimes saw this mysterious woman when we were out looking for cattle but she'd never talk to us. She was believed to have been a 'kept woman' of one of the old mining chiefs who owned a big tract of land down at the Three Mile, and had apparently left her a small legacy for the rest of her life. Whenever we saw Jim on the horse we'd say, 'He's off to see the guzzler again, it must be Sunday!' He'd spend the whole afternoon with her, presumably in bed.

Jim never married. During the war he too moved in with my parents and stayed for many years, even after my mother died in 1944. When I returned home he had practically gone blind. What a great pair we were.

Beechworth Hospital for the Insane – later the Mayday Hills Hospital.
(From the permanent collection of the Burke Museum, Beechworth)

Mayday Hills Hospital

An obvious need for an asylum existed on the Ovens Goldfield where unsettled living conditions, isolation and poverty were liable to induce mental disturbances. The remoteness of the district from Melbourne meant that mentally ill persons, after suffering confinement in gaol until certified, had to endure a tedious journey by wagon to the overcrowded Yarra Bend Asylum in Melbourne. Work commenced on the Beechworth Lunatic Asylum in December 1864. A 200 acre site was chosen on a hilltop behind the benevolent Asylum and commanded a panoramic view of the surrounding countryside which it was hoped would be beneficial to patients. In May 1867 the main building was completed. The Asylum formally opened on October 24, 1867 under Superintendent Dr Thomas Dick and received many patients from Yarra Bend, some of whom were former Beechworth residents. In order to make the hospital as self-supporting as possible, patients engaged in various forms of work including the making and mending of clothes and cultivation of the Asylum farm and garden.

The Lunatic Asylums of Victoria became known as Hospitals For The Insane in 1905 and Mental Hospitals in 1934. Patients at the Beechworth Mental Hospital increased from about 300 in 1870 to 785 in 1950. During centenary celebrations in 1967, the institution adopted the name Mayday Hills Hospital.

Mayday Hills Hospital closed on June 30, 1996. It is now LaTrobe University, Beechworth Campus.

SOURCE: THE BURKE MUSEUM, BEECHWORTH

One very wet Sunday morning we went into the Salvation Army Hall in the buggy and ran into a man called Frank Stephens. He said he was a member of the Army and had nowhere to live. Frank had with him a push-bike onto which all his belongings were crammed. My parents never turned anyone away, so he was soon riding home with us behind our buggy.

The house was already pretty crowded but we set him up in the hay shed on a bit of a bed. He came in for lunch, by which time my parents had decided that it was the wrong thing to put a fellow Christian in the shed, so they found room for him on the verandah. He was a decent man and stayed with us for about five months, helping out with jobs around the place. Eventually he wandered off. I think he got a job collecting for the Salvation Army while travelling around on his bike. He never stayed with us again, but he returned to the area, married and had a family.

People such as these invariably gravitated to the Salvation Army for help and because my parents always believed that everyone was God's children, they didn't turn turn their backs on anyone. My parents gave so much of themselves to other people because they believed that was their duty to the Lord. You can't deny the goodness of people who were so dedicated to others, and so big-hearted. It was an attribute in them I always admired. I have always felt compassion for people less fortunate than myself, and it was due entirely to witnessing their boundless humanity. I was always asking people to come in for lunch or to stay the night, which Kath tolerated quite well.

There was a very fastidious old man who lived near us called Max Tomlinson, who was an artist with his axe. He had a scrupulously clean one room hut. I remember the precision with which he stacked half a cord of wood. You could put a line down from the top to the bottom and there wouldn't be any wood sticking out, not even half an inch on either side of the stack. Everything that Max did was neatness to the extreme. He never married, and we never had much to do with him. However he was always lovely to us kids and bought us lollies from the grocer. He also had an old cart in which he carried sides of meat. The dogs were on to him though. If he called in to our place they would surround his cart, and waited expectantly for him to chop them off a few scraps. He never disappointed them.

The old miners in the district then were mostly of Irish descent with names like Maloney and O'Reilly, and every second one was called Paddy. They lived in tents and bush humpys, and were some of the toughest men I've ever known. All their lives they had been hard working, hard drinking, probably very lonely men. They scrounged for food and made a few extra shillings panning for gold.

Most were quite elderly when I knew them, and only had the pension to survive on. Usually they weren't good with their money, so the local grocer Mr Frank Jarvis controlled their pension books. He'd see that they were fed, had enough for their groceries and would give them what was left over. They had no hope of running their own affairs because they'd drink as much as they could get. The pension came every fortnight, and was about 15 or 17 shillings then. On the Tuesday of the dead week, they'd get a bottle of wine which cost a shilling.

On pension day when their finances were a bit better, I'd see them drinking down at the creek, near where the trout farm is at Silver Creek today. In winter time they lay out in front of their huts covered in white frost, still drunk and fast asleep. The strange thing is they never seemed to die of the cold. When the sun came out they'd get up and go and look for some food. Mum always had a stew bubbling on the stove so she'd give these poor old things a meal.

In about 1931 we got our first big break. There was a property of about 55 acres which joined our land belonging to a man we called 'Stingy' Elliott. He didn't like us very much, but we somehow got a solicitor on side and managed to buy the land for one hundred pounds. By now we had almost 90 acres and ran about thirty head of cattle.

Stingy's land was a whopping paddock which ran right back into the Mopoke Ranges. Alongside it were two broad gullies in which gold had been found, so it had been well and truly sluiced out by the miners. The gullies extended down to about 40 or 50 feet outside the paddock and ran for at least five or six miles, almost right into the town. At the top of the hill at the back of Stingy's paddock was a two acre miners right with a little weatherboard house and a wonderful log cabin. The cabin looked just like the one on the lid of the Old Log Cabin tins of American tobacco which was popular in those days.

At the back of the cabin there was a huge old cherry tree which had masses of fruit every year that we picked and ate by the bucketful. The cherry orchardists Christesens used some of the seeds from this original tree when they started their successful cherry business in Stanley. There were also two beautiful big holly trees. At Christmas time we picked holly to decorate Mum's plum puddings.

An old Englishman called Mr Lewis was living in the cabin with a woman whom we referred to as the 'one-eyed gunner'. I don't know why we gave her that name, but she faithfully cared for Mr Lewis, who suffered from the old miner's complaint of consumption. He was what was referred to then as a remittance man — a scion of a wealthy

British family who had done something shameful. His parents had sent him to the colonies to get rid of him. He was sent a lifelong stipend, or remittance, to live on provided he promised never to go home. Every night after school I took them a pint of milk.

Mr Lewis was highly educated and fascinating to talk to. I chatted with him for hours and he told me fantastic stories about England, different ways of living, and what it had been like working in the mines. He described the Zeppelins going over London during the First World War and the start of the flying era in the early 1920s. This fascinated me because it was around the time of the aviatrix Amy Johnson and the epic flights of the Southern Cross. This wise old man gave me some very sound advice for which I will always owe him a debt of gratitude.

While we were chatting, the old lady stayed in the back room working, and then brought us in a cup of tea and a piece of cake. She also took in washing. Two or three times a week she pushed an old fashioned baby carriage, the sort with high wheels and a big basket, down past One Mile and into town loaded up with piles of her clients clean washing. She was only paid about four or five shillings for her efforts. Her laundry work kept them going, because the small remittance he received from England was barely enough to survive on. They didn't have a horse so she wheeled their provisions back home in the pram. She was a lovely old lady whom also smoked a clay pipe. Many of the older women in those days smoked clay pipes.

Our family bought their land for £15 when they died. I don't remember the exact circumstances of their deaths, but the two of them must have been on the grog a bit because we found lots of exotic bottles at the back of the house, whisky, rum and schnapps, I felt very sad when we pulled their old log cabin down and chopped it up for wood.

Right in the middle of the Mopoke Ranges there was an apple orchard of about six or seven acres tended by a man we only knew as Old Jack. He was a bachelor and spent the week in a bark hut among the trees. On the weekend he'd return to Beechworth where he shared a house with his brother Louis, who was a very talented musician and a most distinguished man. I remember Old Jack's orchard well because it was near Stanley, in the heart of the apple growing area. It had some wonderful old fashioned varieties of apples. This was before wholesalers to the export market were only interested in varieties such as Granny Smiths and Coles which could withstand the long voyage to England.

Most orchards were sprayed to keep the black spot down, but Old Jack's orchard was quite isolated and was never sprayed. Eventually the black spot and the codling moths got in there and that was the end of it. Later the rabbits moved in. The rotten things climbed up four or five feet and ate the bark off the trees. Eventually the scrub over-ran and devoured the orchard.

Old Jack also had 50 acres of virgin forest which our family bought in about 1936. Eventually we ended up owning about 300 acres. I will always remember the magnificent stand of stringy bark trees on Old Jack's block. The property was opened up after the War and the timber was sold for the post-war housing boom. However I thought it was a shame as those trees would have been magnificent today.

Stringy bark trees were perfect for building anything, sheds, houses, the lot. The timber splits like matchwood. There was never any money for buying iron or other building materials, so we used to cut down these incredible trees with a broad axe, split the wood into posts and then cut the tops to sell for firewood. When I was 13 or 14 I helped a couple of blokes cart stringy bark sleepers and shingles with a horse and dray.

We used the bark as well, which we cut into seven-foot lengths. We sliced a bottom edge on the tree trunk and a top edge about seven foot up, then cut a vertical split. Then we put a crowbar in on either side of the split and gently eased the bark off the trunk. You had to take great care. Before you could flatten it out you had to get rid of the gum by lighting it. The heat made the sap run and the tube flattened, eventually straightening the bark out. You left it for a while to dry and then it was completely rain-proof and a wonderful insulator.

Charlie, another old local, owned 44 acres a mile and a half past our place. By the time we knew him he was about 50 years old. In the early days his family had kept bees and he used to work in the mines. He had a very bad stomach which he was always treating with antacid. He lived on his own and talked to himself as he rode his bike along the bush tracks, out of loneliness I suppose. We hid on the side of the gully so we could overhear his running commentary on all the townspeople.

We paid him threepence to sharpen our axes on his grindstone. We were never good friends but for a period of time we saw quite a bit of him. He lived in one of the most exquisite huts imaginable, an absolutely perfect wattle and daub hut which he and his father had built. He never mentioned his mother. The walls were made out of clay and very thin, woven stringy bark poles. Both sides of the weave were plastered with clay which was then whitewashed. It had a floor of slabs split from the best trees and placed on bearers.

His father hoarded the local newspaper, which was similar to *The Weekly Times* today. There were still thousands of these papers wrapped up in bundles of ten and stuffed under the gables of their outdoor sheds, as his father had never thrown a single one out.

The locals used to tell a story about Charlie and his love life. Apparently he had only one girlfriend who lived up at One Mile. Charlie was a good bushman and could fix anything. As the story goes, during his courting days he'd go over every Sunday and visit his girlfriend for lunch. On this particular day just before he set out, his mates laced his breakfast tea and bread with a heavy dose of Epsom salts. Then they asked him to fix something in the dairy, which was built in a log cabin style. When he got inside they locked the door, and predictably Charlie felt an urgent call of nature. He was desperate to escape as he must have felt as if his bowels were bursting, but they pretended not to hear his cries for help. Eventually he prised a log out of the wall, jumped out of the dairy and rode off into the bush on his bike for miles. For some strange reason he never returned to see his lady friend after that.

Later on we had a bit of a falling out with him about a spring on the property. Water was a precious commodity in the area and it often lead to fights. After this altercation he'd cycle past our place and in a loud voice shout, 'By crikey I'd like to get even with those Gee's.' But he never did.

Brockie Gladstone lived in a bark hut near a place called Deep Creek off the Stanley Road. He was old enough to remember the early gold mining days, and he was still panning for gold when I first got to know him. He was a fine old man, and very hard working. I'd see him bootless early in the mornings, trudging along apparently impervious to the cold rough ground underfoot. He often sluiced for gold in the creek with the frost thick on the ground. He must have had a hide like a rhinoceros.

Bob the butcher from Stanley was a mate of Brockie's. It appeared that his horse never got chaff. It was the skinniest, dirtiest nag we had ever seen. Teddy Burke said Bob fed the horse on chopped up dogs. Not surprisingly it had trouble keeping going. But Bob was kind to Brockie and left scraps of meat for him in a kerosene tin on a post. Sometimes the meat would be there for a couple of days before Brockie ate it but he never seemed to fall sick, which was more than you could say for Bob's horse. Brockie must have been terribly tough to live on just meat and bread. I never saw him eat any vegetables, but these old blokes still seemed to live to ripe old ages.

When I was about 12 years old Brockie got a job digging the graves at the Stanley cemetery. Years later I remember my father telling me that Brockie had given up the grave digging job because he said the people in Stanley either died very young, or lived to be too old.

Another old miner I knew when I was about 13 was called Terry. I took him milk and listened to his yarns about the old days. He was an excellent gold panner and kept what he found in a pickle bottle. When he was a bit drunk he'd tell me about the brothels that used to be on the goldfields, which I didn't really understand at the time. He loaned a few books to me including one called 'Nights in London' which I was careful to keep out of sight of my parents. He also sang bawdy songs. One story I remember was about this man peering through the keyhole of the door watching this lass getting undressed. The last line of the Song was, 'It was there that I shot the bishop, through the keyhole of the door. I never realised what the story meant until I was at sea and heard what 'shooting the bishop' really meant! I had fond memories of colourful old Terry who lived until he was 80.

Paddy Delaney was also an old miner. He lived in a tent with a fly in which he kept himself and his belongings very tidy. He had once lived in the Woolshed area and he claimed to know the Kelly boys and the Sherritts, which fascinated me.

Kelly country

Ned Kelly, Joe Byrne, Steve Hart and Aaron Sherritt first met in Beechworth gaol in 1877. Not very far from Byrne's home, but on the opposite side of the creek, was the two roomed shack in which lived Aaron Sherritt and his wife. Sherritt had once been Byrne's friend, but now was acting as a police spy. Towards the middle of 1880, Aaron Sherritt asked for police protection, but in spite of four constables sent to guard him, he was sought out by Dan Kelly, and Joe Byrne. On the night of June 25, 1880, Sherritt was called to the door of his hut, where Byrne shot him. Two months later Beechworth played its final part in the hunt and capture of the Kelly gang, when with his wounds healed, Ned Kelly was sent to Beechworth.

On August 6, 1880, at the Court House in Ford Street there began the initial hearing of the trial under Police Magistrate W. Foster. At this stage the Government decided to change the venue of his trial from Beechworth to Melbourne.

It was Ned Kelly himself who provided the final and grimly humorous touch to the part Beechworth had played in his deadly drama. When being escorted from the Court House back to the gaol, he leaned out of the cab and pretended to shoot at the crowd of children who were running behind.

From *A Background to Beechworth* by Roy C. Harvey [p 49]

I once asked Paddy why he never got married. He replied that he was in love with a wonderful girl whom he had taken to a dance somewhere near Bright. They rode about twenty miles by horseback to the dance and danced half the night. Coming out into the cold air afterwards, she caught pneumonia and died soon after. He said he had loved her so dearly that he couldn't bear to meet or marry another woman. I thought it was a very poignant story.

Paddy once saved the life of our beloved horse Bess when she became very lame. A vet called Mr Knight, who had been in France during the First World War and was badly gassed, said that Bess would have to be destroyed. We were very distressed by this but when I told Paddy, he gave me an ointment called Venus Turpentine to try. The leg healed and Bess lasted another eight years.

POS SHENNAN [*Beechworth resident*]: In the old days Silver Creek was a very close-knit community. Many of the descendants of the old families are still out there. Things were tough but that was our way of life and we were hardly ever sick. Our food was all organic. They didn't use the chemicals then that are used today. We killed all the meat we needed, and salted beans and peas and stored them in stone jars. We stored our marrows and pumpkins for months on an old wire mattress on the verandah. No one ever bought jam. There were plenty of blackberries and plums about. We ate lots of rabbits baked or stewed up in a pot with an onion. The boys caught the rabbits with ferrets or traps. People worked much harder and if you wanted to go somewhere you had to ride a bike or a horse.

My grandmother was a midwife, and most people had their children at home. In my younger days at Mudgegonga I used to go to dances at the local parish halls. My brother played the accordian and I enjoyed riding horses to Wooragee to attend dances with him. I met my husband Harry at a dance. Harry's mother sewed rugs for our beds out of old overcoats and lined them with cretonne. I always milked cows before I went to school. Water for the weekly baths for us six kids, was boiled in kerosene cans suspended on hooks over the open fire.

DAD: Blackberries were the curse of the countryside and still are. Before the new sprays were perfected during the War, blackberries were almost impossible to eradicate. Sometimes they were a boon though. We picked them when they were in season, for which we were paid seven shillings a tin. You had to be a very skilful picker to fill a whole kerosene tin with wild blackberries because they used to sink. If you left them for a while when you thought you had a full tin, it would subside down to half full. I wasn't much good at it but I ate plenty. Hannah was an excellent picker, and could easily pick a tin a day. She took them to the railway station, where they'd be sent off to the jam factories.

Blackberry bushes harboured thousands of rabbits. Sometimes blackberry heaps rose to 20 feet, and covered almost a 100 yards around. It was very difficult to get at the rabbits because the dogs couldn't get in, so we burned the bushes. Unfortunately all burning did was stimulate a bumper berry season the next year.

It was a great sight to see our little fox terriers plunging into almost impenetrable blackberry heaps. There'd always be another half dozen dogs lined up waiting for the rabbits to bolt out. Once out, they didn't have much chance, as our dogs had been born and bred with rabbits in mind and could run down even the swiftest. Rabbits were a significant source of revenue for us, and they also fed the dogs. Nape provided most of the revenue — he sold the skins for sixpence a pair, and we kept the meat. Although it wasn't a lot, it all went into the family pot. One of our most extravagant meals was rabbit stuffed with bacon.

Our next door neighbours, the Trahairs, were very kind people. Their children attended a private boarding school in Melbourne, as they had made a lot of money out of mining. They had a vast property and a grand old home in Silver Creek, and were very well respected in the district.

Mrs Trahair would meet five or six of us kids at the gate on our way home from school in Beechworth, and handed us cakes, scones, cut sandwiches and milk. I suppose it was her way of acknowledging that we were having, a tough time, but their generosity was very unobtrusive. I believe the family now own quite a lot of property in the Benalla area.

The Trahairs

John Trahair was born in 1827, in St Just, Cornwall, England. St Just was famous for its tin mines, and no doubt John had acquired a knowledge of mining which he put to good use on his arrival at the Ovens Gold Fields. John's principal occupation was that of miner — he had claims at various times at Stanley, Silver Creek and Three Mile. Retiring from his mining pursuits about 1880, he settled on his five acres of land at Silver Creek where he spent his time tending his sheep and cattle. John, the father of one son John Henry and three daughters, died on February 25, 1908. He is buried in the Beechworth cemetery.

FROM *SILVER THREADS AND GOLDEN NEEDLES* BY M. ROSALYN SHENNAN

Pigs were always important to our family. I must have been about ten when we got the contract to collect the rubbish from the Beechworth Hospital. I used to drive the spring cart to school and leave it at the old

Presbyterian Manse, close to the prison. The rubbish was dumped in the yard at the back of the Hospital. I used to shovel all the kitchen refuse for the pigs into a 44 gallon drum. They got anything and everything. If we ever had a surplus of rabbits we'd boil them up and feed them to the pigs, as well as fallen apples from the orchards in Stanley. We even grew artichokes for them so they did pretty well, but they didn't live long.

We earned quite a bit of money selling dressed pigs to the butcher, a man called Matt. He'd drive out to pick up the carcases in his cart. He never had less than a dozen dogs which barked violently as they approached the house. Matt was good value because he was a great gossip and told us all the news from the town.

We ended up with four or five sows, and we sold the piglets at eight weeks old for nine or ten shillings each. By the time we killed the sows their bellies would be just about touching the ground. Mum made wonderful bacon and egg pies which we took to school.

When I was a prisoner of war I'd sometimes tantalise the other men about those pies when we were discussing food, 'You wouldn't have known what the Depression was like Allan,' they'd say, 'You were living in the land of milk and honey.' In some ways they were right.

Some of the best pets we had over the years were pigs. From every litter there was always one we called the runt, the smallest and weakest of ten or eleven piglets. A runt could never find a tit on the sow, so if it wasn't taken away from the mother it would die. We fed the runts with cow's milk until they glowed. They were the most gorgeous creatures. The dogs would lie down on them out of jealousy, and the other piglets snapped at them.

We had a piglet called Joe which had a curvature of the spine. We nursed him back to health and felt that we could never eat him. He was incredibly affectionate, like a child really, and we were very fond of him. But he grew bigger and bigger, and he ended up in the cooking pot like the others, which upset me for quite a while.

I'll never forget the day I took three eight weeks old piglets to sell to people at a place called Three Mile. Each piglet was in a brown bag tied at the top tightly with string with just a few holes so they could get some air. Anyway I got paid 30 shillings for the pigs but on the way home I lost the money, which was a fortune. When I arrived home and, with great shame, told my parents the money was lost we all ran out and frantically searched the road trying to find it. Then my father had a miraculous stroke of luck. He found a £5 note which had been washed into one of the gullies. I never got belted for losing the money, but I felt guilty for being so careless.

ALLAN GEE [*Uncle Nape's son*]: My father, said it wasn't uncommon to see men five miles outside Beechworth pushing wheelbarrows looking for wood for their fires. They were very fortunate at Silver Creek because they had the horse and cart, and people in town couldn't keep a horse, let alone feed one. Dad said they ate so much rabbit meat it's a wonder they didn't all have rabbit ears. Dad had hundreds of rabbit skins stretched across a wire rack. Lew's job was to take them into Beechworth and sell them to the rabbitohs.

My father said the family survived quite well, despite Grandad's over-zealous generosity. What little money he had he used to give away to less fortunate people. Dad disliked the Salvos because he felt they let his parents down, but Grandad remained loyal to them to his last day. He always proudly wore his uniform. I have very fond memories of him. He was a very kindly man, and a great story-teller. He had a lovely voice and always spoke clearly and precisely. He was highly regarded as a great orator. I never had the privilege of hearing him preach but everyone said he was very impressive. I don't think he ever saw the inside of a pub.

One day grandad walked this massive sow and a litter of piglets from the markets in Wangaratta and was heading back towards Beechworth, a distance of 22 miles (35 km). Apparently the sow got so tired it just lay down and wouldn't go any further, in spite of much prodding from Grandad. He didn't know what to do, so he tied it up to a tree, went home and returned the next morning to find it had gone. This was a terrible loss to him, a sow and God knows how many piglets. Years later they found out the fellow they had suspected of stealing the sow had taken it up into the bush and bred from it for years. It sounds funny now, but then it was a disaster for the family.

Colourful characters

Beechworth was once a town that was rich, not only in gold, but in colourful characters. Mick Dougherty whose fame spread far beyond this district was a renowned story-teller and coach driver.

Then there is Mr John Brown, the barber. Only in the pages of a Dickens novel would you find anyone to compare with this delightful character. Others that are sure to be remembered are Constable Bones (Old Bones) Hans Susemiehl, the town bell-ringer, Nicholas (Nicky) Dowling, a cabby for the better part of 64 years, Mrs. Connelly of Newtown with her rich brogue and dry Irish wit, and the irascible little man, Billy Poodle.

Other colourful characters included, Cranky Jimmy, Granny Doyle, Patsy Benbow, Cemetery Jack, Jimmy the Dog, Terence O'Connor, Louis Costa and his little dog drawn cart.

FROM *A BACKGROUND TO BEECHWORTH* BY ROY C. HARVEY [P 45]

DAD: Another way I helped make money was by doing a small milk round after school. We were milking about nine or ten cows, which really boosted our income. We had bells around the cows' necks, so we heard these wonderful clanging sounds through the bush early in the morning and at dusk as they gambolled around the hillsides.

Our cattle were as self-reliant as we were and were accustomed to scrounging for food. They had no compunction about barging through fences into other people's properties. The neighbours screamed a bit but mostly they didn't mind. However once they got into a big cherry orchard owned by the Christesen family and ate the tops off 15 acres of newly planted trees just as they were about to flower. There was no way we could compensate Mr Christesen, even though we offered to work for six months for nothing. Fortunately they were very understanding.

We had a wonderful orchard of apple trees out the back of the house. I had a very peculiar experience related to them after I survived the sinking of *Perth* in 1942. One was an exquisite Roman Beauty apple tree which bore delicious fruit. When *Perth* went down I was eventually picked up by the Japs. Being utterly exhausted, I went into a sort of trance sitting on the quarterdeck of the Jap destroyer. I must have been quite delirious because I thought I saw water rushing past me.

I imagined I was Tom from 'The Water Babies' (by Charles Kingsley). It all looked so beautiful, but I was black with oil and all I wanted to do was to jump in after them. Then I had a dreamy feeling that I was sitting under the Roman Beauty apple tree at Silver Creek. The memory of sitting there peacefully has never left me.

The only animals we didn't have on our farm were sheep because they wouldn't have survived the dozens of mine shafts. Sheep also herd tightly together and lose control when they get frightened. I have always thought sheep were incredibly stupid, and that was confirmed when I had hundreds of the bloody things on my own farm in Wooragee.

Once we had a giant Ayrshire bull which was serving one of our cows. I was in the dairy doing something and I decided to hunt the bull out. Well he charged me full on, caught me and tossed me in the air. Fortunately I had a scout belt on because his razor sharp horn caught in the ring of my old style belt which stopped me being gutted, but it did slash into my left side, twisted and just missed my kidneys. The old doctor who attended me sewed me up with a bag stitch and left a dreadful scar. When I had my medical to join the Navy I was terrified the scar was so ragged that it would stop me being accepted, 'It must be alright,' the Navy doctor said, 'You look pretty good now.'

Not only did we practically live off the land, but many of our dealings were done on the barter system. We sometimes traded wood to the grocer, and dropped off potatoes to pay other bills. We even sold pipe clay which we dug out of the hills. It went for about a penny a pound. Townspeople used it for whitewashing their stoves and fireplaces. It was heavy work extracting and delivering it into town on poor old Bess.

We always had chooks for eggs and meat, but when we tried turkeys, which are notorious wanderers, the foxes got most of them. Despite all our dogs around, if we hadn't locked the chooks up at night we would have lost them too.

One of my biggest mistakes was a passion to own a couple of goats. I nagged my parents until they allowed me to buy a pair on the condition that I looked after them. I bought a couple of Saanen goats somewhere in Beechworth for one shilling and sixpence. They became the curse of my life. I had a vision of training them, and driving them but they were impossible to train. I thought they would survive quite well eating blackberries, but they preferred to eat everything in the garden including the apple trees, flowers and vegetables. These goats plagued my life, but they were lovable creatures. They had an appealing way of looking up at you with big brown eyes so you could never be rough on them. I tied them up in front of blackberry heaps and they'd nibble them, but mostly they'd stand up on top of the fence posts and bleat their heads off. I had them for about five months until they decided to go bush, which delighted my whole family. Inevitably they colonised the Mopoke Ranges and their descendants are still there. I never wanted to own another goat!

This was not my first experience of contributing to the population of feral wildlife. When I was about nine I hatched a scheme to make my fortune breeding Angora rabbits for their fur. I had visions of selling these beautiful white bunnies at two pounds a pair, and I was convinced that demand would outstrip supply. Well rabbits being rabbits they multiplied at an alarming rate and before long I had 40 of them. I couldn't really afford to go on feeding them and predictably some escaped. I only ever sold one pair for two guineas. I don't know how many eventually survived in the wild, but they soon became quite a nuisance around our property living under the sheds and everywhere else. The locals found them simple targets because they were so easy to see at night.

Mum compulsively attended auctions. Whenever someone moved or died she'd be at the clearing sale buying odds and ends for sixpence or a shilling. I used to marvel at the treasures that she'd find, especially all the books. We were keen readers from an early age, and the house was always full of books. I remember being thrilled by *Robinson Crusoe* by Daniel Defoe, stories by Edgar Wallace, *Treasure Island* by Robert Louis Stevenson, *Call of the Wild* by Jack London, *King Solomon's Mines* by J. Rider Haggard, Zane Grey's stories, *Sinbad the Sailor* and other seafaring stories, little realising that's where my destiny lay. *Sea Patrol* by Jack London was a particular favourite of mine, in fact I loved any book about early explorers and sailing ships. Even though our parents were very strict, thankfully they never censored what we read.

My whole family liked sitting around and talking about books. I'm sure it greatly broadened our outlook. It certainly enhanced my education, which I needed because I left school when I was barely 13. I have no doubt that my early reading fostered my great love for the sea. Later when I joined the Navy at 17 years old I was very grateful that my parents inspired me to read and follow my dream.

My broad reading knowledge also meant that I could mix with people easily and converse on a wide range of topics. Years later after I had joined the Navy I hung around with Norman Lindsay, the colourful author and illustrator of *The Magic Pudding*, William Dobell the painter, and some of the writers from *The Bulletin* magazine. My kids are all avid readers.

It was a momentous day when Mum returned from one of the auction sales with an old Edison gramophone with big loud speakers and boxes of cylinder records. It was fantastic hearing music other than hymns. We loved listening to those American and English artists singing their hearts out. We played them all the time and learnt the songs by heart.

My eldest brother Napier (Nape) was 14 years old when he got his first job at Jarvis' grocery store. There was a great fuss because he didn't have a proper pair of trousers to wear. Mr Jarvis was very kind-hearted and gave him a five shillings advance on his first pay packet so he could buy some strides for work. He was an incredibly generous man. The Depression hit everyone hard and he used to feed dozens of families in the town who didn't have enough to eat. His son Max later became one of our closest friends.

Nape was a true Depression boy. He'd start work at eight in the morning and wouldn't get home until half past six in the evening. He would immediately go out and cut wood to supplement his income. He became a very fine axeman as a result. At night before coming in for dinner Nape never failed to set his 40 rabbit traps. He was careful with his money but very generous to other family members if they ever needed assistance.

I think Nape was Dad's favourite and he always dreamed of owning his own property which he did as soon as he could afford it. By the time

Nape left Silver Creek in 1951 to move to Gippsland he had expanded his holding to 500 acres. He was a quiet man and a phenomenal shot with a gun. Nape was well respected and later became a very successful dairy farmer in Moyhu. He worked hard all his life.

ALLAN GEE [*Uncle Nape's son*]: When the Second World War broke out my father Nape was an ordinary private stationed in the Army camp near Frankston. He was transferred to a transport division where he drove trucks. He spent most of the war in Alice Springs and Darwin and served in the action zone. His unit was in Darwin for three weeks at a time, then moved back to Alice Springs, so none of his battalion were ever in active service. They weren't in Darwin the day it was bombed. However he saw the Japanese aircraft overhead, and all of the devastation when they arrived the next day. They helped bring out a lot of survivors, many of whom had fled into the desert. Dad once told me that the only thing he enjoyed about the Army was being in the band and playing cards. Unlike the Navy the Army did not always look after its own.

He met my mother Vera at a dance at the Preston Town Hall when he was on leave in Melbourne in 1940. He said to his mate, 'I'm going to marry that girl,' and he did in 1942. When he died they had been married for 51 years.

Non-combatants such as Dad suffered a great deal too. By the end of the War, of my father's group relatively few were still fit for duty. Dad finished up in Melbourne with dust on his lungs. He was discharged from the Army in late 1944 as medically unfit. Because manpower was in short supply in those days and he was a truck driver, he was put to work on the tramway buses in Melbourne. In 1947 he returned to the farm at Silver Creek, where he remained until about 1951.

DAD: My 14th birthday was coming up in October. I left school without any regrets in August 1933 for the school holidays and never returned. I worked on the farm and helped Mum and Dad until I got a job at the Tannery. I didn't miss the teachers, but I missed the company of the other school kids. However, I kept up with my own reading.

My elder brother Bramwell and my older sister Miriam were quite brilliant at school. Miriam worked terribly hard at her lessons but she was frustrated by our family's lack of money. We were always battling to get enough for lessons, books and uniforms. I remember when she was 16 or 17 years old she had no shoes other than some old sandshoes which she had patched up. She completed her Matriculation and later became a teacher then a librarian. She taught at several schools until she married Bert Brewer, later to become my brother-in-law.

UNCLE BRAM: The biggest mistake in my life was that I dropped out of high school. I was 12 years old, and was two years past what they called the Merit Certificate. It nearly broke my mother's heart. I had the brains but there were other factors which came into play. I enjoyed school but people didn't realise how hard it was for us. All I could do at the time was just keep up with my reading.

We were living at Silver Creek and were milking cows. My older brother Napier had gone to work in Beechworth and he didn't have much time to spend helping out at home. Then he bought a paddock of his own and he was too busy with his own affairs, so a lot of that responsibility fell on me. I always seemed to be stuck with milking all these cows before I went to school and again when I got home. And it wasn't as if they were confined to one paddock. They were all over the place, as well as along the lanes. You had to find the wretched animals before you could milk them.

Sometimes people who had no idea of farm life were critical of me for not keeping up with studies. As far as I am concerned family duties came first. I was competing with fellows who had never done a day's work in their life, people who had good jobs and a reliable income with no worries about anything. We were struggling just to keep going. Dad was away a lot selling a variety of door-to-door products. In fact he was only really happy when he was helping someone or delivering the Lord's message.

I had a very good job at Zwar's Tannery in Beechworth for two or three years. I worked in the staining shed and on some of the machines. The Tannery used a lot of water and many people in the town started complaining that too much was being taken out of Lake Kerferd. We were worried that this fuss would close the Tannery down. It would have been a tragedy as it employed almost 200 people.

There was a spring which ran through a piece of our land at Silver Creek, so we always had plenty of water. Because the townspeople were still ranting on about the Tannery using all the water, Dad allowed them to come and collect fresh water from our spring. He was a bit of a sucker and found it hard to turn people down. But he was cunning enough to say to the Tannery owners that they could have the water if his boys could always get a job, to which they readily agreed.

The Tannery

In 1858 Matthew Dodd established his Tannery on Malakoff Road, Newtown. This was acquired by the Zwar brothers in 1888 and continued to operate through Beechworth's decline. The Beechworth Tannery produced every grade of dress leather, and also sole leather, from both local and imported hides. In 1915, most of the buildings of the Tannery were burnt to the ground. This crisis forced a decision, whether to invest further in an industry sited in the country, or to bow to increasing transport costs and the need for nearby markets.

Consultations with railway commissioners and reduced railway freight charges enabled the Zwars to rebuild the Tannery on its original site two miles from Beechworth. 'Local sentiment', it was said had influenced the decision. The image of 'Old Man Zwar' watching the flames engulf his life's work, yet vowing to support his town by rebuilding, became a popular one in Beechworth. In a town which was losing confidence in its own future, no action could have earnt him more respect. As one resident said in honour of Mr Zwar in 1922, 'All remembered the burning of the Tannery.'

Once rebuilt the Beechworth Tannery became renowned for the fine quality of its leathers. The Tannery, as a major employer in Beechworth and a generator of social and sporting activities such as annual picnics and cricket matches, became closely woven into the fabric of community life. Beechworth's first electricity supply in 1926 came from the Tannery's plant, and that service was continued until 1946. The Beechworth Tannery closed in 1961.

THE BEECHWORTH TANNERY 1858-1961. COURTESY THE BURKE MUSEUM, BEECHWORTH.

DAD: I started work at the Zwar brothers Tannery when I was 15 years old. I rode my bike through Silver Creek down into the town, and then to what was called Newtown. I'd turn off Malakoff Road, go down the hill into the gully and on to the Tannery. It was in an area called the gorge which is still a strikingly beautiful part of Beechworth. I saw the trains which ran then between Beechworth and Wangaratta at ten to eight in the morning, and I'd think to myself, 'Someday I'll get away from here for a bit of adventure.' As it turned out I got more than I bargained for during the War.

Beechworth railway

The first train arrived in Beechworth on July 13, 1876, but the official opening did not take place until September 29, when the ceremony was performed by His Excellency Sir George Bowen. After the opening a banquet was held in the goods shed and among those present were the Minister for Railways (Mr Jones) Hon. G.B. Kerferd, the Mayor of Melbourne, Mayors of all the surrounding towns and the French and American Consuls. In the evening 350 couples attended a ball for which a double ticket cost thirty shillings. This however, included a moonlight train trip to Everton and back.

A BACKGROUND TO BEECHWORTH BY ROY C. HARVEY [P 23]

DES ZWAR [*great grandson of the founder of the Tannery*]: I never missed going down to see Allan and Kath in Wooragee each time I returned to Beechworth from England and enjoyed their warm welcome and Allan's philosophy. I don't remember any talk of the War, which I guess is strange. It was always a case of feeding off each other's mind. Allan wanted to know about England and what I thought of things. I wanted to enjoy his unique down-to-earth honesty and the pleasure of having an older man as a friend.

Allan was always serious; always caring about how I thought my parents were faring; always offering to keep an eye on Mum after Dad died. I guess he was the most reliable Beechworth friend I had. There was no doubt in my mind that if needed, he would respond to a call from me and would be by Mum's side in an instant. And so would Kath. In short I loved them both.

DAD: I was lucky to work in the kid leather shed, which was one of the best jobs at the Tannery. My brother Bram was already working there and I knew a lot of the other blokes, who were friends of our family. Twelve months later they closed down the kid shed so I was moved to the staining shed and I had to work the printer and put designs on the leather. There were no unions then and this was a job often given to boys. Nearly everyone else who did this job had lost a couple of fingers in the two great rollers which printed crocodile and pigskin markings on the leather. I made a great friend there, a delightful man called Eddie Martin who was very good to me.

What I remember most about the Tannery is the smell of the leather. You reeked of it for 24 hours a day and nothing could get rid of it. I enjoyed the work and was paid 25 shillings a week, which was enough to buy my food and clothes. Best of all I had enough money to afford to go to the pictures on Saturday night. My mother really frowned on this but I was quite independent then and had started to imagine a life beyond the Tannery and Silver Creek. I thought there must be something more to life than this. I would look down through the pits at the Tannery and see these poor men scudding the flesh off the hides who had been working there all their lives. It was a filthy job and many had started there and had no idea of a different life.

I read every book I could find about the sea and the local theatre showed a marvellous film called called 'Brown on Resolution'. It was a story from the First World War in which Brown's ship had been sunk and he made it to the shore on one of the islands in the Caribbean. The film showed a lot about what happened on ships. As I watched footage of the sailors I thought, 'That's what I'm going to do, I'm going to join the Navy.' Some people at the Tannery talked up how tough the Navy would be, and I remember thinking, 'How would you know you've never been out of Beechworth?' These pessimists had never seen a ship and many hadn't even seen the ocean. Even my brother Bram told me how tough the Navy was and he was very sceptical about my ambitions. Bram knew as much about the Navy as the bloke who took the sewage away, but I suppose he was trying to protect me in some way.

3

'PINEDALE'

The Brewer family home

John Brewer of Trewint, Cornwall and his wife Mary had three adventurous sons, John, William and Richard, and two daughters. In 1849 at the age of 17, his son John migrated to Australia after the death of his parents, finally settling in Wooragee after a stint at sea and on the goldfields. He married Charlotte and they had nine children. His two brothers came to Australia shortly after. William Brewer started an orchard in Wooragee. He married Jane and had six children William, Mary (known as Minnie), Ellen (known as Nellie), Elizabeth (Lizzie), David and Anna.

The younger John Brewer was 'Pop' Brewer's uncle, and was the first Brewer to come to Australia and the district.

Obituary: Mr John Brewer

The ranks of the old pioneers in the district have been further depleted, and it is our sorrowful duty to record the passing away of a highly respected resident who has been associated with the town for over half a century.

Mr John Brewer of Wooragee passed to that place from which no traveller returns on August 13, at Nurse Edwards' private hospital after an illness extending over several months. The deceased gentleman was a native of Cornwall, and in 1849 came to Australia where he was engaged in taking cattle and sheep from this continent to New Zealand in a sailing vessel.

On the discovery of gold in Australia Mr. Brewer relinquished the sea-faring life, and entered on the quest for gold. He was at Ballarat in the early days and was on that field at the time of the Eureka riots. The Ovens Goldfield subsequently claimed his attention, and hither Mr. Brewer wended his way, and for a time was engaged in mining. He afterwards commenced a dairy on the Wooragee Road, about three miles from Beechworth.

By hard work he prospered, and later on bought some valuable properties at Wooragee, where he afterwards went to reside. Although well advanced in years, it was his practice until recently to personally deliver milk to his customers, and he was remarkable for his punctuality.

He always enjoyed good health until about three months ago when he was compelled to come to Beechworth for medical treatment, and although for a while his health improved the inevitable end came on Friday night.

Mr. Brewer passed away peacefully within a few days of being 83 years of age. The late Mr. Brewer was married at St. Mark's Church, Malvern 61 years ago to Charlotte Warren, a sister of the late Mr. Richard Warren, and last year he and his wife celebrated the diamond jubilee of their wedding.

In addition to his widow, a grown up family of nine sons and daughters, all highly respected is left.

Charlotte Brewer died on 11th October 1918 aged 83. They are both buried in the Beechworth Cemetery.

The sons are Messrs. John (Victorian Railways), Richard (Malvern) and William (Wooragee) and the daughters Mrs. Hitchens (Malvern), Miss Ellen Brewer (Wooragee) Mrs. Kennedy (Geelong), Mrs. J. W. Denier (Hastings) Mrs. White (Malvern) and Mrs. Nicholl (Sydney).

The funeral took place on Sunday afternoon and the remains were followed to the Beechworth Cemetery by a large concourse of friends.

OVENS & MURRAY ADVERTISER, AUGUST 18, 1915

Richard Randall Brewer, my Brewer great-grandfather, married Cassandra Parr, aged 30, at Beechworth when he was aged 35, and had four children Mary, Ellen, Richard and my Brewer grandfather Arthur 'Pop' Brewer. Richard Randall Brewer, had earlier started a dairy in Malvern, Melbourne before moving to 'Pinedale', which was then a vegetable farm in Leneva, several miles out of Wooragee. 'Pinedale' became the Brewer family home. Richard Randall Brewer died in Melbourne on April 14, 1897 from cancer of the thyroid.

My Brewer grandmother was Clara May Brewer, who was originally a Phillips. As a child I vividly remember staying at Nana's farm 'Pinedale' at Leneva, ten miles out of Wodonga on the Beechworth Road. This picturesque property, set in rolling green hills flanked by willows and pretty streams, was my mother Kath's childhood home which she shared with her eight siblings. The house was a rabbit warren of bedrooms, sleep-outs, and pantries. Outdoors was dotted with sheds, chook-houses, yards and kennels overrun by a menagerie of animals there to delight us. Nana inevitably greeted us at the front gate in a shapeless floral frock and straw hat, hand watering a bed of dahlias.

She was a prodigious gardener. Apart from myriad flowers, she grew every imaginable vegetable from climbing beans to rhubarb. Nana was famous for snipping cuttings from other people's gardens, and carried a pair of secateurs in her handbag at all times. The highlight for my twin sister Christine and I was sifting through Nana's bedroom, an Aladdin's Cave of bric-a-brac overflowing with flowery hats, knots of stockings, scarves, gloves, jewellery, notebooks, handkerchiefs, lavender bags and perfume bottles. Sheafs of banknotes often tumbled from purses and handbags.

One night we stayed and shared Nana's sagging double bed. Around midnight she heaved herself out of bed and settled on her enormous porcelain chamber pot for what seemed like an eternity. She also snored like a trombone, so all in all we had a sleepless night. The next morning I sprang from the bed straight into her brimming pot! Clara May Brewer was unforgettable.

Arthur and Clara Brewer had nine children, Arthur (Artie), Marjorie (Marge), Albert (Bert), Frank, Reginald (Reg), Gwen, Mary, Kathleen (Kath), and Colin (Ted). My mother Kath and Mary were twins. Mary was born first and had cerebral palsy. The delivery was breech and was assisted with forceps. Her condition was not apparent for several months, but it has afflicted her all her life. My aunts Marge, Mary, Gwen, my uncle Bert, and his son Allan Brewer and daughter Meryl Brown and others have greatly assisted with this chapter.

AUNTIE MARGE SCHUBERT [*Mum's sister*]: The original 'Pinedale' home had four rooms and was surrounded by beautiful pine trees. Dad's full name was Arthur Randall Brewer. Many Brewer sons through the generations were given the middle name of Randall.

ALLAN BREWER [*Uncle Bert's and Auntie Miriam's son*]: Pop's father Richard Randall Brewer initially had a dairy farm in Malvern, which then was an outer Melbourne suburb. Pa Brewer milked cows and sold the milk door to door from a horse and cart to the ladies in Toorak.

He later moved to 'Pinedale' in Leneva West. His Uncle William had already been growing vegetables in Wooragee for some years. Pop Brewer was born at 'Pinedale' in 1884, and he later inherited the property from his father. I've seen a photo taken in 1917 of the back of 'Pinedale' when all the hills were densely timbered. Nowadays most of the area has been cleared. In 1919 Pop purchased Hicks' block, named after a drover from Queensland who used to drive cattle down to the Newmarket saleyards in Melbourne. He would leave his horses at 'Pinedale' then, on the way back to Queensland, he'd collect the fresh horses.

The old Wooragee Hotel

'Pinedale' was a popular overnight stop for many of the old-time drovers herding cattle and sheep because it had a laneway which ran down onto a creek. The drovers would build up herds along the way. Sometimes they would leave as many as 200 head at 'Pinedale' before moving them to market or dropping them off at other properties.

I have very fond memories of Pop Brewer. He started out with only 40 acres, but when he died he owned close to 1,500 acres. He left school when he was 13 years old, and earned his living by shepherding sheep to protect them from wild dogs. He was paid three shillings and sixpence a week which allowed him to save enough money to buy a horse, saddle and bridle.

I remember Pop shooting vealers, pigs, and snakes. There is an unwritten law that the eldest Brewer son from each generation is to receive Pop's gun. It was passed on to me by Uncle Artie who gave it to me for my 50th birthday. Next in line is my son David.

UNCLE BERT BREWER [*Mum's brother*]: Dad, known as Pop by the family, lived at 'Pinedale' with his mother Cassandra, who lived to almost 90, before he married Mum. It was a hard life. He started out with a small holding and there was hardly any money to be made. Their main income was from dairying, but he also ran a few sheep.

ALLAN BREWER: It is unconfirmed, but I believe Nana Brewer's grandmother, my great-great-grandmother had a child out of wedlock. Her original name may have been Lascelles. I heard that she got into trouble with a sailor named Phillips, and she gave the baby the father's name. They may have married later. That's how the Phillips name came about. Perhaps that explain's Nana's reticence about Kath marrying Allan, a sailor!

My great-great grandmother's second husband was a Nankervis, although there is some doubt that they actually married. However, she was always called Granny Nankervis. She is buried with Ma Phillips at Wodonga Cemetery. In 1913 the Nankervis' left Corryong for Wooragee. They travelled by bullock wagon, a journey which took ten days.

AUNTIE MARGE: My mother Clara Brewer's father was Frederick Phillips. Mum was the eldest girl in the Phillips family. Her brothers and sisters were Arthur, Frederick, Winnie, Alice, Maude, Robert (Bob), and William. My grandfather was a tall man, a miner from Bethanga, on the New South Wales-Victorian border. He died of silicosis, the old miner's condition of rock dust on the lungs.

Bethanga

From 1836 until the early 1870s Bethanga was the name of a pastoral run. The appearance of selectors was soon followed by gold prospectors and miners. A government body The Goldfields Rewards Committee, fixed the discovery of the Bethanga Goldfield in May 1875. A gold rush of moderate proportions got under way from the beginning of 1876. During 1877-78 the population reached about 1,500, and it probably never exceeded 2,000.

THE MAKING OF A MINING COMMUNITY, BETHANGA, AND VICTORIA 1875-1885 BY JUNE PHILIPP

Hume and Hovell were probably the first white men to set foot anywhere near Bethanga and Springdale; in 1825 they crossed the Murray just above its junction with the Mitta Mitta River not far from where the Bethanga Bridge now stands. The aboriginal population was left undisturbed for ten years longer. In 1849 Joseph Henry Packer, the son of wealthy London cotton merchants and mill owners, came to Australia to cure his health. When he did not return his family sent his fare.

Instead of returning he married Mary Egan (in Fremantle, WA) whom he had met on the journey out and they bought a small farm below Wodonga. Because he had married a Catholic he was disowned by his family. In 1868, at the age of 38, Joseph Packer died leaving his wife and seven children (Esther, Mary-Ann, Joseph, Julia who was Clara Brewer's mother, Margaret, William, and John) in very poor circumstances.

Mary kept the family together and when he had grown up young Joseph selected 320 acres at Springdale, and built a hut on it. His sister, later Mrs Saunders, selected a further 320 acres; a home was built on it and she stayed and kept house until the residence conditions had been fulfilled and she was free to sell the land to her brother.

When he died Joseph Packer (Jr.) had acquired about 4,000 acres of land. While the land was still heavily timbered he bought 1,000 wethers (sheep); he drove

*them into the hills during the day and brought them back close to the hut at night,
lighting fires to keep dingoes away. Shearing took about two months and the
wool was taken to Wodonga by bullock train. Joseph Packer married Margaret
Toohey of Dederang and they had three sons, Joseph, Francis and Thomas.
(A daughter died in early childhood.) Joseph was a non-Catholic, but his wife
Margaret and three sons were Catholics.)*
EARLY DAYS IN BETHANGA AND SPRINGDALE BY JUNE PHILIPP

*They were harsh times for the men, working from early morning till late at night
clearing land, splitting timber for posts and working on the mines under primitive
conditions. While we look back on their deeds with pride, it is the womenfolk
who have been overlooked. No woman today could ever imagine the terrible
foreboding each pregnant woman had. The reasons were many — the midwife may
not be able to deliver it, the doctor might be in another area or the river might be
in flood and isolating Bethanga. Last but not least there was a terrible fear of
dying from blood poisoning.*

*The poor, over-burdened women with their large families usually lost one or more
children from illness. It was known for whole families to be wiped out by diseases
such as diptheria. One mother set off in the gig to have her baby at Wodonga.
With her husband driving they tried to race ahead of a violent storm which had
blown up. The baby was born in the gig amid torrential rain with no ill effect to
mother or child. Another privation these woman had to endure was loneliness as
husbands were sometimes away working for months at a time. Sometimes illness
struck a family while the husband was shearing or fencing many miles away on
a large station. One of the greatest privations for families living in the bush was
the lack of schooling for their children. On the lighter side, a mob of 40 turkeys
was purchased for these isolated families. It was found to be impractical to load
them onto pack horses. If they were not carried their feet could not have withstood
the many miles over the sharp rocks in the mountains. The men decided to run
tar on the ground and then put sand in front of the tar. The turkeys were run
through and came out with bitumenised feet! To our early Bethanga settlers who
suffered such great hardships — we salute you.*

*Fred Phillips (Clara Brewer's father) selected land at Springdale. In 1897 he
married Julia Packer. In 1901 he sold his property to his brother-in-law Joseph
Packer and moved to Leneva where he again selected land and also purchased*

some. He farmed this property until his death when it was taken over by his sons Art, Bob and Bill — the homestead portion is still owned by descendants today. Julia became a Catholic towards the end of her life.

A HISTORY OF ST FRANCIS BETHANGA BY PAT R. PACKER.

AUNTIE MARGE: My grandmother's maiden name was Julia Packer before she married Fred Phillips in 1897. We called her 'Grandma Phillips'. If you cut a photo out of the paper of the well-to-do Sydney Packers and compared them to our lot, the men bear a striking resemblance. The shape of the nose and the jawline is identical. I remember Grandma Phillip's brother Joe. He was the image of Kerry Packer. Joe Packer was Mum's uncle. I remember when Joe arrived at 'Pinedale' one day in a Fiat car and in those days that was like having a Rolls Royce. Mum's first cousin, Frank Packer, also had a Fiat. Joe eventually moved into Wodonga where we visited him with Mum and Dad. His cottage was where the Wodonga Hospital stands today.

The Packers of Bethanga were well off, and had big families, a few had seven and eight children. In those days they ran some cattle, but they mainly had sheep for wool. Every three or four months they came down to 'Pinedale' for Sunday dinner (lunch) in their big flash cars. The Packer family hosted a big family reunion on October 6, 1980 and Mum received a plaque for being the oldest there.

Grandma and Fred 'Pa' Phillips came to live at Leneva, just down the road from 'Pinedale', in a weatherboard house called 'Loretto'. Pa Phillips died in bed, but out in the open in summer under a cherry-plum tree.

MG: Mrs Pat Packer told me that considerable research has been done into the Packer family and she is fairly certain that there is no family link with the Sydney based Packers.

MERYL BROWN [*Uncle Bert and Auntie Miriam's daughter*]: Grandma Phillips reared turkeys. She ran 20 or 30 at a time, and sold some at Christmas. She loved her turkeys. She was always outside just before dark, feeding the chooks and turkeys and gathering eggs.

Nana's eldest brother Fred was killed in an accident while riding a motor bike over the Sydney Harbour Bridge. He was only in his 30s, and left a wife and young family. Apart from Fred, all the Phillips' lived well into their 80s and 90s.

UNCLE BERT: Ma Phillips was a short lady, and a lovely old soul. She was fond of gardening and turkeys, which she fed wheat. When her son Bill killed a pig, Grandma would catch the blood in an enamel dish as it gushed from the pig's throat and make it into black and white puddings. She mixed the blood with a bit of rice and other meat then hung the puddings on hooks in front of the fire to smoke them. It was a big event for her. She never missed a pig kill.

Dad made beautiful bacon and hams. He would put the cuts of pork in a big wooden box he kept in the storeroom and rub them once a week with salt and saltpetre. It was the best bacon I've ever eaten. The hams were also hung in front of the fire and smoked.

MERYL BROWN: When a pig was killed it was first put into the copper in the orchard where it was boiled to remove the bristles from the skin. Pop had big vats in the stone out-houses where he made delicious silverside, hams and bacons. I used to go out with him and he'd say, 'Now you put a pinch of this and a pinch of that,' as he stirred the vats to turn the meat. Nana Brewer made the most beautiful sausages. She had a machine into which she put all the meat and turned a handle. When they killed the sheep and cattle she kept all the guts, and made the sausage cases out of them.

AUNTIE MARGE: Mum was close to her siblings, in particular to our Auntie Win and Uncle Bill. Win lived with Uncle Bill and his wife Annie and helped raise their three sons and two daughters. Bill and Annie were primarily dairy farmers, but they also grew tomatoes and pumpkins on the rich black flats across the creek. Bill was a good farmer and Annie was a very hard worker. She was still in the dairy milking when she was six and seven months pregnant. She had one baby after the other and was a wonderful mother. They were all ardent Catholics. Uncle Bill was also a great singer and his daughter Kath Fulford sings beautifully too.

Mum's sister Maude was a bit of whinger, and married a man called Fred Stasson. She worked very hard and went around on her bike cleaning hotels. She was a very keen fisherwoman, and often rode her bike down to the Murray River at South Albury. She always seemed to catch something, and would ring up the family to say, 'Come in, I've caught a big cod!' Maude battled on and reared two daughters after her son died at birth. Maude died shortly after Mum. They had both been living at the aged care home Osborne Lodge. Mum died on March 16, 1984, aged 93.

Bob was the youngest of Mum's brothers and sisters. He never married but he had a great life. He was always out and about, particularly dancing. His last days were spent at the Ovens and Murray Benevolent Home in Beechworth.

Mum's sister, Alice (our Auntie Al) became a nun (Sister Christina), but before that she was a schoolteacher at Baranduda. She taught my husband Walter and boarded with his cousin during the week. They couldn't stand her. She rode a bike to school from Leneva after each weekend, and was always late on Monday mornings, probably because of all the cows she had to milk before she set off. By the time she reached the school — population about 17 — the kids would have all been down the river swimming, and no doubt getting into trouble. Walter told me that one day they caught a goanna and tied it to the school gate to frighten her. They were demons. They also pricked her tyres on Friday afternoons, so she'd have a flat when she tried to ride back to Leneva for the weekend.

Auntie Al was a Catholic, as Mum was, and trained as a novitiate at Goulburn. As children she drove us all mad talking about religion. She half lived at the church. She carted us off to mass in a horse and gig about once a month. Afterwards we'd all have morning tea, which was the best part.

I was born at Dr Wood's Hospital in Albury, as were Bert, Frank and Artie. Reg was the first of Mums's children to be born at 'Pinedale'. When Mum gave birth at home she was assisted by a midwife called Granny Kiel who lived in a dear little whitewashed cottage on the creek surrounded by willows. Bert used to pinch her quinces and apples. Because the phone wasn't connected when the midwife was needed, one of us would run up to fetch her. There was mostly only a two year difference between the nine of us, and only 15 months in the case of Reg, Frank, Gwen and the twins (Kath and Mary). Auntie Win also helped Mum when she gave birth at 'Pinedale'. She was as good as a nurse.

ALLAN BREWER: We loved teasing Auntie Win when we were young. We'd hide outside her window and mimic foxes barking. She'd run out yelling because she thought the foxes were after her precious turkeys.

AUNTIE MARGE: Auntie Win was a great character. She loved to dress up and go to the races in Wodonga. She was also the Postmistress for Leneva West and operated the public telephone from 'Loretto'. She had to deliver telegrams to everyone because most people didn't have the phone connected. The mail was delivered in a horse and gig three days a week to Leneva West by the mailman from Wodonga. Urgent telegrams were delivered to Auntie Win, and someone would be dispatched to deliver them by horseback.

I recall Auntie Win would come in from across the creek where she had been picking tomatoes, looking like something out of the ragbag. Suddenly she'd say, 'Oh it's nearly time for the mailman. I'd better tidy myself up.' She'd wash her feet, put on another dress and a clean apron, and come out sparkling.

Auntie Win helped out all the Phillips' and the Brewers, including my father, with the milking. If she wasn't helping one she'd be making pickles and sauce for another. She also grew raspberries and made delicious jam.

She was engaged to a man called Maloney. They were both relatively old at the time, and went out together for years. Mr Maloney came down to Leneva every Sunday to court Win. I was boarding in Wodonga and attending Albury High School, so he gave me a lift back into town on Sunday evenings, usually about midnight after they had finished canoodling. I don't know why they didn't get married, but he eventually married someone else.

My mother Kath told me, 'Auntie Win was like a second mother to us. Our mother was always out in the garden, and was not particularly maternal. Win gave us a lot of affection. I can never remember Mum putting her arm around me. I think Mum had so many kids she was a bit overwhelmed. She had nine of us without much of a break. We younger ones were really reared by our loving sister Marge and Auntie Win. I always felt sad Win's engagement was broken off and she never married and had her own family. She was broken-hearted.'

AUNTIE GWEN ROSS [*Mum's sister*]: I don't think Mum necessarily wanted so many children, but there was no family planning then, and she believed you couldn't fall pregnant when you were breast-feeding. They just hopped into bed, had a cuddle and that was it. Sometimes Mum wasn't even sure when the next baby was due. She once told me, 'I nearly dropped poor little Reg on the doorstep of Dr Wood's Hospital. I had no idea when he was due.' Mum didn't tell us about babies until we were 16 years old.

My twin sisters Kath and Mary were born at 'Pinedale' in Mum's own bed. There were 15 or so men shearing at the farm at the time of their birth. Mum didn't know she was having twins. Dad told us that Auntie Win came down to the shearing shed and said, 'Oh Arthur, Clara's got not one, but two!'

AUNTIE MARGE: Kath was the strongest. She grew quickly and sat up first. Mary couldn't sit up for at least another six months, and she didn't walk until a surgeon in Mt Eliza cut the sinews at the back of her heels when she was eight or nine years old. She spent a lot of her childhood in hospital. Even after the operation her heels didn't touch the ground, so she has always walked on her toes, but she couldn't wear ordinary shoes for a long time. At the time Mum and Dad weren't sure about the operation, because there were no guarantees it would do any good. Despite her physical handicap, Mary was very alert and spoke clearly.

AUNTIE MARY [*Mum's twin sister*]: When I was about seven years old I started going to a special orthopaedic hospital in Mt Eliza.

In those days they believed in treating my condition with sunlight. I had to sunbake for hours on this little patio in a swimming costume. I would return to 'Pinedale' as brown as a berry. I went to that hospital for weeks every year and I always fretted for Kath. I missed her terribly and the rest of the family. A lovely specialist at the hospital called Dr Colhoun operated on me, which enabled me to stand up properly and walk. He was a very kind man and he made an enormous difference to my life.

AUNTIE MARGE: Kath and Mary always liked doing the same things and they were inseparable. Kath always worried about Mary when she was at Mt Eliza for months on end for treatment, and mothered her at home.

Kath had a lovely nature. She was kind and helpful to everyone. She helped Mum a lot and she became a very good cook early on. Kath left school at about 13 and helped at home until she got a job. She worked at the telephone exchange in Wodonga for many years, from the age of about about 16 and throughout the War. She boarded with Mr and Mrs Thompson in Wodonga during the week and rode her bike home on the weekend. She brought home bits of gossip from the exchange and always dressed well.

My mother also told me she later worked briefly on the confectionary counter at G. J. Coles at their store at 586 Burke Road, Camberwell, in Melbourne. Her work reference is dated May 6 – July 27, 1946. Attendance: Very good. Reason for Leaving: To be married.

AUNTIE GWEN: I was only 18 months older than the twins. Mary adored Kath and vice-versa, right through life. There was just some bond between them. Even when Kath started working and later married, they didn't grow away from each other. Kath was always very protective of Mary and stuck up for her if any kids picked on her at school. We were all very supportive of Mary.

Mary was in a lovely little cane stroller until she was five or six years old. She and Kath played together in the backyard. I don't think Mary was fully aware of her disability at that early stage. Prior to her operation she couldn't stand at all and people had to hold her up. She had a lovely nature and people respected her.

We had a sulky and quiet horse in which we took Mary to school. About four of us travelled in the sulky, which we left with a friend opposite the school until we had to go home.

The Leneva School

The Leneva School — then Middle Creek — was completed by January 30th, 1875. The contractor who built the school was Mr Jas O'Keefe and his tender for the school and residence was £245/8s. The first school building was a structure of Murray pine, with a slate roof. The building consisted of four rooms and a lean-to verandah. Three of these rooms formed a residence, the remaining one being the classroom. Classes began with about 40 children attending grades 1-6.

The school was opened on May 10th, 1875 with George S. Manns as Head Teacher. Mr Manns submitted the name of Leneva, being the reverse of Avenel, which was in the news at the time being the railhead for the construction of the north-east line. Manns remained in charge for 20 years. Before becoming a teacher he had been an Army officer in India. During Muriel Young's time (1933-59) as teacher the school had success in the Gould League and garden competitions.

LENEVA STATE SCHOOL CENTENARY 1875-1975 BOOKLET BY ROY McGAFFIN.

AUNTIE GWEN: There were only 15-18 students at Leneva West School. We were all in the one classroom with the same teacher who taught all six grades. The teacher boarded at a residence in Leneva and rode a bicycle to school. The first teacher I remember was Miss Marie Cavanagh. She was very conscientious and patient, a wonderful teacher. Another, Mr Cleaves, was a really nasty person. He had no patience with Mary and quite often had her in tears because she couldn't answer questions. If anyone giggled he slapped them over the head. He had a leather strap. If you did anything wrong, you went to his desk, held out your hand, and received a terrific whack. A lot of parents then thought we deserved to be struck at school.

Kath was a brilliant student and was always top of her class. She had a very good memory, so she didn't have to study much. It was a shame she didn't further her education. We had to learn geography off by heart, then the next day we were questioned on it. History was another big subject. We had a lot of homework to do and Mum helped us more than Dad. She was quite good at spelling. Marge was also very smart at school. We were the only kids from the one teacher school at Leneva who had ever been to Melbourne.

There was not much sport except for tennis and Kath was a good player. We played at lunchtime and recess on the school court and Mary would sit on a bench and watch us play.

Kath and Dad were very attached to each other. I was more Mum's pet. Kath was his favourite and she adored him. She'd sit on his knee and he called her Lyn, from Kathleen. He'd say, 'What have you been doing today Lyn?' They both loved cats. Dad had quite a few around the farm, but he always had a special one in the house. He'd nurse the cat in front of the fire in our big family room.

AUNTIE MARY: Dad was lovely to Kath and I. He was very gentle. He liked all animals, but he was particularly fond of cats. He had eight or ten of them at the dairy. They'd drink the milk slops and catch mice.

ALLAN BREWER [*Uncle Bert and Auntie Miriam's son*]: The last 'favourite' cat I remember Pop having was a black fluffy cat which slept on his bed in the sleep-out. He'd say, 'I'd better take Fluffy with me tonight, because I saw a mouse in the sleep-out.' We all knew it was just an excuse to tuck Fluffy under his arm. He was particularly fond of ginger cats and apart from one called 'Marmalade', he had another called 'Yackandandah', so named because there was a circus playing at 'Yackandandah' at the time.

UNCLE BERT: Dad's cats mainly ate at the dairy, but sometimes when we had rabbits strung up on wire in the trees at night they'd make a real mess stripping all the meat off the rabbits' hind legs. They gorged on those rabbits until they were full. The only way to stop them was to string chicken wire across the rabbits.

AUNTIE GWEN: Kath got along better with Dad than with Mum. I helped Mum in the kitchen. Sometimes when the boys were shearing or harvesting Kath would go down and help milk the cows by hand. I never did as I hated the smell of the milk. When Kath and Allan were married she was a tower of strength.

We used to take our lunch and a couple of dogs and went for long walks, swam in the creek or went rabbiting. We all loved horseriding, and Kath was a good rider. We played table tennis amongst ourselves. Sometimes we had the neighbours over for a game or played at competitions in the local hall. We had an old gramophone, and later played records. We didn't have a radio until we were eight or ten because we didn't have electricity, but we were never bored.

'A tribute to our pioneers' (extract)
by FRANK HUDSON

We are the old world people
Ours were the hearts to dare
But our youth is spent, and our backs are bent
And the snow is in our hair
Back in the early fifties
Dim through the mist of years
By the bush-grown strand of a wild, strange land
We entered — the Pioneers
Take now the fruit of our labour
Nourish and guard it with care
For our youth is spent, and our backs are bent
And the snow is in our hair

LENEVA STATE SCHOOL CENTENARY 1875-1975 BOOKLET
BY ROY McGAFFIN

ALLAN BREWER: My mother, then Miriam Gee, was also a teacher at Leneva West school. At the time she boarded with the Darmody's, a well-known pioneering family. Mum had gone to Teachers' College where she received a Bachelor of Arts degree. She became a general teacher and first taught in 1937 at Upper Thollogolong Victoria, alongside the Murray River, where she was head of a primary school called 'Wandooma'. She boarded with a family at Talmalmo, NSW. Every morning they rowed her across the river and she walked to the school.

MERYL BROWN: After teaching at Thollogolong, Mum went to Boorhaman near Rutherglen, Victoria. They were all one teacher bush schools stuck in the middle of nowhere. Most children rode horses or bikes, or cadged rides to school.

AUNTIE MARGE: Because I was the eldest girl, and Mum was outside milking or tending her vegetable garden most of the time, I was like a mother to the younger children. I bathed and fed them, and put them to bed. Mrs Maude Edney, who lived across the creek from us, was crippled with arthritis and did mending and darning. She would say to people, 'Oh, that little Margie Brewer, you know why she's not very tall? She had to rear all those other children.' Fortunately I loved babies.

Maude and Walter Edney had six children of their own — Eric, Clive, Dorrie, Ruby, Rene and Percy. They were keen churchgoers, very musical and never worked on Sundays.

Mum was a wonderful cook, and what a mob she had to cook for. She never used a recipe. If you asked Mum for a recipe she'd say, 'I don't know, a bit of this and a bit of that.' If she ran out of yeast she boiled up a couple of potatoes and put the water into the dough to make the bread light. We made all our own bread and Mum made beautiful hot cross buns. She'd have all the yeast set out, but 'look out' if you caused it to go flat. It was a heck of a business making bread every few days.

By the time I was eight, I could cook too, and loved making scones and sponges. I cooked cakes and biscuits every Saturday morning, or Mum would tell me to make a batch of rock cakes. We always had hordes of visitors on Sundays for afternoon tea, including the Phillips' and the Kellys, whom we called the Kelly Gang.

Mum bottled a ton of fruit. There were no Vacola bottling outfits in those days. She stewed the fruit and put it in screw top AG jars. We made all our jams — plum, apricot, marmalade, pear ginger, as well as sauce, chutney, relish and pickles to have with our meat dishes.

Clara May Brewer's spicy relish recipe

3 kilos ripe tomatoes. 2 cups sugar. 1 cup vinegar. Dessert-spoon dried chillies. 1 teaspoon salt. Finely chop large piece of fresh green ginger and 12 cloves fresh garlic. 1½ cups currants. Place all ingredients in large saucepan. Simmer on low for 2 hours.

Auntie Esther, whom we called 'Grandma Kelly', was Grandma Phillip's sister, formerly a Packer. She had 13 children, but hardly any of them got married and at least five remained old maids. They'd all arrive and say, 'Oh, I hope Marjorie made a sponge!' They would be dressed up like Queens and wore beautiful hats and 'oohed' and 'aahed' about Nana's exquisite dahlias.

Auntie Esther had a large lake on her property near Wodonga where she had flocks of ducks, turkeys and chickens. Every evening she'd row across the lake in a little boat to feed them. Their property was called 'Melrose', which Melrose Drive in Wodonga was named after.

It was a constant cycle of cooking, eating and washing at 'Pinedale'. Mum always had huge pots of potato and pumpkin on the stove, and often I'd have to catch a chook and cut its head off. I've put lots of chooks on the block then cleaned them. Once after I was married I had to kill a big turkey gobbler for Christmas. Its' head was on the block and I had its legs and claws in my hand. When I raised the axe it wrenched away and gave me a very deep scratch. The wound should have been stitched, and I still have the scar. The turkey gobbler still lost its head!

My father was very appreciative of how much work I did. We had an open fire in the kitchen and nearly everything was cooked in huge boilers and saucepans which stood on an iron bar. Our brothers and Dad always had tomatoes and onions on toast for breakfast. 'She's up at six o'clock every morning and she lights the fire,' he used to say. 'Then she cooks this big pot of porridge and puts on a huge frying pan full of tomatoes and onions. That's my girl Marge.'

Most of the time Dad never wanted to leave 'Pinedale', and there were too many of us to go away together until we got the Dodge. Since we couldn't leave the farm and the animals, the boys usually stayed home.

Auntie Gwen: Mum loved dressing up for weddings or special occasions. Mostly though she'd wear an old dress around the house and garden. But if you announced, 'Mum, there's someone at the front door,' She'd reply, 'Quick, I say, quick, get me a clean apron.'

She grew flowers and practically all our vegetables and fruit, watered from the creek nearby. She worked 11 or 12 hours a day. She didn't have time to tidy herself or wear a clean dress every day. When she was making jam or doing preserves, she'd be up until midnight. She bought boxes of choice yellow peaches, apricots, pears, and cases of 'black heart' (St Margaret or Lewis) cherries from Christesen's at Stanley.

Dad killed all the meat, but the boys also went rabbiting. We ate a lot of rabbits. We soaked them in salted water and baked them. We had fox terriers which were very good rabbit dogs.

Every Sunday regardless of the temperature Mum cooked roast lamb or poultry in her big fuel stove. My brother Artie loved to help with the cooking. The relatives who descended on the weekends demolished an incredible amount of food. These days you're lucky if anyone offers you a cup of coffee and a dry biscuit.

Uncle Bert: Mum and Dad planted a wonderful orchard which is still there. They had peach, pear, plum, apple — Irish peach, jonathon, and granny Smiths — nectarine and apricot trees. The fruit was

'Pinedale', Leneva West

magnificent. I can still see Dad pruning the trees in the orchard in winter on a bitterly cold day after a snowfall. His hands were blue with the cold, and he could hardly close the secateurs. There's no worse job than being up a ladder pruning in winter. They also grew loganberries for jam and had a grapevine. There were six or eight quince trees across the creek and Mum was renowned for her quince jelly.

Dad was a quiet man. The only time he really came out of his shell and talked a lot was when he got tipsy at a 'tin kettling'. These were held when a forthcoming marriage was announced and everyone had a drink, something to eat, and presents were exchanged. They'd always have beer and a jar or two of wine. We once went to a tin kettling for Otto Ziebell. Mr Patterson, a friend of Dad's, filled him up with wine and they both got pretty full. I can still hear Mr Patterson saying, 'Gawd, Arthur you must always watch out for those bloody red-back spiders, they'll bite you.' He started almost every sentence with, 'Gawd'.

AUNTIE GWEN: Dad was very reserved, very much like his eldest son Artie. He was kind, thoughtful and inoffensive. Mum was much more direct. She was the driving force. She'd say to Dad, 'We all need a holiday, and we're going!'

AUNTIE MARGE: Mum was a very difficult woman at times. We loved her but she tested everyone's patience. We'd clean the place up like a new pin and by the end of the week it would be like a pigsty. She was clean but terribly untidy. That's why I'm so scrupulously neat and tidy now, and so was dear Kath. We grew up with Mum's stuff flung everywhere.

Mum loved meat. She cut up sides of beef and corned it in brine, salt, saltpetre, and sugar in a kerosene tin. It would be brought to the boil, covered, put in a sugar bag and stored in the meat safe.

In the old days we drank cold water out of a canvas bag. We didn't have an ice-chest or even a Coolgardie safe for many years. Nana put the cream and butter in a bucket and hung it down the well at night to stop it going off. She'd get up around 4.00am and pull up the cream to make the butter while it was still nice and cold. Bert and Miriam were the first ones in our family to get a kerosene refrigerator.

Zelma and Henry Buntz had a Coolgardie safe. She was Dad's niece and Henry was a blacksmith in the main street of Wodonga. He made the safe himself with hessian and a flat, lipped piece of tin on top. They left it out on their verandah in the breeze. The tin was filled with water, and pieces of towel were draped over it and hung down. The cool water dripped down onto another dish at the bottom. It kept food surprisingly cool. We got their Coolgardie safe after they bought an ice-chest. We kept butter and cheese in it, and you could even set a jelly. Henry Buntz was fond of going to the dog races. One day he had a win so he bought Zelma a 'Frigidaire' refrigerator, which was a big deal in those days.

We finally got an ice-chest. The ice was delivered three days a week, Monday's, Wednesday's, and Fridays, when the cream bus came. We had always run out of ice by Monday.

Before the power was connected at Leneva we had kerosene lamps, and an Aladdin lamp which was a luxury. It was a big, tall, lamp on a stand. We bought it from a travelling salesman. Tinkers were always calling in trying to sell you things.

Auntie Gwen: We didn't have electricity connected until the mid 1940s. Mum wouldn't have candles in the house, as she thought they would set the curtains alight. There was always a strong smell of kerosene from the hurricane lamps. We carried them into the bedrooms at night, and once we were in bed Mum and Dad would take them out.

People went to bed fairly early because they were up so early to milk the cows. In the evenings we sat in easy chairs in the lounge room listening to a battery radio in front of the open fire. I remember the large English chime clock ticking on the mantlepiece. Mum had a timber table specially made to accommodate our large family and in the evenings when the table was cleared, we played ping pong.

Auntie Marge: Mum had a copper out in the yard. Later on they built an inside laundry, but you could never get into it because Mum had so many clothes piled up. You can imagine the loads of washing with eleven of us. She did the washing by hand every day, and even made her own soap. When a sheep was killed she would take some of the fat and boil it up in the copper in a kerosene tin. You needed at least six pounds, which Mum mixed with lux, borax, caustic soda and water. It was quite dangerous to make because you had to be careful it didn't boil over. It was left overnight to set hard, then it was cut into large yellow-brown bars which were quite hard and lasted for ages. It was wonderful pure soap.

The mountains of ironing were done with a flat iron heated on top of the stove or in the ashes of the fire. We were constantly ironing. Sometimes Mum asked old Mrs Lucas to come in and help out with the washing. Later on Mrs (Irene) Rene Ziebell came to help. She was a great laundress and lived until she was 95.

AUNTIE GWEN: Many people had petrol irons, but Mum was frightened they would explode. She starched and ironed her beautiful white damask tablecloths with the old flat iron. People don't know they're alive today. Everything in those days was done manually. It was an immense amount of work.

Because of the shortage of water and there being so many of us, we only had baths once a week. We washed our face, feet and hands every day and on Saturday night we got into the tub. When we were growing up the tub was in the kitchen. We heated the water in the copper, but many people got their hot water by boiling water in kerosene tins over the open fire. Our water came from the well outside the kitchen which had a big windlass to wind up the bucket. Water was never wasted the way people do today. Even the bath water was put onto the garden or the pot plants when it had cooled.

The bedrooms were freezing in winter. Some of us slept in sleep-outs which were really only glassed in parts of the verandah. Mum heated her flat irons, wrapped them in old jumpers and put them in the beds to warm them up a bit. There were no hot water bottles then, let alone electric blankets. Our feet were never warm, and we all got dreadful chilblains.

AUNTIE MARGE: I suffered terribly with chilblains on my fingers and toes from milking cows and feeding poddy calves in the frost.

They were very painful and the only treatment was methylated spirits.

There were plenty of snakes at 'Pinedale', mainly blacks around the house and browns down at the creek. The first house was made of whitewashed mud brick and and we didn't have any wire on the doors or windows then. When they were building the new house, we slept out on the verandahs, but unfortunately the snakes easily found their way inside.

AUNTIE GWEN: We frequently saw snakes in the garden, and sometimes on the verandah. Mum killed them with a spade, and thought nothing of it. You were allowed to kill them in those days. Two or three were even killed inside 'Pinedale'. Dad shot one which had found its way inside Mum's very congested pantry. It was the only way he could get at the snake. Another was shot in her bedroom. Dad knew how to handle a gun.

AUNTIE MARGE: We had to milk cows and do lots of other chores before we walked the three miles to school. There were 30 cows so we milked several cows each twice a day. We separated the milk from the cream and poured it into cans. The skim milk was fed to the pigs. Occasionally someone in a horse and gig would give us a ride to school, but mainly we walked all the way, regardless of the weather, in our big boots.

In summer we'd follow Middle Creek on the way home from school. There were black snakes everywhere, and it's a wonder we didn't get bitten. They'd be coiled with their heads up and poke their little tongues out at us through the watercress, then dive into the water. It didn't stop us hopping into the cool water too, and we'd arrive back at 'Pinedale' with our clothes soaked. Dad would be waiting impatiently for us. 'Where have you been you little beggars?' he'd say. 'Get in and change as quick as you can and get up to the dairy to milk your cows.' Another important job was cutting the wood into small pieces and bringing it inside so it was dry for the fires in the morning.

My father was a wonderful man and we all loved him. He was an excellent farmer and was always worrying about his crops. Sometimes he'd walk up to the house wearing his big hob-nailed boots looking concerned. Mum would say, 'Get on with your jobs. Don't be worrying me about whether it's going to rain. I can't make it rain.' We had a beautiful old lime tree. We made delicious lime drinks from it in summer. The tree was next to our cool room where the meat, beef, lamb, and pork, was hung.

Dad had a market garden over the creek and in September he'd plant hundreds of tomatoes. We all helped. We'd jab a hole with a peg and drop the seedlings in, then irrigate them from the creek. We picked them when they were half green so they wouldn't split. On Saturday Dad took the tomatoes into Wodonga in his spring cart and sold them to the fruit and vegetable merchants J.G. Arnold and Sons. They also packed a lot of tomatoes into big wooden cases and sent them by train down to T. Stott and Sons in Melbourne. Stotts would write the following week and tell Dad how much he was going to be paid. Sometimes there would be a glut of tomatoes and the cheque wouldn't be very large.

UNCLE BERT: Later on Dad carted tomatoes into Albury in the Dodge. He'd pull the back seat out of the car and fill it up with about 20 cases. He'd get an extra two or three cases on the running board as well. He also sold tomatoes to some of the local hotels and sent tomatoes and pumpkins to Sydney. We spent weeks watering, hoeing and picking tomatoes. Later in the season we'd pack tomatoes all day under the shade of a willow tree and Mum would bring us over a cooked hot lunch. Then in the evening we still had to milk the cows, by hand of course.

Mum had a greenhouse built at the side of the house, next to the sleep-out. Flowers were her passion and the greenhouse was chock-a-block full of plants, including orchids and ferns. Mum was as strong as a horse.

AUNTIE MARGE: Nana made a lot of money out of her flowers. She packed them in a huge suitcase and sold them to local hotels. She sold whatever she had in the garden — roses, dahlias, daffodils. She'd say to us, 'Now if you see anyone coming down the road going into town, sing out.' Then she'd run out and stop people in their gigs and horses and say, 'Would you mind dropping my flowers into this or that hotel?' No-one seemed to mind. Country people were very obliging in those days.

Dad had lots of sheep and he rented out a number of his paddocks. The Edney brothers Eric and Clive did our shearing. They arrived about five oclock in the morning and we had to cook all their meals, including a hot breakfast, and give them morning and afternoon tea.

We never had time to be bored like kids today, we were too busy. At night we played cards and went from house to house. Later when we learned to dance in the old hall, we'd go to people's houses if they had a gramophone and dance on their wooden kitchen floors. The Edneys had a gramophone. We danced the fox trot and the waltz and went to balls in Albury and Wodonga.

We bought some of our clothes in Wodonga and Albury, but Mum made a lot of our things. She had a box full of patches and was forever patching and mending. She patched till she couldn't patch the boys' pants anymore. They never wasted anything. They couldn't afford to. Clothes were passed down from one to the other until they were threadbare. Being fashionable wasn't an issue, but we were always clean, tidy and warm.

Mum really dressed up for special occasions. She'd be done up like a queen with her hair set and wearing a top of the line hat and gloves. But as everyone knows, her real mania was for shopping. Sometimes you couldn't see the top of her bed for all the things lying on top of it. Her favourite outing was to go into Schlink and Sons in Albury, where Coles are now. They had groceries on one side and blankets, sheets and clothing on the other. We had an account there and Mum booked up a lot of goods. Dad would go crook when the bills came in and roar at her like a bull, 'Clara, what have you been getting up to at Schlinks? The bill's a couple of hundred pounds!' She'd say, 'Oh, Arthur, I've hardly been in the shop.' Of course we knew she'd been in there having a spree. She particularly liked buying hats and gloves, and even after we were all married she continued buying sheets and towels at Schlinks.

UNCLE BERT: Schlink's were German and had stables at the back of their store where country people could leave their horses and gigs. Everyone booked things up and you paid for them when you could afford to. There were no credit cards then, and no GST!

MERYL BROWN: I recall a commercial traveller, a hawker, who came to 'Pinedale' with suitcases of materials. He wore a grey suit and had his hair slicked back. He was also some sort of preacher and he gave us little religious booklets. He'd lay all his material out in the lounge room at 'Pinedale'. During the war a lot of it probably came from the black market. Another hawker who dropped in was a turbanned Indian called Gamal Singh. He travelled in a horse-drawn covered wagon filled with buttons, material, ribbons, pots and saucepans. He camped on the creek near Uncle Bill and Auntie Annie's. We loved rummaging through his wagon, and so did Nana. There was also an Afghan hawker whom I believe was called Jimmy Bogong.

Nana hoarded more stuff than you could poke a stick at. In the clean-up after Pop died, we found bolts and bolts of hideous black fabric which Nana had stored in the sleep-out. Even when Mary and Nana finally went into a flat in Wodonga, Nana saved every bit of brown paper and string. She never threw anything out, and the place was crawling with silverfish. Nana berated me if I tried to tidy up, 'Don't throw that out!' I'd say, 'Nana, the War's over.' It was the way they were brought up, nothing was ever wasted.

ALLAN BREWER: I remember a tin smith, a real Jack of all trades called Mr Casey who called at 'Willowdale' and 'Pinedale'. He had a draught horse which pulled a caravan and he was amazing. He'd tune pianos, re-upholster furniture, sharpen knives, and solder buckets. He camped down at Mortimer's place on Middle Creek.

AUNTIE MARGE: When Mum died we found hundreds of dollars worth of towels laid out between the wire springs and mattresses on the beds at 'Pinedale'. The towels had rust all over them from the springs. Kath came and helped us sort through everything. I can still see our youngest brother Ted standing there with a wheelbarrow saying, 'Put all the towels in here. All you can do is burn them.' We took them to the wood-heap and set them ablaze. It was a scandalous waste. Mum also hoarded jams and newspapers. She'd say, 'Don't take that paper out, I haven't read it.' They brought mice into the house.

We always had flash horses and a very fancy sulky with rubber tyres. We also had a black-hooded buggy. You were really somebody if you had a black-hooded buggy and a matched pair of beautiful black horses. We took it to the Albury Show, which was tremendous fun.

The Show went for three days and Dad always showed his pigs, of which he was very proud. They were black, shiny stud Berkshire sows. He bathed them and took them in in his spring cart. He was renowned for his boars and sows and sold them to people in the district. He always won First Prize. We looked forward to the Show all year. Dad bought a Member's ticket which cost a guinea and also entitled him to enter his pigs. We'd go in the side gate because we wanted to avoid paying the entrance fee of sixpence. We'd say, 'Our father is Mr Brewer and he has pigs in there.' 'Oh, go in', they'd say and three or four of us would dart in. Then another lot of the Brewer kids would say the same thing. This strategy gave us more money for the penny rides on the merry-go-round and the side-shows.

Mum and Dad also went down to the Melbourne Show after they bought their beautiful navy blue Dodge which, in those days was like a Rolls Royce. It took Dad about two years to decide to buy it, and l ike a true farmer he paid cash. After being used to the horse and gig, it took him a while to learn how to drive. George Buntz, who owned a garage in Wodonga, taught Dad to drive. George was the first certified A-grade mechanic in Victoria. Dad had three go's to get his license. He went to this little house which was the Police Station in Wodonga, and at the first test he shot down over the railway crossing. They reckon he was going so fast he scattered stones as far afield as the Post Office, which was about half a mile away. When he finally passed, he drove us to Melbourne for holidays at his sister's, our Auntie Mary and her husband Jack Croker who lived at Coburg, an inner suburb of Melbourne.

We didn't leave on these long car trips until lunch-time, because

Mum was never ready. When we were going to Melbourne Dad would say the night before, 'Now Clara, we're leaving here in the morning no later than seven.' She'd eventually get into the car, always in the back seat, with one leg in her bloomers and her corsets in her hand. The bloomers were about two foot long with elastic in the legs. As we approached Melbourne she'd wriggle around in the back seat and heave herself into her corsets.

Mum was habitually late. She'd always be weeding the garden or washing, and Dad was forever waiting for her. She drove him mad sometimes, but mostly they got on very well.

AUNTIE GWEN: We loved travelling in our Dodge Tourer, which was considered to be the smartest car in the district. When we left for Melbourne, the Dodge was filled to over-flowing with the six of us and loads of produce for our holiday, including a large stone jar of butter, half a carcase of lamb, preserves, many varieties of home-grown fruit and vegetables, and a case of tomatoes weighing 20 kilos. There was also a metal carrier on the driver's side running board of the car. As there were no trunks in those days, it was the only place left to cram our luggage.

In Melbourne we went to pantomines, the beach, picnics and visited other relatives. Mum spent much of her time in the city buying more clothes, linen, and shoes. She loved the Christmas sales, and lugged all her purchases home on the trams. We helped her carry everything.

The Crokers had an eight bedroom house, which was a mansion to us, and they had a gas stove. Uncle Jack made his money buying fruit and vegetables at the markets and selling them to housewives door to door. He'd leave home to buy his produce at 4.00am. Sometimes one of us kids would go with him, which was very exciting. He always had a big bag of money because he was paid in cash. It's a wonder someone didn't knock him on the head and steal his money.

ALLAN BREWER: Years later I drove Nana down to Melbourne a couple of times. Just outside of Eurora she'd say, 'That's where we stopped to boil the billy.' I've still got their old picnic box, which is lined with 1917 copies of 'The Weekly Times'.

Uncle Bert: My brothers Reg, Frank, Artie, and I loved going to the hut up the hop scrub when we were kids. We stayed up there for a month at a time in winter when we took a break from milking. Dad would visit us in his horse and cart and bring us enough tucker for a week. We stayed in a slab hut, which we built with the help of Uncle Artie Phillips. In the morning when there was a snow white frost we didn't get out of bed until the sun came up. Sometimes water would drip onto us from the tin roof and that always hunted us out of bed.

While we were there we cleared some of the green timber and went rabbiting. We walked or rode around on our ponies and dug the rabbits out, up to a hundred a day. We had a big pack of dogs, whippets and fox terriers which raced after the rabbits, and caught and killed them amongst the ferns. The only trouble was that then we had to skin them. The next morning there were dozens of rabbit skins lying out in the frost. We soaked some of the rabbits in salty water overnight, rolled them in seasoned flour and cooked them in a pan on the open fire. Those young rabbits were delicious.

Allan Brewer: My family were exceptionally good rabbiters and occasionally had 'rabbit drives'. I once saw Clive Edney drive 1,500 rabbits into a trap yard built in the corner of a paddock. The rabbits were so thick they were climbing over each other and getting over the

Arthur Brewer's sister, Mary Croker

fence. Some of my uncles and Clive then beat the rabbits to death with sticks, or in most cases broke their necks by hand. They then had the job of skinning them.

BRUCE GEE: The Brewers loved fox terriers. I remember Bert and Miriam had a foxie called 'Timmy' at 'Willowdale' in Leneva, which was quite vicious. It bit old Clive Edney, who had lived with them for about 17 years. Quick as a flash he kicked Timmy into the open fire to a shower of sparks, and much yelping from the dog. Timmy never bit anyone again.

Baranduda

Bushfires are remembered for many years because of the loss of stock, property, and trees, the sheer terror they cause and the way they bring the community together to fight a common enemy.

Baranduda must have seemed particularly vulnerable to fire when the early settlers were clearing the bush. Goldminers visiting the Yackandandah area in 1853 spoke of a forest still blackened after the great Victorian bushfires two years previously. On May 17, 1927 fire destroyed the original Baranduda school, which was apparently caused accidentally by a swagman who had slept in a nearby shed. Much of North East Victoria was swept by fire in 1939, but it was the fires of February 21-22, 1940 that effected Baranduda worst. The major fire started at Lowden's property in Middle Indigo, near Barnawartha, caused by a spark from a blazing stump blown on to dry grass in a howling wind. Flames raced over the hills to Leneva, killing sheep and cattle and destroying telephone lines, fencing, haystacks, a chaff-cutter and steam engine. Fire fighters saved dozens of houses. Almost one thousand square miles of timber and grass between Barnawartha and the Kiewa River was devastated.

A BARANDUDA HISTORY BY HOWARD C. JONES

AUNTIE MARGE: I will never forget the 1939 fires. It was a very hot morning and my husband Walter and I were up early and did the milking. A hot day had been forecast and we went into town as I also had to deliver a few eggs to the grocer's shop.

Then we heard the Wodonga fire bell. Everyone was running about.

'Leave your groceries!' Walter said, 'There's a fire at Barnawartha.' Walter was Captain of the Baranduda Fire Brigade and we rushed home. My job was to phone as many people as I could to warn them. They didn't have much equipment in those days, just the water truck, rakes, bags, wire cutters and knapsacks. The men took off and by lunchtime the fire had burned right through to Baranduda, and burned paddocks in Leneva and Indigo. It was terrifying and we kept hearing that people's houses had been burnt. Not many people had phones then so it was hard to find out what was going on. They saved the Baranduda school but Walter's mother's dairy was burned. There were fires throughout Victoria that year, and hundreds of houses and lives were lost. I was pregnant with my daughter Dell (later Mrs Rex Jenkins) at the time. Every year there'd be a bushfire somewhere, but not like those big Black Friday ones. Farmers are always looking out for smoke, it's in their blood.

> *Walter Schubert, Marge's husband, was a member of the Baranduda Rural Fire Brigade, of which his father Johann was a founding member. They lived on the property of the Baranduda school, on the Wodonga side. At the time he was first Captain there were only three telephones in the area and he had one. When there was a fire, he would come 'screaming over the hill blowing his horn' and all the locals knew that meant there was a fire to attend.*
>
> CELEBRATING 50 YEARS! THE BARANDUDA RURAL FIRE BRIGADE 1947-1997

ALLAN BREWER: Auntie Kath's brother Artie was a highly skilled shearer, and did shearing work for wages to help Pop's cashflow. He told me a funny story about the time he worked for an old Leneva grazing family when he was about 16 years old. The lady of the house had a drop dunny outside. One day she came into the house complaining that something had bitten her. They worried it was a nasty spider bite so he took her to the doctor in Albury in a horse and gig. The doctor examined her and said it definitely wasn't a spider bite. Artie had a look around the dunny and concluded that an old turkey hen had gotten through the hole at the back. Clearly, when the woman sat down it had pecked her on the behind.

UNCLE BERT: During the war my brother Artie and I were called up by the army. A mob of us went over to Albury, but I was never sent away to camp. Artie trained at Table Top, but he didn't serve because he was needed on the farm.

Eulogy (extract): Arthur 'Artie' Frederick Brewer (Died June 26, 1996)

Born at Albury November 3, 1913. Eldest son of Arthur Randall Brewer, and Clara May Brewer (both deceased).

He was always a keen worker before and after leaving school, helping with ploughing, milking, fencing, rabbiting and caring for sheep. He was well known as a good shearer and travelled long distances in the season to many properties, first with blade and later machine shearing.

In those days people made their own entertainment. In the district Artie was a very good tennis and table tennis player. He was a keen card sharper. Euchre and 500 were played at home, and in Leneva Hall where he was also fond of dancing. He was a voluntary bush fire brigade member. He married Violet at St Matthews Albury in 1943. They lived on a property at Leneva and had one daughter Melody, now Mrs Barry Sproule. In 1960 they moved to their new home 'Wee Hope' on his Huon Creek Road property farming sheep and cattle. Unfortunately Violet passed away suddenly in 1964.

Artie remarried to Eileen Rawson and they lived at 'Wee Hope' until they moved to Wodonga for their retirement.

PART 2

The Navy

4

ABLE SEAMAN GEE

A radically different life

My father left Silver Creek as a young man and before long he was soaking up the bright lights and exotica of New York, Durban, London, and other exciting destinations. All too soon he was caught up in the dramatic events of World War Two.

If it hadn't been for a childhood yearning for the sea, and an adventurous spirit Dad may well have remained in Beechworth for most of his life.

Sometimes I wish he had. Returning home virtually blind at 26, with shattered health and his nerves in a poor state, was a fate he'd never bargained for when he joined the Navy against his parents' wishes.

DAD: Around September 1936 I eventually wrote away for the papers to join the Navy. They sent back various booklets and forms. After all the paperwork was completed I went down to *HMAS Lonsdale* in Port Melbourne, and on March 8, 1937 I did my initial test for the Navy.

I looked very young at the time. Mr Cutting used to call me Sparrow because I had a gap in my front teeth where a dentist had taken three out when I was 14. I was pretty embarrassed about my missing teeth. In those days we couldn't afford to go to the dentist's surgery, but if you went to hospital and paid a shilling the dentist would come and pull

---

The correct Navy expression is serving 'in' not 'on' a ship.

out your teeth, hoping you would come back to the surgery later for false ones. The dentist's name was Mr Vandenberg, whom I always resented because of my mother's sudden death during a dental procedure at the Beechworth Hospital in 1944.

About ten young knockabout boys attended the initial Navy test. I went home disenchanted believing I probably wouldn't get accepted. I was elated they asked me to come back to Port Melbourne. The Chief Petty Officer and Petty Officer were very gentle men and kind to us. We were given an education test, a general examination by the doctor, and an eye test. I think the eye test clinched it for me. I was so nervous I started to read the chart from the bottom upwards, and got a perfect result.

We seemed to be there for most of the day. Finally there were only two of us left and they said that we had been accepted. I officially joined the Navy on March 9, 1937. Lucky me! At this time the Royal Australian Navy were taking ten recuits every two months from the whole of Australia.

I didn't know Melbourne at all, and was staying with people called Mr and Mrs Close who had periodically visited my parents at Silver Creek. I remember the morning after I had been accepted into the Navy. Before I left I went in to say goodbye to Mrs Close who was in bed. She told me to promise her that now that I was a Navy man I would never enter a house of ill-fame. Jack Close took me into Swanston Street, where I caught the Port Melbourne tram to *HMAS Lonsdale*. There was a mob of us waiting there to catch the train to go to Crib Point, the Flinders Naval Depot.

Six or eight boys from Sydney and Queensland and a couple from Tasmania made up the nucleus of our class of about 16. In those days the train used to go right into the Navy Police depot. From there we were picked up and taken into what was known as D Block. This was to be my home for the next nine months.

From the first day in the Navy I was called Elmo, and the name stuck. Even now at 70 years of age I have friends from my Navy days who never knew my name was Allan.

They gave us a very good meal in the mess hall. Afterwards we went up to the third floor where we were given our hammocks. At this stage we were still wearing civilian clothes. It seems strange now but we were sleeping in hammocks only about 18 inches wide, and six foot long with a blanket and a pillow. But I slept very well. Ever since then I have always enjoyed sleeping in hammocks.

Next it was off to the Sick Bay, which was the hospital, where we were given various injections. Talks about the Navy, naval discipline and other matters soon followed.

About eight days later we were kitted up with all our uniforms. This comprised three blue suits, two white duck suits which were dress suits, and working clothes, overalls, a pair of sand-shoes, gym shoes, a pair of boots, and slippers. They even gave us needles, thread and buttons so that we could do our own mending. We also got blankets, toothbrushes, boot brushes, and polish. The kit was probably worth about £35, which was a fortune to me.

After we were fully booted and spurred we did eight weeks on the parade ground. Everything was done at the double. It was great fun and they really whipped us into shape. There was no roaring or shouting. Everything was said in good humour and soon we were fighting fit and could run and jump like brumbies. We also had two weekly physical training sessions and most of us played sport. I played hockey and Australian Rules football as a full-back. I was very fortunate to play against a sailor, a sick berth attendant, who was a full-forward for South Melbourne.

In the entire time I was in the Navy I only struck two 'narks', and they were very bad ones. It was uncommon in the Navy to find bad sports. There was a particular Petty Officer called Bennett who was like a father figure to me. He took me under his wing and was always available if I had any problems. I was able to see him and shake his hand before he passed away at 84 in the Heidelberg Repatriation Hospital.

BRUCE GEE [*my brother*]: Dad told me that as a Depression kid he couldn't believe how wonderful the Navy was. On arrival at the depot they were fed, given bunks and kitted out. He was truly amazed at how well they were being looked after straight off. They gave them an assortment of clothes and he said much to his embarrassment he burst into tears. He loved the Navy from the word go. The only trouble he got into was when he lost the rowlock off a boat and was fined £3/5s. He always said to me the saddest day of his life was March 18, 1946, when he was discharged from the Navy as P.U.N.S. (Permanently Unfit For Naval Service).

DAD: Finally we started actual training, enlisted as ordinary seamen. During this period I remember going down to the Sick Bay with the Chief Petty Officer who gave us a lecture on the dangers of the pox. We were advised to take every precaution against contracting venereal disease. He was quite a serious man. Before he started the lecture he put two marks on the board and said, 'At the end of the lecture I want you to tell me what those two marks stand for.' A half hour went by and most of it went completely over our heads. I had never been with a woman, although I was certainly keen to. Finally he told us what the marks on the board were all about. 'It means that two of you bastards will have the pox within two weeks, and I'm silly wasting my time talking to you, because what you've got between your legs will lead and you will follow.' Everyone thought it was a great joke.

One of the first things we were taught was how to point and graft, which was a sort of fancy rope work. This took a fair amount of time. Our instructor was an ex Tingira man called Alf Coyne, a Petty Officer and a very experienced seaman. He later finished up being Captain of the quarterdeck on *Perth*, and although he survived the sinking of the ship, sadly he died on the Burma Railway in 1943. When *Perth* was sunk Alf and ten of the other Petty Officers and able seamen, including Ray Parkin, got hold of a boat and actually attempted to sail back to Australia. But before long they were captured and ended up in Java. I never saw Alf in any of the prisoner of war camps I was in, and he is buried at Kanchanaburi War Cemetery in Thailand.

The next eight weeks of our training in the Navy were spent swearing in at the drill hall where we learned to march and drill. Most of us had to start by learning to walk properly. During the drill rest periods they used to talk to us about the Navy. I soon realised the easiest way to get on was to follow the rules and never get caught.

I always remember one instructor who took us down onto the quadrangle for the first time and said to us, 'In this man's Navy you can sleep with the Captain's wife, or anything you like, but there is only one sin in this outfit and that is to be caught doing it.' He added that if you did get caught you take your punishment like a man. 'Don't wear the green coat', was the Naval expression for being a coward. They also impressed on us not to blame others for our mistakes. I think that philosophy is what makes the Navy tick. It inspires a sense of individual responsibility and where possible 'doing the right thing'.

I had always had terrible problems with my sinuses but after being near the sea for a short time, and with the great food, friends and exercise I flourished and had no other medical problems.

Reveille (the traditional military wake up call) was always at half past five in the morning. They gave us a hot cup of cocoa and we worked from 6.00am till 7.30am doing chores around the place, cleaning the toilets, sweeping, and working in the different Chief and Petty Officer's messes.

After breakfast at 7.30am, we went to what were called divisions, and the whole ships company used to file into the drill hall at about 9.00am into the different classes. Even the officer cadets participated. We used to say that the Navy at the time was like a religious order. The band played, there would be a couple of hymns, and the chaplain would say a prayer. Saturday was the only day this didn't happen and on Sunday we always had a church parade in which the band and all the classes marched. It was very pleasant and was all part of the Navy training. I enjoyed the Church of England service more than the Salvation Army's.

I recall going to the dentist at the Sick Bay early on in my training. He said, 'Good God, you can't go around looking like that.' I also had teeth missing at the side, as well as the three in the middle. Anyway this dentist fixed me up with a plate which increased my confidence. For another few shillings I also had some gold fillings done. In general I was always grateful that the Navy boosted one's self esteem, and tried to get the best out of its people. There is a saying that the Navy always looks after its own, and in my ten years with the RAN I can certainly vouch for that.

During this time until we reached 18 years of age we weren't allowed out at night. Even if you had weekend leave you had to stay with your parents who vouched for your safety and had to act as moral guardians. If you were out for the day you had to be back at the depot by dark.

I went up to Melbourne a couple of times, and once Mum and Dad came down to Melbourne for a Salvation Army Congress so I was able to visit them on Sunday. Mum was such a gentle loving soul, and Dad was always talking about religion. I think their attitude was that I was doing something which was educational with job security.

Once during this time I had three weeks leave and went home to Silver Creek. It was lovely to spend some time at home on the farm with Mum and Dad. I also saw the men I used to work with at the Tannery going off to work. I considered myself very fortunate that I'd been visiting places and doing things they could never have dreamed of.

I was flat out with my training, which was essentially two month long courses in seamanship, gas, gunnery, torpedoes, signals and rudimentary instructions in wirelesses. They taught us how to sail and how to pull boats. You never got too much time to yourself. If you were lolling around Petty Officer Coyne would come in and send you down in a cutter to the wharf and you'd have to pull a boat back four or five miles. It was a very good grounding in seamanship and most of the stuff I learned I have never forgotten. It was also a very happy and fulfilling time. During this training period I also spent six weeks at sea in *HMAS Vampire*.

I once saw a film on the ABC showing an Army training course and everyone was shouting at each other. The Navy had a different attitude to discipline. I remember Petty Officer Ray Parkin who also became a prisoner of war and a friend, and who held classes next to us. Even if there was some punishment going on he would join in and frog march with the guys or run with them. Ray was totally different to most sailors and wasn't the average run of the mill bloke. He was a genuine intellectual, a thinker and a philosopher.

I thoroughly enjoyed going to school again and improving my

education. We were lucky to be taught by an excellent teacher called Commander Guest, but of course everyone knew him as Beau. Apart from the compulsory classes he taught extra ones at night. I did very well in English and mathematics and I achieved what was the equivalent of the Intermediate Certificate as it was known then. Commander Guest urged me to continue with my studies after I was at sea because he thought I should continue up to Matriculation level. But entertainment and girls became my priority, so I dropped out of the classes, which I later regretted.

My 16 classmates came from all over Australia. I only found out about two years ago that they served everywhere; the North Atlantic, on Russian convoys, and with the British Navy. The only person from our class to die either in battle or as a POW was our instructor Petty Officer Coyne which was quite amazing when you consider what we had all been through.

It is an understatement to say that the Navy was a radically different life to Silver Creek. There was plenty of entertainment, rugby, football, hockey and you could box or work out in the gym. There were three picture shows a night and as I was a film fiend I never missed one. It cost us ninepence a flick and the funds went towards buying recreational gear. Later when I was allowed out on leave I revelled in the lack of restrictions. There were plenty of girls about and I loved talking with people about every imaginable topic.

There were three things I learned at the Navy depot which I was passionate about but was strictly against my Salvation Army background. Smoking which I enjoyed immensely, playing billiards and snooker, and cards, favourite pastimes throughout my naval service. I particularly loved playing cards, and I made a few bob out of them too.

After about three months at the Flinders Naval Depot they asked us if anybody had any experience playing cornets because they wanted buglers to join the band. I put up my hand, and that was it, I was in the Navy band. There were three buglers. Apart from the band work, we were taught how to counter-march and march behind the drummers, which was great. We had band practice each morning.

One day I was summoned to the Police Office at the depot and told to get ready because the next day I would be doing the Last Post at the Shrine in Melbourne for the annual march of the Old Contemptibles, who were members of the old regular British Army who served in 1914 at Mons and Le Cateau. I went up with the Navy band and a Scots band was also there marching along St Kilda Road. It was the first time I had heard the bagpipes and I remember I jumped in the air like a startled rabbit. I was terribly nervous standing alone at the Shrine playing the Last Post and hoping I wouldn't make a hash of it, but it went reasonably well.

I left the depot in early December 1937 and joined the ship *Canberra* on January 2, 1938, a 10,000 ton cruiser with Captain W. Patterson in command. I would have gone to sea a fortnight before Christmas but I failed a signals course and had to do another two weeks of study. We went on manoeuvres around Australia and the Pacific Islands. My salary was £2/10s a week.

I had Christmas 1938 in the *Canberra*, and I've still got the menu for the lunch. *Canberra* was a very happy time for me, and we seemed to earn enough money to manage on. (Menu: Crème giblet broth, roast turkey, York ham, French beans, green peas, baked and boiled potatoes, Christmas pudding and brandy sauce, fresh fruit and cake.)

About six weeks after I joined *Canberra* we were on our way to a regatta in Hobart when we encountered mountainous waves, the worst I ever saw in my naval career, including the hurricane off Bermuda. It was so bad that we lost a man named Harry Storey over the side. He was a leading hand and I was with him when he got washed over. About eight of us had been hit by this huge wave and Storey had apparently neglected to put up a bottom gale rail. The only thing that stopped me going over with him was that I got jammed against the torpedo tubes.

Although we had him in our sights for 16 hours we never got him. We pumped out tons of oil, but with the raging seas one minute we'd be on top of him and then he'd be at the bottom of the trough. My heart went out to him.

I was very lucky that I was never seasick. It was common on the ship to be served pork and onions for breakfast and people sometimes vomited quite violently. I once ate five pork chops at a sitting. In all the rough weather I experienced at sea I never once felt queasy.

After I had been in *Canberra* for about six months I was again made the bugler and I never really got away from it. I bugled in *Perth* and on the Burma railway.

Able Seaman First Class A.H. Gee played the bugle on Canberra *under Commander F.E. Getting who was later to die on the bridge of the ship. Allan was assigned to the quarterdeck under Lieutenant Peek, his action station being in the shell room of Y turret.*
THE SHIP'S BUGLER BY L.F. HOLMES [P 3]

BRUCE GEE: Dad was ecstatic to be asked to play the bugle. Before he knew it he was the Commander's runner, which was a pretty cushy job. Let's face it, if you had the choice of scrubbing the deck, or painting the ship what would you rather be doing?

DAD: Once on leave in Sydney from *Canberra* I spent a week with my Uncles John and Alf and their sister, my Auntie Janet. Her husband, whose surname was Fowler, introduced tin hares to dog racing. He helped start off Harold Park in Sydney, but he lost most of his money trying to sell the idea to South Africa. I walked across the Sydney Harbour Bridge with them and had long conversations with Auntie Janet. Uncle John lived at Marrickville and was a tram driver. They were very warm to me. They were very diverse people but great friends and it was wonderful talking with them about their early lives.

I have very happy memories of most of my shore leave in Sydney. We used to leave the ship at nine in the morning and head straight for the pubs at the lower end of George Street where I ended up spending a lot of time with the writers from *The Bulletin* magazine. They used to go over there for a beer during their morning break. They seemed to accept me because I read a lot, and I was invited to some of their do's. I was also very fortunate at that time to meet Norman and Daryl Lindsay who were fascinating people. I also became very friendly with a cartoonist at *The Bulletin* called Les Sutch who was a delightful man. He was terribly concerned with what was going on in Sydney and the impact of the Depression on ordinary people. There were still a lot of people out of work, and many of the girls in factories were being treated like slave labour.

I realised later that some of these people I hung around with were founding members of the Communist party in Australia. They were disillusioned with the traditional parties and felt there must be a better way to live. Some of these individuals are very prominent in Sydney today. Given my own background it is no wonder that in this environment the seeds were sown for my own passionate commitment to the Labor party. I became an avid reader of *The Bulletin* and other publications and became convinced that the Labor Party was for me.

One story in *The Bulletin* had a profound effect on me. It was about the New Zealand Labor Prime Minister Michael J. Savage (in office from December 6, 1935 – December 27, 1940) who got people work, housing and roads built. Although he was condemned by the British and Australian governments he was the person who convinced me to join the Labor Party. I have remained a dedicated Labor supporter all my life. I also recall going to Hyde Park to hear the speakers which was very inspiring. I went to some very bohemian parties and met a lot of academics, poets, writers and painters. Most of them were probably twenty years ahead in their thinking, but I remember those times with extraordinary warmth. I also met a charming woman called Lorna. She was a sculptress and a true bohemian, and had done sculptures for Luna Park in Melbourne and Sydney. She was an excellent artist, but sometimes she said she was having a rest period. This meant that she went on the grog for a few days.

I was never interested in horse racing but I liked to go swimming at Bondi Beach. I travelled everywhere by tram and often went to the Olympic pool across the Bridge at North Sydney which was great fun. There were always lots of girls there.

BRUCE GEE: Apart from the Lindsays Dad got to know the Department Store heir Mark Foy before the war. Dad had a great time on leave. He had money, and Australia was still in the grip of the Depression. There was about 30 percent unemployment for men, and 65 percent for women. The Navy guys walked around with pockets full of money and they had an interesting fun job. The girls swarmed all over them. The Navy had a lot of style, and Dad was in the band with top musicians. What could be better? Sydney was a real Navy town. It's no wonder he had an enduring love for Sydney.

DAD: In March 1939 I left *Canberra*. In February I found out I'd been picked to go to England, to Portsmouth to collect what was to be *HMAS Perth*. Once again I had been chosen because I was a bugler. There were three buglers on the ship.

After a spell of leave, I embarked on the Blue Funnel Line steamer Autolycus. We sailed for Portsmouth from Sydney on May 13, taking five weeks to get there. Our mission was to commission the RAN's second Improved Leander Class light cruiser *HMAS Perth*, formerly *HMS Amphion*.

Seamen are traditionally superstitious about renaming ships, and in this instance it was proved to be a bad omen. The *Autolycus* was an old coal burning ship. Conditions weren't very good but we were very experienced seamen by this time and handled everything well. She was an old freighter fitted out as a troop ship with mess tables and hammocks. It was very basic but there was a galley on the upper deck and four cooks and we didn't have much to do. It was another very happy time for me.

I left Sydney and we sailed straight to Albany, where a stowaway was also removed. (According to *Perth* Leading Stoker Jock Lawrance, he was a *Perth* crewman called Curly Sutton who was vetted from going to Portsmouth because he had chickenpox.) It was here that I nearly became unstuck because I fell dreadfully ill with pneumonia and they didn't think I'd be well enough to go to England. I met an amazing man in the Sick Bay, a surgeon called Charlie Downward who had a great influence on me. Fortunately I recovered. We sailed from Albany non-stop to Durban, South Africa. Eventually we got to Durban where we spent four very pleasant days. The ship was a coal burner and

*Postcard commemorating voyage on the Blue Funnel Line Steamer Autolycus
to commission HMAS Perth (formerly HMS Amphion) at Portsmouth, UK, 1939*

they had a black crew to put the coal aboard when we arrived. The blacks looked utterly miserable and seemed to be living on scraps of food which they fought for. In South Africa I was also appalled to see black prisoners being taken out to work on the wharves and other places with chains around their waists, ankles and arms. I was shocked at the way the whites treated the black people with no respect whatsoever, and thought nothing of giving them a kick to make them move along.

In the Indian Ocean we encountered huge seas for three or four days but we just kept the ship's nose into the weather and we were alright. We then sailed around the Cape of Good Hope calling at Madeira in the Canary Islands, and on to Portsmouth. It was like a paid holiday, and we had a ball.

Julius 'Judy' Patching was a very interesting man, and a great man amongst men. He arranged tons of PT (physical training) and we had a sing-song for the crossing the line ceremony. There was a band of course and at night there was more singing and always a picture show. We did a fair bit of pistol shooting off the stern of the boat, mainly at bottles thrown over the side.

'JUDY' PATCHING: All I ever wanted to do was to be in the Navy. I finished up as a Petty Officer Chief of the PT (Physical Training) branch in the Navy. I left *Perth* before she went to the Mediterranean and I stayed in the Navy until 1947.

I first remember Allan on the *Canberra*, and then of course on *Perth*. We were also together on the the the *Autolycus*, which took us to Portsmouth for the Commissioning. Apart from the crew the ship carried a huge load of apples from Tasmania. The Duchess of Kent renamed the ship from *Amphion to Perth*. Renaming ships according to the old sailors fable, is a disastrous thing. When we got to Portsmouth, Chad Langdon, Charlie Downward myself and a couple of others, went to Paris for about five days. Fortunately Charlie had told us to pack some 'civvies' (civilian clothes).

Allan and I were great friends of Charlie Downward, the Surgeon Commander on the ship. I played in the Navy cricket team, and Charlie was the Captain. Charlie was quite a remarkable man, and finished up as a Surgeon Captain. Charlie had a regular little private happy hour in the Sick Bay. He would often invite Chad Langdon who later became a Supply Commander in the Navy and several others. Allan was still an Able Seaman and for all of us to have a quiet beer with the Commander was practically unheard of. Even though we had different positions on the ship there was a great feeling of mutual respect.

Charlie was very paternal, and a voracious reader. This partly accounted for the affinity between Allan and Charlie. Charlie had worked his way through Sydney University, paying for it by playing billiards and snooker in the championships.

Danny Riordan was a Leading Steward on the ship and another good friends of ours. Danny got off the ship when she came back from the Mediterranean, because he was pretty sick, but he recovered. He later worked in Veteran's Affairs and did a lot to help the *Perth* guys.

Allan smoked, and we enjoyed a drink. but never to great excess. Charlie was also the Censor so there were probably a lot of things that Allan wrote to his family about and I wrote to my fiancee, and later my wife, Betty which Charlie turned a blind eye to.

Every letter going out of the ship was censored. 'Loose lips, sink ships,' they told us. Before I went away I'd divided the world map up into squares and zones and gave this diagram to Betty. At the top of a letter I might put C3 or C5, and she would know that we were in Halifax or wherever. The naval term for being at the wheel is 'a trick at the wheel'.

Allan and I spent a great deal of time together. He was a very deep thinker and had strong views on any issues that were being discussed. He was passionate about politics and a very dedicated Labor man. We had a common accord. He was an incredible optimist, friendly, bright, and generous. Allan treated everyone as an equal. He was interested in other cultures, and in spite of being a country boy he wasn't narrow-minded.

Many of the Navy guys were very intelligent and responsible people, best described as solid citizens. This was clear in the way they went about their business on the ship, and in wartime. The Navy was better off because of them. They were the salt of the earth.

DAD: I was presented with a silver bugle to mark the occasion of the commissioning of *Perth* on June 29, 1939 at Portsmouth.

The re-naming ceremony. July 10, 1939

At 1.15pm the Admiral Superintendent arrived closely followed by the High Commissioner for Australia The Honourable Stanley Bruce and Mrs Bruce. Lower deck was cleared and everyone fell in to await the arrival of the Duchess of Kent. At 1.30pm sharp the Royal car arrived alongside the gangway. As H.R.H. stepped from the car on to the carpet the 'Alert' was sounded by the ship's bugles, and the Guard of Honour then presented arms and the National Anthem played.

HMAS PERTH BY ALAN PAYNE [p 33]

The same evening with the Hood *and the* Ark Royal *and many other Royal Navy units at the anchorage, Allan mistook the preparatory flag for 'sunset' and engaged in the premature blowing of that signal some five minutes too early, an action which led to the buglers of every ship in the harbour following suit. They didn't make him walk the plank but he got told off in no uncertain terms.*

THE SHIP'S BUGLER BY L.F. HOLMES [p 3]

I remember being 'suitably' spoken to by the Gunnery Officer Lieutenant W.S. Bracegirdle, who told me I was the only person in history who had caused the British flag to be lowered before time. I can laugh about it now, but at the time I thought, 'I've really cocked things up,' and worried about the repercussions.

Later when we returned from the Atlantic the fellows said that the *Perth* was one of the most integrated ships they had ever been on. There was a great *esprit de corp* between all branches of the ship. It was unique because people on most ships tended to stick to their own areas and mates, but *Perth* was different.

The only thing I ever anguished about was that I knew my mother was concerned that I was having too worldly a life. I hoped deep down she was proud of me.

Perth *had a shakedown cruise in the Channel and left Portsmouth finally on July 26, 1939 bound for Australia via New York, where that city's famous Mayor, Fiorello La Guardia, made the ship guest of the city for the day.*
THE SHIP'S BUGLER BY L.F. HOLMES [P 3]

DAD: We sailed for New York and arrived on August 4. We spent 12 days there as the Australian Naval attachment at the World Fair.

The New York longshoremen, led by the much liked Australian born Harry Bridges contributed to our special time in New York.

At 5.30am we embarked the Pilot, and were steaming up the channel towards the Statue of Liberty. Astern there were several large liners also entering this grand harbour. At last New York's famous skyline was showing through the mist, the famous Manhattan skyscrapers being our first thrilling glimpse of New York. At 7.30am we drew abreast of the Statue of Liberty. Here we fired a 21 gun salute to the American nation.

A gift of a koala bear toy for La Guardia's children was presented by the Perth *crew to his secretary Mr Stanley Howe. When receiving the koala Mr Howe referred to the animal as a bunny. This brought forth roars of laughter. He remarked, 'It seems as though I have said something wrong.'*
AGE SHALL NOT WEARY THEM BY ROWLAND G. ROBERTS [P 41-47]

Dad: We had a memorable time in New York, apart from the fact that the ship's company briefly went on strike. It all got sorted out and the Captain said they did such a good job getting the ship together for New York that there would be no punishment.

Jock Lawrance [*Perth Leading Stoker*]: The Captain at the time, H.B. Farncomb, said, 'If I'd been in charge I would have shot the lot of you.' When the strike occurred, Farncomb had been in New York being feted by the local 'Society' and had delegated command to someone else.

Aussie mutiny
One of the several newspapers here caused a mild sensation with poster headings: 'AUSSIE MUTINY, British Officers Too British'. It wasn't a very nice article to make screaming headlines, even if it had been true in any way at all. It was founded on a lot of lies and loose talk and we did our best to live it down.
The bare facts of the 'mutiny' are described in a seaman's diary: '1,200 clear Lower Deck, everybody aft but majority of ship's company went and sat down on forecastle. Complained about having to wear whites ashore. 12.25. Hands fell in on quarterdeck and matter settled. Commander granted 'make and mend' but very few hands went ashore till 1815 when whites were allowed. All hands up in a request to see Divisional Officers to go ashore in blues, but we have to comply with West Indies Station orders.
HMAS Perth by Alan Payne [p 4]

'**Judy' Patching:** We had a ball in New York. Some of us were invited to the Cotton Club in Harlem, where the famous Cab Calloway, Ella Fitzgerald and Bill Robinson were performing. Cab was a very famous black dance band guy. Unfortunately, Allan didn't come to that, because he didn't have his 'civvies'. The guy who organised it for us on behalf of La Guardia, was a fellow by the name of Noel Bronstein, a lawyer who looked after the Harlem district.

Obituary: Cab Calloway
Calloway died at the age of 86 and gained fame with his 1931 trademark song 'Minnie the Moocher.' He played as a song and dance man opposite Louis

Armstrong in Chicago before starting his own band in 1928. His career took off in 1931 when he replaced Duke Ellington at the The Cotton Club. During the Harlem jazz era, Calloway helped the careers of Dizzy Gillespie, Pearl Bailey and Lena Horne. In the 1950s he played the role of 'Sportin' Life' in the George Gershwin movie 'Porgy and Bess' and starred with Pearl Bailey in an all black version of 'Hello Dolly'. His career was revived in the 1980 film 'The Blues Brothers'.

But Allan did come to the Waldorf Astoria Hotel function with us. We were in our uniforms, and Charlie in fact stayed the weekend in a suite. Allan and I were on the same watch together whenever the ship was at cruising stations. We really did New York over. I remember Allan and I sometimes slept at the railwayman's YMCA which was very close to Pennsylvania Railway station. We had to be back on board by 8 o'clock in the morning, and on some occasions by midnight. We also went to the famous boxer, Jack Dempsey's restaurant together.

Jack sat at the entrance to the restaurant and signed menus. I saw him sign, 'From Jack Dempsey to Allan Gee.' We had boxing on the ship and I'm not sure if Allan boxed or not, but I remember him playing deck hockey.

DAD: I'll never forget meeting all the dignitaries and celebrities. Everyone was just so warm to us. As I'd boxed a bit on the ship, meeting Jack Dempsey and Jack Johnson was an unbelievable thrill. Jack had been to Australia and had an amazing fight with Tommy Burns in Sydney.

JOCK LAWRANCE [*Perth Leading Stoker*]: New York was wonderful. We couldn't wait to see the skyscrapers. A *Perth* mate Joe Hartley and I were walking along the street and someone came up and offered us tickets to a baseball game — the Reds vs the New York Yankees. The stadium was packed and at quarter time some clowns invited Joe to participate in a mock cricket much. To the amazement of the crowd he hit the ball right out of the stadium. The capacity crowd of 78,000 gave Joe a standing ovation. It was unforgettable. But it got better. A wealthy Australian businessman based in New York invited us out on the town. He wined and dined us then took us to The Canary Club where we met Mickey Rooney and Dorothy Lamour. We didn't get back to the ship until 5.00am.

One young officer's memories include driving back from the Australia Day reception which followed the march with Australian Sir Hubert Wilkins (the Arctic explorer), Johnny Weismuller, and Esther Williams. Several clubs were made open to the ship's company and officers and men were admitted free to Radio City Music Hall and two theatres.

HMAS PERTH BY ALAN PAYNE [P 5]

DAD: It was a dream come true. The nightclubs were open 24 hours, and we drank and danced practically non-stop. We had an endless party, and girls, girls, girls. They'd call out, 'G'day Aussie', and soon we'd be in all sorts of trouble. We were very naughty boys, especially McQuade! None of us a slept a wink for about a week. Poor old Mum wouldn't have approved of any of it, especially those gorgeous New York girls.

Jack Dempsey

At this time the ship's company was told that instructions had been received from the Commonwealth Government that Perth *had been handed over to the control of the Admiralty, and was now under the orders of the Commander-In-Chief, America and West Indies station.* Perth's *duties would be to give every protection to British shipping and to intercept enemy ships. A large number of German ships were then in neutral ports in the West Indies area, and it would be the ship's duty to capture or sink them when they came out to make a break for Germany.*
HMAS PERTH BY ALAN PAYNE [P 6]

On August 16, Perth *commanded by Captain H.B. Farncomb sailed for Kingston Jamaica, on the West Indies station, and waited in the Caribbean for the by then inevitable declaration of war.*
THE SHIP'S BUGLER BY L.F. HOLMES [P 3]

We stayed in the West Indies until August 26, 1939. During this time we patrolled in the areas of Port of Spain Trinidad, Tobago, Curacao, Aruba, Bonaire, Venezuela, Haiti, and the Dominican Republic.

We sailed down to Jamaica. By then the announcement of war was practically imminent. We waited near Kingston for about a week. There was a lot of German shipping in the area, so we spent a lot of time chasing ships but never got any.

'JUDY' PATCHING: Sometimes it was so flat and calm in the Caribbean I can remember sitting back steering the ship with my feet. Although I was a Quartermaster and organised PT *(physical training)*, fitness and all the sport I still had to keep watches. Allan and I were together a lot and when we pulled into Jamaica with convoys Charlie Downward and I played a lot of golf. Allan didn't play golf, but on occasions he and our friend Bill Bracht used to come along. We'd have local guys as caddies and later have dinner together at the golf club before returning to the ship.

We also frequented a hotel in Jamaica called Constant Springs which catered for American tourists. With the advent of war tourism ceased. The *Perth* boys visited this place a lot. We had quite a bit of dough and our philosophy was to have a good time while we could.

Bill Bracht, a Gunnery Instructor, was a very serious card player. He had a phenomenal memory when it came to playing cards, so did Allan.

They both played a lot of poker and crib. When Bill left the Navy he enrolled in a course in the Commonwealth Rehabilitation Training Scheme and obtained his Accountancy Degree. He forged a highly successful business career and became the company secretary and financial controller of Monier. He was later actively involved in the greyhound industry and was an official of the NSW Greyhound Racing Association.

At the age of 18 Bill enlisted in the Navy and served for almost 13 years, which included active service during the war. In Perth he participated in every sphere of the war against the Axis Forces in Egypt, Libya, Greece, Crete, Malta, Syria and the Battle of Cape Matapan.

Bill was transferred to Darwin when the Japanese bombings took place, just before Perth was sunk in 1942. He was also amongst the first Australians to set foot in Tacloban (Leyte) and Manila (Luzan) in the liberation of the Philippines. He took part in more action, from New Guinea to Borneo. He acted as a Gunnery Instructor in HMAS Warrego, the first allied ship to enter Manila Bay, while the Japanese still occupied Corriegedor after the invasion of Luzon, which enabled General Douglas MacArthur to return to Manila. In 1968 Bill was quoted as saying, 'He gave away the rat race for the greyhound race to be happy in the human race.'

THE GREYHOUND RECORDER

DORIS BRACHT [*Bill's wife*]: Bill was desperate to stay in *Perth*, which he loved, but he was transferred to *Warrego*. Bill told me about one guy in *Perth* who was the type who would give you a punch on the nose and talk to you later. I was a new bride when I met this rather aggressive character and he said to me, 'I paid for your bloody honeymoon!' Bill had cleaned him out at cards. His photographic memory was useful for cards and later the greyhounds.

At 9.30am on August 21, 1939 we anchored off Kingston. It was a beautiful morning and the harbour waters were like a sheet of glass. At 3.15pm that day received a signal from the British Admiralty which practically put us in a first state of readiness for war.

AGE SHALL NOT WEARY THEM BY ROWLAND G. ROBERTS [P 51]

War was declared on September 3, 1939.

DAD: I'll never forget hearing the announcement that signalled the start of the war. It was quite a frightening moment, but strangely exhilarating. We all thought, 'This is it,' and in our guts we all wondered if we'd get out of it alive. At the time of the announcement of war *Perth* was patrolling off St Anne's Harbour, Curacao.

Captain Farncomb was ever a man of few words and this was all he had to say, 'We have just received a signal from Admiralty which reads: 'Total. Germany Total'. We are now at war with Germany.

THREE CHEERS FOR HIS MAJESTY THE KING! *HMAS PERTH* BY ALAN PAYNE. [P 7]

Outside Kingston we were joined by the British cruiser Orion, *then we proceeded at 20 knots and carried out our summary exercises. On parting company the* Orion *flashed the signal 'Good Hunting' to us, as the use of the wireless had been forbidden.*

AGE SHALL NOT WEARY THEM BY ROWLAND G. ROBERTS [P 54]

Orion *and* Perth *spent the first weeks of the war fruitlessly chasing German shipping in the area. On October 4, the Australian cruiser and HMS Berwick escorted KJ.3, a 45 ship convoy, from Kingston half way across the Atlantic to a point roughly 300 miles west of the United Kingdom. They were protecting the ships from German U-boats.* Perth *suffered damage to her superstructure from a hurricane which they encountered on the return passage to Bermuda.*

THE SHIP'S BUGLER BY L.F. HOLMES [P 5]

DAD: The hurricane blew like hell, and we took a real pounding. The seas were mountainous.

'JUDY' PATCHING: Allan and I will never forget that hurricane. It scattered all these ships far and wide. He and I were on the wheel when it struck. Allan was the sort of guy you could trust your life with. What I loved about him was that he never complained about anything. The hurricane was so severe that the Captain was concerned the ship might roll over. It was so bad that eventually the Chief Quartermaster had to take over the steering of the ship. The waves were gigantic. All that we could do was to keep the ship heading into the eye of the hurricane, so that we were facing in the direction of least resistance. There was tremendous damage done. Everything was awash below deck. It took about a week to get the convoy sorted out again, and some ships were lost.

Other highlights Allan recalls from this period include going to action stations after intercepting signals from a German warship thought to be the Deutschland, *but failing to contact same; leaving Halifax, Nova Scotia, and steaming up the coast of Greenland in a vain search for survivors of the gallant AMC Rawalpindi, sunk in action with* Scharnhorst *and* Gneisenau. *'We also heard a running description of the Battle of the River Plate broadcast over the ship's loudspeaker system from a commentary provided live from an American plane over the scene.'.*
THE SHIP'S BUGLER BY L. F. HOLMES [P 5]

DAD: During the battle of the River Plate the British 8 inch cruiser *Exeter* received terrific punishment at the hands of the German pocket battleship *Graf Spee*, which finally escaped to the safety of Montevideo. *Graf Spee* inflicted enormous damage on Allied merchant ships in the Atlantic. We were reunited with *Exeter* in the Battle of the Java Sea.

After searching for enemy warships in freezing conditions we arrived at Halifax, the capital of the Canadian Province of Nova Scotia.

Leave was granted and Halifax was soon invaded by 400 Aussies. The majority were doomed to disappointment as hotels were conspicuous by their absence. The temperature had dropped to 29° Farenheit (-2°C). Halliards on the foremast were covered with ice. After a stay of four days we slipped out of harbour in company with another British cruiser.
AGE SHALL NOT WEARY THEM BY ROWLAND G. ROBERTS [P 87]

'JUDY' PATCHING: In Halifax, Nova Scotia we met up with a guy called Bob Arnett who was my counterpart in PT, in the Canadian Navy. He was a big wheel in Halifax. I had shaved all my hair off by this stage and he invited me, Allan and some others out for the day. He ran the Halifax ice hockey team and drove a dirty big Buick car. He said,

'Bring any of your friends and we'll give you a run around the town.' So myself, Chad Langdon, Allan, and 'Peggy' O'Neale went out with him. We were all in uniform and had a fantastic time.

DAD: We were in Halifax a few days before Christmas 1939. I had booked my passage to go up to Quebec as I remembered the story about Captain Cook doing the sounding of the St Lawrence River, making possible General Wolfe's successful attack on Quebec. It was one of the places in the world I had yearned to see, but fate decreed that I return to the ship. We then sailed a long way up north looking for survivors of the *Rawalpindi* which had been sunk. We never found any and were very lucky we didn't strike the *Scharnhorst*.

Perth was then ordered back for patrol work in the Caribbean and the Gulf of Mexico. We were recalled straight away to Jamaica and arrived on Christmas Eve 1939 staying until December 26. We had a fantastic Christmas day in Kingston. Everybody was pretty merry as people were buying rum off the gun boats. Everyone was all dressed up, the bands were playing in the streets, and all the people and kids, even the dogs, seemed to be cheering us on. The authorities were very welcoming and saw that we were just a bunch of happy sailors enjoying their town.

> *Christmas Day in the West Indies was heralded in by 'Christians Awake' instead of the usual bugle call of 'Reveille'. A church service was held in the forenoon and from then onwards Christmas was celebrated with a real Christmas spirit. Dinner consisted of soup, roast turkey, York ham with french beans, green peas, roast and boiled potatoes, pudding and brandy sauce, fresh fruit and nuts. Some old* Perth *sailors swear that the man in cells was let out for the day on the condition that he was back for Commander's rounds at 9pm, and he was. The youngest ordinary seaman assumed the role of officer of the watch, a customary Christmas event.*
>
> HMAS PERTH BY ALAN PAYNE [P 13]

DAD: On February 29, 1940 *Perth* departed for Australia through the Panama Canal, much to the delight of all of us.

Panama: On entering Limon Bay, Panama, the customary call was paid by the United States Naval Officer of the Guard. We commenced transit through the Canal, passing through Gatun Locks. We had a faint suspicion we were to rendezvous with some British warships, though our destination was unknown to us. However when we steered course 250 degrees the cry rang around, 'There I told you so, Australia!' A day or so out from Panama we rendezvous'd with two Canadian destroyers. After their departure we weighed and proceeded on a patrol, hunting for any stray Nazi shipping that might be attempting to run from South American ports to Vladivostock.

AGE SHALL NOT WEARY THEM BY ROWLAND G. ROBERTS [P 92-93]

DAD: On March 17, *Perth* arrived at Tahiti, and the crew had two days ashore. Tahiti was a true Paradise. I had always dreamed of seeing it, and I could see why Robert Louis Stevenson and painters like Gaugin fell in love with this tropical nirvana. Tahiti was unforgettably beautiful, as were the local girls.

ALAN LAWRANCE [*son of Jock Lawrance*]: My Uncle Arthur 'Olga' Close was a range finder on *Perth*, and according to the late 'Jumma' Brown played a small role in an incident which occurred during shore leave at Tahiti. Apparently one of *Perth*'s crew — it wasn't Olga — stole an icon from a native Chief's hut. The Chief showed up at the ship and demanded that the icon be returned. He allegedly said, 'If you don't give it back this ship will sink.' As they left Papeete the thief threw the icon out of a porthole into the harbour. Jumma also told me that when *Perth* was sinking one of the crew yelled out, 'I told you we shouldn't have pinched that thing in Tahiti.' Olga Close died aged 32, when *Perth* was sunk. Jock and Olga had a pact that if either one of them were lost at sea the survivor would care for the other's children. Jock was drafted from *Perth* onto *Vendetta* in 1941 when *Perth* returned to Australia.

Perth left Papeete on March 20, 1940 for Suva, Fiji arriving at that port on the 25th. Two days later Perth sailed and after carrying out torpedo firings, sailed direct to Sydney. The Heads appeared out of the mist early on the morning of

March 31, and Perth *had reached the end of her long journey. Since leaving Australia in May 1939 her ship's company had covered about 73,000 miles. As Perth entered Port Jackson numerous pleasure craft and ferries circled the ship and followed her to her berth alongside Garden Island. Perth's docking here marked the first Australian fighting unit to return from active service.*
HMAS PERTH *by* ALAN PAYNE [P 17]

DAD: I had experienced problems with my appendix in the West Indies and the doctor was so concerned about it he wanted to leave me in Panama City on the way home. I said I wanted to stay with the ship but if it ruptured, I was happy for him to operate. However I collapsed on top of A turret as we were passing between the Heads at Sydney Harbour. I was in terrible pain, and they were concerned my appendix was about to burst. I thought just my luck, here I am worrying about what could happen during the war, and I'm going to get wiped out with this. I was immediately transferred to the Naval Hospital in Randwick and operated on straight away.

After my discharge from hospital I was sent to *HMAS Penguin*. I was made Cox'n of *Penguin's* motor boat. I got to know every inch of the Harbour, all the little bays and inlets, each beach and jetty. I've been to Venice and San Francisco, and seen other great harbours around the world, but Sydney's the best by far. Later on in life one of my favourite trips was to take a ferry to Manly with Kath and the kids, buy some fish and chips and sit under the Norfolk pines overlooking the beach. Then came the news that I was one of fifty trained men drafted to Britain to run the new N Class destroyers. However, fate had decreed that *Perth* and I belonged together. Before I could sail for the UK I was drafted to the cruiser as ship's bugler under Commander Adams. I was more than happy to return to what the Navy termed a happy ship. There was a fantastic *esprit de corps* which pervaded *Perth*, and it remained right up to the end.

ABLE SEAMAN JIM NELSON: Elmo Gee and I were close and firm friends. I was drafted from Flinders Naval Depot to *Perth* on June 30, 1941 as a bugler, joining in Western Port Bay, Victoria. On boarding I was introduced to Elmo who was the sole bugler at that time when the ship's complement should have been three. Naturally he was pleased to have have me on board and immediately introduced me to the ship's bugling routine. We shared the duties between us, practised together, and sharpened each other's skills.

We were in daily contact on board but never went on shore leave together, because one of us had to be on duty at all times. Between us we ran a Crown and Anchor game on board and often ran foul of the Master At Arms, the game being illegal. Elmo was the gambling half of our union and resulted in us earning some pocket money. This time covered our 'tour of duty' in the Mediterranean encompassing the horror and dangers of actual naval combat, both at sea and on land during which Elmo conducted himself with dignity and honour, truly a good sailor.*

DAD: There was just a sense of being part of a team. We worked hard but we had a lot of fun playing cards, darts, horsing around, which helped allay our anxiety about what might lie ahead. Some ships simply have a good feeling about them, and *Perth* was that sort of ship. We always felt safe in *Perth*.

> *Commander Bowyer-Smyth took command of* Perth *(on June 6, 1940) and after a period spent on the Australian station, which included convoy escort duties with such notable charges as* Queen Mary, Queen Elizabeth *and* Aquitania *bound for the Middle East.* Perth *herself sailed from Fremantle in November to relieve her sister ship* Hobart *on the East Indies station.* THE SHIP'S BUGLER [P 5]
>
> *Captain Sir P.W. Bowyer-Smyth R.N., a baronet, also saw much hard service with* Perth *in the Mediterranean and was to serve longer in command than any other Captain. Prior to the war he had been the Naval Attache at Rome and was no stranger to the Mediterranean.* HMAS PERTH BY ALAN PAYNE [P 19]
>
> *Following a short spell of escort work in the Red Sea* Perth *arrived at Alexandria (Egypt) on Christmas Eve 1940 to relieve her famous sister ship* Sydney, *whose Mediterranean tour of duty was over.* THE SHIP'S BUGLER [P 5]

---

* Onboard ship, Elmo and I were always addressed from the Captain down as 'Sticks', whether on duty or personal. I believe this term originates from Nelson's day, deriving from 'drumsticks', when drummer boys sounded the orders.

It was not much of a Christmas for anyone in the Middle East that year. Perth *in company with six destroyers sailed into the Mediterranean to stand off Tobruk during an Allied air raid, which was a precursor to the British and Australian land forces that attacked the Italian stronghold in Tobruk the following month. After returning to Alexandria on (December 30) she sailed the next day for Crete, to embark soldiers for the Adriatic.* Perth *reached Suda Bay, on the north coast of Crete, on New Year's Day 1941.*
HMAS PERTH BY ALAN PAYNE [P 2]

It was at Alexandria that Perth *took on her distinctive camouflage and began action-studded service with the Mediterranean Fleet working mostly with* HMS Ajax.
THE SHIP'S BUGLER BY L.F. HOLMES [P 5]

From the first day we got into the Mediterranean until we left we seemed to be in the thick of action. The first job was to support the troops going up into the Libyan desert, and then we did a couple of convoys to Malta. All of these were very tough. January 14, 1941, the first day we were in Malta, was the day the Germans got into the Mediterranean in a big way, and we were attacked by about 250 planes over this period. Every day we seemed to be fighting German aeroplanes.

During one massive air raid on Malta on January 16, *Perth* was berthed astern of the transport Essex laden with ammunition. Things got so hot that the order was given to leave the ship, and in the general confusion I mislaid the Commander's megaphone. I simply couldn't find the wretched blower. There was chaos all around and I became confused and couldn't lay my hands on it. I felt quite stupid about it later and the Commander wasn't too happy at the time.

GEORGE JONES: [*Secretary* HMAS Perth *Association, NSW*]: *Perth* was special and I think it was largely due to our bonding in the Mediterranean. We received a bomb underneath the ship in Malta which frightened the hell out of everybody.

They reckon some of the fellows heard 'abandon ship' and scaled about an eight foot wall with broken glass on the top and managed

June 1, 1941. Aboard HMAS Perth *in Alexandria, Egypt, after she had taken part in the evacuation of Crete. Some of the gun crews are relaxing while others clean the guns. Allan Gee is second from right standing. (Australian War Memorial: 008868)*

to get over the other side. I was thrown off my feet. I was between decks and it actually lifted the ship. It was also the occasion when Allan 'Skeeter' Bishop was hit by a bullet. The dive bomber had a rear gunner, and as they made the dive, they dropped the bomb, and as they retreated they fired on the ship. That's when Skeeter got hit. When we left Malta, (referring to the 'abandon ship' confusion) Captain Bowyer-Smyth said in effect, 'You're from the land of the Anzacs and you behaved like that.' That comment really pulled everybody together.

> *None on board* Perth *are likely to forget what happened on that day. Severe air raids were experienced and* Perth *was strained by a near miss off the starboard quarter and MV* Essex *lying astern was hit and set on fire.*
> *The ship shuddered and shook as a thousand pound bomb fell very close. Then all of a sudden the deck lifted a good two feet and the whole ship jumped sideways and settled back in the water with a huge splash.*

Able Seaman Peter Watson noted in his diary, 'As soon as we heard a lull in the action we rushed aft, only to find a large bomb had dropped between us and the wharf, exploding under us. It had blown a hole in the store wharf and showered us with water and masonry. When we at last got to the wharf we found the rest of the ship's company had gone to an air raid shelter just ahead of the ship.

On February 3, the destroyers left to refuel and the two cruisers turned north to contact a south-bound convoy and acted as escort for a time. At noon next day the two cruisers berthed alongside at Piraeus. The two cruisers left for Alexandria at high speed the following day. About noon a violent sand storm so reduced visibility that the ships could not enter the harbour until 0400 the following morning. On February 5, the Prime Minister of Australia the Right Honourable R.G. Menzies inspected the ship's company at Divisions. The diarist commented, 'Ship looks lousy, covered in red dust.'

HMAS PERTH *BY* ALAN PAYNE [P 29]

DAD: There was practically no rest for the whole time we were in the Mediterranean and we were in the thick of things in the withdrawals from Greece and Crete. One day we had 13 hours of consistent fighting and the next day nine hours, and in between time we were usually attacked four or five hours a day.

On March 27, 1941, after a few days of convoying and covering activities between Malta, Suda Bay and Piraeus, Perth *departed Piraeus with orders to make contact with the Italian Fleet which was believed to be on the move. Intelligence sources indicated that the fleet was about to attack the weakly protected convoys to Greece, no doubt as a precursor to the planned German invasion of Greece.*

SHIP OF COURAGE *BY* BRENDAN WHITING [P 7]

The only victory we seemed to have there was during the Battle of Matapan. Nine enemy ships were sunk and 2,400 Italian officers and men were killed. I remember thinking my God Allan Gee, you're a long way from Silver Creek now. (This was a very important battle in the Mediterranean. *Perth* and *Ajax* played a very prominent role in luring the Italian fleet back towards the British battle fleet. The Italians were destroyed and never ventured to sea again.)

Perth's *war diary has little to say about the Battle of Matapan. 'Friday March 28: 0800 sighted 3 Italian 8-inch cruisers and engaged by them. At 0900 enemy broke off action. Squadron turned to westward to maintain touch. At 1059 sighted and engaged by Italian battleship of Littorio Class from northward. Squadron turned away behind smoke and led towards own Battlefleet. At 11.30 this assailant also broke off the action.' HMAS PERTH BY ALAN PAYNE* [P 33]

The battle, lasting more than 12 hours and covering two hundred miles of water, took place between Sicily and Cape Matapan, the most southerly point of the Greek Peninsula. SHIP OF COURAGE BY BRENDAN WHITING [P 7]

On March 31, Perth, *and* Ajax *detached to enter the western Aegean. The cruisers arrived at Piraeus on April 5, 1941. Next day the Germans invaded Yugoslavia and Greece. The onslaughts were accompanied by fierce air attacks on Belgrade and Piraeus. After an air raid warning* Perth *shifted to an anchorage in Salamis Bay during the afternoon when a severe air attack developed. At 2100 S.S. Cyprian Prince anchored next to* Perth *was sunk. One diarist made the following comment, 'I went out on to the flag deck to see an immense sheet of flame and smoke, with black objects of all shapes and sizes raining down like hailstones no more than 50 yards off our starboard bow.*
HMAS PERTH BY ALAN PAYNE [P40]

Perth *saw a lot of that 'big' little ship* HMAS Stuart *and her famous skipper Captain H.M.L. Waller in this period. Neither* Perth's *crew nor* Stuart's *captain could guess of the union later to take place and the events that were to quickly follow. THE SHIP'S BUGLER BY L.F. HOLMES* [P 5]

DAD: We took part in the big bombardment of Tripoli then we participated in the shelling of Derna.

Admiral Sir Andrew Cunningham had planned a night bombardment of the Port of Tripoli at 0500 on April 21, 'The bombarding ships will be Warspite, Valiant, Barham, Gloucester *in that order, accompanied by nine destroyers.*

Formidable *will be operating aircraft in the vicinity and will be protected by* Orion, Ajax, Perth *and four destroyers while doing so. The R.A.F. will carry out a high level bombing attack.'*

It was still dark when the bombardment began with a supporting bombing attack by Formidable's *aircraft. The battleship fired 300 tons of high explosive at the harbour and city while the naval aircraft made repeated attacks. A* Perth *diarist recorded: 'We could see occasional pin points of light and hear very faint explosions, but we were too busy guarding the* Formidable *against underwater and surface attacks to take much interest in other activities.'*

A war correspondent in the fleet flagship called the attack on Tripoli, 'The biggest and most spectacular bombardment in Naval history.'

During the Spring and early Summer of 1941, the fortunes of Britain and the Commonwealth reached a low ebb only surpassed by the defeat of France and the evacuation of the Allied troops from Dunkirk.

HMAS PERTH BY ALAN PAYNE [P 42-44]

DAD: *Perth* was at the Greece and Crete battles and picked up 3,000 troops after the Germans had driven them out. She was hit by a bomb on May 30, on the Southern coast of Crete, on the way back to Egypt. Eventually we evacuated Greece and Crete and took the troops back to Alexandria. Although we had been attacked by a great number of German dive bombers the only direct hit we took was from an Italian bomb. We lost soldiers and sailors. It was an immensely difficult time.

At 0943 Perth *was hit by a bomb straight down the funnel which killed two cooks and two stokers and nine soldiers. Further attacks were made on the ship and she was badly shaken by several near-misses. Alexandria was reached on May 31, and the troops disembarked.*

The Mediterranean Fleet had paid a very heavy price in the Battle for Crete. Three cruisers sunk, Gloucester, Fiji *and* Calcutta *and six destroyers,* Juno, Greyhound, Kashmir, Kelly, Hereward *and* Imperial.

Admiral Cunningham felt the loss of Crete and his invaluable ships very deeply. 'We had been fighting against the strength of the Luftwaffe, and once again it had been borne in upon us that the Navy and the Army could not make up for the lack

*Able Seaman
Allan Howard Gee*

*Captain Hec Waller,
DSO, HMAS Perth*

*HMAS Perth Petty
Officer George Kirtley
'Slim' Hedrick*

HMAS Perth. Painting by Ray Parkin

New York August 4, 1939. Starboard side view of the modified Leander class cruiser HMAS Perth arriving in New York Harbour where she represented Australia at the New York World's Fair. The Statue of Liberty is toward the upper left. (Australian War Memorial: 001107)

Allan Gee and shipmate Jack Teagan in HMAS Vampire, 1937

Able Seaman Allan Howard Gee

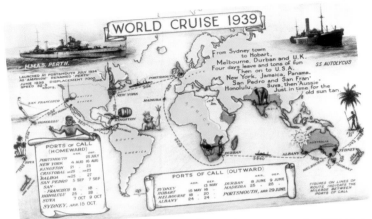

Postcard commemorating HMAS Perth's World Cruise, 1939

Formal group portrait of the crew of HMAS Perth. (Australian War Memorial: PO1915.020)

HMAS Perth shipmate Bill Bracht

Right: HMAS Perth in action Battle of Sunda Strait, 1942. Original oil painting by Dennis Adams. (Australian War Memorial)

May 30, 1941. Breda gun crew of HMAS Perth after a full day returning the fire of German fighter aircraft during the evacuation of allied troops from Sfakia, on the Southern Coast of Crete, to Alexandria. Allan Gee, far right in middle row. (Australian War Memorial: P1345/16/16)

CHRISTMAS GREETINGS 1941

This Christmas I'll spend at sea with the "Perth"
While keeping Australia from harm,—
But Oh, I will long for the rich brown earth
And cheer of the old home farm.

I'll think of you mother, father and Lew
This Christmas at far Silver-Creek,
And send all the best of good wishes to you,
That you find all in life you may seek.

May the harvest be rich, the sun and the rain
Make fruitful the hours of your toil:—
Good health be your wealth, 'til peace comes again
And your Allan comes home to the soil.

From your
loving son
Allan
xxxxx

Christmas Greetings in 1941 (before Dad became a POW)

of air forces. In my opinion three squadrons of long range fighters and a few heavy
bomber squadrons would have saved Crete.' Over 2,000 naval personnel had been
killed. The casualties would have been even heavier if the enemy fleet had
appeared, and it certainly had many favourable opportunities for doing so.
HMAS PERTH BY ALAN PAYNE [P 52-55]

The campaign in Syria opened on June 8, and was directed against the
Vichy French. To the Navy fell the usual task of supporting the Army
along the coast. *Perth* missed the beginning of the campaign as she was
under repair, but on June 25 sailed for Haifa.

DAD: I saw the survivors of *HMS Kelly*, including her captain Lord
Louis Mountbatten, landed at Alexandria in May 1941. I never dreamed
that I would meet this famous man half a world away and in very
different circumstances only four years later. Repairs had to be
completed in Egypt, so *Perth* remained at Alexandria until June 24, 1941.

We had no rest at all during these eight or nine months. On our last
night in the Mediterranean the Germans came and dropped about 50
mines over the ship. They didn't hit any of us but we had to haul the
mines and the lines in. The crew actually pulled the ship by hand along
the wharf, but eventually we got out of there. Even going through the
Suez Canal was tricky. It had been mined by the Germans so we used
to stop the engines and float over the mines so that the vibration of the
propellers wouldn't set them off. Fortunately we got back safely
through the Indian Ocean.

Because of the heavy bomb damage suffered during the withdrawal from Crete,
Perth *was replaced by* Hobart *in mid 1941 and returned to Australia for repairs.*
THE SHIP'S BUGLER BY L.F. HOLMES [P 7]

Ports of call on the way back to Sydney included Port Said, Aden, and
Colombo. We arrived at Fremantle on August 6, 1941 and docked in
Sydney on August 12. *Perth* went straight into dry-dock for the
completion of the repairs. We then had about ten days leave before
going back to sea.

On leave, prior to the sinking of *HMAS Perth*

During lunch hour at Zwar Bros' Tannery on Monday when Pastor J. A. Fullarton's usual weekly lunch hour entertainment was in progress, advantage was taken to tender a welcome to a former employee, Able Seaman, Allan Gee, who is at present on leave from HMAS Perth.

Cr. K.H. Zwar, Managing Director of the company, expressed pleasure on behalf of the proprietors and employees that he had come through what they all knew must have been a strenuous time without mishap. He deserved the thanks of everyone for what he had already done in the defence of the country. Cr. Zwar then made the presentation to Able Seaman Gee of a leather toilet compact as a token of the esteem in which he is held at the Tannery, and expressed the hope that he would return home after the war safe and sound. In a brief response, Able Seaman Gee expressed his appreciation of the gift and their good wishes. Patriotic airs were broadcast through Pastor Fullarton's address system during the proceedings.

ARTICLE (EXTRACT) FROM THE BEECHWORTH OVENS & MURRAY ADVERTISER

Dad's wartime welcoming ceremony at the Beechworth Town Hall

'*Although the Town Hall was filled, many only found standing room. Cr LeCouteur, Shire President, who presided, in his opening remarks stated that the crowd should have been three times as large as it was. Many people in Beechworth did not seem to realise that there was a war on. In childhood days, continued Cr LeCouteur they had read of great exploits such as the charge of the Light Brigade, which were nothing compared with modern warfare, involving dive bombers and submarines. These men had taken part in the biggest scrap the world had ever known, and on behalf of the people of Beechworth he was pleased to welcome them home safe and sound. Cr Dick Nankervis said whenever he saw a sailor in uniform he thought, 'Thank God for the Navy.'*

LOCAL NEWSPAPER

DAD: I was very moved by the honour bestowed on me by my home town, but all I could think of was catching up with pretty Kath Brewer.

Captain Sir Philip Bowyer-Smyth relinquished his command on September 1, and returned to England. On October 24, 1941 after repairs had been effected Captain H.M.L. Waller assumed command of *Perth*.

Captain Waller (affectionately known as 'Hardover Hec' because of the way he handled ships) was born on April 4, 1900. He was the son of a Benalla (Victoria) storekeeper and the youngest boy in a family of six boys and one girl. He began his career at the age of 14 at the Royal Australian Naval College at Jervis Bay. At the passing out he was awarded the King's medal. Waller became an outstanding signals officer, coming first in his 'Dagger' signals course. He served with the Royal Navy in 1918 on HMS Agincourt. At the outbreak of war he was appointed to command HMAS Stuart as Commander (D) and later won great fame as Captain (D) of the 10th Destroyer Flotilla in the Mediterranean under Admiral Cunningham. During World War II, he served with distinction in several theatres of war and was honoured with five awards, the last being a posthumous Mention in Despatches.
HMAS PERTH BY ALAN PAYNE [P 60]

A few days after the Japanese attack on Pearl Harbour December 4, 1941 Canberra and Perth sailed from Sydney to Brisbane and then to the vicinity of New Caledonia to meet an American convoy bound originally for the Philippines, but then diverted to Brisbane. Perth's next job was to escort the Aquitania and two other transports to Port Moresby in company with Australia, Canberra and Achilles.
THE SHIP'S BUGLER BY L.F. HOLMES [P 7]

DAD: We were engaged in anti-aircraft practice in Port Phillip Bay when we heard news of the tragic loss of our sister ship *Sydney*. All of Australia was stunned. It just seemed unbelievable, such a waste of lives and brought home to me yet again that there's nothing nice about war. It's usually a bloodbath and cuts short the lives of brave young men.

We took on board the first troops, mainly militia, who went up to New Guinea. They were the men who first confronted the Japanese on the Kokoda trail. We then went sailed to Noumea, picked up some ships there, then sailed north of Fiji and brought the first Americans into Brisbane. Then we sailed south into the Tasman sea and picked up the first American ships in Sydney that were bound for Melbourne.

MG: My father delighted me as a child with stories about Redlead, Perth's cat and mascot. I have always been besotted with cats and it was a joy to discover that Able Seaman Bob Collins, ASDIC Operator, was Redlead's guardian.

ABLE SEAMAN BOB COLLINS: We were on the wharf at the Man Of War steps in Sydney saying farewell, because we were off to Fremantle on the way to Java. Ray Firminger's two year old daughter Pat was standing there with her mother Betty. She thrust a little grey and white tabby kitten at me. 'Oh, thankyou,' I said. I stuffed the wriggling creature inside my jacket. Ray was a good mate of mine, who sadly died later when *Perth* was sunk. I didn't want the kitten, but felt that I couldn't knock it back. We took the liberty boat out to *Perth*.

Charlie (Pricky) Reid was the First Lieutenant and we never got on. He wouldn't have animals on board at any price, especially if I brought them back. One of the reasons Reid hated me was he was always nagging me to get a haircut. Another reason was because of an incident in Haifa Harbour, in Palestine. We were streaming paravanes, which are used to cut mines. He'd just been made an Acting Commander and he had this beautiful cap on which had recently arrived, probably from Grieves Naval Supplies in the UK. It had lots of gold braid on it and cost an arm and a leg. Reid was up on the focsle and he said to me, 'Stand by to stream paravanes.' I said, 'But it's too early.' He said, 'Collins that's a direct order, stream the paravanes!' With that his cap blew off and went over the side. I laughed, which did not go unnoticed.

Anyway, we hid the cat below deck and I made a little hammock for her. Redlead was so named because she upset a pot of red lead paint on the ship and covered herself with it. When we got to sea Reid had an idea that there was an animal aboard, and he had me pinned as the perpetrator. I still don't know why. Reid didn't have any spies because he wasn't very well liked. I thought the only way I can get the cat included in the ship's company is if the 'old man' (Captain Waller) will officially recognise her. So one day, I'm up on the bridge, and I had Redlead inside my jacket. The old man was sitting in his chair. I put Redlead down and the cat went up to Waller and rubbed against his legs and 'said', 'Meow, meow,' as cats do.' I'll never forget what happened next.

'What have we here Collins?' said Waller. 'It looks like a cat Sir.' What else could I say? 'Well don't just stand there, get something I can give it to play with.' So I passed a piece of paper and some string to the 'old man', and he's going around the deck and Redlead's chasing this piece of string. Then Reid came up on the bridge and boy did he glare at me. I pretended it had nothing to do with me. Once Waller had given Redlead the royal seal of approval, she was free to roam around the ship.

Everyone looked after Redlead, but I was primarily responsible for her. We took scraps to her from the mess. Bob Bland was the Chief Cook from whom we would scrounge little bits and pieces. Bob used to say, 'Where are you going with that meat Young Collins?' I'd say, 'I know, and you will have to find out Chief.' Redlead dined like a king, but she was still a bit of a secret.

I heard from others that Waller had a monkey when he was Captain D of Destroyers in the Mediterranean in early 1941. They went up to Tobruk taking mail and supplies, and fit guys and brought backwounded soldiers. They called it 'the biscuit run'. He probably got the monkey in Alexandria and apparently carried it around on his shoulder. People said the monkey was better than an air raid warning, and screeched its lungs out whenever enemy aircraft approached. Everyone agreed that Waller was a sailor's captain, a very special bloke in every respect.

DAD: Berthing in Melbourne from Sydney, we believed we were going to stay for a couple of days, but we were there for only a matter of hours. The war was really hotting up now, and I can't explain it but I had a sixth sense that something big was looming. I didn't have to wait long for my prophecy to come to fruition.

5

THE
UNDERSTANDING

You're the one for me

As we grew older we were told about some of the 'shotgun' marriages on both sides of my parents' families. But we were in no doubt that Mum and Dad's marriage was based on genuine love and was not a hastily convened nuptial to silence gossip-mongers. Dad would sometimes say, 'When your mother walks into the room my face lights up.' Dad was very exotic for young Kathleen Brewer, because he was worldly and enthralled her with stories about his Navy adventures in Jamaica, New York, and London, and later his more dramatic wartime experiences. Mum always said to me, 'He was different to the other country boys. He had travelled and met a great variety of people. He was tremendously exciting for someone like me who had only really known farm life.' Dad wasn't conventionally romantic but she was passionate about him from the outset.

AUNTIE GWEN: We came to know the Gees when Bert and Miriam married. Allan had just joined the Navy when we first met him in the late 1930s. Kath probably met him first when he visited Bert and Miriam shortly after he joined up. She would have been about eleven years old then.

AUNTIE MARGE: I think Kath first got to know Allan when he was home for a period of leave in 1941. She was already working in Wodonga. They hadn't known each other long before he proposed. He told her he'd marry her when he came back. Mum used to grumble about their romance. Kath still went out to balls and events during the War, but Allan was always at the back of her mind.

Kath sometimes rode her bike home to 'Pinedale' from Wodonga when she was working and boarding there. There was always a muddle in the kitchen at home. 'Those blasted girls,' Mum would bellow from the pantry, 'They come home and then I can't find anything!'

Reference
Postmaster General's Department: June 7th.1946. Miss K. Brewer
Period of employment: 13/5/43-12/4/46.
Capacity in which employed: Telephonist.
Remarks: Services satisfactory.
Reason for Leaving: To be married.

AUNTIE GWEN: Kath worked on the telephone exchange in Wodonga during the War. She was very efficient and she finished up becoming a monitor, in charge of six or eight other women. She boarded with a family in Wodonga who had a son who was quite keen on her. She went out with other fellows, but Allan was the only man Kath wanted to marry.

ALAN CONDON: I met Kath Brewer at a dance in Wodonga and went out with her for two years during the War. We went skiing at Mt Buffalo, had picnics in the Albury Botanical Gardens and went to balls together. She was good friends with my sisters June and Francis. Sometimes when she finished work at the telephone exchange I would meet her and we'd go to dinner at restaurants such as Font's. Because she didn't have to pay for the calls, she would ring me up from the exchange. I also visited her and her family at 'Pinedale'. Kath was a wonderful companion but I always felt that Allan was on her mind. If he hadn't returned from the war I would have married her. My oath I would, I loved her. Later on when we were happily married to our respective partners we'd call in and see Allan and Kath at Wooragee. I drove

Storey's school bus and I remember picking Christine and Margaret up outside 'Lyndale' to take them to Beechworth. They were the last ones picked up on the school run, and the first to be dropped off.

Bruce Gee [*my brother*]: Mum and Dad had an 'understanding' to marry after the war. It was like a pact. Mum's brother Bert had married Dad's sister Miriam in May 1940. Dad stayed with Miriam and Bert in 1941 at 'Willowdale' at Leneva while on leave for about three months, after *Perth's* service in the Mediterranean.

Mum was about 16 years old at the time. Dad liked Bert quite a lot, and being close to Miriam, he always visited them when he came home. In fact during this particular leave he did some work for Bert at the farm, and spent as much time as he could getting to know Mum.

Dad was due to return to *Perth* in Sydney, departing from Albury by train. Bert and Miriam offered to drive him to the station in Pop Brewer's beautiful old Dodge. Before they left for Albury, Mum and Dad were alone and sitting in the back seat of the car. They had a pretty serious talk. Dad said, 'I really fancy you, and I think we get on very well.' Mum replied, 'I like you very much too.' And Dad asked her, 'Will you wait for me to come back from the war? I want to marry you.' Mum told me she said, 'Yes, I will. You're the one for me.' It was a very clear understanding between them. Even though he was listed as Missing In Action, she always believed he would turn up.

They were married on September 7, 1946. Dad was 27 years old, and Mum was 22. At the time of my father's death in 1992 they had been married for 46 years.

Kath and Allan courting at 'Willowdale',
1941, with Bert and Miriam Brewer's daughter, Meryl

6

HMAS PERTH

A happy ship

This year, April 25, 2000 was the first time I had joined the *Perth* survivors for the Anzac Day march in Sydney. Storm clouds threatened, and I hoped the rain would hold off for the march. As I walked down King Street looking for the *Perth* banner I felt the emotion welling up inside me. How I wished my father was still alive, to meet up with his shipmates, to march with them, and to then go off for a drink and a yarn afterwards. Suddenly I spotted the bright blue banner with the gold trim clearly marked with their battle honours: Atlantic 1939, Greece, Matapan, Malta Convoys, Crete 1941, Java Sea and Sunda Strait 1942.

As I approached the men who included George Jones, Al Parker, Gavin Campbell, Frank McGovern, Gordon Steele, Allan 'Skeeter' Bishop, Charlie 'Jock' Lawrance and his son Alan, and Jack Burdon I fought back my tears, 'Hello, I'm Allan Gee's daughter. I've come to march with you today.' I was greeted warmly, and after a few laughs and some photographs, the Navy band struck up with great pomp and ceremony and we took off down Pitt Street. We wheeled into Martin Place, and marched back up George Street. A crowd of around 200,000 had turned out. As the people cheered and the flags fluttered it was hard to hold back the tears. I said to Jack Burdon, 'See, you haven't been forgotten.' He nodded and smiled back at me.

Afterwards at the traditional get-together at the Cricketers' Club stories were swapped, and everyone was enjoying themselves. A relative of Captain Hec Waller was there, and assorted friends and relatives. I felt very nostalgic when I heard the names so often mentioned by my father, 'Buzzer' Bee, Arthur 'Blood' Bancroft, Percy Partington, Knocker White, Ray Parkin, Harry Mee, John 'Macca' McQuade, 'Tubby' Grant, 'Jummer' Jim Brown, 'Tiny' Savage, and 'Judy' Julius Patching. A special day, marred only by the absence of my dear father, *Perth* survivor and POW 'Elmo' Gee.

Elmo Gee [signature]

Some of these men had been with Dad when the end came for their beloved *Perth* shortly after midnight on March 1, 1942 in the Sunda Strait between Java and Sumatra. Four torpedoes sent her and soon after *USS Houston* to a watery grave. (According to Naval Historian G. Hermon Gill *Perth* was sunk about 25 minutes after midnight)

Perth left Sydney for the last time on January 31, 1942, proceeding via Melbourne, and sailed for Fremantle on February 5th, arriving at noon on the 8th. All night leave was granted and the ship refuelled. The next day the ship sailed for Batavia, Java. However on February 10th, orders were received to return to Fremantle, and they arrived that afternoon. The ship remained in harbour until the night of the 13th, but to avoid sailing on Friday the 13th, Captain Waller decided to sail at 0030 on the 14th.
HMAS PERTH BY ALAN PAYNE [P 65]

Perth met that veteran of the Graf Spee action HMS Exeter in Tanjong Priok, the port of Batavia, and sailed with her and the British destroyers Jupiter, Electra, *and* Encounter *(screen to the ill-fated* Prince of Wales *and* Repulse) *to Surabaya to join the main ABDA (American, British, Dutch and Australian Allied Command) force. A few days later came that encounter known as the Battle of the Java Sea when the ABDA units under the Dutch Rear Admiral Karel Doorman met a Japanese force escorting the Java invasion convoy in what Sir Winston Churchill described as 'the forlorn battle'.*
THE SHIP'S BUGLER BY L.F. HOLMES [P 7]

On February 26, 1942 when the Japanese invasion convoys were moving on Java, an Allied Striking Force was already in the Java Sea, that long narrow strip of water between Java and Borneo. The striking force in command of Rear-Admiral Doorman, consisted of the Dutch light cruisers De Ruyter (flagship) and Java, the American heavy cruiser Houston, the British heavy cruiser Exeter, the Australian light cruiser Perth, the Dutch destroyers Witte de With and Kortenaer, the British destroyers Jupiter, Electra and Encounter, and the American destroyers Edwards, Alden, Ford, and Paul Jones.

The Americans called Houston 'the Galloping Ghost of the Java Sea' because the Japanese had claimed her sunk so often since Pearl Harbour.

A 14 ship force like this, with air cover and experienced leadership would have been formidable. Unfortunately it had neither. The Dutch Admiral was as gallant as any in Netherlands naval history, but his battle experience was limited, and he should never have been in command. But on top of the leadership blunder there were other grave problems. The Striking Force had never worked together. It had no common signalling plan, many signals did not reach the other ships from the flagship in correct order, and worst of all, the Force had no air reconnaissance. The Battle of the Java Sea, which decided the fate of Java, was two actions – afternoon and night – spread over more than seven hours. The Battle of the Java Sea began at 4.16pm when the Japanese heavies, Nachi and Haguro, opened with their twenty 8-inch guns at seventeen miles, and the Allied heavies, Exeter and Houston, replied with their twelve 8-inch guns. The battle ended at 11.30pm when the Japanese torpedoed both Dutch cruisers, De Ruyter and Java.

PROUD ECHO BY RONALD McKIE [P XII, XIII]

Captain Waller concluded his report on the Battle of the Java Sea by giving his reasons for withdrawing: 'I had under my orders one undamaged 6-inch cruiser, one 8-inch cruiser with very little ammunition and no guns aft. I had no destroyers. The force was subjected throughout the day and night operations to the most superbly organised air reconnaissance. I was opposed by six cruisers, one of them possibly sunk, and twelve destroyers. By means of their air reconnaissance they had already played cat and mouse with the main striking force and I saw no prospect of getting at the enemy.

It was fairly certain that the enemy had at least one submarine operating

*directly with him and he had ample destroyers to interpose between the convoy
and myself. I therefore had no hesitation in withdrawing what remained of the
Striking Force and ordering them to the pre-arranged rendezvous after night
action — Tanjong Priok.'*

*The withdrawal of Perth and Houston was not opposed by enemy surface
forces, but within 60 miles of Tanjong Priok enemy reconnaissance located
the two cruisers. Waller sent out a 'Help' call and fighter aircraft were
sent out from Batavia and escorted the cruisers into Tanjong Priok, the port
of Batavia.*

*The first surface action in the Pacific War had ended in disaster for the Allies,
largely due to the superb Japanese naval air reconnaissance and their very
liberal use of the world's most powerful torpedoes.*

HMAS PERTH BY ALAN PAYNE [P78-79]

DAD: The whole campaign was a disaster for the Allies. At the end of a
terrible time *Perth* and *Houston* were really left on their own. When we
eventually got back into Batavia the Japs were then very close to the
area. We had taken a lot of bombing and it was obvious the Japs were
about to land. We got whatever oil we could and what provisions were
available, then made a dash for survival.

*Defeat was everywhere. It was something you could almost reach out and touch.
At 2.30pm on February 28, 1942 – invasion eve and only five days before the
Japanese took Batavia – Perth and Houston came in from the Battle of the Java
Sea – came in from defeat to the smell of defeat – and stayed five hours.*

*None of Perth's crew had closed their eyes for thirty hours. Few talked of the
action just over, or of the war, but war was in their minds like suspicion.*

*Most of the younger men, and some not much more than boys, were
optimistic about the future. They had survived a battle, they would get away.
But the older men were not so sure. They were in a landlocked sea, and the
ships and planes of Japan now had command of that sea. They knew they had to
get out, and that Sunda Strait, the closest escape route to the Indian Ocean,
was a narrow laneway of water leading to freedom, or a trap — a submarine
commander's dream.*

PROUD ECHO BY RONALD McKIE [P 1-2])

BOB COLLINS: Redlead had grown up a bit by this time. When we withdrew to Tanjong Priok in Java, we decided to go ashore. 'The old man' immediately wanted to know where Redlead was. Somebody said, 'She's jumped ship Sir.' So Waller said, 'Send a squad out to find her,' and they did. They sent half a dozen blokes to fetch her. They brought her kicking and screaming back on board. The cat was not happy. She had been through the Battle of the Java sea, and like many of us, she was exhausted and fearful.

DAD: For some reason Redlead the ship's cat tried to leave the ship several times at Tanjong Priok. Some of us thought this was a bad omen. Unfortunately for the cat she was brought back on board and she was later lost at sea.

On February 28, 1942 *Perth* with 682 men aboard left Tanjong Priok with *Houston* and sailed for Sunda Strait, the route to Tjilatjap and the safety of the south coast of Java.

> In the dusk at 7.00pm Perth *and* Houston *sailed, and an hour later, when free of the minefields covering the port and heading west, every man in the Australian cruiser stilled. 'This is the captain speaking.' In those seconds as the men waited,*

HMAS Perth taken from HMAS Adelaide, 15th February 1942. This image is believed to be the last photograph taken of the Perth. (Photo by Chief ERA H.J. Elliott, RAN)

the dull pulse-beat of the engines was the only sound. Then, again, Captain Waller's voice came over the inter-communication system to every part of the ship. 'We are sailing for Sunda Strait bound for Tjilatjap and will shortly close up to the first degree of readiness relaxed. Dutch air reconnaissance reports that Sunda Strait is free of enemy shipping. But I have a report that a large enemy convoy is about fifty miles north-east of Batavia moving east. I do not expect, however, to meet enemy forces.'

PROUD ECHO BY RONALD McKIE [P 5]

DAD: The crew had a great feeling of trust and confidence in Captain Waller's ability to lead us to safety. There can be no higher compliment than that for a commanding officer.

I was in the wheelhouse at the time that we actually ran into the Japs, as I had been a helmsman for about two and a half years from the time the war started. We made contact with the Japs about 11.00pm and we all rushed to our action stations. My action station had been changed from the wheelhouse to the bridge. The captain told me to blow the bugle, to signal everyone to go to their action stations on the double.

I had seen a lot of action by that stage, in the Mediterranean and elsewhere, but this was different to anything anyone could ever imagine. We were in the thick of destroyers and cruisers firing at each other with machine guns at a frighteningly close range. I have always believed that we never got enough credit for the number of ships we sunk that night.

We fought like hell, but it was never going to be enough. We were relentlessly bombarded, and it was only a matter of time before we were history. The Captain must have been very worried, because just before we left Tanjong Priok for Sunda Strait he made us load on board (24) Carley floats. That decision saved many lives.

Allan Gee was a service helmsman and Captain's bugler when the ship fought her last battle against overwhelming odds in the Battle of Sunda Strait. He was on the bridge for the whole furious action, and was one of the last to see the Captain when the order was finally given to abandon ship.

THE SHIP'S BUGLER BY L.F. HOLMES [P 3]

Captain Waller was last seen with his 'Mae West' blown up at the front of the bridge looking down at the silent guns. Shortly afterwards the bridge was seen to receive a shell and Perth's *Captain must have been killed instantly.*
HMAS PERTH BY ALAN PAYNE [P86])

DAD: We could hardly breathe from the thick smoke, and the Japs were continually firing at us. We took a lot of shelling up on the bridge. The shrapnel made a terrific noise, and sounded like we were being smashed with chains. All I could see were men moving around the ship, not quite knowing what to do next. Before midnight I felt the cruiser shudder when the first torpedo struck, and there was a shattering blast. By this stage some of the blokes had been hit, and a few were saying to jump into the water. I believed then that the ship was going to go down. I think I piped the 'Abandon Ship' order with my bugle over the loudspeakers.

The final moment of abandoning ship was the worst feeling I had ever had. I was a bit scared but I couldn't bring myself to believe that I'd had it. I remember thinking that my number wasn't up. From the top of the bridge it looked as if we had to jump into this black void. The ship started to list and I knew she was going down. It was an immensely difficult decision to actually leave her.

There was still quite a lot of firing going on, but the thing that I remember was how people were relatively calm. I had only experienced a calm, collected atmosphere like this once before in the Mediterranean when a thousand pound bomb came more or less over the afterbridge. I could have touched the bomb, which almost grazed the guard rail and exploded right alongside the ship. We were all covered in water, but no one panicked unduly.

Just before I jumped I did a strange thing I rushed to retrieve my bugle. I took the mouthpiece out of it, then thought what a stupid thing to be doing and just threw it away. I then walked down on to the flag deck only to discover that the starboard side had been completely shot away. As Waller and myself and others had been on the bridge, we hadn't seen the full extent of the damage.

By the time the last gun had stopped firing there had been awesome carnage. One thousand Australian and American sailors were dead or drowned, floating in the water or trapped inside the sinking ships. Of *Perth's* complement of 682 men, close to 400 were killed during the action. I'll never know how I survived.

> *Please God, not again Lloyd Burgess thought. In the dark he fumbled for his shoes, found his tin hat and stumbled on to the bridge. He was still half asleep. A search-light got them and Waller called, 'For God's sake shoot that bloody light out.' 'A' turret fired again her defiant last, and Burgess' tin hat again fell over his eyes. When he pushed it back the bridge was empty except for Waller, Willy Gay the officer of the watch, and himself. The Captain was standing far forward blowing into his Mae West. As Burgess went down the ladder he heard Waller say, 'Get off the bridge Gay.' Waller was standing with his arms on the front of the bridge looking down at the silent turrets.*
> PROUD ECHO BY RONALD MCKIE [P 46]

DAD: Nobody seemed to be in a real hurry, but eventually we cut off some of the Carley floats. The man that was next to me was a former Tingira boy who had joined the *Perth* when we were commissioned. We were very close friends, and he was a very fine seaman. His real name was George Catmull, but we always knew him as 'Moggy'.

Other people had started to jump, so I joined about a dozen other crew at the focsle, grabbed a life jacket and leapt off the port side with George. We held hands and as we jumped George shouted to me, 'I'll see you in Young and Jacksons' (a Melbourne Hotel famous for its painting of the nude 'Chloe'). George couldn't swim and I never saw him again.

I took a deep breath, hit the water and just seemed to go down and down. I didn't have time to be scared, I was too busy thinking about staying alive and *Perth* moved right over the top of me.

The first time I came up I hit the bottom of the ship and went down again. For the first time in my life I thought I was going to die. It would have been so easy to succumb to the sensation of drowning. That's the weird part. I had this beautiful feeling of floating, and being incredibly light and happy. I had no pain and no fear. I guess I was close to drowning. I remember thinking how lovely it was. Everything in your body tells you to give in and not to fight. It was just like being drunk, a revelation really, that dying wasn't necessarily an awful experience. Another strange memory I have of that euphoric state of near drowning was seeing my eldest sister Miriam laughing at me. That seemed to make me snap out of it, and I struggled harder than ever.

The Master at Arms, 'Jan' (Herbert Rowland) Creber, another close friend pulled me onto a little wooden table which had floated off *Perth*. Sadly Jan eventually drowned. By this time I was just about drowned. Thank God for the table and the Carley floats which Waller had the foresight to bring on board. With so many ships sunk there was masses of oil everywhere.

In 1974 my wife Kath and I sailed to Singapore on board the Greek ship *Patris*. The delightful Captain made us welcome on the bridge. When we passed through Sunda Strait we were shown the exact position of where *Perth* was sunk. It was a very emotional experience.

BRUCE GEE [*my brother*]: Dad and I enjoyed talking for hours about his time at sea, but his voice always took on a different tone when he talked about *Perth* sinking. Like everyone on board he couldn't believe that his beloved ship had had it. Dad said that even though he was a very good swimmer, at crunch point, he wasn't too keen on going into the water. He left the ship at a very late stage, and was worried about being sucked under. He was also one of the last people to see Waller alive, whom he practically worshipped.

He was also upset about losing his collection of hundreds of photos. In Egypt he had swapped his Zeiss binoculars for a Leica camera and he set up his own darkroom. He had a little business taking photos on shore and selling them on board. He was a good photographer, and the Leica was the first successful compact camera.

DAD: We weren't far off shore so I decided to have a go at getting to the beach and came within 50 yards of making it. I had been clinging to a raft for about 15 hours by then and I thought it was my only hope of survival. But every time I got close the tide washed me out again. It was just as well I didn't make it, because we heard later that the Japs were on the beach bayoneting the survivors as they came ashore.

I had no doubt that the action and subsequent sinking had killed dozens of *Perth's* crew, but we were all so exhausted and dazed with shock it was hard to make much sense of what was happening. It was all very strange, and I was wondering which would be worse to get eaten by sharks, to drown or be picked up by the Japs. I remember being very thirsty, and my tongue felt like a piece of wood.

I think it was about four o'clock in the afternoon when a Japanese destroyer sailed near us and stopped. We had to swim about a hundred yards to reach it. I was with another Able Seaman Bill Clifford who joined the Navy about twelve months after me. I remember saying, 'Bill, please don't leave me.' but as it turned out, I reached the destroyer first. When they hauled us on board many of us threw up as we'd swallowed gallons of sea water. I lurched about as I was blinded by the oil. I was sunburnt, and my skin was falling off in handfuls. We were in bad shape, and hardly looking forward to being guests of the Imperial Japanese Army. They gave us water and kerosene to wash the oil from our eyes, and put us down onto the quarterdeck. We were treated alright, by Japanese standards that is. However the bastards threw some of the wounded back into the sea. I couldn't believe it. Imagine coming through that nightmare, only to be tossed back into the sea?

ALAN LAWRANCE [*son of Perth Leading Stoker Jock Lawrance*]: The late 'Jumma' Brown told me that when he was in the water after *Perth* had sunk he witnessed a shocking incident. Apparently some other survivors were in the water and were approached by a Japanese destroyer. They were asked in English by a Jap with a loud hailer who they were. He told me these brave *Perth* men replied, knowing their imminent fate, 'We're Australians and we're fucking proud of it.' The Japs then machine-gunned them.

DAD: They had too many of us on the destroyer so after about an hour we were transferred to the transport *Somedong Maru*. We were unbelievably tired as we hadn't had a wink of sleep for three days. I was totally exhausted. I remember we were all sitting on our haunches, pushed together with no clothes on. The Japs later gave us bits of cloth like G-strings to put around our waists.

On *Somedong Maru* we were treated a bit better. We were given boiled barley to eat and we were able to sleep. In some ways we had a longer sleep there than we'd had for ages. I remember in the Mediterranean there was so much going on that we had become accustomed to only sleeping for two or three hours at a time.

I had a weird experience on *Somedong Maru*, undoubtedly due to exhaustion and delirium. My legs were sticking over the side and I was looking down into the water. My early reading came to mind, and I felt I was Tom from 'The Water Babies'. I felt very dirty and I had this strong desire to jump over the side and cleanse myself. The only other clear memory I have is imagining I was sitting underneath our lovely old Roman Beauty apple tree at home in Silver Creek. I felt very peaceful.

We were taken off the *Somedong Maru* in barges, still mostly covered in oil, as we had been given no soap to wash it off. Not that it would have helped much. I think there were at least 150 of us. Anyway we hit the beach which to our horror was ringed with heavily armed Japs, some with machine guns. We were right at the waters' edge as the barges moved away. We thought we were going to be mowed down by machine gun fire. They seemed to be all set to do just that. I don't mind telling you I was scared.

I'll never forget one prick of a Jap officer. I don't know what rank he was, but he told us that we were now prisoners of war and ought to be ashamed of ourselves. He said that if we were good we would be looked after, and if we were bad we would be shot. With a warning like that, we didn't dare put a foot out of place. We were put into what looked like sheep trucks, about forty of us per vehicle guarded by Japs. This lot treated us reasonably well and they brought us some bananas. We thought things might improve. We were taken to the cinema at Serang (Java) where things changed immediately for the worse.

Newspaper account of the sinking of Perth.

Ray Parkin the Action Chief Quartermaster in Perth *when she went down, likened the battle to a bar room brawl. Imagine a crowded bar and two gunmen enter. Then all you see is smoke, flashes and hear gunfire. When the smoke clears there is nobody left.'*

'Our time in the Mediterranean toughened us up. We survived an incredible 257 air attacks and only lost five men — three killed and two washed overboard. Perth and Houston *survived the initial Battle of the Java sea, but ran into an enemy convoy about 12 hours later. The battle lasted about one hour. You keep going until you get knocked over,' Ray says. Ray was swept by the current to an island where he found a lifeboat with other sailors who had been on the ship. But they were captured by the Japanese some days later.* 'Captain Waller was one of the best and would have been destined for great things had he come through.' Ray said.

Missing in action. Canberra: March 13, 1942

'Information has been received from the Naval Board that HMAS Perth and HMAS Yarra are overdue on their return to Australia from waters around Java', the Prime Minister (Mr Curtin) said today. 'In view of the circumstances surrounding operations in that area, it is with deep regret that I announce that these two ships must be presumed lost'.

'An enemy claim to this effect was made, in the case of HMAS Perth some days ago. At that time however the Naval Board had no information to substantiate this. The position then was that HMAS Perth had fought successfully and unharmed in the battle in the Java Sea. There is no news of survivors. But it is conceivable, in the narrow waters in which they were operating, that members of the crews of both ships managed to make their way to shore, or were picked up by other ships. With so much of the area in enemy hands, communication is naturally difficult. The next of kin of personnel have been informed. My Government and the Naval Board, extend to them our sincere sympathy of the whole nation.'

Roll of honour

There were 682 men in HMAS Perth when she fought the Battle of Sunda Strait — 45 Officers, 632 Petty Officers and men, and six RAAF Officers and men. In the battle 23 Officers and 330 Petty Officers and men, were killed, and 100 Petty Officers and men died in Japanese prisoner of war camps. No officers died while prisoners of war. Of the original 682 in Perth, only 229 returned to Australia at the end of the war. No officers died while prisoners of war.

PROUD ECHO BY RONALD McKIE. [P 130]

According to revised official figures 218 Perth *men were repatriated to Australia, less than a third of the ship's company. A total of 463 men did not return.* Perth *deaths in Burma and Thailand were 58, which included the men killed in Allied air attacks. The worst camp was 55 kilo (Tamarkan) where 13* Perth *men died.*
HMAS PERTH BY ALAN PAYNE [P 117-122]

POS SHENNAN [*Beechworth resident*]: I recall seeing Mr And Mrs Gee preaching on the street corners of Beechworth with the Salvation Army band, and I remember the talk in the town when *Perth* went down and Allan was presumed lost.

MERYL BROWN [*Auntie Miriam's daughter*]: Mum had just given birth to Nancy and was haemorrhaging when she heard that *Perth* was sunk and Uncle Allan was presumed missing. She was sent down to 'Pinedale' to help with the washing up. They said it would keep her mind off the tragic news.

Naval hymn

Eternal Father strong to save
Whose arm doth bind the restless wave,
Who bidst the mighty ocean deep,
Its own appointed limits keep;
O hear us when we cry to Thee,
For those in peril on the sea

O Trinity of love and power,
Our brethren shield in danger's hour,
From rock and tempest, fire and foe,
Protect them wheresoe'er they go;
Thus ever more shall rise to Thee,
Glad hymns of praise from land and sea

PART 3

POWs and Pal's

Allan Gee, Williams Force,
the blind barber of the Burma Railway.
(Illustration by Ulf Kaiser)

THAILAND-BURMA RAILWAY

Source: Hellfire Pass Memorial Book.
Published by the Australian-Thai Chamber
of Commerce, 1998

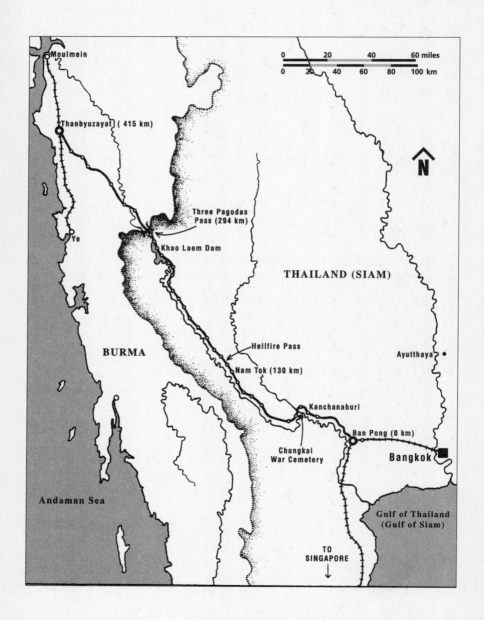

7

PRISONER
OF WAR

'It wasn't as bad as you think and worse than you can ever imagine'.
RAY PARKIN

Growing up with a man who had lost his eyesight and was severely traumatised as a result of his experiences as a POW wasn't always easy, for him or us. But it was only when I was older and had talked to my father in greater depth about his years on the Burma railway that I was able to comprehend the true extent of his ordeal.

I have always been horrified by the brutality and deprivations he suffered, but my sister Christine once said, 'It was the best and worst thing that ever happened to him.' For all the problems it created Dad said being a POW was a club you couldn't join, and he truly cherished his friends from those days like brothers. We grew up hearing about and meeting our 'special' uncles, with names which bewildered our school friends 'Blood', 'Judy', 'Tiny', 'Slim', 'Buzzer', 'Tubby', 'Macca', 'Jumma' etc. Dad always emphasised the compassion they showed each other, and some of the fun they shared, in spite of being in a hostile environment. Other POWs I interviewed for this book expressed similar sentiments.

In 1999 I went to Kanchanaburi in Thailand to visit the Museum, the Kanchanaburi War Cemetery and the remnants of the railway. On a stiflingly hot day as I boarded the local train and chugged over the Bridge on the River Kwai, and through the dense jungle my heart was heavy thinking of what my brave father and his comrades endured. The idea of Dad suffering numerous tropical diseases and failing eyesight without any medical attention, inadequate food and routine bashings was deeply sad. One can only reiterate the inscription on Weary Dunlop's commemorative plaque whose ashes were interred in Hellfire Pass, Thailand at the Anzac Day Dawn Service, April 25, 1994. *'When you go home, tell them of us and say we gave our tomorrow for your today.'*

Allan Gee and thousands of other wonderful young men suffered terribly during their years as prisoners of the Japanese. We must ensure that the same should never be allowed to happen again. To do this we must not allow our history to be forgotten and we must learn from this history.

'A Long Way From Silver Creek' is an apt description of what was to befall the many youngsters who enlisted to serve their country, not only out of a sense of duty but also as a road to adventure. Adventure which few would have experienced had the world remained at peace.

How could Allan Gee, and those other young men, have imagined just how far they were going to travel? Not only in the sense of thousands of miles but into a set of circumstances so far removed from existing experience as to be beyond belief. Little did these young men (nor the leaders of the Allied nations) understand the nature of the enemy they were soon to face and the extent of the long-term preparations made by this enemy. These shortcomings were soon to be apparent at terrible cost. The Allied forces in South-east Asia were rapidly defeated by determined Japanese forces which were numerically inferior but which had a huge advantage

---

* *Background: First became personally involved with the Thailand-Burma Railway in February 1994 when I re-cleared the pathway into Hellfire Pass prior to the visit by then Prime Minister Paul Keating. Erected the plaque unveiled to commemorate the internment of the ashes of Weary Dunlop, Anzac Day, 1994. Offered to regularly maintain and further develop the pathways leading to Hellfire Pass for the Australian-Thai Chamber of Commerce. Accepted the position as Supervisor of the Commonwealth War Graves Commission's cemeteries in Thailand (May 1995). Appointed Project Manager of the Hellfire Pass Project January 1996. Finished my term in 1998 with the completion and opening of the Hellfire Pass Memorial Museum by Prime Minister John Howard. Commenced work on compiling a database on all Allied prisoners of war who worked on the Railway and died as prisoners of the Japanese.*

— they knew they would defeat the Allies. So sure were they that they had planned their offensive to a strict timetable affected by several determined rearguard actions during the battle for Malaya.

It is possible that the Japanese had begun preparations for the occupation of South-East Asia as early as 1934. Evidence of this can be seen in the locomotives and rolling stock, which the Japanese shipped to Thailand for eventual use on the Thailand-Burma Railway. These locomotives manufactured in 1935-36, were built so that they could be re-guaged from the wider Japanese 3' 6" to the narrower metre guage (3' 3") of South-east Asia by the simple process of moving the tyres inwards on the wheels.

The Japanese were so confident of victory that these same locomotives and other rolling stock were loaded onto transport vessels in November, 1941, departed Japan soon after the invasion fleets and they were already being reassembled in Bangkok three weeks before Singapore fell!

The same national characteristics, beliefs and planning, which contributed to the early rapid advance across South-east Asia, were to lead to much of the tragedy of the Thailand-Burma Railway and other areas of incarceration for Allied personnel. The Japanese are expert planners and very adept at planning for the many variables which may eventuate. But on the other hand these plans once adopted are inflexible and if the unplanned for does happen then they have great difficulty adapting to the changed circumstances. An example of this was that the Japanese were planning to build the railway using Asian labour (bearing in mind that the Japanese would never have expected to capture hundreds of thousands of prisoners of war) and their plans were for food and equipment suitable to Asians — not for the Europeans subsequently used. So it is not surprising that these men slowly starved to death.

Also as with most Asian nationalities, the welfare of the Japanese individual is so subordinate to the aims and aspirations of the group, or nation, as to be almost irrelevant — once the individual is no longer an effective part of the group. And so it proved to be for those unfortunate enough to become their slaves.

The differences between Western and Asian concepts and behaviours are numerous and complex. One has to live in Asia for a long time and make a conscious effort to learn before understanding these differences. The chances of this happening in the turmoil of war and captivity is almost zero so it is not surprising that conflict raged whenever the determined Japanese tried to force a reluctant and resentful workforce to build a railway through terrain considered impassable by most of the world.

A most important lesson to be learned from the tragedy of the Railway is that we should understand the nature of our fellow humans and prepare ourselves. A combination of factors, our unpreparedness, Japanese inflexibility and ruthlessness and national ambitions as well as weather, terrain and disease led to the terrible conditions of the Thailand-Burma Railway. May the lessons learned by Allan Gee and his fellow prisoners of war be not forgotten.

ROD BEATTIE*, KANCHANABURI, THAILAND, JULY 25, 2000

The bugler who's lucky to be alive

It was playing the bugle so much that got Allan Gee down in the finish. Like about 1,500 times — the Last Post over the graves of comrades who had perished not in a hail of gunfire, but in the grip of hunger and disease. On one day alone, in the heart of the Burmese jungle, he sounded that melancholy dirge over the graves of 33 men. Had he needed at the time to be able to see what he was doing he would not have been much use. He was almost blind, and still is.

The loss of his sight had begun in the aftermath of the sea battle when HMAS Perth was sunk. Flung into the sea by the force of torpedoes exploding below the waterline, Able Seaman Gee was temporarily blinded as he floundered about in the smoke and fire and burning oil.

Later starvation in the Burmese jungle induced retrobulbar neuritis, an eye disease in which the central vision nerve disintegrated. Today he sees with about eight per cent vision. His war adventures enveloped his youth, ruined his sight, and but for the intervention of a loving capable wife would have ruined his future too. His response to all of that is grateful submission because it would have taken only one better-placed bullet to rub him out and place him among the 'killed in action' casualties of the war.

Survivors of Houston and Perth were put ashore at Serang, Java, where they were incarcerated in a cinema. Dysentery erupted and many men became seriously ill. Some died. From Serang they were taken to Batavia for six months, then Singapore and finally in November, 1942, to Burma to build 'the death railway' line to Thailand. Allan was there for 18 months. It was the worst time of his life — daily signalling on his bugle the death of his comrades.

THE BORDER MAIL, SATURDAY, AUGUST 19, 1989. REPORTER: TERRY MCGOVERNE

DAD: We were taken to Serang from the coast in trucks and unloaded outside a cinema. The Japs broke up the group I was with and people were either moved into the cinema or went to the local gaol.

I never saw the gaol but I believe the prisoners there had a very bad time. We felt very dejected and must have looked terrible. None of us had had a shave, we had no boots, and were still covered in black oil. We were wearing only ragged G-strings. Hundreds of Javanese threw muck at us and abused us, which was terribly dispiriting. They also kept saying the Japs were going to kill us, which didn't make me feel very cheerful.

There was bright sunshine outside but when we entered the cinema it was very dark inside. Jap guards were all around and as we walked in they gave us each a punch or a kick to put us in our place. We spent the next six weeks on the stone floor of the cinema wedged in so tightly that we had to sit between each other's legs. It was unbearably hot, and at night-time we had to lie against each other like rats in a cage. It was a horrible experience. There was one particular Jap Captain who was especially nasty. He kept telling us we should be ashamed, and if we had any courage we would shoot ourselves.

All we got to drink was a cup of rank water and some dirty boiled rice once a day with a bit of miso soup (a thin gruel made from salted soya beans) slopped over it, so we were all half mad with thirst and hunger. We were not allowed out to exercise, and our toilet was a bucket which was constantly overflowing. The stench was unbearable. Dysentery was rife, and many of the men dropped down dead, or just simply didn't wake up. There was no medicine of any description.

I had a badly infected ear which was probably due to the oil we floated in after we were sunk. I was going insane with the pain, so one day I levered a piece of stone out of the wall and prodded inside my ear with the sharp end. About an egg cup full of pus shot out, giving me enormous relief. Luckily it never affected my hearing.

While we were in Serang we were joined by some of the blokes off the *Houston*. They were big guys and we all became close friends. My best buddy from the *Houston* was Jack Feliz from Hawaii.

After about three weeks another Jap Captain arrived from a

different platoon who was more compassionate. He seemed quite upset at the appalling conditions and let us out to walk around a bit. I felt delirious a lot of the time, and in this strange state between waking and dreaming, my sense of reality was blurred from starvation, sickness and general deprivation.

We discovered that we were about to join some hundreds of survivors from the Australian cruiser Perth *and the American cruiser* Houston.

We gathered from other captives, also lined up with us to give their particulars, that there had been many brutal bashings of captives by the Japanese, and that conditions inside the cinema were very grim indeed. A few minutes later we were thrust into the dark interior of the building.

Neither the scraps of information, nor the changed attitude of these Japanese, had prepared us for what we saw inside. Seated on the bare stone in rows, packed together like penguins or seals were hundreds of Europeans, most of them unshaven and incredibly dirty.

With few exceptions they were stark naked except for a small calico loincloth. A guard cleared a space for us with the butt of his rifle and told us to sit. I suppose that with normal seating that cinema would accommodate perhaps five hundred people. About three times that number were now jammed into it.

It soon became obvious that the handful of guards at the back of the cinema had no chance of enforcing the no-speaking order if one were careful. Some of the men had been in this cinema since March 3rd. without being given a chance to wash even their hands or faces. Food was limited to a small issue of almost uncooked rice of the poorest quality in the early afternoon, and a similar issue of a small loaf of white bread in the evening. Anybody who had been in the place for twenty-four hours was ravenous.

Several of the boys from the ships were badly wounded, but they were lying on the filthy floor like the rest of us, having received no bandages, dressings or treatment, despite repeated protests and appeals to the Japanese.

The majority of the other sailors, particularly the Perth *boys were covered with a thick coating of oil fuel, which had also got into their eyes causing pain.*

On the balcony, at the back of the cinema, the Japanese had a machine-gun mounted, and at times a second gun was also trained on us from this point. A large pit had been dug, and across this half a dozen boards and beams had been carelessly laid. This open cesspit was the sole latrine for over fifteen hundred men. We had to sit to attention, which means sitting bolt upright in silence for two hours. When we were at last allowed to talk again, had a great yarn with half a dozen of the boys including 'Slim' (George) Hedrick of Mordialloc, and Allan Gee of Beechworth. We had a marvellous discussion about the merits of Rugby League and Rugby Union which led to the inevitable dog-fight as to whether Aussie Rules is better than rugby, soccer and the rest, as most of us from the Southern states believe. You'd think they were sitting in lounge chairs in the Australia (Hotel) instead of being huddled together in this hole where none of them has had a square meal in the ten or eleven days they've been there.

The Perth boys are grand with their six or seven wounded mates who have to be carried to and from the wretched latrine day and night. Still no bandages, antiseptics or treatment for these boys, although it is now thirteen days since Perth was sunk. But their spirit is unbeatable and except for one chap who is in constant pain, not even a groan escapes them.

I suppose we were lucky they didn't cut our heads off. Some of the Perth and Houston boys saw other shipwrecked mates decapitated as soon as they were washed up on the beach.

I doubt whether any of the men who spent those five weeks in the jail, or cinema, will ever forget the experience. We were all suffering from acute malnutrition and claustrophobia and most of us had dysentery or chronic diarrhoea. We felt fairly confident that whatever lay ahead it could not be worse than Serang.

BEHIND BAMBOO BY ROHAN RIVETT [P 90]

DAD: At the end of our time in Serang I was rotten with dysentery. We were taken from there to the Bicycle Camp at the Dutch Army Barracks in Batavia, named after a Dutch regiment who used to travel around on bicycles.

It was here that we met the 2/2nd. Pioneer Battalion and the 2/3rd. Machine Gunners whom we had worked with in Syria. These blokes were very good to us. Many still had their kits with them, and shared what they had. There was also an American Texas battalion who had been left in Java and were stuck in the same camp. The entire battalion finished up as POWs. They still had most of their equipment, and like true American boys they were smoking cigarettes and all the rest of it.

Although some of the Japs in the Bicycle Camp were alright there was still a lot of bashing. We were working outside the camp most of the time. They had us sweeping up the streets, mainly to try and humiliate us. We thought conditions were quite bad, but with hindsight we were in Paradise compared to what was coming on the Burma Railway. We didn't have much food in the camp, a bit of tinned stuff and some eggs, but we managed to scrounge quite a lot of food from the Javanese on the outside. It was difficult getting the food in, but the Japs were quite stupid and couldn't match the Australians' cunning. I thoroughly enjoyed outwitting the Japs and having little victories over them. Sometimes I was able to talk my way out of the beltings. During that time I hated them with a passion.

We stayed in this camp for about six months and many of us regained our health to some extent. I had recovered from dysentery and slept more than I had slept for years. Then we were on the move again.

When I left the camp I travelled with two *Perth* friends Petty Officer Slim Hedrick and Eric Thompson. We sort of lived together and looked after our own little group. We believed we were off to Borneo and took what we could with us. I had done a lot of trading and card playing, so I left with a good stash of Dutch guilders. We were terrified as the Japs searched us relentlessly. It was quite a job to keep all our contraband hidden from them.

We boarded a ship bound for Singapore. The trip took about eight days and the conditions were atrocious. We were jammed into the holds between each others legs, just like in the Serang cinema.

Once again it was stiflingly hot and impossible for people to get to the toilet most of the time. There were only two toilets on the upper deck which were never cleaned of course. It was a disaster, because you were only allowed up on deck about twice a day. There was shit everywhere.

We reached Singapore on my 23rd birthday, October 10, 1942, and I was extremely ill and very weak. We were taken by truck to barracks close to Changi Gaol. I have a stark memory of a thin European woman's arm waving a lace handkerchief through a slit window in one of the gaol turrets. She was about 50 yards away and we all felt very despondent, stuck here under the control of the Japanese, knowing that so many of our blokes and women were also their prisoners.

Changi was a very disturbing time for me. I thought we were there for two or three days but Slim Hedrick said we only stayed one night. He told me I was so delirious I didn't know where I was half the time. However I do remember that Slim got hold of a tin of milk from somewhere and put it in boiling water. He opened it for me and I drank the lot in one go. Whatever it was, it settled my tummy down.

At one stage I was so crook it seemed I would be left in Singapore, but I stuck with our little group and we eventually joined a ship, the *Mayebassi Maru*, to be taken to Burma. Unfortunately torrential rain kept the ship in Singapore for five or six days with us stuck on board. Conditions were frightful and we were all dreadfully sick, and riddled with dysentery. Finally we sailed. We were joined by another ship loaded with prisoners as we went up the Bay of Bengal. We were escorted by a small gun boat which was always on our port side. A few planes flew over us but we were never bombed, thank God. We heard that other ships after us were bombed and sunk, with tragic loss of life.

The notorious Thailand-Burma railway, built by British, Australian, Dutch and American prisoners of war and impressed Asian labourers, was a Japanese project inspired by the need for improved lines of communication to maintain the large Japanese army in Burma. During its construction more than 12,000 of the 60,000 Allied prisoners of war died — mainly of disease, sickness, malnutrition and exhaustion — and were buried along the railway. The Asian labourers, predominantly Tamils, Malays and Burmese, also suffered high death rates, and between 80,000 and 100,000 of the more than 200,000 Asian workers perished. The Japanese kept no records of these deaths and it was not possible for anyone else to do so. The graves of the Asian workers remain unmarked.

Japanese communications depended upon a long and exposed sea route to Rangoon via Singapore and the Straits of Malacca, and a road (totally unfit for prolonged heavy traffic) from Raheng through Kowkareik to Moulmein. The decision to complete the railway connecting Moulmein to Ban Pong, which had been commenced before the war but abandoned by the two countries concerned, was taken in June 1942. More than 403 kilometres of railway, from Thanbyuzayat in Burma to Ban Pong in Thailand, remained to be constructed, much of it through mountainous jungle country, in a region with one of the worst climates in the world and subject to almost every known tropical disease. The British Army had originally surveyed the route in 1903. Although the Japanese used aerial photographs, they did little on-the-ground surveying, and the final route chosen was close to that determined by the British.

The Imperial Japanese Army was responsible for the acquisition of material and labour for the project. A total of about 15,000 Japanese and Koreans were employed on the project.

Following their victory in Malaya and the fall of Singapore in February 1942 as well as that of the Netherlands East Indies shortly after, the Japanese found they had a large number of Allied prisoners of war. In many ways, these prisoners were a significant problem for the Japanese military administrations. In many of the areas captured, there were no detention facilities outside civilian gaols. Moreover, their immediate removal to Japan would have diverted vital transport and administrative resources from the war effort. The Imperial Japanese Army therefore found it had acquired a potentially strong and well trained workforce, much of which it subsequently transported to Thailand and Burma to be put to work.

The Japanese aimed at completing the Thailand-Burma railway in 14 months, or at least by the end of 1943. From June 1942 onwards large groups of prisoners were tranferred to Thailand and Burma from Singapore, Java and Sumatra.

Those sent to Burma were transported under extremely bad conditions, by ship. These troops included the relatively small number of Americans (700) to be captured in this area of conflict. The prisoners selected to work in Thailand were crammed into small steel box-cars and transported by rail to Ban Pong under equally inhumane conditions.

When the first of the prisoners arrived, their initial task was to construct camps at Ban Pong and Kanchanaburi in Thailand and Thanbyuzayat in Burma. Accommodation for the Japanese had to be built first, and at all staging camps built subsequently along the route of the railway this rule applied. The cookhouse and huts for the working parties came next and accommodation for the sick last of all. Frequently men were sent to work on the line long before their accommodation was completed.

Throughout the building of the railway, food supplies were irregular and totally inadequate. The rice was of poor quality, frequently maggoty or in other ways contaminated. Although it was sometimes possible to supplement this diet by purchases from local traders, men often had to live for weeks on little more than a small daily portion of rice. Malaria, dysentery, pellagra (a vitamin deficiency disease) and later cholera attacked the prisoners and labourers.

The Japanese engineers demanded a certain number of men from each camp for each day's work irrespective of the number of sick. For those who fell ill there was generally very little that could be done for them since the Japanese refused to provide even basic medicines or other supplies. At main camps such as Tarsau, Chungkai, Tamarkan and Thanbyuzayat there were 'base hospitals' which were also only huts of bamboo and atap, staffed by such Allied medical officers and orderlies as were allowed by the Japanese to care for the sick prisoners. Only the devotion, skill and enterprise of the prisoner-of-war medical staffs saved the lives of thousands and gradually evolved a system which could control disease and mortality.

Work on the railway started from Thanbyuzayat and Nong Pladuk in October 1942 and reached a frenzied climax during the infamous 'speedo' period from July 1943. This happened to coincide with the wettest monsoon season in memory causing even greater difficulties. The rails were joined near Konkoita in October 1943 and the railway was completed by December. Allied reconnaissance flights had started over the Burma end of the railway in late 1943 and were followed by periodic bombing raids.

These became more frequent after the line was completed and trains full of Japanese troops and supplies began to go through Thailand to Burma. Many of the camps were located close to the railway track and some, such as Tamarkan, were close to major bridges. As the Japanese refused to allow the prisoners to construct a symbol (a white triangle on a white base) indicating a POW camp, these bombing raids added their quota to the deaths on the line.

By March 1944, with the bulk of the prisoners relocated to the main camps at Chungkai, Kanchanaburi, Tamarkan, Tamuang and Nakorn Pathon, conditions temporarily improved. Some of the fitter prisoners were returned to Singapore and shipped to Japan and other destinations. Unfortunately, several of the transports carrying these prisoners were unknowingly sunk by American submarines causing great loss of life. The few survivors rescued by the same submarines carried word to the world of the uncivilised treatment they had undergone at the hands of the Japanese.

It appears that the Japanese began to feel apprehensive about the reaction of the world and made efforts to counter this by improving conditions and slightly increasing supplies to prisoners. But this phase soon passed and from May 1944 until the capitulation by Japan on August 15, 1945, parties of prisoners were again being employed under harsh conditions on road and airfield construction and other defensive work.

HELLFIRE PASS MEMORIAL: THAILAND-BURMA RAILWAY,

COMPILED BY KEN BRADLEY AND UPDATED BY ROD BEATTIE

DAD: I was told 850 of us left Singapore for the railway at that time. Our arrival in Rangoon was one of the few times during the war that I completely lost my nerve. It was stiflingly hot and we were left in the bottom of the ship's hold as we tied up at the wharf at night-time. The stench was horrendous and the mosquitoes descended upon us in their thousands. I pretty much went to pieces but Slim talked me out of flipping my lid completely. I felt I just couldn't take any more.

We were transported from the ship to the Moulmein gaol where I think we stayed for about ten days. I met some very interesting people. Slim and I talked to a lot of British prisoners and the Burmese who told us what total bastards the Japs were, but we already knew that!

There was nowhere to cook, so we all had little fires going fuelled with the wood from the gaol itself. We burned the stairs, the doors and half the floors. If we had stayed in that gaol much longer it would have fallen down. One day we had the chance to walk through the streets of Moulmein and it was a wondrous sight. The Burmese had realised by this stage the Japs would never be their friends and they waved at us, even though they were often knocked down and clubbed by the bastards. The Burmese gave us everything they had. Sugar, cigars, some sort of rice loaf, whatever they could manage. I have often thought when people are talking about Christian ethics that these Burmese who were extremely poor themselves showed us immense compassion. They took enormous risks to help us, and we had nothing to give them in return.

Soon enough we were off again. The POWs were broken up into groups or 'Forces' by the Japanese under the command of various commanders (Kumichos) including Brigadier A.L. Varley, Lieutenant-

Colonel G.E. Ramsey (2/30th. Battalion), Major Charles Green (2/4th Machine-gunners), Lieutenant-Colonel Chris Black (2/3rd Reserve M.T. Company), Lieutenant-Colonel Charles G. Anderson (2/19th Battalion) and Lieutenant-Colonel John M. Williams (2/2nd. Pioneers). I was in what was called Williams Force. We walked to some place and caught a train. There were so many of us that if you couldn't fit into a carriage you sat on the roof. We then had a four hour trip by truck and eventually we arrived at Thanbyuzayat, 43 miles (70 km) south of Moulmein. This was the base camp for the POWs and was a station on the existing Moulmein-Ye line which had been built in 1925.

I recall we stayed there for about three days and were addressed by the Japanese Lieutenant Colonel Y. Nagatomo. He spoke to us in French some of the time. Through the interpreter we were told that we were the remnants of a defeated army, we were rubbish, and ought to be ashamed of ourselves for being prisoners. The same old message. He also said we ought to be ashamed for looking so degenerate. Our loin cloths were torn and the only food we had was what we were able to scrounge. It was a disgusting speech given the treatment they had meted out to us. (After the war Nagatomo was hanged as a war criminal.)

The camp names related to the distance from the starting point of the railway, Thanbyuzayat, and the camps were referred to as kilo (kilometre) camps. Throughout the building of the railway POWs were frequently moved up and down the line, staying in a variety of kilo camps. Our first camp after Thanbyuzayat was the 35 kilo camp (Tanyin) which looked a bit more promising. We had to clear away the jungle and try to get water and basic sanitation organised.

The Japs divided us up into groups called 'kumies' which were groups of fifty men. 'Kumies' is the same term used in Australia for a platoon. All the Navy men were put into one kumie which included great friends of mine Joe Deegan and Percy Partington. The *Perth* guys more or less stayed together.

I worked on the railway then for about six weeks straight. One particular day we were managing all right, although it was unbearably hot, and Joe said to me, 'I think we've got too many bloody brains for doing this. We've got to get off this damn railway and stay in the camp if we're going to make it.' I knew he was right. I couldn't last indefinitely on the railway.

Luckily for me when I came back into Tanyin camp that day, Lieutenant Colonel Williams the camp commander asked me if I would be the bugler for the camp, which I gratefully accepted. Another bugler in this camp was an American from the *Houston*, (a top flight jazz trumpeter from New York) called J.B. Cole III. I used to play the Last Post to signal the burial of every one of our blokes. My heart went out to those poor blokes being buried in unmarked graves so far from home.

ARTHUR 'BLOOD' BANCROFT [*a fellow* Perth *survivor*]: 'We used to hear Allan playing the Last Post. Too often as far as we were concerned, because every time you heard it you knew someone else was being buried.'

45 kilo camp (Anakuin): A Japanese film unit had been in the area during the week, making films of the 'happy workers for the Co-Prosperity Sphere'. This unit wanted to film the camp at dawn on Friday and, in addition, they wanted the Australian bugler to sound Reveille. But on Thursday night a 'purge' was put on the sick personnel, and in the purge the bugler was ordered out to work. Colonel William's protests that the bugler was wanted in camp were brushed aside. When dawn came on Friday morning, the bugler, with the rest of the working party, was several kilos away dropping sleepers on the embankment. The Jap in charge of the film unit soundly berated Sgt. Shimojo, the Jap in charge of our camp, who in turn vented his spite on Colonel Williams. The Colonel was then beaten up and stood in front of the Japanese guardhouse, a simple but terrible punishment. After being bashed all day Friday, he stood to attention outside the guardhouse from 11.00pm on Friday until 5 o'clock on Sunday morning. [P 75]

The memory will always remain with me of the dismal rain that fell unceasingly; of the sad groups which day after day slowly passed my hut on their way to the burial ground; and of the slow, mournful notes of the Last Post and Reveille through the murmur of the rain. I grew to hate these bugle calls. Day after day men were buried, and sometimes the bugle call would sound three times. Many Williams Force men died in 80 kilo camp, most of them being naval men from HMAS Perth.

SLAVES OF THE SON OF HEAVEN BY ROY H. WHITECROSS [P 88]

DAD: Sometimes instead of playing Reveille at daybreak, I would stir the Japs up by playing a jazz number. They thought that it was an Australian Navy tune. It gave us a bit of a laugh, and cheered us up. In spite of all the horror, there were some good times. We told jokes, and tried to keep each other going.

Shortly after I started the bugling job I teamed up with a bloke called Stan Rixon. He was a very good barber and he gave me a few tips on how to cut hair and shave the blokes, which I quickly became very proficient at. We had literally hundreds of people to shave, so we were flat out the whole time. Little did I realise that this skill would one day save my life.

PERCY PARTINGTON [*fellow* Perth *survivor*]: One day Allan came to me and said, 'Percy I'm full of these crabs. Will you shave my crutch for me so I can get rid of them.' So, we went off to this quiet place in the camp, and I'm soaping him up. He's spread-eagled on the ground, and he said, 'Now don't you cut me!' Anyway by the time we're finished there was an audience of about 150 guys all standing around laughing. It was a great joke in the camp. It could have been all doom and gloom, but we saw the lighter side. We did all we could to cheer each other up. Those laughs kept more of us alive than anything else. Allan and I also collected large 'elephant' leaves off the trees which the POWs used for toilet paper.

> *The* Perth *boys were a happy bunch who stuck together. They never talked, they 'nattered'; there was no such thing as the floor or the earth, there was only 'the deck'; the latrine became 'the heads', a second helping or 'back up' became 'gash', a soldier was a 'swatty', while a sailor could only be referred to as a 'matelot'. One of their number, A.B. Keith Mills, was savagely attacked by an engineer on the railway because he had driven a spike in crookedly.*
> BEHIND BAMBOO BY ROHAN RIVETT [P254]

DAD: Christmas 1942 came and went, a very sad day for us all. I thought of everyone back home at Silver Creek having a roast dinner with all the trimmings, including Mum's delicious plum pudding with the holly perched on top. In January 1943 I first realised I was having eye trouble. I was reading a book called 'Arcadia' which I had picked up in Singapore. I couldn't see the words on the page very clearly and it's a problem I have been stuck with ever since.

I was shocked, as reading had been my favourite pastime since I was a young boy. I later found out I had a vitamin deficiency called beri-beri which caused retrobulbar neuritis, a degeneration of the main nerve to the eye.

JOHN 'MACCA' McQUADE [*fellow* Perth *survivor*]: I was at a loss to know how to help Allan as his eyesight gradually deteriorated. I arranged for him to stay off the railway and have lighter duties, sweeping, cleaning the toilets, helping in the kitchen. However, often the Japs forced him at gunpoint to return to work on the line. One day he came to me and said, 'Macca, if I go back on that stinkin' railway one more day I'll die. I can't see any more, my eyes have gone. I've almost had it. You've gotta' find me a permanent job in the camp. I can't go back there. If I do, this time tomorrow I'll be dead.'

Because us officers were treated marginally better by the Japs and didn't have to work on the railway, I was always trying to think up things to save one of our blokes from being worked to death. I needed a barber because the Japs had an obsession with short hair. If they saw that your hair was getting too long they'd stand you up and give you one hell of a hiding. I didn't think Allan could cut hair because he was pretty blind. He couldn't see anything. He was stumbling around in the heat. It was pathetic. 'I can cut hair,' Allan said. 'You couldn't have anyone better to do it. I'll get some scissors and I'll start today.' He wouldn't take no for an answer. I didn't really care if he could cut hair or not. I wanted him off the railway, so I said, 'You're hired'. He rushed off and found an old pair of clippers. They may have even been made from a knife and fork. Everyone was very resourceful in the camp, and there were lots of Army blokes who were tradesmen. It was amazing the useful tools that were made from all sorts of metal scraps, even radios.

Allan was a fairy rough barber but it didn't matter. He didn't put a basin on their head but cut the hair purely by touch. He felt around the head, fumbled with the scissors, and clipped away as if he were shearing sheep back on the farm. It was amazing really. All things considered, he did a pretty good job. Because he was the barber he was talking to every Tom, Dick and Harry so he always knew what was going on in the camp. He had a happy disposition in spite of our circumstances.

BOB COLLINS [*fellow* Perth *survivor*]: I remember Allan cutting hair at Thanbyuzayat. He cut mine and he didn't charge me! I asked him where he got his scissors from and he replied, 'Don't ask. Do you want a haircut?'

JOHN 'MACCA' McQUADE: Christ Allan was tough. He was determined to get out of the camp alive, even if he was blind as a bat and half dead. He just wasn't the sort of bloke that would lie down like a dog and die. The only ones who came out of the camps were fellows like Allan. They never gave up. You couldn't kill them. I also noticed the country kids survived much better than their city counter-parts. In my opinion they were more adaptable.

Propaganda postcard
Dad sent this to his parents at Silver Creek but the card was not received until after his Mother's death in 1944, so she never knew he survived the sinking of *Perth*.

From Imperial Japanese Army
I am still in a POW Camp near Moulmein, Burma. There are 20,000 prisoners, being Australian, Dutch, English and American. There are several camps of 2-3,000 prisoners who work at settled labour daily.

We are quartered in very plain huts. The climate is good. Our life is now easier with regard to food, medicine and clothes. The Japanese Commander sincerely endeavours to treat prisoners kindly.

Officer's salary is based on the salary of Japanese Officers of the same rank and every prisoner who performs labour or duty is given daily wages from 25 cents (minimum) to 45 cents according to rank and work.

Canteens are established where we can buy some extra food and smokes. By courtesy of the Japanese Commander we conduct concerts in the camps, and a limited number go to a picture show about once per month.

DAD: In the first 12 months we were on the railway, about half of the 850 who came with me from Singapore had died. You'd be talking to a bloke one day, and next day he'd be gone. You'd say, 'Where's Ronnie?' You'd be told, 'He's dead,' just like that.

The ones who died looked like sticks, wide-eyed staring heads on emaciated limbs. The awful part was that I knew I looked just the same. These once handsome blokes, many of them strong country lads, were reduced to skeletons. Proud men, good men, with sweethearts, and families they loved.

There was one incident in this camp which could have been disastrous for me. I had sold a watch to a Jap called Hana who up until then had been reasonable to us. He said I was a very bad man, and he called me into his hut. He was completely drunk. 'You have sold me a watch that doesn't work,' he said. 'Now I am going to shoot you.' He put a couple of Jap soldiers on either side of me and told them to take me out the back and do it. I have never been so terrified in my life. I believed completely they were going to shoot me. I froze from my neck all the way down to my spine. Hana was standing there grinning at me, no doubt enjoying my terror.

I thought I only have a few seconds left to plead for my life. I bowed and said, 'Mr Hana you can't do this to me. It's wrong. I am a number one warship man and you are a number one Japanese soldier. You can't take me out and just shoot me like a dog.' He said, 'Alright I won't shoot you this time, but I will tell everyone that Mr Gee is a very bad man.' I went away a bit of a psychological mess, rejoicing just the same. But it affected my nerves, and I never completely got over it.

Later on things got even worse for us. They sent in about ten or fifteen Korean guards. They were animals and the whole tone of the camp changed. I didn't want to cut their hair, although I was ordered to, or have anything to do with them because they were so vicious. One day they lined us all up in front of a big fire and belted us continuously. It was terrible. There was almost a riot after this, and the Japanese troops moved in to restore order.

Things were really hotting up now, and there was increasing pressure — 'speedo' — to get on with the work on the railway.

Overnight it seems things had really deteriorated and our conditions got worse and worse by the day. We never stayed in a camp for longer than five months, and usually we were on the move every five or six weeks as we completed a section of track. The first thing you had to do in a new camp was clean out all the excrement that was everywhere. There were often twenty to forty decomposing bodies lying around as well, and flies in their millions. The bodies had to be either burned or buried. It was pretty desperate at times.

As we moved down the railway line the Japs got crankier and beat us relentlessly to work harder. There were a lot of ugly scenes, which have been written about by Rohan Rivett and Ray Parkin. The blokes were sick all the time. Malaria, beri beri, appalling dysentery and all the time we had to work 12, 14 and 16 hour shifts. I was lucky that I didn't get malaria until late 1943.

We also suffered terribly with the cold at times, and you'd lie in the huts at night one minute shivering uncontrollably, then sweating with fevers the next. Further up the line we were lucky to have a couple of very good doctors which made all the difference. One camp full of British soldiers was not so lucky. They had poor medical help and died in their hundreds.

The Japs cared nothing for our health. After the war I learned that they had stolen our precious Red Cross medical parcels which included vitamin supplements that could have prevented my blindness. Once at the 60 kilo camp they were examining everyone to see if we had cholera, which they did by putting a piece of wire up your rectum. Slim Hedrick said, 'There is no way they are going to do that to me', so I lined up for the procedure twice. I didn't like it very much, but Slim was a very determined man. I am certain he would rather have been shot than have that wire stuck up his backside.

Slim and I were very upset when we lost our mate, Harry Thomas another *Perth* man. Then we lost another dear friend, Seamus O'Brien. Seamus had joined the Navy about the same time as I did. So many died I don't like to even think about it. This particular day I had buried quite a few people and I went over to see Seamus who was extremely ill. 'Seamus, is there anything I can do for you? 'No,' he said 'I am going to die tonight.' We didn't have a Catholic priest but a man called Mike Taylor looked after the Catholics. I asked Seamus if he would like me to get Mike over to see him, but he said, 'No, Elmo. I would like you to talk to me about all the happy times we had in the Navy, and the fun we had in Jamaica, and tonight I will die peacefully.' I buried him about ten o'clock the next night and cried my eyes out. I will never forget that very cheerful, wonderful man.

RAY HEGARTY [*fellow* Perth *man*]: Both Alf Coyne and Seamus O'Brien were real 'Old Navy' guys. When he was a kid for a number of years Seamus served on the old salt clippers which sailed from Adelaide to Hobart. Seamus knew every sea shanty that was ever written, he could sing them too: 'Sailor, blow the man down', 'Me father ran off with Charlotte Brown'. He also sang 'Shenandoah' beautifully. They both should have been born a 100 years earlier and roamed the seas on the old sailing ships. Alfie was a fantastic seaman. He was a hard bloke, but a good bloke. When Alf was an instructor at the Flinders Naval Depot he had the nickname, 'The Black Prince'.

DAD: I used to ask myself over and over, 'God where are you now? How can I believe in you when you let this horror go on, day after day?' No wonder I came out of the war with my faith in religion severely shaken.

For the first time in my life I wondered if I was losing my mind. There was so much dying, and death. We couldn't even bury people properly in the mud. All we could do was dig a trench and lay branches and leaves over them. The smell of the bodies was so bad sometimes that we used to vomit. The worst part of it was when we were trying to bury the poor blokes with some sense of dignity and ceremony and the Japs stood around laughing. I thought they were sub-human.

July 20. There came into the hospital camp at Retpu (30 kilo) 120 sick men from the mobile force. Many of the men were from the 2/2nd Pioneers and Perth, and I had not seen them since Moulmein gaol. A number whom I had known well were totally unrecognisable. Slim Hedrick and Alf Thomas of Perth were cadaverous wrecks of their former selves.
BEHIND BAMBOO BY ROHAN RIVETT [P 268]

ALLAN GEE [*Uncle Nape's son*]: Uncle Allan's mother called him 'Reynard the Fox' when he was a little boy in Silver Creek. Coincidentally he told me that one day on the Burma railway he stole a chicken and was caught and sentenced to death. They had to steal to live, but they all knew that there was a real risk of being executed if they stole something as valuable as a chicken. When Allan was caught he knew he was facing execution, cuts to his back and then decapitation. Ultimately because he was the bugler in the camp, and they needed him, he was spared. But he was brutally bashed with the flat of a Jap's sword which explains the scars he had on his back. Undoubtedly this incident contributed to his acute post-traumatic stress disorder after the war.

DAD: Somehow we struggled through 1943 and into 1944. We had built the line right up to a place called Nikki (130 kilo camp) which is 20 kilometres past The Three Pagoda Pass (114 kilo) on the Burma-Thailand border. There we endured four or five months of the monsoon and most of us developed dreadful trench foot, basically footrot from never being dry.

The work pressure was intense and conditions were very bad. When this section of the line was finished we moved further south in Thailand to a place called Tamarkan (55 kilo), not far from the town of Kanchanaburi. It was a gruelling trip, and took us about six days to get there, even though the distance was less than 200 kilometres. We travelled by train sitting on top of the freight cars. I was sitting on the roof, on top of the wood for the engine, but there was no rest because the sparks kept flying up.

Slim Hedrick had gone ahead of me. Much of this trip was through inpenetrable jungle. Sometimes you could only see about 50 yards. Then we crossed the River Kwai across the bridge that there's been so much talk about, and into flat country until we arrived at Tamarkan. To my delight Slim was waiting to greet me. He was rotten with dysentery and fever. Diarrhoea was running down his legs and he was blown up with beri beri. He was standing there with this big smile. He said, 'I've got your wardrobe here, your urn for boiling water and a bamboo container for washing. And I've got you a new pair of pants made out of a piece of canvas. But the best news is I've got you an egg!'

That was the great affection we shared as prisoners of war, and it never left us. We have always said that if you didn't have a mate on the railway you died, and Slim was my mate. I owe him my life. I loved Slim.

MRS MAUDE HEDRICK [*Slim's wife*]: Allan was in a bad way, almost blind by then. My husband told me he would wait for Allan each day when he came off the railway and wash all the dirt off him. George was the one who really looked after him. You can see by Allan's face in this sketch that he was in pain. George is looking at Allan with a smile that seems to be saying, 'Come on, you'll be alright. I'm going to take care of you.' Allan looks as if he was feeling that he couldn't go on any more. It's a wonderful sketch and says more than words can ever say. George (Slim) used to say, 'Once a sailor always a sailor.'

BARRY HEDRICK [*Slim's son*]: This is a sketch (by Jack Chalker) of my Dad helping your father. Weary Dunlop wrote to Mum to confirm it was your Dad and George.'

POWs on the Burma Railway by British war artist and POW Jack Chalker

JACK CHALKER [*British War Artist*]: I was born in 1918. I'll be 82 this year. I was in Thailand at Konyu camp and Hintok with Weary Dunlop and the Australians. This is a little pen sketch I did in the early days at Konyu. It was very special to me, but it wasn't of anybody in particular. I drew it to show how people looked. I was very impressed with the way everyone helped each other. I wanted to show the extraordinary tenderness of people out there. People were often so terribly sick and very young and the POWs nursed each other with great care. I remember one who died on his 21st birthday.

Around this time I was making a few notes and drawings about the camp, which was strictly forbidden. One day a Korean guard caught me hiding them in a section of bamboo and started shouting and screaming. He tore my drawings up, bar two including this one. I was sitting or lying on some rags as I had very bad dysentery and malaria, and fortunately I was able to conceal them under me. The guard knocked me about and I was dragged down to the Commandant (Shuban) where I was tied up and bashed some more. It was a pretty bad couple of days, and the two drawings hold a special memory for me.

Despite the horror and chaos in the camps there was a lot of fun and humour. At Christmas time at the final base hospital camp we had a race which Weary organised and took part in. The stockier prisoners carried the lighter ones on their backs. Years later Weary took me to a Melbourne Cup, which was something of a contrast!

Ghastly as it was I wouldn't have missed my time with the Australians for anything. I think I was regarded as a sort of fringe Anzac which meant a lot to me. When we were free I went down to Bangkok as a war artist attached to Weary's unit to finish some of the records. It was an enormous privilege. Like so many people I owe my life to Weary.

DAD: Sometimes when I look back I think we were fortunate to go through what we did. It was a stage in our lives where we showed each other great affection and deep caring, and what it is to be truly human.

We stayed in Tamarkan for about six months. My condition picked up a bit, although my eyesight never improved. However, it didn't affect my ability to cut hair, although it was probably lucky for me we didn't have any mirrors. It wasn't until I returned from the war that I realised I had a permanent vision disability.

About 50 of us from Tamarkan were sent back up the line a bit to Chungkai where I met up again with a man who became one of my closest friends, Tommy Wittingslow. Tommy went on to run one of the biggest carnival operations after the war, which his son Des has taken over.

Thanbyuzayat: Christmas Day, 1942. Today the Japanese did for once allow us a reasonable quantity of meat and vegetables with which the camp cooks, headed by Sergeant Wittingslow, achieved a triumph.
BEHIND BAMBOO BY ROHAN RIVETT [P 210]

BRUCE GEE [*my brother*]: Tommy Wittingslow was instrumental in helping to keep Dad and many others alive. He was an Army Sergeant in Black Force and was in charge of the kitchen in various camps along the railway. Tommy told me that when they arrived at one camp the British officers were strutting around in uniforms and boots, while their enlisted men were in loin cloths. Apparently at that stage the British had charge of the food and the Australian Lieutenant-Colonel Chris Black, who was Supply Chief for Black Force in Java, felt not enough was being dished out to the other POWs. In short, after a hell of a stoush with the Poms the Aussies, with Tommy in control, took over the kitchen and the dispersal of food.

Tommy was a genius at making a little bit of food go a long way. He wasn't a trained cook, but he was a natural leader and organised getting the food in, and topping it up with as much as he could off the natives. He was also meticulous about hygiene.

Tommy also ran the two-up schools in the camp. He told me that Dad was appointed as the 'picker up,' the one who went into the ring and called out whether it was 'heads or tails', which was ludicrous because he was as blind as a bat. One night he lost his job when some of the guys yelled out, 'Get that fucking blind bastard out of there.' Tommy and Dad remained lifelong friends. They had a special bond forged in those horrendous circumstances. Running the carnivals after the war was indeed child's play for Tommy after dodging the Japs in the camps and the logistics of feeding thousands of men.

Tommy Wittingslow

Tom is Mr Showman in Australia. You will see his sideshows from Melbourne to Adelaide to Perth, to Sydney, Brisbane and Cairns. There were 40 Wittingslow sideshows at Moomba this week.

Tom's career began in 1932. He had a fruit stall in the Victoria Market which he rented for 2/6 a day. There was no money in that, but wait there was a long arcade in Bourke Street, called Penny Lane, where the Commonwealth Bank is now. He got a job there, supervising penny slot machines and a shooting gallery. His first show was at Bunyip and he travelled by horse and cart which he hired for five shillings a day. He remembers vividly the first car he owned. It was an ancient T-model Ford which he bought for £21. Tom began with all the standard shows, games of skill, shies, shooting games. The prizes were those great China dogs. He travelled to every agricultural show in Victoria and this was the Depression. Side-shows were different then. There was the snake show, the pin-headed Chinaman, the half-man, half-woman, the tallest man in the world and the fattest lady.

There was one character who specialised in bringing out African pygmies. There was always a girlie show. 'Can you imagine? In those days they didn't show anything. There was one fellow who always announced that the last show would be something special. Rosie would show a bit of pussy. Of course the tent was packed. The ultimate came when Rosie would lift the side of her knickers and reveal a little pussy tattooed on her thigh. If you didn't go for Rosie there was always Big Chief Little Wolf, the American Indian. He had this wrestling troupe. Tom joined the Army on June 13, 1940. He was born on June 13. Indeed almost everything happened to Tom on June 13. He was captured by the Japanese in Singapore and went to work on the Burma railroad. He was an army cook.

He used to make terrible black stews out of eggplant. They were supposed to get a fixed ration of rice, but often the rice bags would arrive nearly empty. He was 11 stone 7 pounds (72 kg) when he went into the army. He came home at 8 stone 5 pounds (55 kg).

He was in hospital for nine months and he was discharged, of course on June 13, 1946. He came out of the army with £200 deferred pay and the absolute conviction that if you want to succeed in this world, go into food. Yet somehow the old show business had a fatal attraction and gently he moved into it again. (Tommy died aged 86 on April 2, 2000).

EXCERPTS FROM *SUNDAY AGE* INTERVIEW WITH KEITH DUNSTAN, MARCH 15, 1992

DAD: We stayed in Chungkai for three or four months. There is no doubt that Tommy's superb organisation of Chungkai once again saved my life and many others. We had a few things going on the side here and accumulated a bit of money in the camp kitty which made an enormous difference to our ability to buy extra food.

Just before Christmas 1944 I was sent further back into the jungle to Hintock. At this camp we were cutting wood to fuel the engines that were working on the railway. It was a very bad camp and we lost a lot of good officers. We were under the command of the British there, but they were very inexperienced in these conditions, and many died, despite us having quite a lot of food. The problem was that the organisation of the camp was poor which made it harder to make the best of what we had.

We stayed at Hintock until the day before Christmas 1944. Then the Japanese told us that the war was nearly finished. We left there by train. After a long ride, once again on the top of the train, we arrived at Tamarkan (55 km) again where we stayed for a short time. We then walked abut 200 kilometres to a place called Ratchaburi in Thailand where we waited out the end of the war. It wasn't a bad place compared to some we had been in. Our guards were mainly airforce personnel and were not nearly as brutal as the Jap Army or the Koreans. Ratchaburi certainly would have been a difficult place to escape from. There was a big water-filled trench around it and surrounded by Japs.

There weren't too many incidents which I can recall, but they had an annoying habit of counting us day and night. These were called 'tenkos'. At this late stage American planes were constantly flying over the camp which was both exhilirating and frightening. We hoped like hell they wouldn't bomb us. The Japs would not allow us to paint the roofs of our huts with the sign POW.

Just before the Allies reached us we heard news from Japan that all the POWs were to be shot when the Allies landed. We were stricken with fear. We thought after all this, just when we're about to be saved, the Japs will exterminate us. It was a very depressing thought to say the least. I had an opportunity to escape about three or four weeks before the war ended when American commandos who had been dropped close to the camp made contact with us. My eyesight was very bad by this time, and I was stumbling around. Slim had been sent somewhere else and I was planning to get away with two blokes including one called McLean. When I was making arrangements McLean said he decided not to go with me because he had promised Colonel Williams and Brigadier Blackburn that he would stay with the troops until the end. A few Australians and Americans got away with the American commandoes, but I decided to hang on until the war was officially over.

We had built an aerodrome while we were at Ratchaburi and another one was built at Phetchaburi. (The towns of Ratchaburi and Phetchaburi are about 50km apart on the railway line to Singapore just South of Ban Pong.) They were ready just in time for the Allied planes to land. Then suddenly it was over. Leaflets were dropped into the camp once the Japanese surrender had been announced (August 15, 1945). We were eventually flown from there to Rangoon by the Americans.

To all Allied prisoners of war:

The Japanese forces have surrendered unconditionally and the war is over

We will get supplies to you as soon as is humanly possible and will make arrangements to get you out but, owing to the distances involved, it may be some time before we can achieve this.

YOU will help us and yourselves if you act as follows –

1. Stay in your camp until you get further orders from us.

2. Start preparing nominal rolls of personnel, giving fullest particulars.

3. List your most urgent necessities.

4. If you have been starved or underfed for long periods. DO NOT eat large quantities of solid food, fruit or vegetables at first. It is dangerous for you to do so. Small quantities at frequent intervals are much safer and will strengthen you far more quickly. For those who are really ill or very weak, fluids such as broth and soup, making use of the water in which rice and other foods have been boiled, are much the best. Gifts of food from the local population should be cooked. We want to get you back home quickly, safe and sound, and we do not want to risk your chances from diarrhoea, dysentery and cholera at this stage.

EXTRACT FROM REUNION BOOKLET COMMEMORATING THE 50TH ANNIVERSARY OF THE BATTLE OF THE SUNDA STRAIT. PRODUCED BY THE *HMAS PERTH* SURVIVORS ASSOCIATION WESTERN AUSTRALIA. REUNION CHAIRMAN: ARTHUR BANCROFT.

BRUCE GEE: Dad told me that when he finally crossed from Burma into Thailand in 1943 he thought he was going to be okay. The food was better, they were trading a few things with the Thais, and the work wasn't as brutal as it had been on the railway.

It didn't become really nerve-wracking again for him until towards the end of the war when the Japs started moving them around in more restricted areas. It became apparent that the Japs were looking for a convenient place to shoot them. They were constantly on the move for the last two months. Dad said the Japs were so terrified of the local Thais they sometimes slept in the POW quarters, with the prisoners forming a protective ring around them. But not half as terrified as were the prisoners. Dad said another reason they knew they were going to be killed was because they had been forced to dig deep trenches, just like the Nazis in Poland made the Jews do.

There is no doubt that dropping the Atomic bombs on Hiroshima and Nagasaki saved the POWs lives. Dad's attitude to the atomic bombs was, 'It stopped the war, and saved thousands of Allied lives.'

DAD: The American Navy wanted to take us and other survivors back to Australia via the United States. The different authorities were all trying to claim us. We were in Rangoon for six weeks, and were treated very well. I was put into an eye hospital in Rangoon under a brilliant eye specialist by the name of Major Riddell. He wanted to take me directly to St Dunstan's, the renowned eye clinic in London, but I hadn't been home for four years and I was desperate to see my mother and Kath Brewer. At this point I was unaware that Mum had died in November 1944, believing that I had not survived the sinking of *Perth*.

I shared my ward with a number of Mountbatten's Burma Army men, mostly Captains and Colonels who had been shot in the eyes. They were outstanding people and wonderful to us. One day Lord Louis Mountbatten was visiting the ward and asked if there were any seamen present. I answered in the affirmative, adding that I had served in *Perth* alongside *Kelly* in the Mediterranean. Waving his party on, Mountbatten spent half an hour talking with me which was very uplifting.

The doctors didn't want us to leave the eye hospital until we had attendants, because we could hardly see. As soon as they assigned some sisters to travel with us we were flown to Singapore. When I arrived at the airport we ran into another sailor who had had a very bad nervous breakdown. He was supposed to travel on a plane with lots of other psychiatric cases, but he couldn't bear to travel with this bunch of 'loonies'. I changed places with him and travelled on the plane with all these people who were half out of their minds. One was a big horsebreaker from Queensland, who was barking mad. I had to help restrain him in his seat. It's the worst flight I've ever had in my life.

Welcome to Rangoon!

At last the day has come. Three years of darkness and agony have passed, and a new dawn is here, bringing with it for all of us deliverance from danger and anxiety, and for you above all freedom after bondage, the joy of reunion after long separation.

Through these long years we have not forgotten you. You have not been at any time far from the thoughts of even those who had no personal friends or relatives among you. We of the Red Cross have tried every way of establishing contact and relieving your hardships. Some provisions have been sent, and many messages despatched; but we do not know how much has reached you, for the callous indifference of the enemy has made the task well nigh impossible.

But now that the enemy is beaten and you are free once more, we are doing all we can to give you the welcome you richly deserve and to make your homeward path a pleasant and a joyful one. If our preparations in Rangoon leave something to be desired, it is only because the end has come sooner than we dared to hope and has found us unprepared. These deficiencies will be more than made up by your welcome in India and your homeland.

On behalf of the Indian Red Cross and St John War Organisation we welcome you. May God bless you and send you home rejoicing!

RED CROSS LEAFLET GIVEN TO DAD ON ARRIVAL IN RANGOON

Letter from Rangoon from Dad to his sister

Dear Miriam,

The rest of the sailors are leaving here in a day or two. The specialist told me I could go with them if I wished to, but advised me very strongly to wait as it will be only a matter of a few days.

I am very concerned about the condition of my eyes although I have already had a slight improvement. I would be very foolish not to wait as I will be able to get the proper diet and treatment that is necessary for my eyes at the moment.

I have seen some very good films here. I go to them almost twice a day. Rangoon is a very dead place except for entertainment arranged by the British Army. Do not write any more as I shall be home before they get here. The days are dragging a bit now. I can hardly wait to get home in spite of the fact that the Japs taught me a lot about the word patience.

Love to everyone, Allan

Letter from Singapore from Dad to his sister

Dear Miriam,

I flew from Rangoon yesterday. We had a pretty hectic time for nine hours. It was good flying out, but we had two violent madmen with us, one a big horsebreaker from Queensland. I was the only one who could approach him after he got loose from his strait jacket. I struggled with him for about two hours and eventually got enough dope into him to give him the knockout. Just quietly I never ever want to get in another aircraft again. I hope to get a ship here in the next few days. Do not try and meet me when the ship docks as we will be messed about for a couple of days. I hope you will pick me up in Albury. Give my love to the children and I will try and get something for them if we get the opportunity. I will be discharged from the Navy for certain, however something will turn up I suppose. Give my best to all the crowd, and tell Bert (Miriam's husband) I'll be seeing him. Love to all, especially Mum.

Your loving brother, Allan

MG: My father arrived in Singapore and was sent to Changi barracks where the prisoners were being marshalled for return to Australia. I was told by Alf Spencer from Beechworth, an Army man helping to organise the repatriation of prisoners of war, that he heard a voice ask, 'Is there anyone here from Beechworth?' I replied, 'Yes', and was surprised to see Allan. He looked quite well all things considered. Alf didn't realise until later that Dad's sight had been affected by his experiences as a POW. Dad was very keen to hear all the news from Beechworth of course. Alf said, 'Some of the prisoners were in a shocking state, just skin and bones.' After the war Alf was a butcher in Beechworth for 32 years, and he is now aged 92.

Sun News Pictorial

Among the 33,000 prisoners of war released on Singapore Island are 6,300 Australians. The majority of prisoners are in poor condition, but they are now enjoying their best treatment for three and a half years.

Hospital ships and transports have already pulled into Singapore Harbour, and the Australians will leave in a few days. Some may fly home. Singapore went mad with joy as the liberators marched through the city. Civilians and prisoners waved tree branches and uprooted palms, shouted, sang and threw flowers.

Most of the prisoners were unshaven, undernourished, and poorly clad, but nothing is wrong with their spirit. The most moving moment came as we left the jetty. As we trudged up the main road we heard cheering in the distance. Two hundred yards ahead there was a prisoner-of-war cage with the Union Jack fluttering proudly over it. All along the wire men in tattered shorts and loin cloths pressed forward waving and shouting. They had recognised our digger hats and jungle-green battle dress – the first link with home they'd seen. A few came running to meet us, the rest sang, 'Pack Up Your Troubles'.

Some of the men were as thin as those I saw in Nazi horror camps and many were suffering from beri beri and chronic malaria. Most of them were survivors of the dreadful Siam jungle camps.

MELBOURNE, SEPTEMBER 7TH, 1945

When our minds go back to these years which stretch like a deep abyss across the plateau of our lives, we will tend to think of the brighter side. Yet, now and then, a word, a sound or a meeting with old friends will arouse memories.

Again the great yellow Burma moon will drench the jungle with its light; the midday sun after tropical rain will make the matted vegetation steam like a Turkish bath, again we will feel the icy fingers of the November monsoon clutching at our thin half-starved bodies clad in rags. And once more we will hear the poignant notes of 'The Last Post' as it rang out across the little jungle cemeteries each time one of our mates was laid to rest. These things have been a part of our lives. We will never quite forget.

BEHIND BAMBOO BY ROHAN RIVETT [P391]

Extract from The Sydney Morning Herald

This morning Sir Edward ('Weary' Dunlop), Ray Parkin and his son John Parkin, and about 50 other Australians will gather for an Anzac Day dawn service in Hellfire Pass which was, when the sun went out of men's hearts in World War Two, a cutting on the Burma Railway.

Sixty eight men are believed to have been battered to death by Japanese guards in Hellfire pass. Of 22,000 Australian prisoners of war, 7,000 were killed or died of starvation, cholera, and malaria, many on the railway.

'You can still see the marks where the poor wretches drilled,' said Sir Edward. They worked day and night. It was very like Dante's Inferno. It measured up to the name 'Hellfire'. It measured up except for a crucial point. The inscription at the entrance to Dante's hell said, 'Abandon all hope, you who enter!'

Weary Dunlop and his doctors, Ray Parkin and his fellow Australian prisoners of war walked through hell but clung to hope.

If 304 people died for every mile of railway built, Parkin worked it out that a man died for every 17 ft 6 inches (about five metres) of the 420 kilometre line. That's why it became known as the Death Railway.

Yet this survivor of the sinking of HMAS Perth *found much to marvel at – the beauty of the countryside, the loyalty of man's body, which enabled it to heal and renew itself.*

Dunlop felt sickness in his soul as he 'witnessed the agonies and exertions of those gaunt, chronically starved, diseased, gallant men.' Yet he said, 'To this day I feel uplifted and born up by their unquenchable spirit and patient endurance of suffering.'

BY TONY STEPHENS, APRIL 25, 1991

BRUCE GEE: One night during the trip home to Australia by troop ship from Singapore, Dad went up on deck, probably for a leak or a smoke. A section of the guard rail was down and he very nearly toppled over the side in the dark. He got a hell of a fright. It was a very near miss.

8

SHIPMATES

'No Australian died alone'

From the time I was a little girl I can remember gazing at Ray Parkin's beautiful watercolour of *Perth* which hung in pride of place in our lounge room at Wooragee. Dad purchased the painting in 1946 for £4. Whenever I asked my father to tell me about *Perth* and the War, he always said, '*Perth* was a happy ship, and the crew were a family.' This sentiment has been echoed repeatedly by my father's former shipmates. Their close bond has endured, and was a mainstay during the tragedy of the sinking of *Perth* and when the survivors became prisoners of war. It remains to this day. It was a pleasure and privilege to finally meet with Ray at his home in Melbourne. My only regret is that I left forgetting to see his save-all which was miraculously recovered from the sunken wreck of *Perth*.

Ray Parkin

Ray was in the Royal Australian Navy for 18 years, including three as a prisoner of war. He was Action Chief Quartermaster in *HMAS Perth* and spent 15 months on the Thai-Burma Railway. Ray is renowned as a maritime painter and is the author of *Ray Parkin's Wartime Trilogy* comprising his works: '*Out Of The Smoke*', '*Into The Smother*', and '*The Sword and The Blossom*'. He is also the author and illustrator of the award winning book *H. M. Bark Endeavour*.

RAY PARKIN: I was a Petty Officer in the Navy, and Allan was an Able Seaman, but that didn't make any difference, except that our duties separated us. He was one of the Navy family. We didn't necessarily live in each other's pockets but we were all conscious of each other.

We used to call him Elmo, and there were always stories going around about him. Elmo was one of the characters of the ship. We had contact in many ways because he was one of the buglers. Allan frequently trotted around with the Commander (not the Captain, the secondary officer) and with the Commander's man. They were like a trio. I had long yarns with Allan at *Perth* reunions. He was quite a reader and had a very open mind. He accepted the things that happened to him during the war.

The Navy had a way of disciplining you and of bringing you together. The ship makes you a family. She holds you, and you don't want her to sink. That is a big advantage over the Army, which is only just a unit. It's a kind of distillation in your mind of experiences shared. You cannot separate the experiences from the ship. She becomes an identity and you have a feeling for her. The ship was the job. She came first before any personalities, and your job was what you were judged on.

When Dave Burchell, author of 'The Bells Of Sunda Strait' located *Perth* at the bottom of Sunda Strait, 25 years after the sinking he found my little save-all and returned it to me. It was a small metal container with a lid in which I used to keep a small amount of water. If I was smoking, which was forbidden for safety reasons, and someone came along, I slipped the cigarette into the save-all to extinguish it. It had a great association for me. Being the Chief Quartermaster I dealt with the navigation and steering of the ship. Dave found my save-all in the wheelhouse where I had worked.

At just after midnight March 1, 1942, with about one third of our ship's company, I lay in the water coated with oil fuel watching our ship sinking. Exposed and helpless in the glare of searchlights from surrounding Japanese warships, she had come to the end of as violent an hour's action as was ever fought at sea. Not many minutes before I had been on board, steering her through this last battle — a vessel complex, expensive, and extremely efficient in speed and action. I had lived in her for two years and nine months, which was her whole life as an Australian warship. She had been hit by torpedoes and shell-fire had shattered her boats. We watched the ship go out of the searchlights' glare into the unknown blackness below, taking almost two thirds of our shipmates with her.'

FOREWORD BY RAY PARKIN. *THE BELLS OF SUNDA STRAIT* BY DAVID BURCHELL

I was steering *Perth* when she was hit by the first torpedo and I heard Captain Hec Waller say, 'That's torn it.' Hec gave the order to abandon ship but later he amended it, realising that the ship was getting blown to pieces. There was no point in people trying to go to their abandon ship stations, because they probably wouldn't be there, so he gave an order, which is rarely given, 'Abandon ship, every man for himself.'

John Harper was the Navigator and was on the bridge with the Captain when the abandon ship order was given. They were removing their jackets and putting on their life-jackets when a shell struck the top of the compass platform. John remembers nothing else until an hour later when he found himself in the water with a groove across his cheek and the middle of his ear missing. That is how close he came to being killed.

The Captain must have been killed outright. He and John were both standing by the standard compass which was covered by a big brass hood. One of the relics which Dave Burchell recovered was this cover, peppered with dozens of shrapnel holes. I took Hec Waller's wife Nancy to the ceremony when the relics were being presented. She had always wanted to know exactly what happened and we told her John Harper's story. Dave also recovered two cylindrical brass lights, one electric and the other kerosene — they always have a backup in the Navy. Dave had mounted one of these lights on a piece of teak which he gave to Nancy. She used to put a Christmas candle in it. Nancy Waller was like a mother to us.

Hec was very practical and he was very good to me. Once I received a message that the Captain wanted to see me in his cabin up on the bridge. I thought, 'I wonder what he wants to see me about?' His cabin had two portholes. When I arrived Waller said to me, 'Oh, Parkin I thought you would like to see this.' He beckoned me to look through the forward porthole. He knew I did a bit of drawing and thought I would like to see the image. We were in company with *Canberra*, and there she was just ahead of us, perfectly framed with all the foam around her. He was like that, very personal.

When *Perth* was hit and sinking I remember thinking, 'This is it.' There was nothing else you could do. You couldn't exactly say, 'Oh well, I'll see the union about it.' It was a matter of coping with what we were trained for. All we could do after *Perth* was sunk and we were adrift in a lifeboat was try to get somewhere and do something. We just had to hope. It struck me then that this is what it is really like when something of this nature happens. No heroics. You just have to make the best of what you have got. That was the reality of it.

We were finally captured by the Japanese about 300 miles down the coast from where *Perth* had sunk. Then we were taken to the gaol in Serang. I once wrote of the experience of being a POW. I called it 'a sort of freedom', because during that time I had the opportunity to think. From the outset of the War anyone of us could have been knocked off. For the entire time we were in harm's way. The prospect of death was always there at the back of your mind. You would see a ship blow up alongside you, and you'd think, 'That could have been me.' There was violence in everything.

Being a POW was different. It was just a matter of survival. We had nothing but a G-string, and we had to compete like the animals do, with what we had within us. It wasn't so much a matter of our humanity, it was a case of having to think clearly, realising what was what. But we did retain a lot of what might be termed humanity within that environment. That was part of our means of survival. In peacetime most of us have the privilege to 'play' with our lives.

Some people only want to hear about the dark side of the War. They want an excuse to hate the Japanese even more. I wrote my book 'The Sword and The Blossom' because people were always asking me what it was like, and they wanted to know all the morbid stuff. I used to tell them, 'It wasn't as bad as you think and worse than you can ever imagine'.

In my trilogy I have tried to talk about the ordinary little things in life during our time as POWs. The common things that people ordinarily take for granted, and the wonderful humour which gave us a sense of perspective about it all. We looked at ourselves in a very wry way. We laughed about how ridiculous it all was.

Sometimes for example, you may have been out with a Japanese surveyor and you would have a yarn with him. He would tell you something about Japan and you would tell him something about Australia. At that point we were both human beings. Then there were times when they were being cruel to us, but that was their form of discipline. They had been brainwashed into it. On the Burma Railway the pressure was on the guards from the top of the Japanese command to get the work done. The Japs guarding us didn't want to be there any more than we did. I saw it in reverse when we were coming out of Manila. When our blokes were in charge some of them treated Japanese prisoners very violently.

In my opinion the big country blokes were the most handicapped of the prisoners because they had been used to such a good diet, three meat meals a day. They needed more protein and it wasn't available. The younger men needed more food too. I always remember Allan's friend 'Slim', George Hedrick, on the railway. He had the Japs baffled. He was always skinny, and they couldn't make him any skinnier. Slim was a character all of his own.

I was very sad when my close friend Alfie Coyne died in the camps in the jungle. We had been together for seven years. Before some of the blokes died on the railway they would get a certain sinking look in their eyes. They just didn't want to go on anymore and they died of pure exhaustion. You grieved for these men as if they were brothers. That was the norm of the times. People don't realise there is a norm to every occasion, and if you can fit into the norm — even as a POW — you have a bit of a chance.

I remember one man who just 'up and went mad'. When the POWs returned home the doctors didn't have a clue how to treat them. Many of the POWs were released too quickly, when they should have been re-assessed.

I was married and had two children when *Perth* was sunk. My wife went to the Navy Office and said, 'I want to send a telegram to my husband.' Well, how do you send a telegram to a POW camp? But five months later, on December 22, 1942, just before we went to the railway

I received it in Singapore. It told me that at least she knew in her heart that I was alive and safe. The telegram, which I still have, says:

To: Ray Parkin *HMAS Perth*

DARLING TERRIBLY GLAD TO KNOW YOU WERE SAFE. ALL WELL HERE. SEND OUR LOVE DO NOT WORRY. KEEP HOPING. LOVE THELMA.

Thelma and her sister had heard over the short-wave from Batavia the names of four survivors including someone called NRE Park. She knew that was me. The Navy wouldn't admit it, but Thelma said, 'That's him!'

Captain N.H.S. Knocker White

My father had fondly spoken of Knocker White and I thoroughly enjoyed meeting this 'true blue' Navy man. Knocker was in the RAN from 1936-1964. At the time of the sinking of *Perth* he was a Sub-Lieutenant doing gunnery training. He subsequently became a Captain and a navigation specialist. We had lunch together at his local RSL club, where I was fascinated to hear his eloquent description of the sinking of *Perth* and his heroic attempt to sail to Australia, a story my father had often alluded to. Post-war, Knocker regularly extended the hand of friendship to Japanese business leaders because he firmly believes, 'In wartime every country shows an ugly face. In peacetime you have to safe-guard your economic interests, your customers. I have always believed in the 'Palmerston Principle*' that a nation doesn't have permanent allies, a nation only has permanent interests. Japan was our ally in World War One; what a pity it was that they became our enemy in World War Two.

KNOCKER WHITE: I joined the Navy as a cadet midshipman in 1936 when I was 13 years of age. Just like Allan Gee, I was intrigued by the book 'Brown on Resolution' by C.S. Forester and the film.

I have total recall of the night of the sinking of *Perth*. I was in the same action station as 'Tubby' Grant. I had no sense of foreboding before the Battle of Sunda Strait whatsoever. Had I thought about it I may have had. Twenty-twenty hindsight's a wonderful thing.

---

* *Henry J.T. Palmerston 1784-1865 former British Prime Minister*

I remember Redlead the cat very clearly. I saw her racing down the gangway at Tanjong Priok, on the afternoon of the night that we were sunk, and the Commander of *Perth* Bill Martin (father of the former Governor of NSW Rear Admiral Sir David Martin) saying, 'Get that bloody cat back!' Sadly Bill perished with the ship.

When a ship was sighted by the *Perth* lookout, Waller said, 'It's probably one of our corvettes.' The ship, later identified as the Japanese destroyer *Harukaze*, which means 'spring breeze', turned away without replying to our challenge. Waller immediately recognised the silhouette of a Japanese destroyer and ordered, 'Open Fire.'

Waller himself handled the ship throughout the action, altering course violently and repeatedly, with Houston *conforming and also engaging the enemy.* Perth *and* Houston *continued to fight with every effective gun as they steamed at high speed, and zigzagged erratically over a sea whose still surface was torn by the giant splashes of exploding shells and torpedoes, and made vivid by the lightning blue glare of gun flash, the cold radiance of star shell, and the cold blue brilliance of searchlight.*

R.A.N. 1939-1942, VOLUME ONE BY G. HERMON GILL

Bob Collins and Perth's ill-fated mascot 'Redlead' leap for their lives. (Illustration by Ulf Kaiser)

I was in what I call the Gunnery Control Centre. Tubby and I and the others were around the fire control clock. We were no more than 50 feet from where the first torpedo hit in the forward engine room. There was a most enormous bang and we were flung onto the deck. All the lights went out, then the battery operated secondary lighting came on. We could see shattered tables and a lot of white-faced people gradually getting to their feet. From the bridge we got the order to prepare to abandon ship. A second torpedo hit on the right starboard side aft, then the order was given to abandon ship.

The first three torpedoes hit on the starboard side so the ship was listing for the most part to that side. But by the time we reached the upper deck we had been hit by a fourth torpedo which struck on the port side. It must have made such an enormous hole that the ship came back to the upright position, and she now listed very heavily to port.

I walked down to the port waist where all I had to do was kick my shoes off and step over the gunwale into the warm waters of Sunda Strait. I swam away from the ship, lay on my back and watched the ship sink. About a mile away from where *Perth* was sinking I could see *Houston* on fire illuminated by searchlights and firing at the enemy. I felt like cheering. I didn't have any flotation, not even a lifebelt. I didn't want to wear one because they were too hot. I had gone for comfort. One never thinks one's own ship is going to be sunk.

We had a great deal of confidence in Waller. Two comments are attributed to him when *Perth* was hit. One in the Navigators Report by John Harper quotes him as saying, 'Christ, that's torn it.' However, one of the lookouts told me that he heard Waller say, 'Oh well, that's buggered the whole show,' which was much more like him. He probably made both remarks.

I knew Captain Hec Waller very well. I was a cadet when he was Commander of the Naval College. He was terribly tough on officers, and he gave me a very hard time. He was tough, especially on young untrained officers who did not have a watchkeeping certificate, which I didn't have then. As Second Officer of the Watch, I copped Hec's very abrasive tongue on more than one occasion.

We all had the greatest confidence in Waller because he had so much experience, and he knew *Perth* well. Gavin Campbell said that Waller had told him that he thought the ship was too big, especially after commanding the destroyer *Stuart* in the Mediterranean. I thought *Perth* was just the right size for Waller. He'd do things that I as a professional navigator wouldn't dream of doing; for example using too much wheel and too many engine movements. He'd duck and dodge and weave, throwing her around like a destroyer. I wouldn't have done it for a couple of reasons. It's a bad navigational principle and it upsets your own gunnery.

Hec commented that he had found being the Aunt Sally in the earlier Battle of the Java Sea particularly trying. For three quarters of an hour we were being straddled by Japanese eight-inch shells, but the Dutch Admiral Doorman wouldn't close the range so that our six-inch guns could have a go. It was a comedy of errors. Doorman was a single ship man, and his bravery is unquestioned, but he didn't have the faintest idea of how to control a disparate group of ships. It was a hell of a mess.

What we did not know until the end of the war was the capability of the Japanese 24-inch torpedoes, which could travel for 20 miles at 35 knots and 10 miles at 50 knots. Our own torpedoes were British, French, Italian, or American. They all had a fairly small warhead which frequently didn't go bang when they struck. Whereas the Japanese torpedoes always went bang when they hit with 450 kilos of TNT in the warhead. Of course they did the most enormous damage.

I cannot think of any other cruiser in Naval history which fired all its' ammunition, and all its' torpedoes before it was sunk. *Perth* fought until her last shell was fired. While I do believe that we inflicted some damage on the Japanese transports during the Battle of Sunda Strait, I think that most damage was caused by Japanese torpedoes running on beyond *Perth* and *Houston* and into their own transports.

In my opinion leaving Tanjong Priok an hour and a half earlier wouldn't have made the slightest difference to the outcome, as we would still have run smack bang into that landing force.

I also feel it was quite wrong that *Perth* was detached from the Australian fleet based in Brisbane under the command of Rear Admiral John (Jack) Crace which was operating in the Coral Sea area. As late as mid February, the British Field Marshall Wavell, previously

Commander-In-Chief of the Middle East, said that any effort expended trying to save Java would be doomed.

The dominant personality in the Allied headquarters at Bandung, Central Java was the Dutch Admiral Helfrich. He basically said to Admiral Collins, 'I gave you all the help I could in Singapore. You lost Singapore, and now you're talking about not providing any help to me.' Admiral Collins was lobbying the Naval Board to send a ship up to Java. I think he wanted to create as good an impression as he possibly could with Helfrich. Who better to send up there than a highly efficient, well worked up ship like *Perth*, commanded by the best captain we've ever had in the RAN. We had a highly efficient Commander, a highly efficient crew, and everything worked. In my view *Perth* should have been on the north-east coast of Australia, and not anywhere near the ABDA (American, British, Dutch, and Australian Allied Command) area.

I was no further than 50 yards from *Perth* when she was sinking with propellers turning. I can still see it. Then I heard the gunner who had been in the Gunnery Control Centre with me calling out, 'Mr White, Mr White.' He was always very formal. I swam over to him. He said, 'I can't blow up my life-jacket.' It was only then that I realised I didn't have a life-jacket on. So I unscrewed the cap on his Mae West and blew it up, and then helped him onto a raft. There was a young Lieutenant on the raft who was terribly wounded. Although I was without a life-jacket, I left the safety of the raft and went off on my own.

I spent about eleven hours in the water without a life-jacket, keeping afloat on a piece of wood. I thought, 'Now I'm drowning. That's okay, that's fair enough.' I didn't think of offering up a prayer or anything like that. I knew I was going to go to sleep. Then I thought, 'Gosh, if I drown now, I'll never have bacon and eggs again, so I'll go on swimming a little bit longer. My greed saved me.'

I was at the point of drowning when I was picked up. I heard a whistle blowing and a lifeboat loomed up with 30 or 40 others on board. It was a 27 foot British steel lifeboat which had floated off one of the sunken Japanese transports. We later tried to sail it back to Australia.

I was hauled in covered with oil fuel. They cleaned my oil-soaked eyes with cotton wool. Where they got that from I really do not know.

Then we rowed this cumbersome boat back against the current for about three and a half hours, double banking on the oars, to Sangiang Island (Indonesian for 'in the middle') in the middle of Sunda Strait.

We were exhausted when we finally beached the boat. I just collapsed and went to sleep. At nightfall we made our way through long grass to a little native village. There were a few huts but no natives. We spent three or four days on Sangiang readying the boat to sail, although we hadn't yet decided where to make for.

When John Thode, Ray Parkin and their party arrived, the idea of sailing to Australia came to fruition. Thode was a New Zealander and very much a leader. He walked up to the boat, put both hands on it and said, 'How many will she take?' Parkin has said how astonished he was by the coolness of that.

The following day the natives started drifting back into their village. They weren't happy that we had butchered and eaten one of their sheep. Japanese destroyers were patrolling Sunda Strait, but by this stage we looked like natives.

We set out for Australia. Fourteen days later I and nine others, John Thode, Ray Parkin, Horrie Abbott, Alf Coyne, Keith Gosden, Harry Knight, Jack Willis, Harry Mee and 'Darkie' Griffiths, were captured by the Japanese at the port of Tjilatjap. We had travelled roughly 600 miles from where *Perth* was sunk.

I got to know Laurens van der Post and Weary Dunlop very well. Laurens was a good friend of Lord Louis Mountbatten, and because of that was introduced to the Royal Family. He was the most intelligent man I have ever met. I never thought of Weary as a doctor. He was a leader, a wonderful leader.

When I spoke to people before the War finished about when it might end many said to me, 'I just don't know. I don't see any ending.' If the bomb had not been dropped the Japanese would never, have surrendered, and the war would still be going on. Australia and Britain would have collapsed, but not Japan. Everyone knows how deeply they despised the POWs for surrendering. When my wife and I visited Japan in 1985 I spoke to a woman guide who said that during the war they were given sharpened sticks to defend Japan.

Able Seaman Robert 'Bob' (Buddy) Collins, ASDIC Operator

I first met Bob on the telephone. Apart from the joy of discovering that he was Redlead's shipmate, I soon realised that he had other stories up his sleeve. I spent a memorable day with Bob in Brisbane and took an instant liking to this quick-witted, courageous man who has a memory like the proverbial steel trap. After hearing his astonishing naval and POW history first hand I couldn't resist saying, 'I set out to write a memoir based around my father, and at this rate you'll upstage him.' When it comes to 'guts and glory' Bob Collins is swimming in it.

This is the signature of Perth's first Captain, H.B. Farncomb

BOB COLLINS: Our first Captain of *Perth* was an Australian officer 'Fearless Frank' Harold Farncomb, and our Commander was Walter Lesley Graham Adams. Farncomb once said to us in Kingston Jamaica when we left the British West Indies squadron, 'I couldn't wish to sail with a finer crew, but ashore I wouldn't give two bob for the lot of you.'

I think most sailors are rather religious, although they don't go around crossing themselves all the time. In the Navy you have what are called Divisions, and you went to church every Sunday whether you liked it or not. If you said, 'I'm not going to church, I'm a conscientious objector,' you'd finish up painting the funnel, or some other dirty job.

Allan was often on the same watch as me. I took my orders from 'the old man' and I'd transmit them to Allan, who was my bugler. He'd say, 'Yeah, what is it?' I'd reply, 'Allan do the wakey wakey call.'

When *Perth* was sunk I was on watch four decks below at my ASDIC station (Anti-Submarine Detection Investigation Committee). Allan had probably bugled the signal to action stations. I had with me a young 17 year old named Bruce 'Mike' Strange from North Sydney whom I was training as an operator.

I was sending torpedo echoes directly to the bridge. When you pick up an echo you press a button and say, 'ASDIC Office to the bridge, echo bearing.' I'd give them the bearing, and say whether it was going from starboard to port, or port to starboard, and the length of it. Sometimes it was a whale! In the West Indies I picked up the signals of about four submarines. In the Sunda Strait the echoes were coming in so fast from everywhere that I couldn't keep sending them up.

We took the first torpedo and I said to Mike, 'Oh boy, that will put us in Cockatoo.' (Cockatoo Island was the Naval Repair Yard in Sydney.) I kept doing my job. When the next torpedo hit us down aft I said, 'It's not getting too funny now.' Then we started to list to starboard. Things were getting serious. I took the chronometer off the wall but there was no order to abandon ship. I said to Mike, 'We can't leave, there's been no order.' The next thing I knew 'the old man' said, 'We have been hit,' and that was it, no more. Then we developed a list to port, so I said, 'Lets get out of here,' so up we went.

We got out through the mess deck, which was a shambles. On the next deck up the watertight doors were all dogged down with clips. Outside the Petty Officers' mess we ran into four men of the amidships fire and repair party. I didn't know any of them but I said to this Petty Officer, 'Can I go through the bulkheads?' He said, 'No.' I told him, 'You can't hear the abandon ship order because the PA has been knocked out.' He still said, 'You can't go through.' I told him, 'Well, I'm not going to stay here and drown.' I offered to go through the door and dog it down. He said, 'Yeah, alright, but be quick about it.' All of those guys are still in Sunda Strait. When I opened the door 'Happy' Hawkins the Canteen Manager came through. I told him, 'Happy you're going the wrong way.' I think 'Happy' was going below to get his money. He's still there too.

Mike and I then got to the Sick Bay where there were lots of wounded guys. We decided to go to our abandon ship station which was the Carley raft aft on the quarterdeck, but it was gone. Whoever else was in that abandoned ship station just took it. I thought, 'Aagh!' *Perth* was listing badly to port by this time. When we came forward on the port side there was half a Carley raft. We unhooked what was left of it and dumped it over the side. We were already in water up to our waists.

I also had Redlead in my arms. She was understandably terrified, and the poor little thing was covered in oil. I was very anxious to save her, and myself. However, I couldn't hold her as I pushed the raft out. She fell into the water and started frantically swimming so I immediately grabbed a paddle and yelled to her, 'Get on here, you stupid cat, get on the paddle!' Sadly she paddled further and further away from us and drowned. There was no way she could keep up, and we drifted away into the night. I wished so much I could have saved my little furry friend.

Everyone near this raft got in. In fact I couldn't even get a seat. The Japanese destroyers were going very fast and they sliced through us but they didn't pick up anyone from the water that I'm aware of. It was 12.35am on March 1, 1942 when *Perth* slipped under.

Allan Gee told me much later that he had seen 'Fishcake' (F.W.T.) Salmon dead on the bridge. I had seen him too, poor old bugger. He was lying on the starboard side of B turret and he was a real mess. He should have been retired by then. However my mate Mike Strange survived the sinking of *Perth* and being a POW on the Burma Railway.

The Captain of the *Houston* A.H. Rooks was posthumously awarded a Congressional Medal of Honour, which is equivalent to a VC (Victoria Cross). Captain Waller only received a posthumous Mention in Despatches, which I thought was a grossly insufficient tribute to his valour.

I saw plenty of sharks and there were lots of dead Japanese floating in the water. I gave another friend of mine Jeff Latch my life-belt as he wasn't a good swimmer, and I was pretty confident. The sharks seemed to be of secondary importance, although one did have a go at us. I had been clinging to pieces of wood with Sub-Lieutenant Gavin Campbell, Mike Strange, and one other. When the shark went for us we put our feet up quick smart. Gavin Campbell's leg was broken, so I grabbed a piece of driftwood, splinted it and bandaged it with some material which I cut with my trusty sheath knife from Gavin's overalls. A sailor without a knife is like a ship without a rudder. Later in hospital in Java a Dutch doctor told him that whomever had splinted his leg had saved his life.

Before I got to land I had what can only be called a near death experience. Somehow I found myself lying on clear white sand on the bottom of Sunda Strait. I don't remember how I got there. There was this huge boulder alongside me with a piece of seaweed curling around my body. I had on my dungarees and sand shoes, a white t-shirt, my knife and belt. Suddenly I felt I was looking back at myself, and seemed very small compared to this large boulder. A bright beam of light focused on me as I lay completely at peace on the ocean floor. I thought, 'I can't die here. Poor old Mum would be devastated,' so to be more buoyant I took off all my gear except my knife, and floated naked to the surface.

I struck out for the beach which seemed miles away. I could see the land like a postcard in the distance, and I thought to myself, 'There's Java, there's Sumatra. Start swimming!' I ended up swimming 12 or 14 miles over two days and I was exhausted when I came ashore at Labuan, Java. A few of us came ashore at the same spot. We immediately flopped on the sand and went to sleep.

As we were asleep some of the Javanese rushed towards us, thinking we were Dutch, their colonial masters. One young *Perth* fellow jumped up and ran towards the water. The natives, many whom were carrying huge knives, slashed at him and cut his head off. It was a shocking thing to witness. We were more worried about the Javanese than the Japs at that stage.

About twelve of us headed into a village called Menes. I asked a local postmaster if there were any Japanese around. He said there were none. Lying swine! We walked on to another place called Pandeglang, and at a hospital there we met a US Army Second Lieutenant Rogers who had graduated from the prestigious West Point Academy. He had a huge graduation ring on his finger which he said his 'Mummy' had given him. The hospital had been burnt out and the village had been looted by locals. A native approached Rogers and demanded his ring. Rogers said, 'Oh, you can't have that, Mummy gave it to me.' I said, 'Give him the ring or he'll take your hand off,' so he handed it over.

To confuse the natives and keep them away from us I fell everyone in. I don't know how many were there, somewhere between twenty and forty. I fell them in in fours, and started calling out orders like, 'By the right'. The natives had been ready to take us apart, but when we looked orderly they retreated somewhat. I got a shift (sarong) out of the hospital because I was naked, but I had nothing on my feet. Quite embarrassing really, but it was a case of 'take me as you find me.' Modesty was the last thing on our minds. Padre Keith Mathieson was also with us, and I think he felt the same way.

We went back to the village of Menes. There were bloomin' Japs everywhere, with their big 'fried egg' flag flying. By this time there were only 12 of us left. The rest had fallen by the wayside, where many had been finished off by the natives.

A short Japanese officer caught up with us. He was only a little guy and his Samurai sword was nearly as big as he was. I think he picked on John 'Macca' McQuade and I because we were the tallest in the group. The Javanese also spat in our faces, and it was a very nasty scene. Macca and I realised we were both about to be beheaded but neither of us cried for mercy or said, 'Save me!' We kept the old flag flying.

I said to Macca, 'I hope this guy's good at his golf game when he takes our heads off.' The Jap officer had his sword out and he was swishing it around. We knelt down, bowed our heads, and looked at the sand, expecting to get the chop. But nothing happened. The Jap was putting on an act to impress the natives and his subordinates.

His next trick was to order about 12 soldiers with light machine guns to line us up against a big brick wall of a Dutch house. There was a large crowd of natives looking on. 'This is really the end now,' I thought. The soldiers took up arms, put one up the spout, and again nothing happened. The threat of death by firing squad also failed to produce any cries for mercy, which it became clear was the sole object of the exercise. Then a truck showed up and the officer said, 'Lets go.' We piled into the truck and it took off towards Serang.

According to the Japanese bushido (Samurai) code, if you're considered to be brave you get beheaded. If they perceive you are a coward you get shot, and you're a miserable coward if you surrender. They considered us to be less than human because we allowed ourselves to be taken prisoner.

I can honestly say I didn't feel frightened when I thought we were going to be executed. The only thought I had was that my head's going to be rolling around the street and the dogs will maul it, and my mother will never know what happened to me. The one thing that kept me alive throughout the war was thinking about that dear sweet woman. Mum once asked me, 'Whatever kept you alive day after day darling?' I replied, 'The truth is your love for me. I just couldn't let you down and die. I had to live.' When I said that, poor old Mum broke down and cried.

My parents actually received a telegram from the Navy saying that I was missing in action, that was all. But my mother being a mother said, 'Oh no, my Bobbie's okay. He's too hard to kill, too stubborn and argumentative.' When I arrived back from the War I was six stone four (40 kg).

Some Jap guards were wary of Australians because we stood up for ourselves. You'd say, 'Australie', and they'd say, 'Australie' and occasionally they would leave us alone. If you were sitting down and a Jap came up to you, the first thing you'd see were these turned-up shoes. You were expected to jump to your feet, bow to your waist and say 'Kiotski' (Attention). One sunny day I was reading a book called 'Forever Amber' and the 'feet' turned up in my line of vision. I didn't see this Jap guard until he was right on top of me. He screamed in my ear 'Kiotski!' So I stood up, and nodded my head. Bowing to them was anathema to me. I never liked to give them an inch, to show any emotion whatsoever. I nodded to him again, and he screamed at me. I yelled back, 'Can't you speak English Charlie?' He lunged at me with his rifle and bayonet. I had done a commando course and unarmed combat in the Navy. I relieved him of his rifle and bayonet, and pointed the bayonet at his throat. It was a reflex action. His loss of face was tremendous. Some of the POWs were laughing at him, which made the humiliation even worse. He started hitting me with an open hand and I was dodging him. He said, 'Japanese soldiers stand to attention and take their punishment,' to which I replied, 'Australian soldiers don't hit each other for punishment.'

He took me down to the guardhouse and beat the hell out of me. When I came out of the guardhouse I could hardly see. My eyes were blown up and my lips were split. Later I went over to the Officer's compound where Brigadier Blackburn was, and I tore strips off him for not coming over to front for me. Blackburn won a VC in World War

One. In my opinion he had ingratiated himself somewhat with Captain Suzuki who was the camp commandant, who came from a long line of Samurai. He was quite tall, elegant and highly educated, something of a gentleman compared to the average Jap.

Predictably, I got into more trouble. One day the Japs said they needed a winch driver for a ship. I thought, 'Great, this is a chance to get out of this stinking Bicycle Camp.' I said I was a 'number one' winch driver and before long I was put to work on an old Japanese freighter on its way from Tanjong Priok to Japan carrying oil to literally grease the wheels of the Japanese war machine. I dropped about 16 barrels of oil into the drink before they woke up that I wasn't a very good winch driver. Once again they beat the hell out of me and sent me back to the camp. 'Take him back, Speedo!' They made me kneel down in front of the guardhouse, and they put a broomstick behind my knees. A Jap officer stood on each end of it. I was there all day in the heat. I've still got the scars on my knees from the pebbles.

I ended up in Serang gaol for about 32 days. I was crammed with 35 others into a cell designed for 12. It wasn't a very pleasant experience. When we first arrived we were interrogated by this big fat Jap. He was sitting at a table eating herrings in tomato sauce and a large buttered roll. I hadn't eaten for about six days except for a little bowl of rice which I had stolen from where someone had left it in a paddy field.

Another very distressing incident occurred in Serang. The cell that James 'Jumma' Brown, another *Perth* man, and I were in was next door to a cell occupied by a group of Australian Army officers. Somehow they had managed to get hold of a bunch of bananas because they had a bit of money. I said, 'Gee, bananas, at last we get something to eat.' This officer said to me, 'Is anyone talking to you?' I couldn't believe it. They ate the bananas in front of us.

There were a few officers like that. Once when I was in Saipan after we were rescued from the *Rakuyo Maru* debacle, a British Navy Captain flew in from Hawaii to ask me about the survivors of the *Prince of Wales* and the *Repulse*. I started to give him the names of people that I could remember. He said, 'I don't want those, I only want the names of any officers.' I said, 'You bloody British pig. These are people, they've got mothers and fathers just like you bloody officers.' Another threat to be court-martialled.

When we got to Changi before we disembarked for Burma an Australian Brigadier called 'Black Jack' Frederick G. Galleghan A.I.F. tore strips off me, 'Look at you, you're getting around like a lot of half naked savages.' The nerve of him. We had been sunk, all our gear was gone and we'd been stuck in Serang for weeks with very little food and a pitiful amount of clothing.

There was one Jap Lieutenant in Singapore who showed us some compassion, and was instrumental in us receiving some mail. It meant so much to hear from our loved ones. I received a letter from my mother containing a photo of my brother and his wife, telling me he had just got married.

A few days after this a Jap guard said to me, 'I want to look at that photo?' I replied, 'Drop dead, Charlie you're not seeing it.' Next thing I know I'm pinned up against a tin shed with a bayonet at my throat. A mate of mine Bronte Edwards, an Australian Army captain said, 'If you don't let him see the photo he'll take it off you when you're dead.' I showed the bastard the photo and he said, 'You number one.' He thought the photo was of me with my bride.

Once I was stood up for two days outside this guardhouse on the railway at Anganan in the sun and the rain, and was beaten up very badly. A Japanese officer said he knew that I was an ASDIC (Anti-Submarine) rating. I said I didn't know what he was talking about. He burned my arm with a bamboo stick which he had taken from the fire, and he said he was going to burn my eyes out. He eventually let me go, but I've still got the scar on my arm. When I got back to our hut the blokes said, 'Have you been playing with the Japs? What did they give you, saki?'

The Aussie humour was unfailing. Once at a *Perth* reunion in Ballina I was having lunch with 'Tiny' Savage, and Max Jagger. Tiny said to an Army guy at the lunch, 'What force were you in?' The man answered, 'I was in F Force.' And Tiny said, 'Jesus, bloody newcomers. We had the bloody railway line built by the time you bastards got there.' F Force had arrived on the railway about a year after us.

The Aussies never gave up, and never let you down. My brother once sent me a cutting from the Sydney Morning Herald about a survey done at the Australian National University which said that during the War, 'No Australian died alone.' We looked after each other. I washed and bathed blokes, and held their hands when they were dying. I washed their bandages, and did their legs for them. And they did the same for me. They were wonderful men. When I came back I wrote to more than 200 people to tell them about their deceased husbands and sons.

I picked up a bloke once in the monsoon who was lying in the mud. He was a big lump in a Dutch green uniform with a beard and long hair. He would have drowned in that mud. I turned him over, wiped his face, got the mud off him and and dragged him back up to the 105 kilo camp. I said, 'There you go Dutchie, they'll look after you here.' And he said, 'I say, hold on old man, I'm English you know.' His name was Richard Alan Crichton Cobley, the same initials as me. His father had a place, Cobley's Farm, in Surrey where William the Conquerer had landed, and it was also where Agatha Christie lived.

I spent a lot of time helping out in the camp hospitals and assisted a brilliant Australian POW surgeon Colonel, later Sir Albert Coates. I helped him cut legs off with the most basic equipment. I told him, 'You're supposed to have long tapering hands.' Coates had short stubby fingers but he saved dozens of lives in the most appalling conditions. I always felt that he didn't get the recognition he deserved. Coates used the most basic materials. The Army people who had knives, forks and spoons in their packs gave them to us and we honed them down to make scalpels. We cut off legs with a carpenter's saw. You had to hold the poor buggers down with a piece of bamboo between their teeth.

We were pretty resourceful about making life liveable in the camps. We made 'coffee' out of boiled water and burnt rice. If a friend came up you'd say, 'G'day, mate how about a cup of coffee?' Chances are he'd reply, 'I'd love one, thanks Buddy,' and we'd sit around on our haunches like natives drinking this black slop.

The Australian POWs really looked after the camps. Some of the Brits quite frankly didn't have a clue. The Aussies built latrines and our hygiene was good, which definitely kept more of us alive. I think many of the Brits we ran into were conscripts. I remember one camp of about

600 Poms (some were Sherwood Foresters) had contracted cholera. The Japs just burned their huts to the ground. They didn't care if people were dead or alive. I had almost every disease known to man, but I never got cholera.

One day I was feeling more terrible than usual and I was too ill to go to work. At the end of the day this big bloke called Bill Killion came over to me and said, 'Are you still alive?' I was sitting on a bench. I said, 'Yes, I'm still here.' He said, 'Do you mind if I have your rice?' Of course I gave it to him. That was typical of the POWs. They were polite even under the most terrible circumstances.

Some of the camps were truly atrocious. A Flight-Lieutenant called Don Hackett from South Australia came up to me one day and said, 'The Americans are starving to death in the 90 kilo camp.' We had stolen some rice from the Japanese and he asked me if I would take a sack of rice to them. They came to us because they trusted the Navy blokes to do the job properly.

I wasn't too thrilled to be the one asked to go on this mercy mission, but off I went. It was pouring rain and I had to scramble through the mud while I was delivering it. Suddenly the Japs called a 'tenko' (head count.) Fortunately for me, this poor American guy lying in a bamboo hammock had just died. They quickly pushed him out of the way and I flopped into his bed, and got counted, even though I was supposed to be dead.

Getting back was a nightmare too, and I had terrible cuts on my hands from clawing my way through the barbed wire in the dark. A couple of days later Hackett would do it again. I said, 'Let me think about it.' But it was simply too dangerous. I got an egg for my trouble, the only egg I got the entire time I was a POW. It tasted like heaven.

Once a bloke called Ted was brought to us from the 90 kilo camp. Ted was riddled with disease and I nursed him all night. It had been freezing cold. Early the next morning a Dutch man said, 'Vat you sit there for, dat man dead.' It was true. The worst part was to try and straighten him out for burial. Ted was emaciated, and even though he was dead, I felt as if I was hurting him by straightening out his skinny little arms and legs.

Time and time again you'd hear the Last Post. When we were first on the railway we'd lose about six blokes a day. At first you'd stand to attention, and say, 'Who's that?' Then it got that way you didn't bother to stand up, or even to find out who it was. There were just too many men dying. An Air Force guy from Western Australia cut crosses and inscribed people's names and regimental numbers before they were buried.

The Japs seemed to push the Navy guys harder than anyone, and it was the Navy blokes who did a great deal of the laying of the line. Each foot of rail weighed 70 pounds. We used to sneak out at night and sabotage the line, by pulling the rivets out. The only problem was the next day you had to repair the damage, but it slowed the Japs down.

Often we'd be working in mud up to our knees. Many of the Japs were in a terrible state as well. I once saw this Jap soldier pulling a cart through the mud at the 105 kilo, Anganan, camp with all the officers' gear in it. He fell down and the other Japs pulled the cart right over the top of him.

We had some pretty rough guards, but the Koreans were by far the worst. It was as if they were trying to impress the Japs by showing that they were even more inhuman towards the POWs. We had names for them including BB for 'boy bastard' and BBC for 'boy bastard's cobber' I would say to one, 'You number one bastard.' And they'd reply proudly, 'Me, number one bastard' which gave us a bit of a laugh.

When we'd finished the railway, we went to Hintock camp, which was a dreadful place. We called the Commandant there 'Pin Head'. Many of the Commandants were ex-Tokyo policemen, which seemed to be some sort of status symbol. We were cutting wood there. The Japs were pretty stupid because the wood was too green to burn, but at least it split easily. You waved an axe at it and it broke. I once asked for two full gallon drums of petrol for the steamroller. They gave us the petrol and we trotted off. The natives bought it off us and sold it on the black market. I thought the Japs can't be that stupid, believing I needed petrol for this machine which worked on steam not on blooming petrol. I wasn't game to go back and ask for more, because I think they would have twigged.

For a while I was a 'mahu', an elephant driver pulling logs. I saw this young mahu boy sitting on a big cow elephant's head, just behind its ears belting it remorselessly. I told him, 'Cut it out.' I don't think he understood me. I got the boy by the leg and I probably gave him a left hook or something. The Japanese thought this was very funny and sent the boy home, saying to me, 'From today you are the mahu.' So in I go, and I had to learn a bit of Burmese. I think, 'Yo' was to go foward, and 'So' was to go astern. Anyway you kick them behind the knee, and they go down on one knee, and you climb up on their head.

My poor elephant had a great wound in her head from the beatings which I packed with mud that I carried up on enormous leaves. She had a back like a razor blade. She was terribly thin, but she still hauled these great logs to build bridges. She also had this blooming baby with her. At night I'd shackle the elephant, but I couldn't catch the young calf, so I was always trudging off looking for it.

We worked from daylight to dark. When the British were there they had fed the elephants well, but the Japanese didn't bother. The elephants were living on bamboo shoots. Finally after we finished work one night at 105 kilo camp (Anganan), she gave a sigh, sat down and rolled over dead. The poor thing died from exhaustion and malnutrition. This stupid Jap gave me a little shovel and said, 'Dig a hole and bury the elephant.' I said, 'Once I have dug the hole how am I going to get the elephant into it?' He replied, 'Oh, I never thought of that.' The elephant was left to rot in the jungle.

Soon after we went to a big camp at Kanchanaburi in Thailand. Then the Japs wanted fit men to work in the mines in Japan. The camp Adjutant, an Australian Army Captain called Martin, sent a runner to tell me that someone had dropped out of the Japan party. I said, 'I'm not going to Japan, I'm Navy.' This expression sometimes threw them out of gear. I didn't want to go to Japan, because the China Sea was ringed with American submarines. However, fate decreed that I had to go. I thought, 'I'll go where the wind blows me.'

We received embarkation orders to leave for Japan on September 6, 1944 aboard two ships down at Singapore Harbour, the *President Harrison* (renamed the *Kachidoki Maru*) and the *Rakuyo Maru*. The Japanese ordered us to board the *Kachidoki Maru*, but there was no way I was boarding her. She was small and didn't look seaworthy. I was leading our group at the docks, and I ordered, 'Turn Right', so we boarded the *Rakuyo Maru*.

I think there were about 1,500 on board, of whom 47 were from *Perth*. The Japs were stone thick and lousy. The ship should have carried at most a few hundred. We were only given half a cup of water a day, which was completely inadequate in the tropics. I was on deck one day and was staggered to see two prostitutes happily washing themselves in gallons of drinking water from the tank. They were 'comfort women' for the Japanese officers and crew.

On September 12, we were six days out of Singapore when we ran into a US Submarine pack — *Queenfish, Sealion, Pampanito* and *Barb*. We were torpedoed and sunk by *USS Sealion*. I thought, 'How lucky can I be to have been sunk twice in the war?' They sank the whole convoy.

I have absolute respect for most Australians, however, some stupid Army Lieutenant said, 'All over the side.' I said, 'Hold on. We're settling, there's no need to panic. We've only had two torpedoes, one forward, one aft. Let's get organised.' He yelled at me, 'I'm giving you

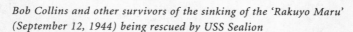

Bob Collins and other survivors of the sinking of the 'Rakuyo Maru'
(September 12, 1944) being rescued by USS Sealion

a direct order. I'll have you court martialled!' I thought, 'Not again.'

I was with the Coburn twins Burke and John. Their father was a bank manager at Crows Nest, Queensland. When we got over the side, the tanker astern of us was ablaze from stem to stern. The Japanese were jumping into the water. John and I swam away underneath the burning oil. It was dead calm and the damn *Rakuyo Maru* was sitting there like a pimple on a pumpkin. John, who was the younger twin said, 'I've got to find Burke.' I said, 'Hang on. It's too far to go. Stay with me.' We were about a mile away from the ship. I don't know if John found him or not, but they both disappeared.

Naturally the Japs had taken off with the life-boats. All we had to grab on to were some wooden blocks about a metre square which were so old and brittle that they broke up in your hands. We drifted around for six days before we were picked up by *Sealion*, the same American submarine which had torpedoed us. Luckily when they surfaced for fresh air and to re-charge their batteries, they saw us floating in the water on our foot and a half by eight foot piece of hatchboard. However at first they thought we were a couple of Japs who had survived the sinking. It's a wonder they didn't shoot us. Noel Day (RAAF) who was on the hatchboard with me yelled out, 'Get that fucking thing over here, you bloody yanks!' The Americans later told us they thought, 'They must be Aussies, they're the only ones who cuss like that.' A big bloke who looked like Johnny Weismuller dived in, put a line around me and they hauled me up like a tuna. My rescuer later received the Navy Cross for this action.

Delighted as I was to be rescued, I was upset because they made me throw away my nice leather wallet, which they were frightened might transmit some exotic disease on board. I was stripped naked and they scrubbed me down in a white tiled bathroom. It was marvellous. I had long hair and a long beard. I looked in the mirror and didn't recognise myself.

Another mate of mine 'Johnno' Frank Johnson and Brigadier Varley and his son (Jack) had taken off in a life-boat on their own. I heard an unconfirmed story later that the Japs caught up with them and they were machine-gunned.

'Blood' Bancroft was rescued by *USS Queenfish* in a similar fashion to me. Apparently the first thing he said, standing there in a thoroughly dishevelled state after days in the water was, 'Permission to come aboard Sir?' You need blokes like Bancroft.

My wartime 'adventures' didn't end there. Before the War ended I was back into service on *HMAS Nizam*, an N Class destroyer. We were sailing between Melbourne and Fremantle. Sailing off Cape Leeuwin, the southernmost point of the Australian mainland, on February 11, 1945, we were caught in the most horrendous storm. The ship did an 89 degree roll. It was the most terrifying experience I had at sea. Sixty one degrees is considered to be the maximum 'safe' limit. I could see the lights of Albany blinking in the distance, but I thought, 'I'd never make it, it's too far to swim.' Those waters are also freezing cold and patrolled by white pointer sharks. The roll was so bad I searched for a life-belt, and several 'greenies' got down the funnel. We lost ten men overboard but I was lucky again, and I didn't end up in Davy Jones Locker.

Despite having her lower deck badly flooded, Nizam *was turned about by her skipper, Captain W.C. Cook, in a desperate search for her lost crew members. No trace of the lost sailors was ever found.*

HMAS Nizam *had an illustrious record during the war. She was one of the ships that escorted convoys to Malta in defiance of the German airforce and Navy. During the evacuation of Crete she was the last vessel to leave Suda Bay — only four hours ahead of the German paratroops who overran the island.* HMAS Nizam *was also one of the ships that helped to keep the beleaguered Allied garrison in Tobruk supplied. Later in the war, she took part in the assault on Okinawa with the British Pacific Fleet. On August 28, 1945, she steamed into Tokyo Bay and was present at the signing of the Japanese surrender on September 2nd.*

AUSTRALIA REMEMBERS, NEWSLETTER

In spite of everything I feel I have had a fortunate life. My wife Norma has been absolutely wonderful to me, and I have great kids. When I came back from the War I was traumatised. I felt very claustrophobic travelling on buses or trains, and I still do not like flying. The anxiety would overwhelm me and I would alight the bus or train I was on, even if it meant walking miles to reach my destination. Norma has been very understanding about these things, for which I am deeply grateful. I am 80 now, and we have been together for 50 years.

Able Seaman Arthur 'Blood' Bancroft

Arthur Bancroft's name was often mentioned when my father was yarning about his *Perth* days, and I was somewhat relieved to hear the nickname 'Blood' was due to Arthur's red hair. Arthur like Bob Collins is one of those rare Navy men to have been sunk twice and survived. Arthur is President of the *HMAS Perth* Association in Western Australia and has tirelessly organised reunions and special events and continues to have close and caring contact with the remaining *Perth* men. Apart from his diary kept at great personal risk while he was a POW, Arthur also smuggled out some grim but graphic illustrations of his experiences. He told me that, 'Allan was our star bugler, he played at all the funerals.' Arthur said, 'The true survivors were our wives. When I was travelling by ship from Saipan after being rescued from the sinking of the *Rakuyo Maru* I wrote a letter to my sweetheart Mirla, and said, 'Dear Mirla, Have you married a Yank yet, if not, I'm on my way home.' She says I proposed the night I got home.'

MG: The following story is from *The Mikado's Guests* written by Able Seaman A. Bancroft and Yeoman of Signals R.G. Roberts after they were rescued, but prior to the end of the War.

A story of Japanes captivity

ARTHUR 'BLOOD' BANCROFT: The stay at Serang Camp ran into the sixth week. One evening the prisoners were assembled in the cinema and addressed by a dapper little Japanese officer who spoke perfect English (apparently a graduate from some English school). He informed the prisoners that this camp was about to be broken up and the entire company was to be shifted. He went on to say how sorry he was for the bad treatment that had been meted out to the prisoners during their stay, but as they were an invading force and we were more or less in the front line, we had to expect a few hardships.

One look at Rangoon was enough. It was immediately christened the 'city of the dead'. Rangoon's beautiful harbour installation was a mass of twisted steel and rubbled concrete and by the size of one crater on the dockyard, it was evident that it had recently been paid a visit by the RAAF. The only visible signs of life were hundreds of black crows hovering overhead like a flock of vultures. Later in the day all the prisoners were transhipped to *Yamagata Maru*, a smaller transport but in far better condition than the former hell-ship.

As this transport stood out to sea the Burmese temples which Kipling raved about showed out clearly against the shore terrain. It was a beautiful sight as the sun glittered on the golden roofs of the temples. During the remainder of the voyage the sea was noticeably muddy, this being due to the Irrawaddy and Salween Rivers.

Moulmein October 24, 1942: The whole city was in darkness as we were marched from the dockside to the Moulmein local gaol. This gaol had previously housed only native prisoners. Imagine our horror on learning we had been allocated the old leper and hospital wards.

This time of the year in Burma is termed the dry season and extremely cold nights and exceptionally cold days are experienced. This added further discomfort to the miseries of the men who for covering only had old rice bags. The force was split up into parties of 600, and with the exception of four sailors, the rest of *Perth's* crew were under the orders of Lieutenant-Colonel Williams who was the C.O. of the 2/2nd Pioneers Battalion. Other units included in our force were the 2/4th Machine Gunners and 105th Transport Unit.

Our immediate future was very vague although we had been informed we were about to entrain for the jungle where we would build a railway line from Burma to Siam.

October 28, 1942 was the date of arrival of the main *HMAS Perth* group at the rail-head of the Burma end of the Burma-Siam Railway, Thanbyuzayat. Welcome speech by Japanese Commandant Lieutenant Colonel Nagatomo, 'We will build the railway if we have to build it over the white man's body.' A real cheer up message!

We finally arrived at Tanyin, the 35 kilo peg before dinner. Lunch for that day consisted of two dry Army issue biscuits. Under the direction of Australian officers the force was divided into what the Japs called Kumis (platoons) consisting of 50 men in the charge of one officer (Kumicho).

We arrived at Tanyin on October 29, 1942, and at daylight on the 30th we were swinging picks and shovels. Our day's task was to excavate one cubic metre of earth. The equipment used was very primitive. Shovels were used to excavate and baskets fitted with bamboo poles took the place of wheelbarrows. The construction of bridges and culverts was also carried out with elephants employed in carting timber and doing all heavy lifts. The only mechanical aid ever seen was a Caterpillar tractor which was driven by Australians. One of the Japanese engineers, thinking he could manage the tractor without any previous instruction, jumped into the driver's seat and threw the machine into reverse with fatal results.

November 24, 1942: Like many other survivors I celebrated my 21st birthday in the Burmese jungle. My diary states: What a lovely way to spend one's 21st birthday in a Burmese POW camp nursing a poisoned foot and an infected ear. Rice and watery stew for a birthday meal with cold boiled water for a toast.

December 8, 1942: Of the 800 men at Tanyin there is a sick list of about 400 unable to work. Only 27 *Perth* men out of our Kumi of 50 fit for work. Japs have cut rations for non-workers down to five eighths of an already inadequate diet.

Christmas 1942: Church service at 0900 (Jap time). Very misty morning, sun not shining through until about 1200. Main part of the morning (a holiday) spent boiling up clothes to try and get rid of the lice which are becoming quite a nuisance.

With the approach of the festive season nothing exciting was expected and Christmas to all would just be another day in this miserable existence. We were informed that we would not be called upon to work and that we could purchase a few pigs from the Japanese.

Owing to the exorbitant cost we were only able to purchase a couple. The pork was boiled in with the melon stew and flavoured it. A further generous addition to our Christmas meal at our own expense was one mandarin per man. Except for a camp concert late in the afternoon we took part in no other celebrations.

New Year was looked upon in another light and every man was determined to stay up in spite of the camp orders which decreed that all fires are to be extinguished by 10pm. Groups gathered around huge camp fires which were kept built up and community singing took place. As the hour approached 11pm the guards decided it was time to break up the party.

The guards orders to retire were simply ignored and the men kept on singing. When it became obvious that they intended to become violent and commenced jabbing their bayonets amongst the groups the parties broke away and made towards Lt. Colonel William's camp fire. No further attempts were made to molest the prisoners who were left alone until midnight. With the singing of 'Auld Lang Syne' the Colonel warned the men to disperse quietly.

1943: Time was producing some very good black and white artists and composers and many theme songs were adopted within the camp. 'The Road To Mandalay' was worked to death so much that even the first bars riled the Japanese. The commandant gave instructions that in future the singing of 'God Save The King' and 'The Road To Mandalay' would be a punishable offence. There was also the Englishmen's version of 'Hap, Hap, Happy, Day'.

> *'It's a Jap, slap, happy day*
> *If you don't kiotske (attention)*
> *You get the boot*
> *If you don't salute*
> *It's a Jap, slap happy day'*

As the sun rises the Japs themselves pay homage to their god, the sun, bearing their heads and bowing in the direction of the sun; they chant an unmusical song which translated into Japanese is as follows, 'We are the chosen people. Who are? We are.'

With the linking up of the Thai and Burmese sections of the railroad on October 14, 1943, orders were received for the closing down of all hospital camps in Burma.

The prisoners were herded into cattle trucks and goods vans, 40 men to one van, and some travelled on the roof. The camps were to join up with their original units, but owing to Lieutenant-Colonel William's and Lieutenant-Colonel Anderson's forces being at the head of the Burma line, men from this camp were taken to Anganan, the 105 kilo peg. Here they joined forces with Lieutenant-Colonel Ramsay's, Lieutenant-Colonel Black's and Major Green's forces. Anganan was the largest camp we had been in and it was well conducted and organised under the direction of the Australian officers. It was October and we had now been captive 20 months. During the wet season the ranks had been sadly depleted due to dysentery, malaria, malnutrition, tropical ulcers and several cases of cholera.

Under the direction of Lieutenant-Colonel Charles Anderson of the 2/19th Battalion which had originally began through both the Greek and Crete campaigns, a high standard of entertainment was provided. It is believed that Charles Anderson*, himself a well known baritone, had sung alongside Australia's own Gladys Moncrief.

As November 1943 drew nigh excitement ran high. The true Australian spirit crept into the camp. Mention of the Melbourne Cup was on everyone's lips. Although cut off from their own world, and perhaps many of their number physically broken, that spark of sporting spirit could not be extinguished. The word was passed around that it was the intention of a racing committee formed for the occasion to hold a meeting within the camp on the same day as Australia's richest

---

* During operations against the Japanese in the Malayan campaign in January 1942, he was engaged at close quarters with the enemy in four days of desperate fighting against heavy odds in the Muar area. He successfully extricated his unit and surrounding troops, which sustained heavy casualties in the withdrawal to Singapore. For his leadership and personal gallantry he was awarded the VC, the only Australian unit commander in the Second World War so honoured.
Source: 'The Oxford Companion to Australian Military History' [p 31]

handicap is run. The reaction to this suggestion was unanimous. Sweepstakes were conducted by enterprising operators. Even in these far-flung outposts of recently occupied Japanese territory S.P. operators flourished.

A six event programme was decided upon. All who were drawn from the prisoners had to be under 5ft 9ins (170 cm) in height. Their 'mokes' consisted of crudely fashioned horses made out of bamboo which were dragged between the legs in hobby horse style. Training was in full swing, and great interest was centred on track gallops conducted on a circular track 70 yards in circumference. It was on these workouts that the S.P. operators carried on their pre-post betting.

The horses nominated for the Cup were taken from old Cup winners and placed horses, and featured such good gallopers as *Phar Lap, Peter Pan, Hallmark, Rivette, Second Wind, The Trump* and *Shadow King*. Other horses bore such original names as *White Slave* out of *Camp* by *Daybreak, POW out of Luck* by *Cripes, Yak* out of *Jungle by Shotgun, Eggs* out of *Canteen* by *Japanese*. The Melbourne Cup itself was to be relayed direct from Australia by a jungle radio.

The set was constructed out of bamboo and in reality housed the commentator himself. Who was he? None other than Private Jim Sutherland, a Melbourne chemist, who had an amazing memory as far as Cups went, including horses, riders, and colours going back over the last 10 or 15 years.

The big day duly arrived and excitement had reached fever pitch. As the first event was not scheduled until 2pm, a grand gala concert had been arranged for the forenoon. To cater for the thirsty a tea and coffee bar was installed on the course — it must be remembered that this is a dry country! Afterwards the crowds began to wend their way on to the course, invading 'the lawn' and the 'paddock'. As this camp had two to three thousand prisoners just how crowded conditions were can only be imagined. The scene around the betting ring reminded one of a bargain sale back home. At approximately 3.30pm a hush came over the noisy throng, and with the announcement that in a few moments they would be crossing to the Flemington racecourse, one could have heard a pin drop.

The stillness was shattered by a voice: 'Good afternoon ladies and gentlemen. This is Jim Carroll, broadcasting from the Flemington Racecourse. We now come to the fourth event of the VRC's second day of its' Spring Carnival, the Melbourne Cup of 1943.'

As the barrier rose for the start of the great race it was quite apparent that the commentator intended to give it all he had. This he did to such an extent that when the 'horses' flashed over the line locked together he collapsed with exhaustion. Medicos were on the scene within a matter of seconds, and it was found that Jim was suffering an acute attack of malaria.

It was a thrilling race and every horse nominated led at some stage of the journey. As they flashed over the line at the finish the excited crowd could do nothing but wait for the judge's decision. As far as can be remembered *The Trump* was placed first, *Wotan* second, and *Phar Lap* third.

The End Of The Line: Reports received from members of Williams' and Andersons' forces who were present at the ceremony of joining both sections of the railway line say it was carried out with pomp and splendour. A Japanese military band played whilst cameramen filmed the whole scene in detail. The actual finishing touches of this work, constructed by the sweat and blood of our prisoners, was carried out by Japanese engineers. As soon as the final dog had been driven into the sleeper, a small Jap staff rail-car carrying high Japanese officials rolled over the joints to the accompaniment of cheers and martial music. At last after 12 months under the most trying conditions and human sacrifice, the great Japanese engineering feat was completed.

The troop train carried the prisoners to their new camp at Tamarkan and made its way through the rugged terrain of Thailand. After the flat plains of the section of Burma we were working in, this rugged mountainous country was a striking contrast. One bridge in particular on the Thai section followed the course of a raging torrent. From reports while under construction some 600 prisoners lives were lost. It seemed incredible that men without mechanical aid could achieve such engineering feats.

Cholera which ravaged the camps in Thailand was responsible for a heavy toll of lives. The past four days in that train was a nightmare. Little water, less food, and filthy conditions. But strangely enough we only had one death, an American who passed on shortly after the journey commenced. His body was turned over to Anderson's Force who were now encamped at Nikki, some 30 kilos beyond Anganan, 105 peg.

The two kitchens had to provide for 3,000 men, so it can be imagined there were some very 'cushy' jobs to be had. The best of all was to belong to the barge crew which went down the river daily to Kanchanaburi to collect supplies. While loading stores the natives lavished bananas on the crew.

In Tamarkan there was a notable decrease in the death toll, and this was a great morale booster. To those doctors responsible for this, they are far greater than national heroes. Amongst some of the 'medicos' were the well known surgeon Colonel Coates, two South Australian doctors Major Hobbs and Major Kranz, Captain Rowley Richards and Major Chalmers. Colonel Coates, who with a Dutch Medical Officer carried out research, discovered that a drug made from native whisky proved a good substitute as a local anaesthetic (spinal injection). Unfortunately, this drug when administered did not localise the pain for very long and in some instances prisoners had to suffer acute pain for short periods should the drugs wear off during the operation. Many other Australian doctors with their Dutch and American colleagues are every bit as worthy of the highest praise.

It was as though a thunderbolt had struck the camp when it was learnt that Japanese doctors had arrived to select the fittest of the men for transportation to their imperial homeland.

MG: Arthur 'Blood' Bancroft was one of the POWs deemed 'fit' to be sent to Japan. Along with Bob Collins and hundreds of others, on September 6, 1944 he sailed out in convoy on the doomed Japanese transport, *Rakuyo Maru*.

ARTHUR 'BLOOD' BANCROFT [FROM: THE MIKADO'S GUESTS]:
At 2.30am on the morning of September 12, an Allied submarine sent over a visiting card and sank one of the escorts. For half an hour the convoy zigzagged furiously and depth charges were dropped by the dozen. At approximately 5.30am the two tankers, only a few hundred yards off our port bow blew up within a couple of minutes of each other. Our transport which was on the tail end of the convoy was silhouetted beautifully against the two burning tankers. Screams from the Japs on the bridge heralded the approach of a 'tin fish' from the starboard side. A minute or two later an explosion rocked the ship.

Before the last prisoner was on deck, the Japs had left the ship and naturally taken all the lifeboats. By this time the ship had lost all way and was drifting towards the burning tanker. Explosions from the tankers threw flames hundreds of feet in the air. Anything that would float was tossed over, even makeshift wooden latrines.

Results of American submarine attack: 2 tankers, 2 transports, 2 escort vessels sunk (one destroyed at 2.10am) Remainder sunk the following day (5 transports and 3 escort vessels) — transport with Englishmen on board (900) believed to have sunk immediately when torpedoed on September 13 with a loss of 300 trapped in its holds. No prisoners were injured in torpedo explosions on *Rakuyo Maru*; total of 1,317 took to the water.

The *Rakuyo Maru* took 12 hours to sink. Many of us attempted to return to the ship, with no success. During the afternoon, two Jap escort vessels picked up Japanese survivors, keeping prisoners off with revolvers. Late in the afternoon a merchant ship hove-to on the horizon but was turned away by destroyer escorts.

September 15, 1944: Three days later. Towards evening a submarine which we later found out to be American started picking up survivors. Just as darkness settled it came within 200-300 yards of us. We later found out she already had over 70 survivors on board. Our hearts sank very low as we heard her engines fading in the distance. At night we paired off on the rafts for warmth, and honeymoon couples never cuddled up closer.

September 17, 1944: During the night the sea became pretty angry and the long awaited rain came with a vengeance. Those without hats used strips of rubber to catch some rain, others caught it in their open mouths.

As the day wore on the sea rose and by midday the waves were from 10-15 feet high. Early in the afternoon another submarine (*Queenfish*) was sighted. Naturally we went a little mad, waving, singing out and doing anything to attract attention. After initially turning away, she at last came directly to us though the sea was tossing her about like a cork. Getting us off the raft onto the submarine was a dangerous job for the crew as well as for us.

The intensity of the typhoon increased, but though the skipper of *Queenfish* cruised for another 12 hours he found no more live survivors. Eighteen of us were lucky to be rescued. The submarine had come 400 miles to pick us up.

These fine husky American sailors were a sight for sore eyes. From then on until we left the submarine nine days later, their kindness, sympathy, and consideration left us with a debt we can never repay.

A British Naval Captain came on board — he had flown from Pearl Harbour. From him I learned that there were only three other survivors off the *Perth* already there, and one of them was A.B. Bob Collins, a pal of mine. It hit me hard to hear that there were none of my other friends amongst them.

We were taken to a hospital where we came in contact with the rest of the survivors, totalling 152, out of 1,317 (Navy and Army combined). Of this number there were approximately 92 Australians. Forty one *HMAS Perth* crew embarked on *Rakuyo Maru*, but only 12 survived the sinking. Four were rescued by US submarines and eight by Japanese destroyers. Apart from myself and Bob Collins they were Jack Horton, Frank McGovern, Derby Munro, Pat Major, Syd Matsen, Keith Mills, Alf Thomas, Max Campbell, Vic Duncan and Tom Johnson. Sadly Pat, Keith, Tom and Max later died in Japan.

The following telegrams were received by Arthur Bancroft on his return to Australia in 1944.

Telegram/cable from His Majesty the King, George VI. November 14, 1944

The Queen and I bid you a very warm welcome home through all the great trials and sufferings which you have endured while in the hands of the Japanese. You and your comrades have been constantly in our thoughts. I realise from the accounts which you have already given how heavy those sufferings have been. I know too that you have endured them with the highest courage. We hope with all our hearts that your return from captivity may bring you and your family a full measure of happiness.

GEORGE RI

Telegram from the Navy and the Navy Board

The Minister for the Navy and the Naval Board wish to convey their congratulations to you on your safe and welcome return. They realise and endorse the thankfulness which your family must feel at your safe deliverance from the hands of the enemy and trust that many more of your comrades will be released in the near future. They wish you a complete and speedy recovery from the ordeal through which you have passed.

MG: According to a US Navy release in 1945 about the *Rakuyo Maru* incident one survivor remarked: 'Matey, we're in safe hands at last!'

It is also worth noting that two *Perth* men Henry A. Kelly, Bandsman (died 20/1/1945) and Able Seaman George B. Morriss from Frankston, Victoria (died 9/5/1945) on the Sandakan death march. These *Perth* men were the only two members of the R.A.N. held as POWs at Sandakan. Of the 2,500 allied POWs held at Sandakan and forced on the infamous Sandakan death marches, only six survived. *(Source: Australian War Memorial)*

PERCY PARTINGTON: Henry 'Ned' Kelly didn't go to Burma with us because he had terrible haemorrhoids when he was in Changi. He was drafted from Singapore to North Borneo.

A. B. Percy Partington, Bandsman

My parents absolutely adored Percy and his wife Margaret and loved catching up with them at the *Perth* Reunions or whenever they visited

South Australia. The bond Dad and Percy forged in *Perth* and as POWs stood the test of time. Their tonic for dealing with their demons from the War was quite simply humour. Dad always emphasised how he and Percy 'talked and laughed' together. Percy and Margaret were professional musicians with the ABC, which included 22 years with the Adelaide Symphony Orchestra. Percy was with the Tasmanian Orchestra for 10 years. Margaret played the viola and Percy played the trombone and bass trombone.

PERCY PARTINGTON: The Japs had told us in Singapore, 'You're going to the land of milk and honey.' At Rangoon we were put on board another ship and sailed the next day for Moulmein, an overnight trip. We then walked five or eight kilometres to the Moulmein gaol.

About four days later we were taken by trucks to Thanbyuzayat, the main base camp in Burma. That was the start of it. We were given a talk by the Jap Colonel Nagatomo who said, 'Work hard and the Emperor will look after you. You will be fed well and given medical attention.' He added that we would be happy.

He spoke for about an hour and a half. We were standing in the sun the whole time. The Japs seemed to really get under our skin, even then. We were broken up into different parties, each destined for different camps. The camps were about five kilometres distance from each other, so you'd work five kilos this way, then five kilos that way. You kept moving up the line continuously building embankments, or whatever was required. Our first camp, Tanyin, was at 35 kilometres. I got sick there and was taken back to Thanbyuzayat. I had malaria pretty bad, and I was covered in sores.

I remember seeing Slim Hedrick at his worst in the 'death hut' at the 30 kilo camp. The death hut was at the edge of the camp and where people were put who were not expected to live. Slim had a long grey-black beard down to his chest and he was terribly skinny and riddled with tropical ulcers. But he said to me, 'I'm coming out of here,' and he did. I'll never know how he survived. Slim was a marvellous, lovable man.

I also got to know the journalist Rohan Rivett very well. He was with me at Thanbyuzayat when we were bombed and his legs were covered in bandages. Rohan was an honorary serviceman so that he could report on the war. He got the story of his life on the Burma Railway.

I met up with Allan Gee and the rest of the *Perth* guys again at Anganan (105 kilo camp.) Allan had been in the mess next to me in *Perth*. We had nattered and played a lot of mah-jong together. He was playing the Last Post all day long at Anganan because so many fellows were dying, 15 or 20 a day. That's where we lost Alfie Brown, one of the bandsmen. He died because he couldn't eat his rice without salt, and we didn't have any salt.

The 105 kilo camp was also where I first saw Allan's barber's hut, built out of bamboo. The camp was up by the border of Thailand and Burma, close to the Three Pagoda Pass. Allan built his barber's hut alongside the main hut, and that's where he first cut my hair. He had a pair of clippers and he just used to lop the hair off. The barber's hut was a bit of a congregation point. There were always about 15 people waiting to get their hair cut. Allan was very amiable, always laughing and joking. People liked to hang around his barber's hut and natter to each other. Barbers like to talk, and he always had an audience. I got to know him very well. Allan was well known because he cut everyone's hair, not only the *Perth* guys, but also the British Army Officers.

He was a clever fellow. He had razors and a shaving brush and a little jug and he used to shave blokes as well. He ended up doing a good job, even though he couldn't see! On average he was barbering twenty or thirty guys a day.

Allan and I were both at Nikki when the railway line was finished in December 1943. The trains were going through to Burma from Thailand and crossed to 'the land of milk and money' Tamarkan. It was a good camp (55 kilo) in comparison to the camps in Burma. About 60 or 80 of the *Perth* guys, Tubby Grant, McQuade, Joe Deegan, were all there in a gang. We all got on well together. We were like a band of brothers.

Tubby Grant
Born the second youngest of eight children at Koondrook on the Murray River, his mother died when he was three. In 1923 Grant met a neighbour who was home on leave from HMAS Tingira. At the age of 15 he signed on. In 1925 while on

HMAS Melbourne *he joined the ship's band playing cornet, trumpet and bugle.*
Back home he was posted to Flinders Naval Depot and when on leave he played
in the cinema pit for the silent films and at dance halls.
Perth *was hit by several torpedoes and Grant knew it was doomed. He said later*
he could have kissed the Japanese sailor who eventually pulled him from the water.
He and other allied prisoners of war were sent by ship to Rangoon. Grant's eyesight
worsened rapidly and because he couldn't see well enough to drive the spikes into
the sleepers, he was frequently beaten by the guards who thought he was avoiding
work. He reckoned he survived because he and his mates never let each other down.
EXCERPTS FROM THE OBITUARY OF TUBBY GRANT, SAILOR 1907-1999

PERCY PARTINGTON: We still had our work to do, unloading barges
of pumpkins for the kitchen. We were in work gangs of 4, 6, 12, or 20.
McQuade's job was to get a party of guys together for that day's work.
He'd say, 'You, you, you,' and the Jap guard would take us off for
the day. We'd come back at night, have a talk, have our bowl of rice.
Gee was always there. At Tamarkan one of the *Perth* boys, Ken Ikin,
got shot. The Japanese had a machine gun nest up on a hill and they
were firing at the allied liberator bombers when poor Ken was struck
down by a stray bullet.

From Tamarkan I went up Hintok way to cut wood for the trains,
because there was no coal. That was a job and a half too. After Hintok
we went to a camp called Rin Tin. 'Stumpy' (Neil) Biddel, one of the
Perth guys was there as the camp cook, and also Harry Mee and Buzzer
Bee. There was Gee, Mee and Bee! I became jaundiced there with
gallstones. We were up there for about five months. For some of that
time Allan returned to Tamarkan as the bugler.

I was sent to Chungkai next, about five kilometres from Tamarkan.
I was there when they bombed the bridge. The planes came down along
the railway line from Burma. Allan was evacuated to Chungkai from
Tamarkan after the bombing.

We knew we could survive if we didn't get blackwater fever or
(cerebral malaria) which killed so many poor chaps. We were also
extremely frightened of tropical ulcers because the infection could

Tamarkan, Thailand, 1944. Allied POWs on sleeping platforms in an atap long hut in the Kanchanaburi ('Kanburi') camp. Each man had 30 inches of bed space. (Photo by Col. J.M. Williams. Australian War Memorial: P1502/03)

Thailand-Burma Railway – POWs carrying rice (Australian War Memorial)

POWs laying
track on the
Thailand-Burma
Railway.
(Australian War
Memorial:
P406/40/34)

Below: Batavia, Java. Lieutenant Colonel J.M. Williams,
Commanding officer, 2/2nd Australian Pioneer Battalion.
Photographed by himself in the Officers' Compound at the Bicycle
Camp after his release from the Kempei Tai. June 1942.
(Australian War Memorial: 030391/10)

HMAS Perth Reunion. L-R: Ron Reece, Bob Bland, Sandy McNab, Jummer Brown, Allan Gee, Al Parker

Tommy Wittingslow. (Photo by Melbourne Age photographer Mario Borg)

Margaret Gee with HMAS Perth, Burma Railway and Rakuyo Maru survivor Bob Collins, Brisbane 2000

Margaret Gee at
Kanchanaburi War Cemetery,
Thailand, 1999

Souvenir postcard
River Kwae,
Thailand

A sense of humour
won the day –
Kun Knit Kway
POW Camp 26 kilos.
April 1943.
Illustration by Arthur
'Blood' Bancroft

spread. I was lucky, I never saw any cholera. It was critical that we remained clean. You never drank water unless it was boiled.

We always knew what day it was. We kept track of time from a secret radio we had in the camp, which we called 'Dickie Bird'. We all pinched things to survive. I'm still sweating over it. If I had been caught I could easily have lost my head, and bashing was an everyday occurrence. The Japs used to bash each othere too.

Then we went to Ratchaburi, 50 kilometres south of Ban Pong, where we built two aerodromes for the Japs, a fighter drome and a bomber drome. Allan was bugler there too. (Another aerodrome was at Phetchaburi.) The aerodromes were never used by the Japanese because the War finished, but we flew out from there to Rangoon when we were liberated.

It was marvellous to see such friendly faces. We just said to each other, 'Thank God, we're going home now!' I'll never forget the first of our rescuers. He was an American Major who looked like Butch Cassidy or Buffalo Bill. He had guns everywhere, as well as knives and grenades. I could have kissed him. There was a concert party that night, and we were singing. I don't think any of us went to sleep. The Red Cross provisions were a godsend. We heard plane after plane coming over and landing. For the first time in ages we had bags of stuff, boots, clothes, plenty of smokes and as much food as we wanted. Until then we had had nothing, absolutely nothing. It was great.

We had to stay put for about three weeks because the Yanks took the really sick guys out first. There were so many to evacuate that we had to take our turn. Allan and I went together to Rangoon. We were amongst the last of the *Perth* guys to leave. I was alright, and Allan was in reasonably good shape, except for his eyes. I think Allan's bugling and haircutting helped to save his life. He was also young, strong and had a good attitude.

At one stage Macca McQuade flew the plane, a DC3, over the Bay of Bengal. He said to these two young American pilots, 'Can I have a go?' We thought they were boys. When we arrived they got out of the plane and were so exhausted that they lay under the wings and went to sleep.

Allan was very sick at the last reunion he attended in *Perth* in March

1992, the 50th anniversary of the sinking of *Perth*. He wasn't coming, and then he said, 'Damn it, I am going.' He had his fawn suit on, and I switched the name tags at the table at dinner so I could sit with him. I think he wanted to say goodbye to everyone. Biddel got up and made a speech and mentioned that Allan and Kath had come over especially. He had this enormous will to live.

John 'Macca' McQuade DSM, Chief of the Watch

If Dad had had a twin brother he would have been like 'Macca', gallant and garrulous. We grew up hearing about this *Perth* man and POW called Macca who seemed to have status beyond our other uncles and friends. In later years when our parents saved hard to us take on holidays to Sydney we always visited Macca at his home for poolside parties — which was pretty impressive for a couple of eight year old country kids. He was everything I had imagined him to be — suave, charming, worldly, and handsome. But more than that he was a brave shipmate and a loyal lifelong friend of my father's. We loved Macca, we still do. I interviewed Macca at his home in Port Macquarie, NSW.

MACCA McQUADE: Although Allan and I were both in *Perth* from her commissioning at Portsmouth, I didn't get to know him well until we were POWs, shortly after we were captured. However, I do remember one incident in the Mediterranean with Elmo as we used to call him. One of the officers called up for one of the buglers. I remember he asked Allan who he was. 'AB Gee,' was the reply. The officer said, 'I asked you who you were?' Allan answered, 'Gee, Sir.' The Officer became confused and didn't realise that Gee was his surname. He probably thought Elmo was trying to be a bit smart.

My job on the ship was called Chief of the Watch. I was all over the ship really, but I was primarily responsible for the auxilliary machinery. I was on the upper deck when the first torpedo struck us amidships. I was thrown in the air and landed on the deck. When I stood up I saw all these sailors running around. I said, 'What are you fellows doing away from your action stations? Get back to where you came from.' They started to say, 'But, but...' I responded very definitely, 'No but's about it, get back.' Their reply was a real shock. They said, 'The Captain has given the order to abandon ship.' I couldn't believe it because I hadn't heard it over the intercom, but they told me that he had shouted it out. From then on we started abandoning ship and blokes were jumping into the water.

Before leaving I went down to the engine room where the Engineer Commander asked me how things were going. I said, 'It looks like the end,' but he didn't believe me. 'From every point someone is having a go at us. It really is that bad,' I told him. He still did not grasp how serious it was because he replied, 'Just carry on and call back every half hour or so and let me know what is going on.' I told him that they couldn't stay there because they would be trapped in the engine room.

At this point we had been hit so badly that I knew it was time for me to go. I was searching desperately for a good place to jump when I came across a bloke who said to me, 'I can't swim!' I told him to get a life-jacket quick smart, but he said he couldn't find one. So I said, 'You're crazy, you're at action stations and you haven't got a life-jacket.' I took mine off and gave it to him, because I could swim a bit. 'Quick, away you go, and make sure you get out of the way of the propellers,' I said and then I left him.

When it was my turn to jump, I did precisely the wrong thing. I was swept by the tide back towards the propellers, and they almost got me. I could hear them turning above my head, and I was terrified I would get smashed up. I thought this is the end. I was swallowing salt water by the bucketful. The ship was still moving, but somehow I got out of the way and came to the surface vomiting sea water. I came alongside this sailor and grabbed hold of him and his life-jacket and yelled, 'I've got no life-jacket.' He said to me, 'If you don't let go you're going to drown both of us.' I was unwittingly dragging us both under the water. I came to my senses a bit and fortunately saw a lifeboat drifting by, so we headed for it. With the tide going with us I was able to climb on. I was damn glad to be out of the water.

I will never forget looking up at *Perth* just before she went down. I saw this fellow standing on the bow still firing. There were a lot of guys lying dead in the water, which was very sad.

Many of us were picked up by the Japanese destroyers. The Japs were also looking for their own survivors who were wearing white uniforms. They picked up one bloke who was dressed in white who turned out to be our cook. They were going to throw him back but they changed their minds. But it is true that some of the Japs did throw some wounded back into the water, which was a terrible thing. The first thing our boys had to do was to strip off completely. The Japs were frightened they would bring a bomb on board or something.

I was in one of the last boats. Suddenly the destroyer that was due to pick us up just veered away and left us, so we drifted around on the tide without any food or water for another two and a half days. Luckily it rained one night. We were trying to make for the shore without success. A couple of the fellows who were very good swimmers said they were going to swim for it. We never saw them again. The tide just took them out.

We eventually reached the shore, although one of the fellows had died in the boat. Despite being very frightened of running into Japs, we dug him a grave in the sand. We were stark, bollocky naked but fortunately some of the Javanese village women gave us sarongs to wear so we regained a little of our dignity. They were kind, courageous and gave us something to eat. We were so exhausted that we passed out and slept.

We were terrified that the Japs would come across us and shoot us outright, so we surrendered when they eventually found us. We were loaded into a truck and taken away to the gaol in Serang, which was a wicked place. The toilet was one bucket for the lot of us, and all we had to eat was a small bowl of rice. Then the Japs said they were going to move us, so they lined us all up outside. A Jap guard aimed a rifle at us and one of our blokes fell to the ground pleading, 'Please don't kill me, please don't kill me.' I picked him up, and the guard left us alone.

We were taken by truck to this big Army camp, the Bicycle Camp. There were a lot of other prisoners there, Australians, Americans and Dutch. Many of them were still in uniforms. The Japs kept telling everyone the war was over, but no-one believed them.

I marvelled at the ingenuity of the Australians in that camp.

We scratched and scrounged and managed to find biscuits and sweets, and even some whisky which we sold to the Americans who were used to heaps of luxury items and found the going very tough. As the food became scarcer the Yanks started to drop like flies. They didn't seem to have the same stamina as the Aussies, because their ships had been extremely well provisioned.

Before we were taken to Rangoon we had a brief stay in Singapore. I remember a terrible incident there. There was a dog in the barracks which we were very fond of. As soon as the Japs realised this they took the poor thing out and chopped him to pieces in front of us.

By the time we reached Rangoon we realised we were to be a slave labour force. We often had to dig holes as wide as a table. Four men would be allocated the task, one was on the pick, one on the shovel and two others to carry the dirt away in bags. We could not go back to camp until we had finished. If the Japs got the idea that we weren't working hard enough each day, they gave us even more jobs. It didn't matter how sick or exhausted we were. They wanted to push us to the limit, so they constantly increased our work quotas to break us.

At first Allan was just one of the crowd, but when we got onto the railway and came under our Army control we came to know each other very well. We had our own authority structure within the camp even though we were under the ultimate control of the Japs.

My naval rank was equal to a sergeant. Each day one of the sergeants was rostered as Duty Sergeant. His duties were working out rosters and chores, which was a bit of a break from working on the railway. You weren't always popular because you chose who was sent out to work.

Once one of our blokes stole a bag of sugar from the Japs. Since sugar was practically unobtainable, the Japs went berserk and took Colonel Williams and they stood him outside the guardhouse with a bayonet to his chest and one at his back. They said he had to stand to attention for as long as it took for the sugar to be returned. I ran around after lights out that night trying to replace the sugar, but of course no one wanted to volunteer to return it because they knew they would be tortured. So we decided to place the sugar on the parade ground at night and hope we didn't get caught.

The next morning the bag of sugar was standing in the middle of the parade ground. Suddenly the Japs were all around us with fixed bayonets. One of the Japs' main rules for the prisoners was that you had to bow to them. This one Jap must have sensed I had a lot to do with returning the sugar, and he started coming towards me, so I bowed at him, and he bowed back. That was the protocol. I kept bowing, and so did he. This bowing went on for a while and then they walked away because it was becoming farcical. Although I was terrified, they eventually released the Colonel.

I was then made a Regimental Sergeant-Major by Lieutenant-Colonel Williams and put in charge of the camp.

About two months after arriving in Burma, Colonel Williams decided to appoint a Sergeant-Major to run the camp. The qualities required were entirely different from handling men under normal conditions. 'Therefore those in charge in a POW camp must be of special calibre,' recorded Colonel Williams. 'I selected John McQuade because I felt he had the required ability to handle men under difficult conditions to say the least. I was proved right as John did an excellent job as Sergeant-Major of Williams Force.'
HMAS PERTH BY ALAN PAYNE [P126]

I had a little bunk of my own and was entitled to an orderly to do jobs for me in the camp. Allan found out I needed someone for this job. He was very persuasive and I agreed to take him on. He was an excellent orderly. Nothing was too much trouble. We also had an affinity because we'd both been brought up on farms, and we became good mates. He had to be on light duties anyway because by this time his sight was badly affected and he was desperate for a job in the camp.

Allan used to go up to the cookhouse and scrounge for food for us which we'd put in buckets and share around. Then one day the Japs said they wanted a bugler, as the one they had had before had left the camp. Allan and Tubby Grant, who had also been a bugler in *Perth* got the job. So from then on they took it in turns to announce wake up, lights out and so forth. It was great because it gave them another job in the camp, and probably helped save their lives. They also had to play signals for the raising of the Japanese flag and the Japanese national anthem. One day I said, 'Allan how can you bear to play those Jap tunes?' He turned to me and replied, 'I'm alive aren't I?'

Food was all we thought about. Getting enough food. Sometimes the workers on the railway would bring back snakes and frogs and we'd eat them. Cats, rats, insects — we ate anything that flew, moved or crawled. It was all tucker to us. Sometimes we'd get a few vegetables and some fruit, mangoes and coconuts from the locals, but mostly it was this bad rice and slops.

We once dragged a dead and festering cow into the cookhouse which we had come across in the jungle. It was green, and so pulsating with maggots you'd swear it was still alive. I thought we'd have to throw it away, but the cook said, 'No way, it may be green but it's meat.' We boiled it for hours until the maggots floated to the surface then we ate it with some rice.

On another occasion when we were out in the jungle with a Jap guard he spotted some kind of cow he wanted to shoot. I think it was a water buffalo. He was banging away and missing so without really thinking I asked for the gun and brought the cow down with one shot. The Jap guard was so pleased he didn't mind, and he had his gun back. We dragged the carcase back to the camp, but typically all they gave us was the guts, including all the tripe. I was going to ditch it but Allan and the other blokes said, 'Tripe's delicious.' We cooked it up into what I recall was the best meal I had as a POW.

The Japs were always bashing us for any reason. They used rifle butts, or anything else that came to hand. The worst thing was when they made us kneel down with bamboo sticks behind our knee joints. It was unbelievably painful, and very cruel. They derived a perverse pleasure from seeing people or animals tortured and in pain. They'd get drunk in the villages at night and come back and bash up a few prisoners just for fun. Their favourite trick with me was bashing me on the kneecaps. Once I was bashed until I sank to the ground bleeding. I couldn't walk for three days. I now have arthritis in both knees.

It was very difficult sometimes not to become depressed because due to my rank I had to attend a lot of grisly events. I've never seen bravery like it. The pain blokes endured was horrendous. We became like skeletons, and the guys who were dying were magnificent. If there was any medicine around they'd say, 'Don't give us anything. Give it to someone who's going to live. We've had it.'

The blokes with massive tropical ulcers knew they were facing amputation without any anaesthetic. It was either that or die, as the gangrene would just rot the leg right up to the thigh. Later on we discovered an amazing alternative for some cases of bad tropical ulcers. The usual routine was scraping out all the pus and muck with a knife. However one day when it was especially hot a guy with bad ulcers went down to the river to cool off and while he was sitting in the water, all these little fish came along and started to eat the rotten flesh. To his astonishment they ate out the suppurating flesh and cleaned up the ulcers. The doctors thought this was miraculous and sent everyone with ulcers down to the river for the fish to feast on. It certainly prevented many amputations. I saw your father treating his leg ulcers that way lots of times.

There would always be a joke, a laugh, or we'd sing a song to alleviate the misery. Those lighter moments made all the difference to our survival. Sometimes we'd put on little productions — vaudeville acts, and musical numbers, all dressed up in rough costumes. Of course the Japs would take the front seats. But it helped keep us going, and distracted our minds from the day to day hardships. We even celebrated people's birthdays when we could. Christmas day was hard though as you'd think of all your loved ones at home.

It was my duty to try to maintain records of deaths, illnesses, next of kin etc. This is something the Japs didn't permit, but I kept them in this case-bound diary which I guarded throughout the war. It is a complete record of the *Perth* blokes medical history, and lists those who died and what ailments they had at the time of their death. I have recently donated it to The Australian War Memorial.

I was about 23 years old at the time I became a POW and I honestly believe that coming off the land made me more resilient. I was brought up in Merredin, Western Australia. I had worked on farms ever since I left school at 14. It was a tough life in some ways, but I think it helped me survive in the camps. There was also a lot of luck. Some made it, some didn't. If you cracked up you were gone. Once blokes were mentally broken they curled up and died like dogs. The country kids seemed to have this incredible optimism and mental toughness. They never gave up, they always believed they were going to get home. The city blokes were a bit softer, although not all of them of course.

Allan had a great sense of humour. Even when things were rough he'd crack a joke and keep going. He didn't break down. He always believed he would get out alive.

One day some of our blokes whom I had despatched to clean the Japs' toilets came back terribly upset. They had found photos of Australian women pasted up in the Jap latrines. One even recognised his own wife. Letters and photos had been sent to us in the vain hope that we were still alive. It was depressing enough not to have received any of these letters, and this incident added insult to injury.

We had a radio in the camp which was strictly forbidden. Our technicians had made it out of scrap bits of wire, which was quite incredible when you think how primitive the materials were. The Japs suspected we had one, because from time to time we let slip we knew of the progress of the War to the natives, and sometimes it would get back to the Japs. They were constantly on the alert for radios and sometimes would spring a search on us at two o'clock in the morning, hoping to catch us with it red-handed. We had ingeniously planted the radio in the bamboo leg of a bloke who had recently been amputated. Fortunately the Japs never found it otherwise I wouldn't be here today. However we did have some near misses.

> Perth's *chief telegraphist, Harry Knight took the supreme risk of making and operating an illegal radio set in order that the camps should have news of the war. The penalty for this if caught was execcution.*
> *HMAS Perth* by Alan Payne [p128]

Only a few of the officers knew about the radio. If the regular blokes had known they could have unwittingly endangered the lot of us, by an unconscious slip of the tongue.

There was one Jap who was determined to catch us out. One night he came back from 'drinking and whoring' in a nearby village, when we were working on the Burmese side. He went berserk bashing us horribly and demanding that we hand over our radio. We thought there was a definite danger this particular night that he would extend the search, discover the radio and shoot the lot of us. There is no doubt in my mind that we had no choice but to 'skittle' this guard to safeguard the lives of everyone in the camp. The big problem was how to dispose of his body. The ramifications of being caught with a dead Jap guard in our midst didn't bear thinking about. We put him in the one place we knew he would never be found, down the camp latrine. The next day the Japs were all over us and the camp trying to find him. It was extremely nerve-wracking. They eventually gave up, assuming the guard had deserted.

There was one Aussie soldier in the camp whom we nicknamed 'Christmas' because he was forever saying, 'We'll be home for Christmas.' One day he was working outside the camp and said he was going to the toilet. He disappeared into a native village and got away.

At a certain point I knew the War was about to end, because I heard it on the radio. We couldn't take the risk of leaking the news because we were terrified there'd be a ripple of excitement through the camp which the Japs would have picked up on. Another guy asked me about escaping and I told him to wait three days and then I would cover for him. Thank goodness he waited. Anyone who attempted to escape was highly likely to be caught and shot.

Three days later the Allies landed. The last two or three days before our release were bizarre. Suddenly the Japs invited the Commanding Officers to lunch. The Japs who had previously bashed us were now waiting on us at the table. Of course they were trying to ingratiate themselves to us at this eleventh hour. At the end of the meal the Jap Commander stood up and said, 'I want to wish all men friends.' We knew what was coming by this point, and he told us that the war was finished. He said, 'All men friends, hooray, hooray.' It was rather ridiculous, but now we could tell the men the War was over.

We were still very frightened because we had heard that the Japs were going to follow an old World War One dictate that at 11 o'clock at a certain date all prisoners of war were to be shot. There was even some talk that they were going to poison us, to stop us from telling the world how evil they were. The Yanks knew about this possibility and they had warned the Japs that if the POWs were wiped out they were going to drop more bombs and obliterate Japan from the map. It would have been shocking to have survived so much to be killed at the last moment. We decided if they started attacking us we would go on the attack too, and go down fighting. Only the final broadcast from Emperor Hirohito stopped us from being exterminated.

After the Allies landed we were taken to a hospital in Rangoon and had lots of tests. The nurses were absolutely fantastic and I recall them saying when we first arrived, 'You all stink.' We sure did. We hadn't had a shower or a bath for over three years, and we were filthy. They bathed us, and dressed our wounds. Just having a cup of tea was an incredible luxury, and there were all these beautiful nurses to look at!

Once at an anniversary 'do' for *Perth* I made a speech and at the end I said the reason we're still here is because of the wives. When we came back from the War we were not little gods, we were a mess. We were probably the hardest people to get on with in some ways, and the women had to put up with a lot. They never get enough credit for that.

Being a POW was part of your duty as a member of the Forces. I think in the beginning some people thought we were lying about what we went through. They just couldn't believe how bad it was. You never know what you're capable of until you are tested in the extreme. Only people who were there know what it was like, you can't really explain it properly. Years after the War I was taken onto a Japanese destroyer. I thought I was okay, but then my guts just started churning, and I had to leave. The emotions are still there, they'll never go away.

The last word from Bob Collins...

There's an old Russian aphorism which I think sums up the experience of being a POW — 'If you weren't at the table you can't judge the meal.'

PART 4

Coming Home

9

THE WEDDING

A love match

Dear Miriam,
We arrive in the West tomorrow, and from there through to Melbourne. The ship's name is Circassia *so you will be able to find out what day she arrives in Melbourne. As soon as we arrive I am being taken to the ABC to give a broadcast, so listen if you can.*
   Love, Allan

LETTER WRITTEN TO DAD'S SISTER MIRIAM ON HIS HOMEWARD VOYAGE FROM SINGAPORE TO AUSTRALIA, DATED OCTOBER 27, 1945

Dad arrived back in Australia in November 1945, emaciated, almost blind and very traumatised. The symptoms of Post-Traumatic Stress Disorder include acute anxiety, temper tantrums, nightmares, sleep disorders and panic attacks. My father had his fair share of all of them, and they afflicted him to varying degrees for the rest of his life. As a result of the loss of 92 percent of his vision due to privations endured while a prisoner-of-war, he was discharged from the Royal Australian Navy on March 18, 1946.

DAD: I was aching to see my family. Little did I know the awful news I was soon to hear. When the ship berthed in Melbourne some of the family were there to greet me which was wonderful, but I frantically searched for my mother's face.

'Where's Mum?' I said, and then I got the dreadful truth that she'd died the year before while being treated by a dentist, a Mr Vandenberg. She was only 60, and hadn't woken up after they gave her the chloroform. I was devastated. It seemed like the last straw. One of the few things that had kept me going in Burma was the thought of seeing Mum again. I loved her very much.

WES BENNETT [*a family friend*]: I went to school with Lew and used to go to the Gee's home to play. I remember Allan walking home along Stanley Road to Silver Creek on his first leave after he joined the RAN. He was wearing his uniform and carrying his kitbag. He looked so proud, the uniform was snow white, head held high, even now I can see him going past our house. The worst thing that happened to him on his return at the end of the war was when he came ashore and his father was there to meet him and he was told in a very blunt way, 'Your mother is dead.'

MERYL BROWN [*Uncle Bert and Auntie Miriam's daughter*]: Nana Gee died on November 1, 1944. Today they wouldn't have given an anaesthetic to a woman with her heart problems. It was a case of gross negligence and it came completely out of the blue. Mum found out she was pregnant with my brother Allan the same day. Years later Mum and I met an old Chinese man who, much to our horror, said that he had seen Alice Gee on the slab in the morgue at the hospital. It was terrible that Nana died not knowing that Allan was still alive. Granpa lived for another 30 years, and Lew never got over it.

UNCLE BRAMWELL [*Dad's brother*]: I saw Mum the night before she went into hospital to have some teeth taken out by the local dentist. I had to go to work of course and I don't remember the exact circumstances, but she said she wouldn't be at home the next night and that we musn't worry about her. I never saw her again. The fellow who gave her the anaesthetic said she just went in an instant and that was it.

I was working at the Tannery at the time. The head man Barnes came up and told me at about 11 o'clock in the morning. Lew was very keen to visit her the night before, but I had said we'd go the next day. However it was too late. I always regretted that we didn't go up to see her. I don't believe the rumours about her being over-dosed by accident. She had something wrong with her heart. It was horrendous for the family. It was terribly sad for Allan when he came back and found out Mum had died in the meantime.

AUNTIE VERA [*Nape's wife*]: When he first returned, Allan came to stay with us at Preston, in Melbourne. When Nape went to meet him off the boat, Allan didn't come down the gang-plank with everyone else. The Navy took Nape aside and told him Allan was waiting in a room. They said he wasn't right in the head, and that he was very traumatised by his experiences as a POW. He was that thin, and had these tiny wee arms. He used to sit on the floor at our house cross-legged, or on his haunches as he hadn't sat in ordinary furniture for years. I'd never seen anyone sitting like that. He found it difficult to eat normal Australian meals as he was used to rice. Every day the Navy picked him up and took him away for tests and treatment. He just looked beaten and he was terribly upset about losing his mother, and the fact that she went to her death never knowing that he was still alive.

BRUCE GEE [*my brother*]: The worst days of Dad's life were when he came back from the War. He was still very sick, and recuperating from the effects of a number of tropical diseases. He was almost 'stone blind' as well which must have been shattering for him, because he loved reading. The Navy took excellent care of him. He was in the Repatriation Hospital at Heidelberg for almost six months where they pumped him full of vitamins and food, which restored his sight a little, but he never had more than about ten percent of normal vision. His central vision had gone, so he only had some peripheral vision. He could distinguish between light and dark and see vague figures, but no detail whatsoever.

Dad recovered much of his strength and about eight months later he had another shot at the Navy medical. He had wanted to be a sailor since he was a child, and could see no other way to live. Due to his poor eyesight, Dad was finally discharged from the Navy as a PUNS, Permanently Unfit for Naval Service.

As an ex-serviceman he was eligible to free further education and training. He chose to attend an agricultural college where he completed a six month course. He got into terrible trouble there. He was out hoeing a garden one day when one of his mates trailed a hose over the back of his legs. Dad whipped around thinking it was a snake and chopped the hose in half and then went for the guy. He was still very nervy.

---

* *Tubby Grant: My mate Allan Gee and I flew out of the POW camp to Rangoon, on a Friday on the 21st flight out. Neither of us had ever been in a plane before. There were no seats and the aircraft was so full it only just got up in the air. We flew through this terrific, fearful tropical storm and Allan was concerned (about the lightning) because there was a lot of oil on one of the wings. When we arrived in Rangoon there were tents at the aerodrome and ladies from the Red Cross met us and gave us tea and sandwiches. But we couldn't chew the sandwiches because we were so used to gulping down rice.*

We were at the British General Hospital having lots of tests. This is also where we met Lord Louis (Mountbatten) whom I remember was a very tall bloke. Apparently we should have been sent to Bangkok with most of the other Australian POWs. After a few weeks Allan and I asked the hospital personnel to contact the authorities (Canberra) and say, 'We are lost, we are here and nobody wants us.'

One day the head sister told us she was going down to the harbour to see her boyfriend who was on a merchant ship. She came back with a bottle of brandy and Allan and I mixed up a vat of brandy with sugar, eggs, and milk and handed out this lovely egg-nog to everyone.

We had another terrible eight-hour flight to Singapore. This guy on a stretcher went berserk and Allan and I had to restrain him until medical staff tied him down. In Singapore Lady Mountbatten came and visited us which was very nice. We were given a bottle of beer a day which made us drunk because we hadn't had grog for three and a half years.

We sailed home on this beautiful big Dutch ship and we passed through the Malacca Straits between Sumatra and Malaya. To avoid any sea-mines we went right up to the tip of Sumatra and down into the Indian Ocean.

Allan and I were in a mess with a lot of airforce blokes who knew nothing about shipboard life. They wanted someone to dish up the meals so Allan said, 'That's our job Tubes.' He always called me Tubes. He told them we would take over the mess if they gave us a bottle of beer a day. Allan was the greatest scrounger of all time. He went into the galley and got a big meat dish which he filled with ice to keep the beer cold. About four or five o'clock we'd all gather on deck and I would play the trumpet – all the new tunes from before the war. It was lovely. One night we played for an Officer's dance and we rigged up a nice band – piano accordian, trumpet, and saxophone. The army blokes and the nurses were the dancing partners.

After arriving in Adelaide we got shore leave and had a big party there. Two days later we set sail for Melbourne – that's where I left the ship and lost Allan, because he lived down Melbourne way.

His sight had come back a bit, but he was still technically blind and he qualified as a blinded soldier. However he didn't want to go on a pension. He was very proud and wanted to be independent and stand on his own two feet. He only went on the TPI (Totally and Permanently Incapacitated) pension in his 50s out of economic necessity when things got too tough on the land.

There were also other allowances which made our lives so much easier. Assistance with school books, scholarships at university, and a special rate for buying a car were all available. The TPI scheme was a genuine attempt by Veterans Affairs to compensate these guys in some way for their war disabilities. It wasn't like winning Lotto, but it took a lot of financial worry off Dad's mind.

My father's overall attitude was that he was lucky to be alive. He always said no matter how bad it was for them, it wasn't as bad as it was for those poor old World War I diggers. He was never self-pitying, and he had great admiration for the way the Navy blokes stuck together, especially when they were POWs.

ALLAN GEE [*Uncle Nape's son*]: Dad was always confident that Uncle Allan would come home. 'Allan is strong and determined and he will simply refuse to die as a POW.' Uncle Allan always conveyed to me that he harboured no hatred or bitterness towards the Japanese. He also said that in his own mind he never left the Navy, as that was all that he had ever been trained for. He was so like so many young men of his day. If you were called up by your country, you put your hand up.

DAD: It's over now. Hating never helped anybody. War does terrible things to people. It twists their minds so they're capable of doing anything and feeling nothing. Mind you I still don't like the Japs very much.

MERYL BROWN: Uncle Allan bought his mother a beautiful Swiss gold watch on the trip back home. It was clearly very expensive. He also bought my younger sister Nancy and myself beautiful big cloth dolls. We had never seen anything like them. They had eyes, eyebrows and mouths painted on. You couldn't buy anything as exotic as that then. In fact there was nothing to buy in the shops. You had to save coupons if you wanted to buy a length of material or even the basics like sugar.

Shortly after Uncle Allan arrived home he came to visit Mum and Dad at 'Willowdale' in Leneva. Mum was terribly excited about him coming up. I can remember Uncle Allan, Nape and Lew sitting around the table with Mum and Dad in the kitchen laughing and talking. Us kids were mad with excitement. I walked around parading this 'proper' doll. Previously I only had dolls and golliwogs made by Nana Brewer out of oatmeal calico bags.

BRUCE GEE: Another big disappointment for Dad was discovering that his bank account was empty. His family had access to it, with his permission, and since they thought he had been killed in action, it had been used to keep their small holding going. Dad remembers asking my grandfather about the account, 'How much is there Dad?' 'A goodly sum,' Grandfather replied. 'Dad, tell me what's left for chrissake.' Dad came home with nothing, but as he always said, 'It was a lot better than being dead.'

UNCLE BRAM: There was a bit of a fuss about the money Allan thought he had left in his bank account, but honestly we wouldn't have managed without it. There was no way it could ever be paid back. Anyway getting money out of the old man would have been like getting blood out of a stone.

AUNTIE MARGE SCHUBERT [*Mum's sister*]: When Allan returned from the War, Kath was nearly 21. They were a real love match. She was crazy about him. We had thought he wouldn't come back when we heard that *Perth* was sunk. We didn't know he had survived and was a POW in Burma. He turned up a real wreck. He was so skinny. We weren't aware of his sight problems until Kath and Allan moved to the farm at Wooragee.

They told Mum they were going to get married, which Mum wasn't happy about and she made them wait. I heard her saying to Kath, 'Well, you're not getting married until you're 21!' When Kath travelled overseas in later life and had to produce a birth certificate, she found out she was a year older than she thought she was. She knew Mum had tricked them to wait that extra bit and Kath was very hurt by that.

BRUCE GEE: Nana Brewer and Dad never got on. I think Nana felt that Mum was marrying beneath herself. It was that simple. Nana took secret delight in delaying Mum and Dad's marriage by lying about Mum's age. In those days you needed your parents' consent if you wished to marry under the age of 21.

MERYL BROWN: Nana Brewer had a bit of a thing about the Gee's. She would say, 'The Gee's had nothing.' Nobody had anything in those days, everyone was poor. She had the same attitude to Annie, her brother Bill's wife. 'Oh, mountain bred,' Nana would say. Anyone who was from the hill higher up was 'mountain bred'.

AUNTIE MARGE: Allan and Kath had a big beautiful wedding at St Matthews Anglican Cathedral in Albury on September 7, 1946. Our sister Gwen and Helen Kothe were her bridesmaids. Unfortunately on the day they married my husband Walter was in Albury Base Hospital. A boiler had exploded in our dairy and his leg was badly burned. Kath and Allan took the trouble to go and visit him. The nurses were clambering to see the beautiful bridal couple. Kath looked gorgeous! Bram Gee's wife, Lillian sang at their wedding. They spent their honeymoon in Sydney. They had their problems like any couple, but they were very happy and very loving. It was meant to be.

MG: Mum told me that her honeymoon in Sydney was a dream come true. 'I had never been to Sydney and it was like going to New York for me. We stayed at a nice hotel in George Street and Allan took me everywhere. We went to Taronga Zoo on the ferry, Hyde Park, and visited Allan's Auntie Janet at Mosman. We had a fabulous time. However one night we went to a movie, and Allan suddenly walked out of the theatre. I said, 'What on earth is the matter?' He said, 'I want to go.' Incidents like this happened occasionally and were anxiety attacks as a result of his wartime experiences. He always had trouble sleeping.'

BRUCE GEE: I was born at Frankston on September 6, 1947. Dad's first job was working at Mr A.A. Dennis' Jersey Stud Farm, Ballan Park, Victoria.

Allan Gee has been with me eleven months and I have found him reliable, trustworthy, in every way, and kindly helpful. Is extremely good with the cows and thoroughly cleans the milk leaving a practically sterile bacteria count under 20,000 per millilitre. Is quite able to undertake the management of any farm in my opinion. He can also drive a tractor.

A.A. Dennis, November 26, 1948

His next job was for a Dr Leo Doyle as a general farm manager and labourer. Part of the deal at Dr Doyle's was that at the end of his work contract he was given the right to purchase three acres of land. Mum and Dad bought this small property and they were mostly very happy there. Mum had a black and white fox terrier called Trixie. Unfortunately he was killed when some men who were cutting firewood on the property accidentally backed over him in the driveway. Mum was broken-hearted.

This is to state that Allan Gee worked for me on a small property at Frankston. He had charge of some animals and worked on the layout and construction. He worked very well and I also found him honest and capable. He left of his own volition when an opportunity came to improve his status. I hope he has every success.

Leo Doyle, 45 Spring Street Melbourne, May 4, 1948

Allan and Kath Gee – a love match.

ALLAN BREWER [*Auntie Miriam and Uncle Bert's son*]: Once when Nana and Pop visited Allan and Kath at their new house in Frankston, Nana took a hen and chickens down on the running board of the Dodge. They were secured in a box and wired to the side of the car. The had to stop every so often to water these chooks. It was a two day trip, so they stayed overnight at a hotel in Kilmore.

BRUCE GEE: Mum and Dad bought a new Morris which they adored. One day Mum drove back from Frankston along a freshly tarred road, covering the hubcaps and the bottom of the car in a sticky mess. She spent the entire afternoon rubbing it off with kerosene. My first memory is when I was about 18 months old, lying in a basket in the back seat of the open top Morris watching the trees race by overhead. Those were halcyon days.

On Friday evenings Mum and Dad took me down to Frankston pier and bought fish and lobsters from men selling them from barrows. It was our weekly treat. Lobster was a working man's meal in those days. Frankston was also where my parents forged enduring friendships with Arch and Nell Neale, Chook Fowler, Clarrie Owen, The Levy's, Doug and Eileen McGregor, and Anne and Bill Lardner. Dad always said, 'Bill had more breaks than Walter Lindrum'. Mum and Dad also spent a lot of time with his great *Perth* and POW friend Slim Hedrick and his wife Maude who lived nearby at Mordialloc. Dad and Slim were in the same lodge.

As well as rehabilitative job training, ex-servicemen were also entitled to something called 'soldiers settlement'. In effect they could borrow close to the full purchase price of a property with virtually no interest, one percent if that. The idea was to help returned men get back on the land. Mum and Dad investigated going to the Western District but they didn't think they could tolerate such a harsh climate, and it was terribly flat.

They had always liked the Beechworth-Wooragee area. It was familiar territory and close to both of their families. They bought 'Lyndale', a 238 acre property, from George and William French. I was about four when we moved from Frankston to Wooragee.

10

'LYNDALE'

The Gee's from Wooragee

Christine and I were born on August 13, 1954 ending my brother Bruce's seven year reign as the only child. Or, as we sometimes referred to him behind his back, 'Baby Bubby Brucie.' It must have been a bit of a shock for my seven year old brother to lose my parent's undivided attention to two premature female babies. My mother once told me, 'When we brought you girls home we were so busy it's a wonder Bruce was fed. I even used to tie his shoelaces.' My father said that he caught Bruce holding me over the top of the well when I was about six months old.

'Lyndale', our farm at Wooragee was a special place to grow up. Whenever I drive past there now, I crane my neck to see if the lilac is out, and the hayshed is still standing, and follow the twists and turns of the creek canopied by willow trees. I peer at our old brick house with the green roof on the Beechworth Road and Mum's Queen Elizabeth roses at the front gate and get lost in a haze of nostalgia. Our property, now owned by the Jacka's, was purchased by us from an old Wooragee family, the French's.

ALAN FRENCH: My family had come to Wooragee in the early 1850s. They were originally from Penzance, Cornwall and on arrival in Melbourne sometime in 1852, they went to Ballarat. My great grandfather George Edwin French and my great grandmother, Jane

Warren, were married in Penzance before they came out. They were basically farmers, but they might have been smugglers. I'm not exactly sure, however when they came out they were officially classified as semi-literate farm labourers. My great grandmother's brother Richard Warren, who had done his print trade in England, published the local Ovens and Murray Advertiser.

The original French's settlement was up the Laserina. Old George French, my great grandfather was a wood carter, and he was run over with a horse and dray on the Chiltern Road. He gave 100 acres of land to each of his sons. The 100 acres which he gave to George Edwin French (Jr) became 'Lyndale', later owned by Allan Gee. My father, John French was born in 1882 and left school when he was ten to go cutting wood. My father told me that when he was growing up he was friends with an old aboriginal called Jimmy. He taught my father how to catch possums and he was probably one of the last surviving Wooragee aboriginals from the Mount Pilot tribe. In the early days Wooragee was often visited by blacks, King Billy and his tribe from the Kiewa district. It is believed that they went there to catch and eat Bogong moths.

The Brewers and the French's are distantly related. My great grandfather and John Brewer married two sisters of Richard Warren. Their two families held most of the land between Beechworth and Chiltern where they ran cattle. The Brewers had the dairy called 'Rosehill' at the Rising Sun, the site of an old hotel of the same name in Wooragee, about two miles from Beechworth. It is rumoured they put water in the milk to extend it.

The Chinese got most of the Wooragee gold. They worked in Wooragee for about 25 years. There were about 3,000 Chinese gold miners in the area. They did a tremendous amount of underground mining. My father used to say their main drive was big enough to drive a coach and six horses along. He also said they wouldn't dig square or oblong holes like the Europeans because they believed that the Devil could hide in the corners, so they only dug round holes. The Chinese were still here around the turn of the century because their barge was operating on the Magpie Creek in 1895. They took a ton of gold out of there during one ten month stint.

The old timers reckon that hundreds of Chinese walked to the mines at Wooragee from Beechworth in single file and were the first ones down the mines in the morning and the last ones to leave. At night they carried fire buckets on poles and apparently it was quite a sight to see them leaving the mines in the darkness in the glow of their buckets. I heard stories of one old Chinaman called Ping who was extracting gold by himself at Wooragee with a pick, shovel and a wheelbarrow. We were also told that when an important Chinese gold miner died he was sent home to China for burial, but not before being filled up with gold. If it's true it was a cunning way to smuggle gold out. When I was a boy in Wooragee I knew some of the old Chinese miners who remained and they were mainly involved in market gardening.

Some chap from Canberra was researching a book and he believed that all the gold from the area came from Beechworth. We took him around Wooragee for a few hours and I showed him all the old Chinese workings. I told him, 'Beechworth's only a parasite on everybody else's history, because the alluvial Beechworth gold was all worked out in about three weeks.'

There were lots of murders on the goldfields and at Reid's Creek once a teenage girl disappeared. The girl's body was never recovered and there is a legend that if you walk along Reid's Creek on a stormy night you will hear the sound of a young girl crying. But I am not all that keen on ghosts so I've never checked it out. Another well known Wooragee ghost is sometimes seen crossing the road in front of Bert Nankervis's place. They say it belongs to a grave that was dug under a big apple-box tree. Another ghost, a cooeeing woman reputed to have lost her child is sometimes seen travelling the bush at night near the old Wooragee settlement of Running Creek. Many years ago my father was coming home late one night on a horse with his dogs and he saw a ghost not far from 'Lyndale'. He said it gave him, and the dogs, a hell of a fright and he turned around and went home the long way around Magpie Lane.

There were a lot of people in the district who were sympathetic to the Kellys and people were careful what they said about them. However, recently I was discussing them with a local and this woman said, 'Don't talk to me about those Kelly mongrels, they shot my uncle.'

An old bloke we knew reckoned that the Kellys made the armour down at Greta, south of Wangaratta. He said he knew where it was made and where some of the bits that hadn't been up to scratch had been thrown in a dam. Ned's mate Joe Byrne delivered meat around Wooragee.

In my opinion Joe Byrne just happened to be in the wrong place at the wrong time and Ned Kelly was made into a criminal because of the system. There was one story going around that the bushrangers Smith and Brady once held up the Wooragee post-office and general store in 1872. They then held up a nearby hotel and shot and killed the publican Mr James Watt. His wife Margaret was so terrorised by the incident that she died shortly after. Smith and Brady were subsequently hanged for the murder in Beechworth in 1873.

There was another bushranger from the Woolshed area called Buttrey but he wasn't very bright. He held up the Eldorado mail coach, stole the gold and then rode back into Eldorado to have his horse shod and the troopers picked him up. Interestingly enough the gold that Buttrey stole was never recovered. He apparently hid it under a rock before going into town.

I also remember the Wooragee railway station known then as a Mallee shelter and locker. There was no-one in attendance and if you wanted to stop the train at night you had to light a red lantern, in the daytime you had to wave a red flag. But the train service was never destined to last, and around 1952 it accidentally started a serious fire. My mother's Uncle Ted Falck used to drive the train and he told us as he drove along he threw bits of coal at kangaroos to keep them off the track.

The first school at Wooragee was opened in the early 1850s and the first teacher was a woman called Miss Cook. Four generations of French's attended the school.

I lived in Wooragee for 78 years and my wife Lorna, who was originally from Toorak, lived with me in Wooragee for 54 years.

LORNA FRENCH [*Alan's wife*]: Lucky is our ginger cat and he thinks he is a dog. He used to help Alan round up the sheep and cattle at Wooragee. One Friday night before we left Wooragee to retire to Wodonga, we gave Lucky away to friends at Woolshed. He walked ten miles and arrived back at our place on Monday morning, so we kept him. Lucky only eats rabbits which Alan shoots for him. We also had a cat called Tiger who recently died at the age of 25.

BRUCE GEE [*my brother*]: Dad had gone ahead to put 'Lyndale', our house at Wooragee, in some sort of order. Mum and I arrived late at night and the moving van was already there. We could see two pairs of feet sticking out of our bath which was still in the van. The movers were inside fast asleep.

The farmhouse was very primitive. There was no electricity or running water and just bare floors. The first thing Dad did was put in running water. We had a chip heater in the bath and an outside toilet for at least the first year. I had just started school, and went to the Wooragee Primary School — population 15 including the teacher Mr Peter Dinsdale. (Peter was later killed in a tragic car accident in the Mallee. According to the current School Principal Sherril Hodgens the enrolment for 2,000 is 43.) The following year I enrolled at the Beechworth Primary School, which Dad had attended, and later the twins.

During the first year at Wooragee we had to deal with a mice plague. They were everywhere — in the beds, the cupboards, running over everything. They were eating all the wiring, and even got into the water tanks. Dad stuffed poison soaked oats into cracks around the house, but nothing made much difference. At night you'd lie in bed and hear them scuttling all around. Mum hated them. In the morning we were greeted with dozens of dead mice and the smell was appalling. The plague was so bad in North Eastern Victoria that they sent the Army in to try to eradicate them.

Sheep were booming when my parents started farming at Wooragee in 1951. For the first couple of years they made great money. The Korean War was on and wool prices were soaring. The farmers were being paid £1 per pound for their wool and even on our relatively small holding we were clearing about £10,000 a year, which was a fortune. But then as they say in the bush, 'the guts dropped out of wool' and they moved into 'the cattle job'.

A few years later I remember going down the creek with Dad in the morning to start the pump motor. As we drove over the hill and headed down we saw that the entire creek flats were covered with hundreds of rabbits. As we approached they came off the paddocks and surged back to their burrows like a brown flood. It's a pity there wasn't a market for them.

Although Dad was eligible all along for the TPI pension, he didn't accept it until 1961. The one day I saw him in tears he had been to the doctor and was told that his sight was deteriorating again. The awful coincidence was that was the same day he had collected a new car. He had to hand in his license. He was allowed to drive on the property, but not on public roads, at least not when anyone was looking.

MG: 'Lyndale' was always shipshape. Dad knew where everything was down to the last tin of nails. Because of his blindness he had to be highly organised. He was always disgusted when he saw ramshackle farms with rusting sheds and farm equipment and old bits of cars strewn everywhere. He was tidy and disciplined, something he no doubt retained from the Navy. Dad was also scrupulously clean and his clothes were immaculate. He was always busy on the farm and there was a sense that nothing was wasted. There were no wild shopping sprees, or impulsive purchases. Dad knew that your luck could change in a day on a farm, so he and my mother were careful with their money. Things were bought on a needs basis, never on a whim. But there was ample food. Boxes of fruit and vegetables, a freezer full of meat, and we had lovely clothes. Every year we'd either go for a trip to Melbourne or Sydney, and we'd save hard so that we could splurge a bit in the big smoke. And we always had great cars, the latest Holdens or Falcons. Dad loved telling people we were 'the Gee's from Wooragee.'

'Woorajay' 'Wooragay' 'Wooragee' 'Worragee' 'Worigee'
The Place of Peppermint Gum Trees, by Alan French

The 'Woorajay Run' of 40,960 acres became known as Bowman's Heifer Run in 1839 when the lease was granted to William Bowman, the first squatter in the district. He arrived on his run at Tarrawingee in 1837, a year before the Reids and Dockers and held the lease for almost 50,000 acres until 1846.

He only held Woorajay for approximately one year as in 1840 it was taken over by David Reid, who had arrived at 'Reidsdale' near Wangaratta in 1838 at the age of 18. At Wooragee, Reid established a station homestead on what is now Jim Elliott's 'Fairlawn' paddock and the run became 'Reid's Run'. Reid became a prominent personality in the surrounding districts. He gave Beechworth its first name 'Mayday Hills' when it was part of his station and contained only a shepherds hut. He was also a storekeeper and gold buyer. He established the flour mill on what is now 'Mill Park' at Allans Flat and built the 'Hermitage' at Barnawartha. He brought to Wooragee and Reidsdale a young Yorkshireman named Richard Goldsborough experienced in the woollen mills in England. Richard classed the stations wool, transported it to Melbourne and arranged the sale to the English mills.

Thus began the pastoral firm of Goldsborough Mort and Co. now absorbed in Elders IXL. In public life he was a J.P. M.L.A. for the Victorian seat of Murray, prominent in farmers unions, the Railway League of Corowa, and the first President of the Ovens and Wangaratta Agricultural Society. His wife Mary Romaine Barber, a niece of Hamilton Hume, also had strong connections with the area.

Mary's uncle, Ben Barber of Barnawartha, was blamed for the introduction of the terrible spikey weed known as cockspur to the district. It almost took over Wooragee in the 1930's, and was known as 'Ben Barber's Curse'. With the cessation of intensive cereal cropping and the improvement of pastures, it has disappeared.

With the discovery of gold in the 1850's came the invasion by thousands of people, horses, and bullocks. The animals ate most of the available grass and as the miners destroyed the land the creeks became drains of muddy water. 'Reid's Run' became as David Reid wrote 'rendered useless for the profitable pasturing of stock'.

For mining purposes Wooragee was worked in the Magpie Creek area intensively by the Chinese both sinking and driving, and the hydraulic sluicing of the alluvial gold leads. They established their own barge which, in eleven months of 1985 recovered one ton of gold.

Wooragee must have been a thirsty place in the 1850's with some seven hotels through the valley. However by 1853 at least one, 'The Junction Hotel', was being sold up including furniture, pigs, cows, sheep, chooks, and goats due to a decline in custom. However, the 'Wooragee Star' 'Rising Sun', 'Half Way' and 'The Gap' survived for a few more years.

With the decline of mining people turned to farming. Holdings were small, in some cases a few acres or a residential right, so orchards, gardens and small dairies developed. Some hawked fruit, vegetables, butter and jam to surrounding towns as far as Rutherglen by horse and cart. Larger farmers grew oat crops for sale as chaff to storekeepers, teamsters or as wheat for the flour mills. The establishment of a butter factory or creamery in Wooragee provided the opportunity to milk a few more cows.

Wooragee stringy bark timber was in great demand for the saw-mills and also for firewood by industries, hospitals, and private homes.

The Wooragee Post Office opened in 1872 at the Bakery and Store of Mr Henry Gale who became the Postmaster with a salary of £10 a year. John Payne and his wife later took over, and after his death his wife continued the service giving Wooragee 50 years as Postmistress and telephone operator.

The Wooragee Railway opened on July 23, 1891 at a cost of £62,612/10/9. It closed July 2, 1954 due to damage to the trestle bridge over Commissioners Creek at Yackandandah in early 1952.

In the mid 1950s a Progress Association was formed specifically to obtain S.E.C. power for Wooragee. This was arranged under a self-help scheme. In 1957 at a big celebratory evening in the old school, the kerosene lights were turned out for the last time, and the power and light was turned on by Mrs Payne.

When Zwar Bros. Tannery in Beechworth closed in 1962 the Amenities building was purchased and after much dedicated effort became the Wooragee Centenary Hall. Wooragee School celebrated its Centenary at the beginning of 1962.

ALLAN BREWER [*Uncle Bert and Auntie Miriam's son*]: Kath and Allan and a carload of us went to Wagga to see Queen Elizabeth in 1954. The others were Bruce, Dad, Mum, my elder sister Nancy and myself. Allan read 'Dad and Dave' to us. We were all jammed into my parent's brown Holden. Kath and Allan owned a little green Consul at the time.

AUNTIE MARGE SCHUBERT: The year Margaret and Christine were born, 1954, was a particularly freezing winter. The twins would have died except Allan kept all the fires going in the bedrooms. He was wonderful. They had only expected one baby, so it was a big surprise when Dr Nicholls in Yackandandah delivered Christine half an hour after Margaret. The twins' heads were tiny, about as big as a teacup because they were six weeks premature.

There were lots of twins on the Brewer side of the family. Our great-great Grandfather John Brewer had twins. Reg had twins, Donald and Wendy-Lee. Frank had five children including twin boys, Ian and Graham, and Uncle Richard had twins Doris and Donald. My sisters Kath and Mary were twins, and then Kath had twins, Margaret and Christine.

Eleven months after they were born Kath and Allan came to visit Walter and I. Kath was crying as she was exhausted from looking after premature babies, and they both desperately needed a break. I said, 'I'll take them, you go and have a holiday.' The twins stayed with us for five weeks. Margaret was already walking and Walter taught Christine to walk. Kath cried again when they returned to pick them up because they didn't recognise her.

BRUCE GEE: We nearly lost the twins when they were three years old. We had stockyards and a post and rail fence which ran down the side of the house, and Dad was leading the twins around the fence on Joan our huge Clydesdale horse. Joan was heading towards the gate post when Dad realised she was about to cut the corner and crush Margaret. He pulled Joan up but she must have shied a bit. Margaret fell off and broke her leg, and ended up underneath the horse. Christine landed on top of her. The horse was clomping around and could easily have trampled them. Her hooves were nearly a foot wide. Dad

Bruce Gee and the twins at 'Lyndale', Wooragee.

had nightmares about it for months and Mum said he'd wake up screaming. Margaret spent six weeks in a cast and frame at the Yackandandah Bush Nursing Hospital with a greenstick fracture.

MG: I have wonderful memories of going mushrooming in winter with my father when I was about eight years old. One of Dad's favourite songs was, 'All Things Bright and Beautiful' and his melodious voice resonated in the crisp late afternoon air. He'd carry a large metal bucket and we'd both slosh through the mud and grass in our gumboots seeking out the bulbous russet mushrooms. Sometimes in the twilight I'd see an enormous ginger hare bounding across the paddocks. 'That's the Easter Bunny,' Dad would say as we watched the blur of fur diving down a burrow. We'd proudly take our laden bucket back to Mum and she'd fry the mushrooms in butter for our tea.

BRUCE GEE: We often visited Grandfather Gee at his old house at Silver Creek when we first moved to Wooragee. It always looked a bit run down and was surrounded by long, dry, silvery grass. Hannah was still there. She was a lovely woman and very kind to everybody. She had a special tin of lollies for visiting children.

Grandfather Gee read the Bible constantly, but he could never be described as a Bible-basher, although some members of the family will probably disagree. He sang hymns around the house and was very accomplished on the pedal organ and the harmonica. He was the mildest man I ever knew. Light seemed to shine from him. He was totally pure, a delightful old guy. In every sense he was a believer. When he was sick in hospital he once said to me, 'I am not worried about dying. I am not frightened. I just know when I awaken I will be with my beloved wife in heaven.' She was the love of his life. He had embraced their 40 years of marriage, not endured it.

Whenever we drove down Gee Lane to visit grandfather I marvelled at the enormous box thorn hedge running its' full length. That same hedge almost cost him the sight in one eye when his horse pig-rooted and pitched him in head-first.

He wasn't all Christian charity though. He didn't like the Chinese or the Irish. He once told me, 'When a white woman has been with a

MERYL BROWN [*Auntie Miriam and Uncle Bert's daughter*]: We often stayed with Granpa Gee and Hannah. They had no electricity or running water. For bathing, water was brought in buckets and boiled on the stove, then put in the tin bath. Grandpa had an enamel basin in which he washed. There was an outside toilet and we had a potty at night. Hannah had to light the wood stove to cook a meal, even if it was 110°F in summer. There were fireplaces throughout the house so at least it was never cold in winter, and they put hot water bottles in the beds at night. There was a small pool near the creek where we collected beautiful fresh water mussels which Hannah cooked.

A big day out for us was when the whole Gee family went to Stanley blackberrying. We had to put up with green biting ants and the adults would always say to us kids, 'Watch out for snakes.'

Mum used to cut down her clothes and other peoples to make our clothes, even pleated skirts. She even made our underwear. I can still see her sitting for hours at the old treddle sewing machine and then pressing the clothes with the flat iron. Later she made beautiful dresses for my cousins Christine and Margaret. She'd go up to 'Lyndale' and sew all day and she used Enid Gilchrist patterns. She was also a superb knitter. The day my dear Mother died in October 1992, while my brother Allan and I were sitting in the hospital, I turned my mother's hands over and I said to the nurse, 'I can't help thinking of all the work that these hands have done.'

ALLAN BREWER: Grandfather Gee was a very clever man. Mind you, he'd talk Christ off the cross, then talk him back on again. He loved to talk endlessly. He was a great oracle, good at telling other people what to do. He occasionally stayed at 'Willowdale' when I was a child. I'd get up early and run down to the dairy so I could escape being 'trapped' for hours.

Auntie Carmel went to a nursing college and at one time was the matron at the Beechworth Hospital where I am told she assisted my birth in 1945. Auntie Carmel and her husband Len, who worked with the railways, lived at Bendigo then Moe before they moved to Port

Fairy. Auntie Carmel called my mother Miri, and they were very close.

AUNTIE CARMEL WARWICK: My father came close to re-marrying. There were a few people he was interested in, two in particular. But sadly the one he liked the most and was keen to marry died. He was very lonely, and lived for nearly 30 years after Mum died.

ALLAN GEE [*Uncle Nape's son*]: Grandfather played the trumpet in the Salvation Army band, and he played the mouth organ when he retired and was living on his own. He was an excellent musician, but no wonder because all they did was march and play, march and play most days.

The only time I saw Grandfather get worked up was when he was staying with us in King Valley and some Jehovah Witnesses turned up. They were regaling Mum at the door, and Grandad said, 'Let me go out and talk to them.' They were in full flight quoting from the Bible but Grandad just stood there saying, 'Oh Yes, Oh Yes, Oh Yes.' Then he launched into them. He finished every sentence, knew every parable, and quotation backwards. He ran rings around them because he practically knew the Bible by heart from reading it every day of his life. He had a great time debating with them for about three hours, and he never once mentioned his Salvation Army background. 'Well Mr Gee,' they finally said, 'We'd like to continue this discussion with you, and we'd like to bring one of our preachers from Melbourne to see you.' So they brought this guy over and Grandad sat in the kitchen, while they stood and went at it again for hours. Mum said Grandad had the best time. After at least four hours the Jehovah Witnesses finally retreated looking very dejected. Mum said she was standing in the kitchen listening and couldn't stop giggling.

The death of M. Napier Cowdroy Gee occurred in the Ovens and District Hospital Beechworth last Friday August 31, 1973. He was aged 91.

Mr Gee was born in Bega NSW, and brought up on his father's property 'Rosedale'. He was the youngest of the family. Later as a young man he moved to Inverell where he joined the Salvation Army. He became a Salvation Army Officer and served in South Australia and Victoria for 17 years. On January 9, 1913, at Kilkenny S.A. he married a fellow Officer Alice Harriet Haywood who died in 1944 at the age of 60. He retired from the Salvation Army and settled in Beechworth and (Silver Creek) where he lived for 47 years.

For years he gave religious education in Beechworth schools and was a preacher in the Salvation Army and the local churches. He was well known and respected. He is survived by his children Napier, Bramwell, Miriam, Carmel, Allan, and Lewis. There are 13 grandchildren and 12 great grandchildren. Services were held in the Salvation Army Hall, Ford Street Beechworth, and at the Beechworth cemetery by Rev. Bramwell Gee, assisted by the Corps Officer, Captain Burton.

OVENS AND MURRAY ADVERTISER, SEPTEMBER 3, 1973

MG: On Sunday afternoons we regularly visited Nana Brewer and Mum's twin sister Mary at 'Pinedale'. On the drive over Christine and I would quiz Mum about her early life and her family. During both my primary school and high school years I can't remember any school friends whose parents were divorced. I was brought up with the view that once married it was basically 'a death till you part' arrangement. In those days though frankly most women didn't have the economic flexibility to bail out of unhappy marriages, and it was morally and socially frowned upon. My mother told me that she clearly remembered hearing her parents fighting about sex. Nana Brewer was obviously reluctant to be pregnant again after nine children, and not averse to denying Grandfather his conjugal rights. They had separate bedrooms for many years but they both enjoyed family and farm life. I remember asking Nana when I was about five years old what the difference between boys and girls were, and she said with a chuckle, 'A man's got a teapot.'

Nana was delightfully eccentric. She had an amusing habit of repeating sentences. 'That's a nice dress Kath, where did you get it? I say, that's a nice dress Kath where did you get it?'

Christine and I also stayed at 'Pinedale' during what can only be described as the 'golden era' of telephones — when the ironically named party lines were operating. Party lines operated in quite a bizarre way. Every phone in the district was connected on a single line, so every phone call would ring in every home attached to that line. Of course everyone answered the ring, but if the call was for someone else you were *supposed* to politely hang up. At the age of nine years I can tell you it was irresistible to listen to these country folk gossiping away. Predictably you'd hear, 'Well Mavis I'd better go, I think there's big ears on the line.' If Nana ever caught me eavesdropping she'd scold, 'That's very bad manners Margaret,' and then break into a mischievous grin and ask, 'But, did you hear anything of interest dear?'

Her lack of punctuality was legendary. One weekend when I stayed with her, we were running late, of course, for a barbecue at a relative's property some distance away. Nana had promised some of her renowned delicious rissoles. I watched in amazement as she squashed the blood stained ball of raw seasoned minced meat, already seeping through the brown paper bag, into her handbag. 'I'll make the patties when I get there,' she cried, flying out the door with her bloomers in her hand.

MERYL BROWN: I half lived at 'Pinedale', I was there most weekends and went everywhere with them. If we were going to Auntie Marge's for lunch at Baranduda, Pop would get the car out and we'd be all dressed up and ready to go. We'd sit in the car and endlessly wait for Nana. Pop would say to me, 'A man ought to drive off Mel,' but of course he wouldn't dare. Once he said, 'I might just drive down to the bridge, that will scare her.' Nana would finally come rushing out pulling up her stockings and saying, 'Come on, come on.' She had no idea of time.

ALLAN BREWER: One day Nana and Pop had arranged to visit Auntie Marge and Uncle Walter. As usual Pop had been waiting in the car, and he started blowing the horn. Nana finally came out of the house, but just to snap at Pop, 'I'll be back in a minute.' Fifteen minutes later she returned with a freshly killed chicken. She'd gone down to the henhouse in her good clothes, cut the head off, plucked it, dressed it, and wrapped it in newspaper. 'I thought Marge might like a chicken for tea,' she said.

Nana would say to me, 'Put three tablespoons of fat over the lamb chops, and keep turning the pan love.' That was my job when I stayed at 'Pinedale'. I'd turn the pan with a poker and then Nana would drop about ten eggs in. Sometimes I stayed there for two or three months at a time. It was a second home for me.

I can never remember Nana needing to go to the doctor or even having a cold. She always told me to eat a piece of dry bread after a meal because it takes the fat off the lining of your stomach. I still do it. Nana died in 1984 aged 93.

I feel very nostalgic about Christmas nights at 'Pinedale', where the whole Brewer clan converged including hordes of Phillips', and assorted friends and relatives. There were never less than about 70 people, some of whom only ever showed up at Christmas. Billy Phillip's son young Billy (Nana's nephew) would dress up as Santa Claus and ride in on his horse. Everyone would bring their left-overs from Christmas dinner, and there would be an immense feast. It was wonderful. I think the last time they celebrated like that was about 1964. Christmas doesn't seem the same anymore. There are a lot of empty chairs.

MERYL BROWN: Auntie Al (Sister Christina) visited 'Pinedale' every Christmas. A cousin of Auntie Al's, Dennis Toohey, would drive her and another nun to visit all the relatives. They weren't allowed to eat with anyone else. At 'Pinedale' we had to set up a card table in the front room so that these two nuns could have their sandwiches and tea on their own. Nana said, 'Now don't you kids be peeping in!' Of course we couldn't wait to hide behind the hydrangeas and peer at them through the window. We couldn't work out why they had to eat by themselves. Uncle Allan was astounded that when the American evangelist Billy Graham first visited Australia in the 1950s Auntie Al knew all about him. They listened to him on the radio at the convent.

ALLAN BREWER: In February 1956, Pop Brewer and I drove about 1,400 of Ted and Artie's sheep into Wodonga. He asked me to ride Peter, a chestnut who used to shie a bit. He rode old Don. His other beloved horse Bonnie was retired by then. I was 11 years old at the time and I was flattered that he thought I could ride such a difficult horse. Soon after Pop became ill with heart disease and I visited him in hospital just before he died on April 12.

In his will he gave the boys the properties. Frank had already set up on his own in Indigo. Bert had his own place 'Willowdale' and he shared half the hop scrub with Reg when Pop died. Artie and Ted got the house creek property 'Trudewind', which Pop had bought off an old Leneva family of the same name. The girls didn't receive any land.

AUNTIE MARGE: Dad died of a heart attack aged 72. One day the doctor said to us kids, 'You know your father's not going to live very long. He has heart disease'. He died a week later in the Wodonga Hospital, and we were all shattered. My brothers then took over all his properties.

Mum and Mary were able to stay at 'Pinedale' as long as they wished. Reg and his wife Kath lived with them for a while after they were married. Mum almost bought a house in Wodonga but changed her mind. Eventually she moved into a flat in Wodonga with Mary.

Mum was very annoyed that Dad hadn't left her the Dodge car in his will. It was sold after Pop died. She couldn't drive but she had this bee in her bonnet to own a car. She bought a blue Holden model around 1959, just before my daughter Betty married Laurie Robinson. Clara arrived at the wedding in this new car, driven by our Uncle Jack Croker from Melbourne. Everyone said to her, 'Where did you get that car?' 'It's mine, it's mine, it's my new car,' she crowed. Maybe she bought the car to carry her chooks to Melbourne, I don't really know. She never learned to drive.

Mum was never sick although as she grew older she became as deaf as a beetle. Occasionally she had a bilious attack from eating too much fatty meat. She loved to wipe out the baking dish with a round of bread, before the roast dinner was served. On Sunday I'd carve the meat and before I made the gravy Mum scraped out the bottom of the dish. She'd say, 'Don't tip that brown bit out, I love that.' Years ago people kept the dripping from their meat meals for cooking, particularly for roasting vegetables. Mum ate like a horse and at afternoon teas she'd scoff scones and cream and ham sandwiches. She had an amazing constitution.

AUNTIE GWEN: The five boys worked on the farm and got paid their keep and some spending money. From time to time they received money in a lump sum. They had a great start in life because they were all given a property when Dad died. In those days land was usually given only to male heirs.

MG: My mother thought it was a travesty that her brothers inherited all her father's property, and the girls were only given an amount of cash. She told me, 'We all worked extremely hard at 'Pinedale' and in my opinion it was wrong that the property was not divided up evenly. The inference was that 'girls would marry and be looked after'. Pop would never have deliberately done such an unjust thing, but I have always felt it was unfair.' However Mum was not a person to brood on things, and she remained close to her brothers.

Mum was a very keen golfer and Dad encouraged her to play as often as possible as a way of having a break from the farm. Later in life she was elected President of the Wodonga Golf Club and once scored a hole in one. When we were around six or seven my parents became friends, through Mum's golfing at Beechworth, with a family called the Mays. Mum played golf with their adult daughter Shirley. Sometimes when Mum and Dad went away, we stayed with Wally, May, Shirley and her brother Alan. Everyone referred to Mrs May as simply May. The Mays were avid Bing Crosby fans.

Wally had a big vegetable garden, just like the one I imagined in Beatrix Potter's classic *Peter Rabbit*. Christine and I spent many happy hours with Wally pulling out carrots, cutting rhubarb, picking peas and navy beans, and squashing snails around the cabbages. Evening entertainment in those days was usually home visits to play cards or sitting around talking and drinking tea with iced vo-vo biscuits. Wally always went to bed just on dark, so May, Shirley, Christine and I would visit either the McAnanlys or the Coyles along Alma Road, beside the Beechworth racecourse. Shirley remained a close friend of Mum's through golf and the Labor party.

Mr McAnanly, a widower, lived with two of his adult children, Pat and Peg. They were all lovely to us. Mr McAnanly let us climb his beautiful old mulberry tree and pick the fruit. I recall once smearing myself with the indelible red juice, then cajoling Christine into playing cowboys and Indians.

The people down the road from us at Wooragee were Peg and Bill McGuinness. They were warm, loving people and great characters. They liked to drink, and enjoyed their own home-brewed beer. They had a farm and from time to time they grew tobacco, had sheep and cattle, and a small dairy.

Christine and I frequently rode our bikes down to McGuinness' farm. Despite his affection for home-brew, Bill was very definite that he had a cure for heroin addiction. 'If the government took notice of me they'd fix heroin addicts for good. You think I'm joking don't you? I'd lock them in my tobacco kiln for ten days without any food or water. It's as hot as hell in there and they'd sweat out their craving in no time.

They had an outdoor toilet at the end of a long path at the back of their house which I assiduously avoided, especially in summer. It was almost obscured by long grass, and infested with cobwebs, and in summer, no doubt, there was the occasional snake. My cousin Lynette Clark, Uncle Lew's daughter, recalls a memorable visit to this toilet when she was a little girl. 'My bottom popped through the seat and I was suspended over the toilet can. I was saved from plunging in by clutching the sides of the seat with both hands. I yelled my lungs out and my parents came and rescued me.'

BRUCE GEE: One Saturday morning when I was about 12, Dad and I went down to Bill and Peg's farm, a mile and a half from 'Lyndale'. When we arrived Peg told us, 'Bill's up the dairy.' Up we went and found Bill, his son Mick, and Bill's older brother Jack sniffing and screwing up their noses. Bill told us there was a terrible smell in the water. Now this was the water they used for drinking, washing out the dairy and hosing down the creamery. Believe me, the smell was disgusting.

No-one could work out where the stink was coming from, but finally we got a torch and shone it down the well. There was a lot of gunk floating on top and there was no doubt this was the source of the vile odour. Then we saw what looked like coils of rope, and realised it was a big black snake which must have fallen into the well, died and rotted.

At first they tried to retrieve it with a bucket and rope, but the snake had putrefied so badly that it fell to bits. Another solution was required. Bill and Jack were big blokes so there was no way they were going to go down the well. Mick was about 13 at the time, and considerably thinner than either Bill or Jack. Despite his protests, they put a rope around his waist and lowered him into the stinking abyss.

As Mick inched down the well the stench was too much for him and he started yelling, 'Oh, it's terrible, let me up!' He was heaving his guts and screaming, 'Pull me up, pull me up!' to no avail. They lowered him right to the bottom and said, 'You're not coming up until you get all that muck.' The poor bugger was down there for about an hour scooping up the remains. You can only begin to imagine the stink of the snake and Mick's vomit all mixed up together. In fact Dad and I felt a bit queasy ourselves. Everyone had a good laugh about it, except Mick.

MICK McGUINNESS [*Bill's son (Michael)*]: The well was 80 feet deep, with about twenty feet of water in it. By the time I reached the snake I was 60 feet down and I was terrified that it might still be alive, but there was no way Dad would let me up until I'd cleaned it out. We had been wondering why our drinking water had a funny taste.

Our well was always trouble for me. Another time Bill lowered me down to fix the pump. I had a rope around my belly which was tied to his tractor. In order to haul me up he started driving the tractor away. I was hanging onto part of the pump and realised that if I got tangled up in the rope I would be pulled in half. Bill was oblivious to all this, and kept driving. I quickly detached myself from the rope and slowly crawled up a thin pipe to the top.

The McGuinness family were amongst the original selectors at Wooragee in 1857, as were the Poyntz' and the Fannings. We were essentially dairy farmers. That was our bread and butter. The Frenchs', Adlams', Jones', Morgans' and Wardens all milked cows. The milk was taken to Springhurst, which was later taken over by the Kiewa Milk Co-Op.

There was a terrible fire burning at both ends of Wooragee in 1954. From Mount Pilot to Beechworth the entire sky was red. Kath was heavily pregnant with the twins and was probably worried about having to make a dash to the hospital through the path of the fire. All of Yackandandah was alight, and there was a big fire burning from Chiltern to Barnawartha. They had a hell of a battle to save 'Yak'. A change of wind saved Wooragee from being burned out. There were a few hard times for the residents of Wooragee, but none of them would have swapped their lives there for anything.

I had one of the first transistor radios in Wooragee. One day we were shearing our sheep at old George French's. I turned the radio on and he nearly had a fit. He said, 'How do you run that, without wires?' He thought you had to have wires running through your property to power a radio. He had never seen a transistor before. Bill bought a television before the electricity was connected in 1958. He had to have one, but it sat in the box for about three months. Before electricity we used Tilly (kerosene) lamps.

My father Bill regarded his beer like gold. However one hot summer's day he arrived home from the pub carrying a dozen bottles of beer in a cardboard carton to find that just outside the back door a huge black snake was sunning itself on the verandah. Bill smashed the carton down onto the snake and killed it stone dead. Amazingly he only broke three bottles. The next day Bill told the publican at the Commercial Hotel who was so impressed that he passed the news on to Carlton and United Breweries in Melbourne. Bill was sent a congratulatory dozen bottles of beer.

He also home-brewed terrible beer. The first batch was excellent, but it was downhill after that. He got his original recipe off an Army bloke who was on one of the first major expeditions to Antarctica.

I enjoyed helping Allan out at 'Lyndale' cutting wood, fixing the water pump, and rounding up cattle. He used to get pretty cranky sometimes as he couldn't see well enough to fix things easily. Obviously his poor eyesight caused him great frustration. When he blew up he'd say, 'Don't tell me what to do. You can go and get stuffed!' But it would all be forgotten the next day.

BRUCE GEE: Bill made good money from the dairy and Peg had a senior job at the Mental Hospital. They had about 100 acres of ground. They also had pigs, and Bill cured delicious bacon.

The Wooragee cream scandal was a hoot. Mum and Dad knew the family at the centre of the fuss very well. They were rather flashy for Wooragee and collected the cream for the Milk Co-Op. They always seemed to have money, a beautiful farm, smart cars, and glorious dams. Soon everyone believed they knew why. The police were suspicious about them and hid in their hayshed where they allegedly observed them taking a dipper of cream out of everyone's cans. This gave them an extra couple of cans a day. They were never convicted but the rumour at the time was that they had 'creamed' off thousands of pounds worth. The alleged scam had been going on for years. They were represented by Frank Galbally the big gun barrister from Melbourne. The prosecution failed and the cops were furious. Dad was quite amused by it, and remained on friendly terms with the family.

One day when I was about 14 years old I arrived home from school and noticed a fire behind the large hill on our property, which we referred to as the aeroplane strip because the super-phosphate pilots landed their planes there. I immediately rang the Wooragee Fire Brigade, grabbed two knapsacks and raced across the paddocks. Oddly enough Dad was nowhere to be seen. My sense of foreboding increased. The knapsacks each carried about five gallons of water, so it was lucky I was a strong kid. It was a stinking hot day and I'm pounding along trying not to panic. As I charged over the hill a familiar face appeared. Dad was there frantically beating out this raging fire with a bloody bag or something, which was totally useless. It was like something out of a bad movie.

He was a bit of a pyromaniac. He liked nothing more than lighting a fire in the paddocks, usually just on the cusp of summer, under the pretence of burning off. I think it was the one time he was pleased to see me. By this stage the fire was into McGuinness' as well and it's a wonder he didn't burn out Wooragee and beyond. He was terribly embarrassed, especially when the Fire Brigade turned up and ticked him off for lighting a fire on such a terrible day.

The Ravdels were another colourful Wooragee family. They were European Jews from Melbourne and had been in the rag trade. They bought Adlam's place but they were typical Collins Street farmers. They were very cosmopolitan, had a flash car, and were an intriguing reminder that there was a whole other world outside of Wooragee and Beechworth. However they were like fish out of water and only stayed on the property for about three years. They sold it to the Fergusons.

Jack Ferguson was a magnificent horseman who had married an heiress by the name of Pearson. Her widowed father owned a string of pubs. They poured a fortune into the property. I was once out shooting rabbits with their son Gary and I tripped and ripped my leg open on a coil of rusty barbed wire. I was worried about an infection so we went back to Gary's place and he poured iodine on it. It stung like hell. I looked at the bottle and saw that it was veterinary iodine for horses.

There were plenty of snakes around, blacks and browns but we never killed them unless we had to. They ate mice and rats so they did a bit of good. Dad was scared of them because of his poor eyesight, but didn't mind them so long as they were away from the house. He hated the idea of killing any wild animals. I think it went back to being a POW and seeing so many sick and dying people. I never once saw him mistreat an animal, and he was never deliberately cruel. Dad never let the twins keep anything in cages, not even the odd ginger or black rabbit which turned up. He particularly hated the old country custom of having a sulphur-crested cockatoo in a small wire cage.

He got cranky with the dogs sometimes, but he never hit them, and he was extremely affectionate towards them. We always said our dogs should all have been called 'Get behind bastard', because that was Dad's usual command to the dogs when he was rounding up sheep or cattle. He wept when he shot our red kelpie 'Bozo' which was about 20, and crippled with arthritis.

ALLAN BREWER: I was helping Uncle Allan on the farm once when I noticed his arm was bandaged. I asked him what happened and he said, 'My dog wouldn't do what I told him to do. I blew up and tried to choke him and quite rightly he bit me.'

BRUCE GEE: Dad was very fond of his sister Miriam, a librarian, who was married to Mum's brother Bert. Needless to say they both had a passion for books. Sadly, later in life Dad and Miriam drifted apart. I have great memories of staying at their farm, 'Willowdale'. Years later Miriam and Bert divorced. Miriam married again, but pre-deceased her second husband Percy Boyes.

I once had this disgusting competition with my cousins Hadyn and Allan. We lay on a bed and competed for who could spit the highest, the aim being to hit the ceiling. We had lots of good times swimming and yabbieing in their dams, but Hadyn nearly died once from meningitis he caught there.

One time Auntie Janet (Dad's aunt) and Grandfather Gee were looking after us at the farm for a few days as Mum and Dad were away. Janet was a rather tall, gracious lady who lived in a house near the beach at Mosman, NSW. This particular day at Wooragee, Grandfather had gone for a walk and paid a visit to the wooden toilet we had outside next to the chook-house. When he sat down he was bitten on the backside by a red-back spider, just like in the song. He was in a bit of a panic about it and nearly died of humiliation when he had to show Janet and me where he was bitten. He was rushed up to the hospital at Beechworth. Margaret, Christine and I were walking around trying, not very successfully, to suppress our laughter. Red-back bites can be fatal, but we couldn't help but see the funny side of it. Grandfather wore these old fashioned woollen Long Johns 365 days a year, but not the same pair fortunately.

MG: Like most little children we believed there were fairies, pixies and goblins at the bottom of the garden. Christine and I delighted in making fairy houses under the lilac trees where there was always a sprinkling of tell-tale toadstools. At night we'd leave out tidbits of cheese and biscuits and charge out in the morning to see if they had eaten our offerings. Daddy would scribble little thankyou notes and leave them on the plates for us to find. I think one of the more distressing moments of his life was levelling with Christine and I when we were eleven years old that Santa Claus, the tooth fairy and

Easter Bunny only existed in childrens' imagination.

We were very inventive when it came to entertainment. This was before TV, the Muppets and Pokemon. Christine and I launched Gum Tree Theatre in 1960 which comprised a little wooden stage, a bedspread curtain, and a few chairs assembled on the sandy floor of one of my father's sheds. Dad painted a sign on the shed and a rough drawing of a gum-tree. We pieced together some raggle-taggle costumes and whenever people visited, friends, family and the occasional vet or Jehovah Witness, they were subjected to our 'amateur' acts. These included singing, dancing, juggling, ventriloquism, and magic tricks. The dogs and even the cat were worked into the show. Our long-suffering patrons were charged a modest entrance fee, which entitled them to a home-made ticket, a glass of cordial and one of Mum's lamingtons.

One Sunday afternoon we had a girlfriend called Lyle Russell visiting for the day. Lyle was the daughter of The State Savings Bank Manager, Wally Russell, and they lived in a double storey mansion in the main street of Beechworth. It was the smartest house I had ever been in with a marvellous sweeping staircase, and they all had impeccable manners. Lyle was a treasured friend, and I'm sure she thought a day at a farm with the Gee girls would be a treat. All went well for a while. We happily showed her around the property, beamed with pride at Gum Tree Theatre, introduced her to our menagerie of animals and taught her to make daisy-chain jewellery from the yellow kapok flowers.

But this rural idyll suddenly turned into a disaster. I decided that it would be great fun to toast some marshmallows over a fire. Christine, Lyle and I crammed lots of wood and newspaper into an abandoned forty four gallon drum, and I struck a match. Boom, Boom! There must have been traces of petrol left because the explosion almost blew our heads off. Fortunately we were blasted back by the fireball, and escaped being fried alive, although there were several singed eyebrows. 'We're not dead, oh dear we could have been killed,' I cried.

But even that potential crisis was no match for the furore caused over the blackened laundry. I had forgotten that my mother had spent most of the morning washing practically every white sheet and pillowcase we owned, not to mention a separate line of clean towels flapping in the breeze on her clothes-line. Once I realised that my head was still attached to my shaking body, I saw to my horror that every piece of washing visible through the swirling smoke resembled burnt toast.

Mum and Dad came hurtling out of the house. They checked to see we were alright, and then erupted in a fury about the sooty washing. 'Bloody kids. Jesus Christ, we should thrash the living daylights out of them. You could have burned the house down. If I catch one of you I'll take to you with the razor strap.' Dad could match any shearer when it came to colourful language.

BRUCE GEE: We had a steam engine on our property which the Frenchs' from across the road had brought over. They had asked if they could park it at our place for a few weeks, but it stayed there for years. When they drove it into our place I thought it was the best thing I had ever seen, a relic from a bygone era. It was parked close to the chook-house. One day Hadyn Brewer, Mick McGuinness and I decided to get it going. Being teenagers we couldn't start the fire quickly enough. It's a wonder we lived to tell the story. We stoked it up with wood but we didn't realise that over the hours it was slowly building up a huge head of steam. It shuddered and shook, then suddenly there was an almighty gush of steam. We thought it was going to explode any minute. Dad was absolutely fuming, because he had told us under no circumstances to fire it up. You can imagine the language.

ALAN FRENCH: The steam traction engine 'temporarily' parked at 'Lyndale' belonged to the old French brothers. It was an old chaff cutting engine which had also been used for timber milling. The brothers used to travel around the district with it, down the Murmungee, Beechworth, Wooragee, Indigo and Chiltern. In the off-season they drove it from Wooragee to Bacchus Marsh to work on the roads.

You could actually move it around on a property. It was a traction engine and was fired up with wood. I can remember cutting chaff with it at my Grandfathers. They used to put treacle on the belts to stop them from slipping on the pulleys. At dinner time I would take the tin of treacle, which by then would be full of haydust and straw, and have it on bread and butter. We couldn't afford to buy treacle to eat, so this was a real luxury. In the end they couldn't get a pound for the steam engine at the clearance sale. They didn't even get an offer for it. Steam traction engines are worth thousands now.

~

MG: I have had a life-long love of cats which commenced during a school holiday visit to my Auntie Marge and Uncle Walter's dairy farm, 'Avenel' — Leneva spelt backwards — at Baranduda. We loved staying with them, but Dad always said, 'They're tied to that dairy like dogs'. They had to milk dozens of cows at dawn and dusk 365 days a year, so holidays for them were rare. Uncle Walter was one of nature's gentlemen, and a keen fisherman. He loved to spray us with milk and we helped feed their poddy calves. They had silos of grain, which attracted mice and cats. One day just as we were preparing to leave their farm to return to 'Lyndale' with Mum and Dad I heard a kitten mewling. I found a tiny tortoiseshell kitten alone under an orange tree and begged to be allowed to take it home. I remember picking the kitten up, her fur perfumed from the bed of violets in which she had been lying. Tootsie was with us for eleven years and produced innumerable kittens. Her first litter, a ginger kitten, was eaten by a tom

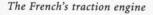

The French's traction engine

cat, which broke my heart. She also sorted out the dogs, even the feisty blue heeler. My current tortoiseshell cat is Sardine, a worthy successor to Kit Kat.

BRUCE GEE: Ralph and Maria Tremonti came out to Australia with the first wave of Italian migrants after the war, probably in the late 1940s. Dad heard that Ralph was an excellent stone-mason who in our less sophisticated district had turned his hand to concreting and tiling. He commissioned Ralph to do the front verandah at 'Lyndale'. He streaked the concrete with a rainbow of colours which still looks attractive today. He and his boys spent weeks at our farm doing the work, staying in the shearing shed and going home on weekends. Mum and Dad got to know them very well. The two boys Joe and Sandro (Butch) were always with them. They were delightful people. We visited their home in Albury for parties and sat around drinking red wine. In those days many people referred disparagingly to 'new Australians' as 'wogs', and they appreciated our friendship.

On November 30, 1963 the family had been casting votes at the Tumbarumba Post Office and were driving home to Albury. A ten ton truck came around a bend, lost control and smashed into their car. Joe aged 27, and 'Butch' aged 21 were killed and Joe's wife Anne was critically injured. Anne's two young sons were also injured. The Tremonti's were shattered by their sons' deaths and never got over it. Mum and Dad were very depressed by it and people in the district felt sad for months. Anne remarried. She was Dutch born and said her children, Joe's sons, Mark and Robert, now laugh if anyone dares to call them wogs. They say, 'We're not wogs, we're clog-wogs'.

Just three months later, our family was deeply saddened by the tragic death of Mum's brother Frank.

ALLAN BREWER: Uncle Frank was killed in a motor vehicle accident in February 1964. He was driving home one night when his car went over the side at the intersection of the Brewer and Beechworth Roads, at the top of the Indigo Gap. My eldest sister Meryl and I were the ones who went to 'Pinedale' and broke the news to Nana. She was devastated. Uncle Reg was never the same after Frank died. The day he had to put Frank's dog Nipper down some time afterwards, he said, 'I've just shot Frank.'

AUNTIE MARGE: We never got over Frank's death in that dreadful car accident. He was only 43 years old. He died in hospital the following day. I rushed in to see him, but he wasn't conscious. Auntie Win was a real worrier, and everyone said, 'Don't take Win in it will upset her too much'. Frank was a real gentleman. Dad used to call him 'the bank manager'. He was a smart cookie all his life. He saw a lot of action in the war, especially in Greece, Crete and Borneo. He was lovely to Mary and was the one who instigated Mary moving into a flat in Wodonga after Mum died. He also taught her to smoke.

AUNTIE MARY: I loved Frank. He had a lovely nature. He always called me 'John'. When his marriage to Doris broke up he lived at 'Pinedale' again with Mum and I. We often stayed up until after midnight talking. At the time of his death he was working as an insurance inspector.

BRUCE GEE: Another of Mum and Dad's lifelong friends were Frieda and Peter. Peter was a Russian bomber pilot during the war and was shot down and taken prisoner. The cannon shell which downed his plane also blew off his big toe. At parties Peter would take off his shoe and show everyone the amputation. Peter found himself in the American zone of Germany after the war and fortunately was not repatriated to Russia. Most of the Russians were rounded up and sent home and went straight into the gulags where the majority perished.

LUDMILA [*their daughter*]: My parents eventually moved to Belgium where my father worked in the coal mines for several years. It was terrible work. They felt there was no future for them in Europe and they came out to Australia in 1950.

BRUCE GEE: Most European migrants arrived by ship at Station Pier in Melbourne, and were sent by train to Bonegilla Migrant Camp on the outskirts of Wodonga with all the other European migrants. They were called DP's (displaced persons) when they arrived. The locals usually referred to them as 'refos' or 'New Australians'.

LUDMILA: It was difficult at times at the Bonegilla Migrant Camp because families were sometimes separated for varying lengths of time. Mum briefly went to Mildura to pick peas. The migrant women there were terrified of the goannas, which they thought were crocodiles. My father was on his way to Castlemaine to seek work in the coalmines when he was stranded in Beechworth because of a train strike. He wandered into a local pub and was immediately offered work. He worked at both the Murray Breweries and the Tannery, and chopped wood to make extra money.

We lived in seven houses in the nine years we lived at Beechworth. Dad would buy an old house, fix it up, and move us into another one. Mum worked as a ward assistant at the Mental Hospital. She later trained as a fully qualified psychiatric nurse. They retired to North Eastern Victoria.

FRIEDA: We had many happy days with Allan and Kath. When Peter took Allan fishing he loved to help out by putting the worms on the hooks. Sometimes we looked after the farm when the family left Wooragee for a holiday. Allan thought it was very funny that when Peter tried to milk the cow it kept putting its' foot in the bucket.

BRUCE GEE: Through Peter and Frieda Mum and Dad became friends with the Rucins family in Beechworth. George Rucins had been a pilot in the Luftwaffe, and was later the conductor of the Beechworth Music Group. They spent a lot of time together and had fabulous parties, drinking vodka, wine and dancing.

We eagerly awaited Peter and Frieda's visits to Wooragee when they had their delicatessen. They'd arrive laden with exotic foods — caviare, herrings, salami, fragrant cheeses, and olives. They were great days.

MG: Christine and I were also in the local Music Group, continuing the Gee tradition of playing in local town bands. I had wanted to play the trumpet, but we both ended up learning the clarinet from the age of ten from Mr Harry Walker in Albury.

For years Mum drove us in for weekly lessons and both our parents waited patiently in many cold local halls while we practised or turned up for another gig. We played at country shows, important town events, and even rodeos. But our most responsive audiences by far were the patients at the Mental Hospital and the inmates at the Training Prison. They were somewhat starved for entertainment, and when the concert was over they went wild. The patients at the Mental Hospital would applaud throughout the performance, and sing and dance to the tunes. It was fabulous. We also visited Melbourne and played at the Yooralla Crippled Children's Home, and the Heidelberg Repatriation Hospital where we visited Michael Sinclair who was recuperating from injuries he sustained in Vietnam.

George Rucins was a very dignified conductor and as proud as if he were conducting the Moscow Symphony Orchestra. The Music Group is still in existence and Geoff Crossman, one of our classmates, a trumpeter and fellow band member, is now the conductor. His parents Herb and Joan Crossman, who were also in the Salvation Army, founded the band in 1963. It was one of the first concert bands started in country Victoria and is entirely self-funded.

Geoff recently told me they played to 15,000 people at Beechworth's annual Mayday Hills Festival. He recalled the time my father drove a tractor loaded with hay and paying customers through the town and down to Wooragee to raise money for the Music Group. Some of the original members included Robert, Boyd and Neil Collins — Boyd and Neil still play in the band — Arnie Leitch, Janice Leitch, Viv LeCouteur, Diana and Jeddah Wyatt, Marie West, Alec Webster, John Brunken, Peter and Edgar Rucins, John Paul, Greg Crossman, Diana McCracken, Peter Fartasinski, John McLurg, Bob Charlton, Norm Hancock, Terry Durling, Betty Hornsey, Peter Mimm, Ron Gray, Arthur Clayton, Bob Galbraith, Alan Johnson and Richard Bonatesta.

11

A COUNTRY COP

The Beechworth follies

The Dixon family, Reg and Maria, and their boys John, Alec and Greg contributed enormously to the happy memories our family retains of Beechworth and Wooragee. Reg was 'an honest cop' but he had a sense of humour and the right mixture of 'clout and compassion' to keep a country town on the rails.

REG DIXON [*former Beechworth Policeman and family friend*]: I took up duties as Sergeant in Charge of Police at Beechworth in May 1958. Beechworth is Australia's best preserved gold town and 27 of its buildings are classified by the National Trust.

The Prison, originally built as a wooden structure, housed many famous, or infamous, personalities including Ned Kelly and the Kelly gang, Henry Power, (said to have been Ned's bushranging teacher) Joe Byrne and the Kelly sympathisers who were locked up for sheltering him and many others.

The origin of the present massive building that is today the Beechworth Training Prison was indeed a humble one. Originally it was only a rough slab unit, built somewhere near the Police Camp. This, of course, was in 1852, and only a few months after the arrival of the first few miners.

The procedure in those early days was to send all prisoners down to Melbourne with the fortnightly gold escort. They were conveyed by means of an open dray, irrespective of the weather.

In 1853 the Government architect, Mr. Nixon, supervised the erection of suitable prisoners' quarters. These took the form of five or six long wooden buildings, with shingle roofs, the whole being enclosed by a stockade of 8 feet slabs topped with spikes. By now there were a great many criminals on the goldfields, and within five years, this gaol was neither big or strong enough to hold all of those who were caught. In 1857 the present gaol was started and was practically completed by the end of 1860. Until 1861 prisoners under sentence of death were sent to Melbourne. The first person to be executed in the Beechworth Gaol was the bushranger Shehan, in 1865, for the murder of Kennedy at Yackandandah. Other executions carried out at the Beechworth Gaol were John Kelly (1867), James Quinn (1871), James Smith & Thomas Brady (1873).

Ned Kelly was twice a prisoner in the gaol, his mother once, and at one stage 22 Kelly sympathisers. The bushranger Power was placed in the gaol and his arrival in town was something of a triumphal entry. Although manacled and in a dray, he still managed to bow to all and sundry as he came down Ford Street.

During the First World War the gaol was closed and the building taken over by the Police Department, when it was mainly used as a lock-up. In 1951 it became a Training Prison. The old gaol is as much a landmark as ever it was, with its massive walls and turreted sentry boxes giving it the appearance of a Norman keep.

A BACKGROUND TO BEECHWORTH BY ROY C. HARVEY [P 30]

REG DIXON: One of my predecessors was Robert O'Hara Burke, who was the Police Inspector, before setting out on his ill-fated journey with Wills to the north of Australia. At the time it was reported that the locals were surprised at the nomination of Burke as leader of the expedition, because he had become lost on a well-beaten track from Beechworth to Yackandandah, a distance of about 14 miles (23 km). At the back of the Court House there is a bricked-in square where Burke is said to have taken open-air baths.

When I took over the Station from Leo Ryan, Herbie Crossman and Leo Newbound were among the Constables. Leo Newbound was a solid policeman, but unfortunately he soon transferred to Wangaratta. Herbie was a local who grew up in the town. He was a member of the Salvation Army and in his spare time he established a brass band. He did a fine job teaching local musicians with some talent, and lots of youngsters with no talent at all, to play several types of musical instruments. They all purchased their own instruments and practised regularly until they were accomplished enough to put on a good show.

To raise some money and gain publicity for the band and for Beechworth itself, the band decided that they would pull a rickshaw from Beechworth to Melbourne where they were scheduled to perform at the Royal Melbourne Show. First they needed permission for the journey down the Hume Highway so application was made to Police Headquarters in Melbourne, which the organisers assumed would be a routine matter. However permission was refused, not on the expected grounds that it would cause a traffic hazard as they walked down the highway, but on a different basis altogether. Some 'brain' in Police HQ's decided that the rickshaw was a vehicle so it had to travel on the left hand side of the road, whereas those pulling it were pedestrians so they had to walk on the right hand side. Only a real R.A. (red-arse) from constantly sitting on an office chair, could come up with a solution like that.

In country centres in those days the Police had to gather annual agricultural statistics from farms. The forms had to be taken out to all the farmers, then collected and returned to the Bureau of Statistics in Melbourne. They had to detail all acreage, stock on hand, and produce. A dear lady called Ethel, who was about 90, had a few acres outside town. Despite having no produce or stock, she still had to fill in the forms. She listed 27 black and brown cats and five bearing litter, 22 non-producing.

One night, Herbie Crossman came over to the residence at about 11 pm to tell me that he had received a phone call from Albury Police to warn us that a gang of about twenty motor-cyclists were on their way to wreck the town. He was really worried and wanted to call in reinforcements from Wangaratta and Myrtleford, 'There's only the two of us here, we won't be able to stop them.' I said, 'Well, we'll just wait and see what happens Herb.'

As we headed down to the main intersection in town, I noticed a loaded semi-trailer leaving for Wangaratta. I asked the driver if he wouldn't mind being delayed for a while. I directed him to turn his semi around, park in the middle of Ford Street, the main thoroughfare, and put his headlights on when he saw the motor-cycle gang approaching. We went on ahead about 100 yards and waited outside the Town Hall where we stopped the bikies. Their leader said, 'It would be a good idea for you to make yourself scarce.' When I asked why, he replied, 'Well we're going to wreck this town and you might get in the way.' 'You know, that might not be a very good idea,' I said. His yelled to his mates, 'Hey guys, this cop doesn't think wrecking the town's a good idea.' He asked me why I didn't think they should proceed.

'Well, you see that semi revving up with its' lights on up ahead. He's a bloody awful driver, he just hates motor-bikes and he runs right over them every time he sees them. He'll even drive on the footpath to get one. I'll try to stop him but he's a very nasty type.' Without another word the leader and his entire gang wheeled their bikes around and headed back to Albury.

Reg's wife Maria formed an extraordinary dance troupe in Beechworth in the early 60s called the Beechworth Follies. As a young girl I thought her dancing girls were the most glamorous creatures I had ever seen, and dreamed of becoming a dancer and running away to Paris to join the 'Can Can' girls at the Moulin Rouge. When money was scarce the costumes were sometimes made from crepe paper. The troupe ended up with engagements in Albury, Melbourne, and even a nightclub in Sydney. They danced to packed houses for four years, and produced some wonderful musicals. Apart from the 'Can Can', they danced the 'Charleston', 'Samba', 'Bob-Cat', and the 'Shimmy'.

When Maria first arrived from Alexandria in Egypt to marry Reg in 1944, her father-in-law Frederick had been so struck by her natural musical talent that he bought her a piano and paid for piano lessons for three years. But she was essentially a self-made musical director. Maria told me, 'I listened to the songs, and remembered them, it was that simple. That's the way I worked out the steps. We had a lot of fun.'

Old-time Cabaret acts were performed in various groups over the years with Joan Anderson, Anne Pancur, Jeanette Weeding, Judy Zwar,

Jeanine Methven, Maree Shennan, Brenda Lawton, Marta Meizes, Magda Rosengren, Margaret Wells, Margaret Blair, Marianna Hofstetter, Margaret Baltus, Yvonne Burridge, Judy Barrett, Andrea Ferguson, Bea McGuffie, Merilyn McIntosh, June Methven, Nan Jaboor, Judy Beatson.

Anne Pancur married Maria's brother Evan and was a star attraction with her belly dancing in a harem scene.

The costumes were designed and made by Maria with help from renowned seamstress June Powell, Joan Anderson, Eileen McIntosh and Sheila Parkinson. Ian McGuffie was the sound recorder and lighting expert, and a radio personality from 3NE Wangaratta compered the shows. Maria also briefly worked as a singer for the ABC in Albury, and sang on Sunday afternoons, live to air. 'I was paid five guineas a week.' Maria is also an exquisite cook and she was the first person I had ever seen cooking with olive oil.

JIM KENNEDY [*family friend*]: Allan was a Legatee from the mid 60s for ten years, and then went on the reserve. I was a Corporal in the Infantry and had been captured by the Japanese in Singapore and was a POW for three and a half years. I was in F Force and worked on the Burma railway for nine months. We walked 200 kilometres from Ban Pong in Thailand to the Burmese border. Allan and I understood each other because of our POW experiences. He was a very generous man, but he didn't like people to think that he was soft. Some POWs feel stigmatised because of their experiences, but Allan and I thought we were just doing our job. However there's no doubt about it, someone was looking after us over there. I went with him to POW reunions at Numurkah (the Goulburn Valley POW Association) and Melbourne on several occasions.

It was Jim Kennedy who first involved Dad in Legacy. The Deverys were one of Dad's Legacy families. I remember one incident related to the Devery family in which Dad was very pro-active. Their son Damien was very young at the time and attended the local convent. One of the nuns once gave Damien a real thrashing and he was very traumatised. Dad went up to the convent and saw the nun in question and allegedly said, 'If you ever hit this boy again, I will do to you what you have done to him.' Problem solved.

MRS PAT DEVERY: I had five children Judy, Anne, Rosemary, Bernadette and Damien. Life was tough for war widows, which is where Legacy came in. Last Easter as we sat at the table, the conversation was about the Gees'. We all feel not only a deep gratitude to Kath and Allan but real love for them. Allan was the greatest Legatee of all. He helped us through very difficult times. Kath worked so hard and endured uncomplainingly at great personal cost all Allan's efforts for other people. She was a real angel and we remember her lovely appearance, her soft glowing skin and her gentle ways. People pass through our lives, some are forgotten and some like the Gee family will always be with us.

JUDY (DEVERY) SNELL: I remember Allan wanted to create a bird sanctuary near the creek, 'Birds shouldn't be caged,' he told us. He took Damien to father/son nights at Cubs, and I remember him concreting our driveway one bitterly cold Beechworth day. He taught Mum to drive her EJ Holden around the paddocks at Wooragee, and organised Pat's house to be painted by the prisoners from the gaol.

He talked to us about the War. 'We all have to do our best to make sure those things never happen again.' He was a peace-maker. They raised our standard of living, but much more than that, together with Mum they instilled self-worth. Allan once said, 'I'm so proud of you kids.' I must have been about 30 at the time. It was one of the nicest things I've ever had said to me. Their influence is always present and they remain in our hearts.

⁓

BRUCE GEE [*my brother*]: Dad believed in the RSL but at times had mixed feelings about the local membership. He used to say that the less fighting some of its' members had done the more they seemed to know about the War. He referred to some of the RSL guys as Camp Street (Beechworth) Commandoes. He was amused by one bloke who was forever talking about how many Japs he had killed from the safety of

Australia's shores. Dad tried to go with Mum to as many *HMAS Perth* reunions as he could.

I recall Dad listening to 'Pig Iron Bob' Menzies on the radio once, a man he absolutely loathed. Dad told me how shocked he had been when he saw the appalling conditions of the average working people in Britain when he spent several months in England for the commissioning of *Perth* at Portsmouth. He couldn't believe how poorly the British Navy treated their naval ratings. In fact Dad said some of them were actually hungry. He said it was pathetic, as there was always tons of food on *Perth*. 'We were treated like princes.' In fact in general he thought the average Briton was living about as well as people in the Dark Ages.

Being brought up in tough circumstances himself, he had a lot of empathy for ordinary working people and the way they lived. It also shows that he was pretty radicalised at that time, even though he was only about 19 years old.

Dad didn't join the Labor party until the late 1960s or early 1970s. I remember he and I spent most of the 60s arguing about the rights and wrongs of Australia's involvement in the Vietnam war. His initial view was, 'We have to support our boys.' Before he finally became disillusioned like most people, we had had some tremendous rows. I had been to lots of demonstrations in Melbourne and Hobart, even before the Moratoriums, and Dad was furious.

Mum and Dad made no secret of the fact that they were dedicated Labor supporters. Some of the people in the district despised them for their political views, but they were undeterred. They avidly read the newspapers, and were always glued to the radio, and then the television news programs.

Dad's brother Lew was mixed up in the Australian Labor Party from his early days of being a staunch unionist, and once stood unsuccessfully for a seat in the Victorian Upper House. The funniest thing I ever saw with Lew was when Frank Wilkes was the Leader of the Labor Opposition. Wilkes cut a Les Patterson type figure and had a glamorous research assistant at his side. It was all a bit flash for Wodonga. Wilkes made a pathetic speech, then Lew stood up and asked him a scorching question about abortion. Wilkes hedged and Lew floored him with an absolutely brilliant speech. Wilkes wilted. Lew was one of those guys who could have gone anywhere if his circumstances had been different. He was a very talented speaker, and well known and respected in the Labor party, Australia wide.

Lew was an enormously hard worker. He worked six days a week his entire life, and his wife Clara worked hard too. Apart from his work as a psychiatric nurse 'Up Top', at the Mental Hospital he had a bit of a farm at Silver Creek, and kept ferrets for rabbiting. They were devoted to their only daughter Lynette. Clara had arrived in Australia in 1938 from England as a child and was sent to Fairbridge Farm School at Molong, NSW. Her mother had died giving birth to her. Clara became a Life Governor of the Royal Childrens Hospital for fund-raising, and was a 'Brownie' leader for many years in Beechworth. She died in 1990.

ALLAN BREWER [*Auntie Miriam and Uncle Bert's son*]: One night in the early 1980s Lew had a turn. Peter Goonan a good friend of his was with him when it happened, and said, 'I'd better get the ambulance.' Lew replied, 'No, bugger the ambulance go and get another bottle of beer. If I'm going to go. I want to go out happy.'

Extract of Obituary for Lew Gee

Beechworth has lost a great townsman, and working people have lost a friend and champion in the late Lew Gee. Lew and his wife Clara, never wavered in their support for the unions and the ALP, and Lew was actively involved in ALP fund-raising at the time of his death, June 6, 1986. He was 61.

Born in Wangaratta in 1924, Lew's family moved to Beechworth the following year. Lew began work at the Mayday Hills Hospital in 1951, and became a charge nurse in 1972 just two years before he retired due to ill health.

In all his years as a nurse and a member of the Hospital Employee's Federation No.2 Lew was known for his compassion in carrying out his duties, his fair-mindedness in dispute situations and his strong support for fellow unionists. A whole generation of shop stewards and HEF2 officials at Beechworth owe their industrial education to Lew Gee, who was always consulted, even in retirement, as the elder statesmen of Beechworth unionists.

Kath and Allan Gee's wedding
Albury, September 7, 1946

Kath and Allan Gee and their dogs
in Frankston, 1946

Allan Gee at
Frankston Pier
with son Bruce

The Brewer sisters and friends

Above: Kath Gee with son Bruce, and sisters.
L-R: Mary Brewer, Gwen Ross and Marge Schubert

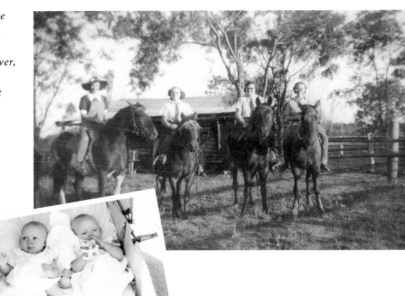

Margaret and Christine Gee at Yackandandah, 1954

Nape and Vera Gee with sons Allan and young Robert

Christine and Margaret with Grandfather Gee at Wooragee

Kath and Allan Gee and twins at 'Lyndale' with Ralph Tremonti and sons

Beechworth Shire Council, 1973 Back row, L-R: H.H.Warner, H.C. Lucas, L.W. Powell, L. Leentjes, R.C. Sewell, T.J. Carroll.Front row: G. Gray (Shire Secretary), R.P. O'Connor, D. Nankervis, D. McKenzie-McHarg, J.J. McCaulay, H.R. Sinclair, D. Pope (Shire Engineer)

Beechworth in the Autumn (Photo: Vivienne Harvey)

Former Beechworth Policeman Reg Dixon and his wife Maria at home on the Central Coast, 2000

Lynette Gee with Grandfather on her wedding day, 1970

Right: Beechworth Police Station and Court House (Photo: Vivienne Harvey)

Lew Gee with Grandfather Gee, Bega, mid 1960s

The Gee twins and Tootsie at 'Lyndale', Wooragee

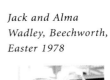

Jack and Alma
Wadley, Beechworth,
Easter 1978

Meryl Brewer's wedding, December 9, 1959.
L-R: Bram and Lillian Gee, Carmel and
Len Warwick, Vera and Napier Gee, Kath
and Allan Gee, Miriam and Bert Brewer,
Clara and Lew Gee

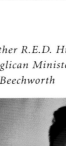

Father R.E.D. Hull,
Anglican Minister
at Beechworth

Beechworth Music Group. L-R: Robert
Collins, Arnie Leitch, Margaret and
Christine Gee practicing at hall, Mayday
Hills Hospital

Bram, Clara and Lew Gee at Lynette
Gee's wedding, September 1970

Above: Lew and Allan Gee with their sisters
Miriam Brewer and Carmel Warwick

Left: Alan French who lived in Wooragee for 78 years. (Descendant of first owners of 'Lyndale'). Below: Young Alan French skinning rabbits with his father's cousin, William John French

Allan Gee, Legatee with Judy Devery, Beechworth, April 1970

Lew Gee rabbiting with a family friend

Allan Gee, outside 'Lyndale', Wooragee

George White's Tiger Moth at Wooragee

Above: Miriam and Bert Brewer's eldest son Allan Brewer – 'I am living every mountain cattleman's dream'

Bert and Mary Brewer with their sister Marge Schubert, Wodonga, 2000

Pop Brewer at 'Pinedale'

Clara May Brewer at her 80th birthday party, Albury

Right: Michael and Dot McGuinness

Far right: Peg and Bill McGuinness, with home-brew, at Michael's 21st birthday party in 1965, Wooragee

Kath (Gee) and her second husband Jack Davies, Melbourne, 1993

Margaret Gee during Silver Creek snow-storm, May 2000

The balance of the acreage at 'Lyndale' for sale, 1994

Uncle Nape's son, Allan Gee

Bruce, Christine and Margaret Gee in Ford Street, Beechworth, November 1999, for their mother's funeral

For almost forty years, Lew was an active enthusiastic member of the ALP. He held office in the Beechworth branch, usually as secretary; he attended state conferences representing Indi for many years, and he stood for Parliament, polling well in his home town, despite North Eastern Province being traditionally conservative. Lew was an example for younger members to emulate and his advice, eagerly sought, was always both principled and practical.

Instrumental in the establishment of the Beechworth and Ovens Credit Union Lew believed that workers should control their own financial future, and he ensured that the then Federal Treasurer Frank Crean, came to Beechworth to open the Credit Union. The State Government recognised Lew's talents and commitment to the welfare of others, by appointing him as an official visitor at Mayday Hills Hospital. He was pleased with the appointment and set about his duties with customary gusto.

LINDSAY RANKIN HEF2 AND JEAN MEMERY, BEECHWORTH ALP BRANCH

I think one of the high points of Mum and Dad's lives was going to Albury in the late 1960s to see Gough and Margaret Whitlam. It was held at the Travelodge Motel, then the smartest venue in town. Inside there was a frenzy of excitement as everyone pressed towards the Whitlams for a handshake and a few salutary words. I remember Dad beaming at Gough and saying, 'Welcome to Albury Comrade.' When Malcolm Fraser's Opposition blocked supply in 1975 and Gough was unceremoniously removed from office the atmosphere in our house was as if there had been a death in the family. Mum and Dad were not your average Joe country cockies, they were highly politicised. One of Mum's jobs was to read sections of the Melbourne Age to Dad so he knew what the editorials were saying. If she was too busy he'd pore over the paper with a thick magnifying glass given to him by The Royal Victorian Institute for the Blind, which had also supplied him with thousands of talking books over the years. Mum was also a fervent, unapologetic Labor supporter. Our mealtimes were frequently the scene of vigorous and often heated discussions about politics. Locals invited to dinner would sometimes be sitting at the table eating their shepherd's pie wondering what they'd struck with all of us holding forth about some contentious issue.

A Beechworth guy, Paul Navarre was killed in Vietnam, and another local Michael Sinclair was injured in a land mine explosion, which I think shook up the town and made them question what Australia was doing being involved in such a 'dirty war'. Michael and Dad saw a bit of each other. Michael was quite traumatised from his service in Vietnam. He told me, 'I returned to Vietnam for a visit. It was really hard to go back, but it was very healing.' About 18 Beechworth guys served in Vietnam including Walter Methven, who now lives at Bill McGuinness' former place at Wooragee, and Kevin Parkinson. I was threatened with suspension from Beechworth High School in 1970, when I and a Catholic boy I was besotted with called Andrew McDonald, left the school grounds to print an anti-Vietnam leaflet. There was a bit of a stink about it, but Dad went up to the school and smoothed things over with the headmaster, a likeable man called Warren Telfer. I think Dad was secretly proud that my political conscience was stirring.

REG DIXON: The Rector at the local Church of England was Father Robert Hull, a brilliant man and a credit to his profession and the church he so ably represented. He could turn his hand to anything. When Maria decided one year to train some local girls for a floor show at what turned out to be an annual Cabaret Ball on Boxing Day, Bobby made and painted the most spectacular stage back-drops. That was no easy task as the Civic Hall had a broad stage and a high ceiling. The back-drops of the period depicted in the dances were absolute masterpieces. Bobby also loved a beer and he excelled at darts and pool. He always cleaned up at Dooley Wallace's Hibernian Hotel.

A Police motor-cyclist once pulled Bobby over for slightly exceeding the speed limit near Wangaratta. It was a highly technical offence and one which called for a reprimand. Despite hearing his identification, explanation and plea that it was surely a minor infringement, the patrolman insisted on booking the good Father. After the usual paper work had been completed, Bobby asked him, 'Are you married Constable?'. The young officer curtly replied, 'What's that got to do with you?'. 'Well, have you a mother and father?' Bobby persisted. 'Yes, I have, but I don't see what that's got to do with you either.' 'Not much

I suppose' answered Bobby, 'But I just wanted to invite you to bring them up to Beechworth sometime and I'll marry them.' Bobby told me later that the patrolman didn't seem to appreciate the joke at all.

BRUCE GEE: Father Hull, known as Bobby, or Red because his initials were R.E.D., arrived at the Anglican Church in Beechworth in the late 1950s with his wife Winnie and their five children Cordelia, Greg, Deborah, Crispin, Damian and Simon. They were a breath of fresh air for Beechworth. He revitalised the Anglican Parish in every sense. He was highly educated, and they were cultured people. They organised Shakespearean plays, and musical events. Winnie was a brilliant teacher and devoted to Red. They worked tirelessly for the church community.

Red was a true intellectual, a stunning orator and actor, and Beechworth had never seen anything like him, before or since. There is a Japanese saying that the nail that is sticking up will be hammered flat. In my opinion Beechworth to a certain extent wore down Father Hull. He arrived in the town as a real activist but he went away somewhat disillusioned.

CRISPIN HULL: Dad arrived in Australia from England in April 1959 from Chichester. Before he joined the ministry he had worked in the West End theatre district of London, including at the Old Vic doing make-up and other jobs for productions including *The Ghost Train*, *Charlie's Aunt*, and some Shakespearean plays. He loved Shakespeare and was always rattling it off in the Rectory.

My parents were at Beechworth for almost 20 years before semi-retiring to Yackandandah in 1977 for five years. His main work in Beechworth was as chaplain to the Beechworth Training Prison and Mental Hospital. I think his attitude was that you had to make the best of Beechworth, although he probably felt a bit trapped. My mother taught science at Scots School in Albury.

Dad was at this church in the 60s and there was really nowhere else for him to go. His work at the gaol and the Mental Hospital, where he was more of a social worker than a minister, sustained him. Dad told me about a funny incident when he was once attending an Anglican Synod at Yarrawonga. He arrived early at the Rectory and the local

Minister's eight year old son greeted him at the door and said his father was over at the church. Dad was invited in and the boy asked him if he would like a drink. Dad accepted the offer and was brought a pint glass of water. Dad took a sip, and the boy looked at him in complete puzzlement, so Dad said, 'Is anything wrong?' The little boy replied, 'My father said you drink like a fish.' I think he half-expected my father to have scales and fins. They moved to Chiltern where Dad died in 1985 at the age of 67. My mother is now in an aged care home in Yarrawonga.

As a young girl whenever I knocked on the door of the Anglican Rectory I found myself confronted with the long grey snout and yellow eyes of the Hull's imposing deer hound. Christine and I were tutored by Father Hull before being confirmed in Wangaratta by the Anglican Bishop. Much to my mother's chagrin I insisted on wearing a red vyella dress I had made myself, although it was *de rigueur* to wear white. Dad had served on the church vestry for a number of years, but Mum was the one who bundled us into the car on Sunday mornings for church, but not before the joint of lamb and spuds were popped into the oven of the wood stove. Bruce served briefly as an accolyte at the church. Sometimes at Christmas Christine and I played carols in the church on our clarinets, accompanied by Viv Payne.

A highlight of the year for us would be the annual Anglican fete which was preceded by a frenzy of cake and confectionary cooking — toffee apples, chocolate crackles, merengues — and much sawing and hammering as various stalls were erected. It was like an old English fair replete with a ghost train ride, fairy floss, wood chopping events, old wares, pet's parade, pony rides and even a fortune teller.

BRUCE GEE: Beechworth was very different to most country towns because of the high level of unionisation which was partly due to Lew's activities, especially at the Mental Hospital. Beechworth was one country town which was not dominated by the squatters, 'the big hats', and the squires, despite being comparatively wealthy. People were very well paid, and there was lots of shift work. Many people had two jobs or there were two wage earners in the family, so there was plenty of cash around.

Dad was heavily involved with the Beechworth Training Prison through the Guide Dogs For The Blind training scheme which he helped instigate. The prisoners were also making toys for Legacy, and fixing up old bikes for disadvantaged kids. Dad became a great friend of the Governor of the prison, Jack Davies.

Jack was very involved with prison reform, and was a modern criminologist. He was previously Deputy Governor of Pentridge Prison, that imposing blue-stone monument to incarceration in Melbourne. His other claim to fame was as the officer in charge of the hanging party at Ronald Ryan's execution. He was in the prison service from the late 1940s, and served for about 40 years. He died of a heart attack in 1993, less than six months after marrying Mum.

Dad befriended one particular prison inmate, one of the Melbourne Security Service robbers who with his accomplices had dressed up as cops and got away with the loot. He was caught because one of the witnesses remembered the diamond in his front tooth. When convicted I think they spent many cold winters in the Beechworth Training Prison.

MG: Jack used to let some of 'the boys' out on day leave to work at our farm. Some were more enthusiastic than others. They mainly helped with fencing or doing the rabbits. We always invited them home for lunch, which had its moments. We'd sit with Jack and the prisoners eating our silverside and carrots and wondering 'what they did'. They seemed delighted to escape the confines of the prison for a day out.

From time to prisoners escaped from the gaol and one of the first places they seemed to turn up was in our hay barn. I vividly remember one bitterly cold winter's night hearing a noise in the front garden around midnight. I looked out and saw a man peeing on the roses, a ghostly figure across the white carpet of frost. I rushed into my parent's bedroom, woke them and Dad sprang into action. He kept a loaded rifle under the bed and charged out the front door in his underpants. He pointed the gun at the man and said, 'Don't try to run or I'll shoot you.' I think the man, who turned out to be the escapee, received more of a fright than we did. The cops came down and collected the shivering prisoner but probably failed to tell him Dad was blind. Before the prisoner was put in the van Dad cooked him bacon and eggs and gave him a packet of cigarettes.

BRUCE GEE: Jack spent a lot of time at our place and became great friends with Mum and Dad. Somebody dobbed Jack in to the Department about prisoners working on our farm. There was high drama about it. Although it blew over, it nearly cost Jack his job. However the biggest fracas was connected with the annual Labor Party fund-raising barbecue which Dad held alongside the creek on our property. There was always gambling of course but no cop in his right mind would think of busting a Labor fund-raiser, not until 1968 anyway.

Around two hundred people lined up at Dad's fantastic barbecue for chops, sausages and hamburgers. They had a lovely time under the gum-trees. There was lots of grog, ice-creams and games for the kids. Dad spent months planning it, building toilets and praying for a sunny day. He also organised some adult gambling games, including pontoon and Crown and Anchor, an old favourite from his Navy days. We always thought that Jack was set up this particular year. A local detective from Wangaratta must have been tipped off that prison labour was on loan for the picnic. The coppers were up on the main Beechworth road with a telephoto camera, although not a very good one because all the shots they took were blurred. Putting it mildly there was a hell of a stink.

The main problem was that Dad was selling grog and had gambling games without a license, with prison labour to boot. Dad had never been that great under pressure, and after the detectives arrived unannounced to interview him, he rang me terribly worried that he might end up in gaol. I said, 'I hope you didn't say anything to the detectives.' He replied, 'No, I told them nothing.' I could hear Mum calling out something from the kitchen. The next day they went to see Joe Murphy, our lawyer in Wodonga. According to Mum, Joe asked Dad exactly what he had said. Dad blurted out that he had 'spilled his guts' and admitted everything. Joe replied, 'Well, that's a fucking great start.' It is very funny in hindsight. Mum said Dad looked like a kid who had been caught stealing apples.

Dad was eventually charged with illegal gambling and the sale of grog without a permit, and the trial was held in Beechworth. He was absolutely beside himself, and in a dreadful state on the day. He hadn't slept for a week, but Mum was her usual stoic self. The Magistrate's courtroom was packed with gawping locals. The prosecution blathered on with all the evidence, and everyone was lined up to give their testimonies. It was bigger than Ben Hur.

Joe was pretty cool and rose to his feet. He had everything planned to the minute and was almost sadistic in his approach to the beak. 'I would like to draw Your Worship's attention to the fact that under Section xxx of the Act that it is not an offence to permit offences such as these to occur. One has to actually participate in the said offences.' Dad of course was not personally selling grog or gambling, he was only guilty of allowing it to happen. The Magistrate agreed and the case was dismissed. The souffle sank. The cops walked out shaking their heads in disbelief, and Dad nearly passed out with relief. Mum liked a brandy and dry each evening and I think she mixed an extra strong one that night.

REG DIXON: Fred Warden lived on a farm at Wooragee and often came into Beechworth where we'd share a few ales, usually at the Hibernian Hotel or my place when he joined in games of solo. He was a very quiet type. Fred never uttered a word of criticism, abuse or a swear-word of any description. Quite often we'd go to Melbourne for a football game where we enjoyed the hospitality and company of my old friend Alf Foley, then the head of the VFL Tribunal and the Chief Magistrate of Victoria. Fred was a member of the Melbourne Cricket Club but I had to rely on the good graces of Alf to get me into the Members' Stand.

On one occasion we were invited into a pre-match dinner in the Holy of Holies, the Members' Dining room. Alf as Chairman welcomed us and remarked that we had come all the way from Beechworth. Called on to reply to his welcome I thanked him and the Committee for their hospitality and told them that we had left Beechworth early that morning. 'Fred Warden is one of nature's gentlemen. He picked me up in his car, let me drive all the way down, paid for all the petrol and on the way he bought me a big breakfast. He has paid for all the beer we've had since we arrived. Furthermore I can drink as much as I like, because he said he is going to drive us home.' Fred, who had obviously nodded off, suddenly woke up, leapt to his feet and shouted, 'Pig's fucking arse he is.' This brought the house down. Over a few more beers after the game, one of the old Members came up to tell me he'd enjoyed Fred's reaction more than the football game.

Whenever possible, I always had a policeman on late duty on Saturday nights, and I usually made it a practice not to go out myself in case I was needed in an emergency. However one Saturday night Mark Sewell, the son of Ronald Sewell, Secretary of the Hospital, and a schoolmate of our number three son, Greg, turned 21. We were invited to a party at Corowa on the NSW side. A great night was had by all and we returned slightly the worse for wear after midnight.

I had just got into bed when Herbie Crossman came over to the house in a very nervous state. 'You'd better come out boss, there's a 'flopping' peanut down the road shooting at motorists.' Although I was not critical of Herbie's style of living, never drinking, smoking, gambling or swearing, I sometimes thought he would have benefited from a few choice words to fill out his vocabulary. 'What's he using Herb?' Herb replied, 'A flopping .22 rifle, and he's fired at several motorists.'

I accompanied him in the police car along the highway towards Wooragee. On the way I asked him if he knew who the rifleman was. He thought it was a local youth, the son of a hard worker and from one of the most respected local families. We were stopped by two other motorists who complained that they had been accosted and fired at as they drove past. As we neared the youth I told Herb to drive up to him and I'd shine the search light in his eyes. 'No flopping fear, boss, he'll flopping well shoot us.' I said, 'We only die once Herb. Give it a go.'

After a bit more persuasion Herb drove alongside the youth and I shone the light in his eyes. He levelled the rifle straight at Herbie and pulled the trigger. The gun went click but there was no explosion. I thought we were very lucky because I was sitting alongside Herb in the front seat and he probably would have cleaned up the pair of us.

Herbert was understandably a bundle of nerves by this time but I told him to keep behind the youth, and I'd slip out the side door and tackle him. 'No flopping fear boss, I'm not going anywhere near him again.' 'You don't have to Herb', I said. 'Just keep behind him and I'll give it a try from the back.' Quietly I slipped out the door, nipped behind the car, managed to bring the guy down with a flying tackle from behind, and grabbed hold of the rifle. I loaded him into the back seat and escorted him back to the Police Station.

The rifle which I thought was empty had a bullet jammed in the breech. Herbie was a wreck. I was pretty rattled myself. 'What was the cause of that little demonstration?' I asked the gunman. 'I had some trouble at home and guess I just went berserk,' he said. 'Do you realise that if that bullet hadn't jammed you'd have shot Herb Crossman in the head?' He replied, 'I'd made up my mind to shoot someone tonight. It didn't matter who it was.'

The real disaster came soon after. Herbie never did another day of police duty. He resigned on the spot telling me, 'I never joined this flopping job to get flopping shot.' It was a pity as Herbie was a good policeman, with a great store of local public knowledge. I was sorry to see him leave the flopping job.

POS SHENNAN [*Beechworth resident*]: I worked as a nurse at the Mental Hospital before I married in 1942. There were a thousand patients when I was there. Some of the patients in the refractory ward used to fight. They didn't have the range of psychiatric drugs then that are used today. All they had to give them was milk of magnesia and epsom salts. Sometimes late at night you could hear them screaming out, especially when there was a full moon.

REG DIXON: Much of our work involved the Mayday Hills Mental Hospital. Apart from all deaths in the Hospital which were the subject of Coronial Inquests we were kept busy with frequent escapes, or what were classed as such. It was really simply a matter of the patients walking off the unguarded grounds. Most patients were harmless and were usually soon picked up somewhere along the highway.

One old lady used to go missing from her ward every week or 10 days. She always came to the Police Station after wandering around the town shops, and would insist on giving me £2. She said it was the booking fee for the St Kilda Town Hall for her engagement party. I'd make out that I was ringing the St Kilda Town Hall and have to return her money as the hall was booked 12 months ahead. She always promised to come back again to make another booking.

~

MG: There was a Mental Hospital patient who came to church whom our family befriended. His surname was Rembriak. We called him Rembrandt because he was a gifted landscape and portrait painter. Dad sometimes invited him for Sunday dinner — lunch — after church, and made Rembrandt feel very much at home. We'd all sit around in the lounge room and natter with him about art.

REG DIXON: The Police were warned never to try to pick up a particular young female patient called Edith who was allegedly extremely violent. She escaped repeatedly, and every time it took at least four nurses to transport her back to the Hospital.

I was returning in the Police car alone one day from Wangaratta when I saw Edith walking down the centre of the highway near Tarrawingie. I pulled over and called her to the car, 'Hey Edith where are you going?' She replied, 'Don't think I'm going back to that fucking Mental Hospital, those female fucking nursing sluts are real shits.' I said, 'Edith, just calm down. I'm going to call at Everton Hotel on the way. Hop in, I'll buy you a beer then we'll go back to Beechworth. How about that?' 'No, Sarge I'm not going back to that fucking hole, not ever.' 'Come on Edith, it's hot as hell, a beer will do you the world of good, hurry up hop in.' 'Oh alright Sergeant, as long as I don't have to put up with those fucking nurses.' She got in the front seat of the car. We had one glass of beer at Everton Hotel then drove back to the Mental Hospital without any trouble at all. I think Edith just wanted a break from the monotony of daily life in the hospital.

Reg Dixon: There was another real menace who regularly threatened women and children in town. Reports had it that Jake had been ill-treated by some out-of-town police and left outside the local hospital with serious injuries. Severe public condemnation was levelled at police and disciplinary action followed for those responsible. We received numerous complaints that he was a dangerous threat, wandering about the town area wearing a black coat, armed with a seven foot long pitch-fork and guarded by a pack of vicious dogs. I spoke to Herb Crossman about him and was told that the police were reluctant to touch him after the previous public outcry.

One day he terrorised some local school girls in the playground of the park on their way home from school. He threatened them with his pitch-fork and tried to set his dogs on them. I said, 'This is it Herbie, we'll grab him this time and put him before the Court.' 'It's a waste of flopping time,' Herbie replied, 'I tell you, the flopping Court will never back us up.'

We came upon Jake walking along the Myrtleford Road surrounded by his pack of dogs. I hopped out of the car and walked up behind him. He pointed his pitch-fork at me, as he yelled to his dogs, 'Get him, get him!' Before they had a chance to lunge at me I grabbed the handle of his pitch-fork and got him in a headlock. We loaded him into the car and drove to the Police Station without further resistance.

The local JP's were obviously ill at ease and reluctant to convict, so I asked for him to be remanded in custody to a later date. The case was heard before Magistrate 'Jockey' Jack Bell, who remanded him for psychiatric examination. He was later committed to a mental institution out of Beechworth.

Harmless Henry, a regular escapee from the Mental Hospital, would always make his way to El Dorado near Wangaratta, where he'd hole up somewhere in the old mine for four or five days. Needless to say he would become extremely dirty and smelly. Bringing him back in the Police car could be a very unpleasant experience. Constable Bruce, 'The Atom', Grant was a thoroughly likeable man but he was new on the job.

We'd had plenty of experience with Henry in the past, but Bruce didn't know what to expect.

A call came through that Henry had escaped again and sure enough after five days he was reported to be wandering down the back road out of El Dorado. 'Come on Atom, you'd better take your own car because he always takes off across the paddocks whenever he sees a Police vehicle.' This decision suited Bruce because he got a mileage allowance if he used his own car in an emergency, and this was a real one. 'What do you want that hospital mask for Sergeant?' Bruce asked me. 'I always carry it for this patient so I can make out I'm a doctor from the hospital. It keeps him quiet.'

We picked up Henry a few miles from El Dorado. He seemed glad to get into the back seat of Bruce's car. Bruce had a very weak stomach which reacted violently whenever anything out of the ordinary upset him. No more than 30 seconds later Bruce started, 'Byrrrrh-byrrrh.' He kept it up all the way back to the Hospital. 'I'll never get the stink out of my car. You bastard, I'll bloody die, you bloody bastard.' 'Don't let it worry you Bruce, 'It's not that bad, I can't smell a thing,' I said through the hospital mask. Later I remarked, 'Bloody hell Bruce, I didn't think anyone could be so sick without dying.' Days later the Atom was still complaining that he couldn't get the smell out of his car. I said, 'Think of that extra mileage you'll get in your pay packet in a few weeks time.' 'It's cost me more than that for deodorant,' he grizzled.

BRUCE GEE: We never went up to the Mental Hospital, previously known as the Asylum, then gentrified to Mayday Hills Hospital, not for personal reasons anyway. It seemed that everyone at school had a parent, cousin, or brother working there. It was like having a factory at the top of the hill. There was one great story that did the rounds. The hospital switchboard was manned 24 hours a day. Late one night the superintendent rang and couldn't raise anyone. He left his house, an old mansion on the grounds, and walked across to the office. The story goes that he found the male nightshift switchboard operator in bed with two of the female patients. Some people in Beechworth thought it was very unsporting that he got the sack.

George White was a real character. He was a cop in Albury, and a very experienced ex-RAAF bomber pilot. The first time I flew with George he stood me in the hopper of a super-phosphate plane with my head sticking out. The super pilots came to the farm during the summer. It was fantastic watching them fly over and land on the strip in their old Tiger Moths. Another time I went up with George and he dropped into the Beechworth gorge from 3,000 feet down to about 60 feet in a flash. I swear I left claw marks on the seat frame, as I could hardly stay in the seat. It was terrifying, and may explain my middle-aged flying phobia.

Although George did *occasionally* fly when he'd been drinking, he was generally very safety conscious. His only serious accident was not his fault. He had sold his hot pink Tiger Moth and the buyer asked George if they could go up for a spin. The punter was in the back seat, which is where the full controls are located and George was in the front. They were flying over Leneva when the engine cut out. George could do little else but hang on while the plane plummeted to the ground. George broke his back and the new owner of what was now a tangle of wood and fabric also survived for his trouble.

Sometimes when George landed at our place for a long Sunday lunch, he'd forget what time it was. Suddenly he'd notice the sun sinking towards the horizon so I'd drive him flat out across the paddocks to the strip so he could fly back to Albury before dark. He'd fire up the plane, swoop over the house to say goodbye, and disappear into the clouds.

I will never forget my first aeroplane flight with the friend Dad affectionately described as 'that mad bastard George White.' I was 13 years old and it was unforgettably wonderful. It's the first and only flight in my life when I had a true sense of flying like a bird. George swooped and dived, and had me squealing with delight. I once flew from our property to Albury with him and being the dare-devil he was he flew low over a herd of cattle and chased some kangaroos up a gully. I adored George White and his fabulous flying machine.

George took Dad for a spin once and really put the plane through its paces, including the odd acrobatic stunt. Dad wasn't strapped in properly and came close to popping out of the plane. When the plane landed Dad was green and said, in extremely colourful language, that he was never going up in another plane. In fact he said, 'It was more frightening than being with the Japs'.

JOHN LeCOUTEUR [*family friend*]: Jerry Mueller, the local sanitary contractor, often talked about flying. George thought he was pulling everyone's leg, so one day he said he'd take Jerry up in the Tiger Moth and scare the daylights out of him. Little did they realise that Jerry had been a rear-gunner in the Luftwaffe. At the appointed time much to everyone's surprise Jerry turned up in his wartime leather flying helmet. He hopped into the Tiger Moth and George took him up. They loop-the-looped and rolled all over the sky. Jerry was like a kid on the roller-coaster at Luna Park. He reckoned it was great.

BRUCE GEE: George White was a great friend of Reg Dixon. They used to go all over the place together, and sometimes they'd take Dad out for the day in the police car. Their colleague Bruce Grant frequently accompanied them. They'd tear off to Wodonga, or Bright, Corowa, or Wangaratta, do some police business, and of course have a couple of drinks or more, along the way. Reg was a bit of a maniac at times and not averse to having fun.

Dad told us he'd be sitting in the back pissed as a fart, and they'd come up behind people at about 90mph. The poor guy in front would be ambling along half asleep on his way home and the next thing Reg or George would put the siren and the lights on. People nearly ran off the road with fright. George claimed it woke up the sleepers and kept them on the ball. I think most of them were stuck to their seats. Then George and Reg would belt back towards Wooragee at an ungodly speed and put the sirens and lights on again just near McGuinnesses' turn-off. Reg wisely wasn't game to get out of the car. Dad would lurch down the front path past Mum and us kids who would all be standing there looking very judgemental.

Despite this, Dad rarely drank much, and whenever he did Mum wouldn't speak to him for about two days. He couldn't handle beer. He'd stagger through the front door, pick up pace along the passageway, and catapult out the back door to spew on the lawn. He'd return looking pale and shaky, but five minutes later he'd be back on his hands and knees praying to the lawn.

His biggest disaster was at the inaugural Mayday Hills Festival. The main event was a parade and pageant in Ford Street and Dad was one of the notables in an old-time costume complete with bowler hat and moustache. He had taken our horse and dray up to the town for the parade and he was joined by John Maher our family chemist, David McHarg the local solicitor and a keg of beer. Much to the delight of the large crowd by the time the parade reached the main street they were all obviously roaring drunk, appropriately as the event was a celebration of Beechworth's gold-rush boom days when there were 61 pubs. As the day progressed things became worse and worse, and finally ended with Dad making a complete spectacle of himself at the racecourse. Fortunately, he had plenty of good company. Dad didn't show his face in town for weeks. To add to his humiliation he couldn't remember a thing and spent days asking me what he had done. To my eternal discredit I took great delight in progressively embellishing his antics. He finally stopped asking.

REG DIXON: Tobacco growing was the big industry in the area in the early 60's, particularly at Myrtleford where the Italian population was into it in a big way. Growers made a fortune as tobacco prices reached record highs. Local farmers decided to cash in on the boom. Crops were planted on every available acre of land. Jack Ferguson, Tommy Bartel and Bill McGuinness of Wooragee decided to explore this new venture. The quantity and quality of tobacco they turned out was comparable with the best in the other districts. Several of us gave them a hand with cultivating, picking sorting, curing, stacking and baling the crops.

Tommy Bartel, a likeable trier, was without many facilities for the process but with help from Bill McGuinness we got his crop through the kiln, dried and baled ready for the market in Melbourne. Several times when we went down to help Tommy kiln dry the tobacco, we found there was no wood to fire up the kiln, so we went over to Allan Gee's farm for a load of firewood. Tommy Bartel was a champion axeman and had won several championships at the Royal Easter Show in Sydney, yet he didn't have a cord of cut wood in the place.

Allan, Kath, Maria and I put in hundreds of hours helping out. Once the tobacco leaves were picked and tied in hands they were hung in the kiln on racks to dry. Back we'd go a few nights later to pull it all out and stack it ready for sorting. Naturally Tommy Bartel didn't have a suitable shed either, so he stored it in the lounge-dining room of his little old house at Wooragee. We were at the window level when Tommy asked if he should take the curtains down before the tobacco reached any higher. 'Don't do that Tommy, it adds a bit of tone to the joint,' Allan told him.

By the time we got it to market, the sales in Melbourne were proving to be a disaster. Obviously supply had exceeded demand and prices, even for the established growers, had fallen sharply. There was also a cartel at Myrtleford who were obviously determined not to let outsiders into the market. Bill McGuinness went up to a group of the strongest buyers of the Myrtleford product and handed one of them a few leaves of tobacco, 'Can you tell me what's wrong with this?' he asked. After carefully inspecting the leaves, the buyer said, 'Well, it's poor quality, immature, badly graded, not properly cured and the leaves are under-sized.' Bill said, 'Is that right? Well why did you just buy it and pay top prices. I just took it out of that bale from Myrtleford.'

BRUCE GEE: Around then everyone was crazy to get into the tobacco business, just like when Nape and Lew were kids. It was like gold-rush fever, but you needed very heavy soil to grow it. McGuinness' and Ferguson's in Wooragee went into it, and they all lost money. It was great casual work for us because we got a bob an hour for hoeing the tobbaco, shifting irrigation, and picking it. Dad and I would return home from picking tobacco covered in sticky, black resin. I think we made about 30 quid between the two of us.

Jack Wadley was born at Wangaratta and raised at Bobinawarrah, Victoria and was a brilliant engineer. He came to Beechworth with his wife Alma in 1940 via Milawa. In the late 1950s Jack, who had known Dad from Zwar's Tannery before the War, got him a job at the Ovens and Murry Benevolent Home for about a year as a general assistant and roustabout. Jack used to run a big steam system up there for heating and cooking. Dad wasn't very well physically or mentally at the time, and the work and Jack's kindly influence was very stabilising for him.

Jack was a genius with anything mechanical. He had a shed at the back of his house in Beechworth full of fascinating contraptions. He built himself a fully functioning metal work lathe. It looked like Big Ben and had hundreds of little wheels spinning around. He could make anything. He made these amazing steam traction engines. If you couldn't obtain a particular metal part for the car or tractor, he would make it for you.

He always looked dapper with a hat and a three piece black suit, with a waistcoat, collar and tie. He was an utterly delightful man. His daughter Doris is a seamstress. She made all the curtains for 'Lyndale' and sewed clothes for Mum and the twins. Today she makes clothes for charitable organisations including the Smith Family. Jack Wadley died in 1983 at the age of 75.

DORIS TURNER [*Jack Wadley's daughter*]: Prior to moving to Beechworth Mum and Dad lived at Milawa where Dad was the boiler attendant at the Butter Factory. His Dad had collected the cream from the farms in the area for the Factory. When they moved to Beechworth Dad worked in the engineer's department and later the boiler-room at Zwar's Tannery until about 1955. He saved the place on more than one occasion from what could have been disastrous fires. One Friday afternoon he hammered frantically on the Main Office door for the manager who at the time was the redoubtable Mr J. J. McCaulay. Dad yelled out, 'There's a fire!' J. J. wasn't interested and didn't even open the door. 'Call back at the office on Monday morning.' Dad replied, 'By Monday there'll be nothing left. The Tannery's ablaze.' On hearing this the door flew open and J.J. raced out, and the Tannery was saved.

Dad spent the next 18 years as a boiler attendant at the Ovens and

Murray Benevolent Home. He cut a fine figure, and always had a pocket fob watch which I had bought him. He was very bright and resourceful, and peered intelligently at people over his glasses. He had made a small traction engine which he sometimes rode down the street, with Mum sitting on the back in a little trolley. He even had his own home lighting plant. I can still see Dad and Allan Gee talking, and Bruce as a child tagging along, a boy listening to man talk. Allan liked nothing better than yarning to Dad in front of the fire for hours about cars and engines.

I was I believe, Australia's only female garbage truck driver. My husband Fred and I collected the garbage at Beechworth, Myrtleford, Chiltern, Yackandandah and Barnawartha. We also collected garbage at Mount Beauty and Bright at one stage. We started in 1967 and finished in 1998, and I was only going to help out for three or four months.

BRUCE GEE: It's interesting that most of Dad's close friends were returned blokes, including many of the migrants in the district. The migrants of course had mostly been on the other side. Dad was often criticised by the stay-at-homes for being, 'friendly with those wogs, Balts, and refos'. Conflict and suffering forged a special bond between them and created a special wisdom. They were worldly guys and had totally shrugged off any small town parochialism.

As well as being in Legacy Dad was also a dedicated Mason. He probably joined when he was in the Navy. The Navy's full of Masons, it's one of the reasons why they're all so close. Slim Hedrick was very high up in the Masons. Dad didn't discuss religion much but he couldn't have been a Mason unless he believed there was a supreme being. (Slim was born in 1911 and died on July 20, 1985.)

Ron Knight was one of Beechworth's great characters. He was always immaculately dressed and a real man about town. He was very suave and distinguished for Beechworth. Ron arrived after the War, and had a heap of medals. He had been a senior officer in the Army, and had seen a lot of action in the Pacific. He was very friendly with Reg Dixon and Jim Kennedy and they were all proud of their service.

Ron had a stunning wife called Val who was English. She was a real star, very pretty, very chic, but she sometimes had young boyfriends to which

Ron seemed to turn a blind eye. Ron was besotted with Val but was quite content to run his pub. He had the constitution of an ox and could drink all night. Val was probably about 30 years old then, and every guy in town was dazzled by her. One day coming home from school in the bus we suddenly saw this young guy, totally naked, running out of the bush with Val, who was also starkers. I thought the bus would tip over as everyone rushed to one side for a better look. Although I was only about nine years old I can tell you it was an unforgettable sight.

Reg Dixon: Ron and Val Knight had an invitation to attend a high society wedding in Melbourne. They were going to stay there for a few days. I saw them just before they left and was surprised to see Val packing their two prized pet goats in the back seat of the station wagon. As it was a very hot morning, I couldn't begin to imagine the smell those wretched goats would create on the drive to Melbourne. After they returned I asked Ron how the trip had gone. 'It was a bit dicey when we got to the Church. We tethered the goats in the front of the Minister's house and they ate all his flowers. When he came out of the service I'm sure I heard him say, 'Oh, bloody hell!'

Bruce Gee: From memory poor, Mrs Robinson was a nurse. She became convinced that she had cancer, although no doctor had made that diagnosis. She apparently decided to kill herself and couldn't bear to leave her four children behind. So she drove them to the Woolshed Falls which are about one hundred feet high. They all got out and she pushed the kids over the Falls then jumped herself. It was a terrible tragedy, and the town was deeply shocked. It was a big story so all the newspapers sent reporters up to Beechworth from Melbourne. Apparently Bruce Grant found them and was very distressed by it.

MG: Trevor Robinson was in our class at Primary School and I remember being told that he died and wouldn't be coming to school anymore. I remember feeling very sad. Mrs Robinson and her children were buried together at the Beechworth Cemetery.

12

MOVING DOWN THE TRACK

An unshakeable survival spirit

The best thing about Bruce leaving home was that I claimed his room, a fibro structure attached to the back verandah. For nine years I had shared a bedroom with Christine which was located opposite our parent's room. The advantages to being out the back were considerable. I could stay up until all hours reading and listening to the radio, sleep with the cat, and smoke. I had purloined one of my parent's ashtrays and routinely pinched cigarettes from them. I would recline on my bed like a midget Marilyn Monroe dragging on these disgusting cigarettes and imagine I was a Hollywood starlet. Sometimes my mother would enter my smoke-filled room and say, 'You haven't been smoking have you?' I would deny the charge, but I once over-heard her saying to Dad, 'I wish Margaret would stop smoking, it's not good for her.' Much to Dad's amusement I later decorated the walls with textured graffiti: 'Make love not war', 'Jimmy Hendrix Forever', 'Tune in, turn on and trip out', and 'I love Paul McCartney'. Dad was a great Beatles fan and and whistled an excellent rendition of 'Yesterday'.

BRUCE GEE: I left Beechworth High when I was aged 16 and moved to Wangaratta High, because I wanted to do a mixed science and humanities course. I boarded in Wang at the hostel for country boys run by the Anglican church. About two thirds of the kids went to Wangaratta Technical School and the rest went to the High School. It is also where I met my future wife Janene Dart. We had two sons Alan and Antony.

One night a group of us decided to climb to the top of the Wangaratta Anglican cathedral. It was a bit of a dare, an initiation rite to climb to the top of the steeple. We thought the ascent would be easy going because they were doing some work on it, and there was scaffolding everywhere. It wasn't difficult, but another night when we were up there, Brother Ted came around with a torch and shone the beam on the steeple. He knew someone was up top but he couldn't pick who. We weren't coming down and he certainly wasn't coming up. We were up there for what seemed like hours until Ted gave up, before we were able to sneak back to the hostel. We almost froze to death. Believe me 130 feet above the ground on a steep slate roof is not a good place to be on a wet wintery Wangaratta evening.

We had a very nice guy supervising us at the hostel called Charlie Helms. They'd had a lot of trouble with maddening teenagers over the years. He sat us all down and said, 'Look we are sick and tired of trying to discipline you kids, so just try and be sensible.' He treated us like adults and to everyone's surprise we responded very well. The Bishop, the Dean, and poor old Brother Ted had trouble coping with this philosophy. It was my first experience of sensible leadership.

The only trouble was that we were hungry all the time. The food was good and plentiful but kids of that age are always starving. We were forever breaking into the kitchen and stealing a bite to eat. To counteract this the kitchen staff removed all the labels from the tins so we had to take pot luck. Peaches were the best because you could slurp down the entire tin in about three minutes. Occasionally you'd rush back to your room only to discover you had nicked a tin of beetroot. We had fires in our rooms, and sometimes we cooked up baked beans. One of my best friends was a terrific guy called David Mott. He was highly artistic and was doing an Arts course at Tech. when he was tragically killed in a hit and run accident.

BRUCE GEE: George French had a paddock on the creek next to ours. The year he died there was hardly any feed for the cattle and our place was as bare as a billiard table. I was home for the weekend from school in Wangaratta and Dad and I noticed that George's paddock had unusually lush grass up to the top of the fence. Nothing had been done about the paddock yet, because there was some delay due to probate. Dad moaned, 'Oh, look at all that beautiful grass in there.' I said, 'Why don't we cut the fence and let our cattle in.' Dad replied, 'I couldn't possibly do that.' What he *meant* was, 'But it's okay if you do, since you don't live here anymore.' I cut the fence and 80 cattle streamed through. We had a very good summer all things considered. We repaired the fence about eight months later when the hole was discovered.

You can't talk about Beechworth and Wooragee without mentioning women like Doreen Blake and Vivienne LeCouteur (Payne). Doreen and Ken Blake ran the local paper, the 'Ovens and Murray Advertiser' for 20 years. Viv was on numerous committees, and to this day plays the organ at the Anglican church. For many years she was the double-bassist in the Music Group. People were sometimes critical of Doreen and Viv but they were strong, capable women who made amazing contributions to the town. They were in everything and knew everybody. In small towns it is very common for people to sit back and criticise, and like anywhere 'the movers and shakers' are an easy target. Viv and Doreen were very public spirited and very nice to Mum and Dad.

According to her son John, Viv's husband Fred died of a heart attack during a heat-wave in 1961. He was only 52 years old. Viv raised their three sons, John, Howard and Geoff. She later married Ron Payne and they live at Wooragee. Ron's mother was the long-serving post-mistress at Wooragee. John and Geoff married and moved away from the area and Howard is with the Anglican Order, the Little Brothers of Francis in NSW.

The Blakes owned and published *The Ovens and Murray Advertiser* from 1960 to 1980. They had bought it from the Laidlaw's who had run it for nearly 20 years.

KEN BLAKE: I was at the *Border Morning Mail* in Albury for four years after doing a printing apprenticeship at Tumbarumba. I then worked at

Narrandera before moving to Beechworth. My wife Doreen was a nurse and learned about newspapers 'on the job'. *The Ovens and Murray Advertiser* is now compiled at Myrtleford and printed at Wangaratta.

At one stage Tom Porritt's father, Andrew owned the other local paper — *The Oven's Register* — before it was amalgamated with the *Advertiser*. Tom worked for me as a printer for 15 years. A lot of people in Beechworth have TV's, washing-machines, refrigerators and televisions that Tom kept running for free. He wrote everything up in his little black book, but he never chased his outstanding debts.

The Porritts owned property in Corowa, and Beechworth. His elder sister Amy who is almost 90 still lives in the original family home. Their young brother Lennie was killed in World War II.

REG DIXON [*former Beechworth Policeman and family friend*]: Tom Porritt and his sister Amy were longtime identities in Beechworth. They lived together in a big old house in the town and had waged war continually against each other. They never interfered with anyone else, were seldom seen in the shopping centre, and never went out socially. They were apparently reasonably well-off but they lived quite frugally.

Tom was an expert fixer of everything mechanical and electrical. The house, front garden and backyard were littered with all sorts of electrical appliances and machinery. Used and old vacuum cleaners, irons, radios, television sets, antennas, refrigerators, washing machines, bicycles, electric wire and cable, spare parts and machinery for anything. It was like a wrecker's junk-yard.

Once I called him to install a television and after he did the job asked him how much I owed him. 'I'll let you know later,' he said, but I never knew him to send anyone an account. I think he just loved fixing things and helping people out. The only punishment his clients had to endure was when he finished his work he loved to sit and talk for hours, smoking his stinking pipe.

I was stationed at Beechworth for over 15 years and either Tom or his sister would frequently call Police to adjudicate on their endless domestic disputes. Tom was certainly no cat lover and it seemed that Amy's innumerable cats were one of the main causes of their conflict.

In one incident he came home late one cold winter's night, stoked up the fire in the kitchen stove, closed the oven door and went to bed. The next morning Amy stormed into his room, 'What did you do that for you bloody bastard? You knew my young of kittens were in the oven to keep warm. I'll get even with you.' Tom was unrepentant. 'They shouldn't be in the bloody oven, it's for roasting food, not bloody cats.' The following morning Tom woke to find that several of his televisions sets had been wrecked with an axe and two new sets, still in their boxes, had been immersed in a bath full of water.

A few days later he arrived home when Amy was out, gathered a heap of her clothing, lit a big fire in the laundry copper and burned the lot. Amy retaliated a week or so later by placing two radio sets Tom was repairing for customers, up a tall tree at the front of the house. Tom said he didn't know how she got up to the top branches as his ladder wouldn't reach within ten feet. He had to climb up two branches higher to get them down. When he recovered the radios, he replaced them with two cats which he somehow managed to secure to the high branches. He waited in anticipation of Amy making the dangerous climb again, but she was too shrewd to capitulate and called the fire brigade to rescue her cats. Tom said, 'I had hoped she would try to scale the tree again and break her bloody neck.' He seemed genuinely disappointed.

Tom arrived at my house early one morning before the Station opened. 'I've lost my wallet and thought it might have been handed into the Police Station', he said. I asked him when he last saw it. 'About a week ago,' he replied. 'I was on a job at Stanley and it just disappeared out of my coat. I don't think anyone there would have pinched it.' He told me there was about two hundred dollars in the wallet.' I said, 'Tom have you been fighting with Amy again?' He answered, 'Every bloody day and night, but that's nothing.'

We headed off to his home where we found Amy in the kitchen. 'Amy, Tom tells me he's lost his wallet, what did you do with it?' I said. Amy replied, 'It's behind the bloody wardrobe. He threatened to pull my cat's teeth out with his pliers. So I hid the pliers and his wallet.' I pulled the wardrobe out, recovered the wallet and told him to check if the money was still intact. It certainly was, close to one thousand dollars. And he didn't just recover the pliers, there were a lot of his missing tools behind the wardrobe as well.

MG: Our family had a love-hate relationship with the legendary Tom Porritt. Whenever we saw his truck or bicycle outside 'Lyndale' we'd groan because we knew we were in for a marathon. Tom would huff and puff his way up the path then pat me on the head and say, 'Hello girlie.' Before I could reply he would head into the lounge-room. His timing was always impeccable. As my father rose from his comfortable lounge chair, Tom would greet him and then with one swift movement plonk himself from where Dad had just risen. He wouldn't budge then for several hours. There was a ritual to conversations with Tom which went something like this.

'So any news up in Beechworth Tom?' 'Nothing Allan, it's as quiet as a mouse.' 'So you've got nothing to tell us then?' 'Nuh, dead as a doornail.' 'Hmmn. There must be something, Tom.' At this point Tom would scratch his shiny pate and the stubble on his chin, painstakingly tap tobacco into the bowl of his pipe, sigh and say, 'Well I did hear, and it's for your ears only that... bird's got a bun in the oven. She's a real jam tart that one is.' 'Go on, who's the father Tom?' 'Well, you never heard it from me but I reckon it's... I was riding my bike around the lake late one night not so long ago and I saw him chock-a-block up her in the back seat of his car. There'll be merry hell when his Missus finds out.'

Several cups of tea, fruitcake and sometimes a bit of dinner later, Tom would rouse himself with much wheezing and spluttering and tackle the television. By this time it would be approaching 11 o'clock. Mum would have gone to bed, and Dad would be slumped in a chair almost obscured by a cloud of Tom's omnipresent pipe smoke. About 1am Tom would nudge Dad awake and say, 'Allan I came down on the bike, any chance of the Missus giving me a lift back to Beechworth.' Mum would usually have to drive 'bloody Tom Porritt' as she called him back in the dead of night. The only way we could ever get the upper hand with old Tom was to ask him about Amy's cats. 'Don't talk to me about those flamin' cats, one of the bastards pissed in my tool box the other day,' he'd grumble.

Phil McQuigan was another colourful character from my childhood. It was only when I was older that I realised just how colourful Phil really was. He was a large man, had a wonderful beaming smile and an engaging personality. Everything about Phil was big, his car, flashy house and swimming pool in Sydney, and his wallet always seemed to be stuffed with bills. We loved Uncle Phil, who was an SP bookmaker, and it was typical of my father not to take the high moral ground about Phil's shady deals. Mum and Dad saw the bigger picture. Phil was loyal and immensely hospitable to friends and family, and generous to people in need. Reg served with him during the war and introduced him to my parents.

REG DIXON: Once Phil, who used to run an SP bookmakers at the back of the Marrickville Hotel, had checked in at the Brighton Beach Hotel. After a stay of three or four days he asked the manager how much was owing. I forget how much it was, but Phil said, 'I don't have any money but I have got a boot-full of toilet rolls, will you accept that? In fact he had even more. The back seat was filled with them as well. The manager replied, 'Oh alright I can always do with toilet paper.'

Phil and Allan Gee once went out to an auction sale at the Bandiana Army camp just out of Wodonga and bid on a few things. Phil ended up with thousands of Army webbing belts, all with brass fittings. He said to Allan, 'I have got to get rid of these webbing belts. We'll have to pile them up and burn them. I can get good money for the brass.' Allan offered to do it at his place, so Phil carted truckloads of these webbing belts out to Allan's and dumped them in his front paddock. Before long there was a massive cloud of black smoke covering the countryside for miles, even though it was an Extreme Fire Danger day.

Fortunately Allan rang me at the police station and told me what was going on, because the Fire Brigade kept ringing me up in a great panic. I told them, 'Don't worry about it, they are just burning off some scrub and a few rubber tyres.' The belts smouldered for days. Allan was a rough and ready diamond and an amazing creature. All he asked for after the war was the love of his wonderful family, his farm at Wooragee and the opportunity to help others in need, though this time he was pushing his luck.

Another of Phil's escapades was when he bought a submarine which was moored in Darling Harbour. This shifty bloke told him he'd make big money because it was loaded with lead, brass and copper ballast. Well Phil was well and truly conned, and paid a lot of money for it. Before long the harbour authorities gave him notice that the derelict submarine had to go. Phil bought some workmen in who stripped out the ballast, but it wasn't lead, brass or copper. It was just rotten old cast-iron, worth absolutely nothing. In the end he had to pay to have the sub taken out to sea and sunk. It cost him heaps.

JOHN LeCOUTEUR [*family friend*]: My grandfather Fred was a former Shire President at Beechworth. My brother Geoff was in the same class as Christine and Margaret at Beechworth High School.

Les Wells owned the property adjoining ours at the Rising Sun, and Gee's place was on the other side of the road. One day Les was moving sheep across the main road from one paddock to the other with his sons John and David. A car came belting down the road at about 70mph and missed the boys but ploughed into the sheep. A number were killed or maimed. Allan didn't hesitate to rush down and help clean up the mess.

Once during a Golden Hills Festival, joy flights were being run as a fund-raiser from Allan's airstrip. On this day two planes were in action when a near tragedy occurred. An Auster came in to land on the strip and struck a rabbit burrow which snapped part of the suspension. The pilot did a brilliant job completing the landing without further mishap. Not surprisingly custom for the flights dropped off dramatically after that.

When Allan's eyesight deterioriated further he was ordered to stop driving. He copped a fair bit of ribbing about being chauffeured around by Kath. In spite of his vision problems, he never complained and was very independent, but the hay-making season was a bit of a challenge. He insisted on mowing his own hay. I did the raking followed by Harry Poyntz on the Fodder Co-Op baler. Because of

Allan's poor eyesight he often missed strips which made it difficult to rake. This sometimes led to heated exchanges. Allan insisted his cuts were straight and it was Harry and I who were blind.

———

MG: In cities one looks forward to the summer, tantalised by the idea of going to the beach, and the swimming pool. Even after all these years of city life I still have an instinctual fear of fires. At our farm when those hot north winds blew we kept the hoses on around the house, had the knapsacks filled, and didn't dare leave the property in case we returned to ashes.

I remember attending a dreadful fire at the back of Tully's cherry orchard in the early 60s on the outskirts of Beechworth. Bruce and Dad were volunteer fire fighters, and Mum, Christine and I went with them this particular day to cut sandwiches for the men. As we prepared tea and snacks they disappeared to fight 'the red steer', an old bush term for a fire which gets away.

It was late afternoon when we raced to the scene of the fire and by nightfall the sky was filled with a terrifying beauty. The surrounding bushland looked like a volcano erupting, with great spires of orange flames and an inferno of sparks and red embers. The noise of the trees exploding was cacophonous, and I felt as if the heat would melt us like candles. The men appeared as stick figures beating back a giant dragon lashing at them with a fiery tongue. Suddenly the wind changed, and the fire switched back towards us. All hell broke loose as we scrambled into cars and trucks and fled for our lives.

Calamitous bush fires in Beechworth

The town and district on Christmas Day, and the days before and after, were terrorised by disastrous bush fires. One fire ignited at Everton on Wednesday week when a Chinaman, endeavouring to smoke a rabbit from a log, set fire to the grass. The Chinaman was old and feeble and unable to cope with the flames, which spread with great rapidity, and soon encompassed an extensive area as it sped towards Sebastopol. This fire burnt briskly on Thursday and Friday, when dense clouds of smoke could be seen from Beechworth and where little heed was paid to the outbreak.

Almost simultaneously another fire was observed near Mr George William's paddock at Bald Rock, six miles from Beechworth. Near the Chiltern Road, Messers George and John French, J. McFeeters, H. Stalker and others in that locality went out at daybreak to combat this fire.

All Thursday and Friday they laboured, and throughout Friday night and Saturday morning. Mr B. Roper manager of the Asylum farm at Wooragee, sent word to the Asylum authorities and three men were promptly despatched to assist. When all chance of saving the farmhouse seemed gone, Mrs Roper and the children were driven off in a wagonette and although great damage resulted to the farm buildings and fences, the house itself was not consumed.

On Saturday morning accompanied by several young men Mr Peter Birtles went from Wooragee to a point 3.5 miles beyond the Asylum farm. In the early morning there was little wind, but towards noon it blew in a perfect hurricane and the brave little band ran for their horses and galloped before the flames for their lives. But fast though they sped the flames were in Wooragee when they arrived. Mr McGuinness' crop, and Murrays, Ropers, McFeeters, and Birtles' grass paddocks were all ablaze. Mr Birtles galloped into Beechworth, and as the trees on either side of the road up to the old 'Rising Sun' hotel were all on fire, his ride was a trying one. He arrived in Beechworth almost speechless.

Inspector Sainsbury promptly engaged all Crawford and Co's and Phillip's drags and the town crier called for volunteers. (A 'drag' was a horse-drawn covered wagon.) The temperature was then 103 degrees in the shade. Tradespeople were busy with Christmas, but when the seriousness of the situation was realised, the drags were filled with volunteers.

Harry Porter, reporter for the Ovens & Murray Advertiser, was one of the first to set out on horseback and upon arrival at Mr John Brewer's farm, met a number of vehicles filled with crying women and children who had hurried away for safety. At Brewer's 'Stone House', on the Beechworth Road, a wagonette packed with harnesses and the more portable and valuable of the household goods stood ready for flight. Despite the warning that the road was impassable, our reporter and Messrs J.H. Delphin, J. Vines, E.H. Coombes, and T. Brunning pushed on, the last four named being in a buggy.

Harry Porter overtook Mr Chatfield, an aged wood carter, whom he persuaded to return to Beechworth. Riding on he met Mr J. Newey. An attempt was made to check the fire at this point, and to save Brewers. This was accomplished subsequently by the Beechworth volunteers.

The old 'Rising Sun' hotel was then burning, and Mr Newey and our reporter galloped past the burning building into the paddock to save the cattle and sheep. The scene in the thickly timbered paddock was one of awful grandeur.

Immense trees had no sooner ignited than their limbs came crashing to the ground. Opossums and rabbits, shockingly blinded and burned, could be seen on all sides, and birds fell, suffocated to the ground. The heat was awful. The clouds of smoke and ashes filled the air and almost blinded the men and horses. The sheep had all run into a swamp where they huddled together.

Pushing on towards Wooragee, our reporter met Mr Fulford of Yackandandah, who had a narrow escape when riding through Magpie Lane past Chatfields farm (opposite 'Lyndale' and now owned by George Johnstone). The fences and trees on either side were on fire in front of him. Finding his retreat blocked, he galloped his horse through and his coat was burnt off his back.

Mr J. McFeeter's house was burnt to the ground and Mr B. Murray's soon followed. At Mr J. McGuinness' and G. French's almost superhuman efforts saved the houses, but all outbuildings were consumed, as well as several pigs.

Mr McGuinness lost 84 acres of crops which had just been stooked. At Mr J. French's several pigs were roasted in their sty, and Mr French who had been beating the flames for 14 hours, narrowly escaped the same fate in trying to liberate them as the smoke overpowered him.

He was only saved with difficulty by Mrs French, and a man who dragged him to a place of safety. Mr John Smith was burnt out, and Peter Birtle's ornamental hedges were ruined, but the house and outbuildings were saved.

Mr Birtles lost 2000 acres of grass and a great amount of fencing. At the Post Office the fire was defeated only at the back door. The Misses Nall in the next house had an anxious time before their mother, who lay ill in bed, was removed to safety

An idea of the panic which prevailed may be gathered from the fact that mothers ran from their homes to waterholes on ploughed fields. They remained there with their children, in some cases for hours, until the danger passed.

The fire burnt Mr John Brewer's farmhouse, grass and fences, also the old wooden bridge in the lane. Mr Brewer was milking 52 cows and his loss of grass is of grave concern. This was one of three houses John Brewer owned in Wooragee.

But the saddest incident of the catastrophe was that in which John Elliott, the 15

*year old son of Mr William Elliott, the well known farmer, lost his life. The
lad galloped off to release a number of cows from a bush paddock. His father is
one of the largest suppliers to the Wooragee Butter Factory. The lad had turned
out all the cows, except two, before they were smothered by the flames.*

*After burning considerable grass and fencing in Mr H. Poyntz's back paddock,
the wind which still blew with terrific force at 6.00pm brought the fire through
Newey's to the farm of Mr M. Maloney, a well known exhibitor at district shows.
Here 20 men including the railway fettlers on the Yackandandah line saved
the house and orchard.*

*After crossing Mr Birtle's large hill paddock, the fire overtook and roasted, hares
and rabbits that fled as it approached the bark houses and worksheds of the
Chinese miners.*

*Careering up the northern end of Magpie Creek, four large bark houses and
storerooms owned by some aged Chinese gardeners were demolished. The poor
fellows left with only a few boxes and blankets passed the night under a pear tree.
They were without food and even their planted vegetables were dried up in their
beds and the fruit roasted on the trees.*

FROM THE *OVENS REGISTER* DECEMBER 30, 1899. ABSTRACTED BY ALAN FRENCH

ALAN FRENCH [*family friend*]: The old fire fighters like Dick
Nankervis were different. They fought the fires by geography. They
knew about weather conditions and when the wind was likely to
change. They knew the topography of the country, and that a fire
would burn quickly up a hill and slow down when it got over the top.
They invariably stopped the fire by raking breaks using the sheep tracks
around the hills as a starting point. Sheep always go around the
contour of a hill. That's the easiest place to rake the grass away, leaving
the bare earth so the fire can't take a hold. Raking is done in advance of
the fire, then a break is burned back towards the fire.

I have an old knapsack in the shed which I first used in the 1940 fire
in Leneva. My mother wrote my name in pencil on the bottom of the
knapsack before I went off to fight the fire.

The big fires sometimes burned for up to a week. We always
reckoned they weren't safe until it rained, because often the stumps
were still burning, and the scrub roots were still alight underground.

At any point it could all flare up again.

Back in the 1920s and 30s with so much native grass around, wallaby and kangaroo grass, a big fire was very dangerous. The native grasses loved to burn. We used to burn off around the roads at Wooragee. If you got a shower of rain there'd be green grass a foot high in about a fortnight. With thick clover that high, you have terrible trouble putting a fire out because it will burn underneath. When you put water on it, you'll only wet the top. We had to use rakes to get it out. The only way you can stop a clover fire is to get behind it and drench it with water from the back. The problem is that taking the water tanker to the back of the fire, can be quite hazardous.

Funnily enough old Dick and Bert Nankervis used to unintentionally burn us out almost every year. They would come over, throw a match into the rushes to clear them out, then go home. They'd forget about it and the next thing it would be blazing away in our paddock. Dick was one of the greatest fire fighters we ever had, but he was a bit of a firebug. He also used to drive from Beechworth down to Wooragee in his old Vauxhall car with the dogs in the back, then he'd ride his horse around the paddocks. He'd see about 100 rabbits go into a blackberry bush so he would chuck a lighted match in and we'd have to put the fire out. He'd be back in Beechworth and we'd still be frantically beating out his fire.

I remember one very hot day in 1940 when a fire came in by Edney's at Leneva West. We saved their house, but then I saw the most incredible thing, something I'll probably never see again. Green Hill as they called it in those days was full of green timber right up to behind Charlie Boyes' place. We managed to head the fire off at the top over the creek, but while we were there, it crossed the peak of the hill and got into Leneva.

Somewhere up behind Jack Elliott's the whole hill on the opposite side of the valley just exploded. It was like a bomb going off. I can still see it. All of a sudden the hill went 'boom' and you could see all these traceries of dust and smoke. The eucalptus oil had created a firestorm which blew all the leaves off the fruit trees. There were just red burning skeletons of trees and smoke everywhere.

ALLAN BREWER [*Auntie Miriam and Uncle Bert's son*]: I was lucky to be born when I was. I caught the end of the horse era, and the remarkable people associated with that time, including my grandparents Clara and Arthur Brewer and Alice and Napier Gee. I did a man's work from the age of ten. Stock work, working in dairies, hay-carting, and cutting chaff. You didn't need the money then which you need today to run a property. My grandparents and their families more or less lived off the land. The drovers, and stockmen, and old style farmers have just about died out.

I was the Executive Officer of The Mountain Cattleman's Association for five years up until 1997. The mountain cattlemen are part of Australian folklore. The primary aim of the organisation is to look after members rights in regard to their cattle grazing leases. My wife Marian and I have a 5,000 acre bush lease next to our own freehold property. I live every mountain cattleman's dream.

I was almost killed by a stallion in 1991 when I went to shift some cattle at a property I had leased down on the Murray River. I had a young bloke working for me, but he was away at the time and he'd taken the dogs. I'd never ridden the particular horse I was riding that day in the same paddock where this stallion was.

He raced out from amongst a group of mares and came towards me. I cracked the whip a couple of times, and I thought, 'Hell, you're not going to stop.' There was an opening in the fence at the river's edge. I thought if I can get down there I can escape. The horse I was on was a good swimmer. The stallion galloped up behind me and I couldn't stop him from coming in under the whip. He was biting at the other horse and grabbed me by the leg. He sank his teeth into my thigh and ripped off one side of it. If he'd gone for my arm, I reckon he would have pulled it out of its' socket. He wouldn't let go of my leg. I swapped the whip from my right to my left hand, and changed the reins over. Then I turned my horse into him and belted him in the eye with the whip handle.

I galloped over to the crossing, which was quite deep water and the bastard kept coming after me. I have no doubt this stallion was trying to kill me. I was battling to get away from him for half an hour. The old boss mare saved my life. She galloped over and took him away, and I escaped. I had high leather boots on and the blood was gushing over the top of them. I cut off my shirt sleeves with a pocket knife. I used one for a tourniquet, and stuffed the other sleeve into the wound. It took me an hour to get back to the house. I knew if I stopped for a moment I'd be dead from blood loss and shock. I was in hospital for two weeks, and came close to losing my leg. When I recovered my good friend Rusty Connley shot the stallion, who was called 'Reflection'.

We'll be back

by ALLAN BREWER

They are missing from the mountains
These men who blazed our trails
Gone forever is our mountain heritage
With it's folklore and it's tales
Now we have a new breed of mountain folk
Greenies is their brand
How they fooled the politicians
To close these grazing lands
Sadly nought but National Parks
Is what they crave, and that's enough
To make the man from Snowy River
Turn right over in his grave.
Take a man like Wally Ryder
Who lives near Mongan's Bridge
Wally knows and understands the mountains
Every gully, every ridge
But they drove him from the Bogong
And now they'll drive him from the plains
In caring for the mountains
Once men like Wally leave
Just who will hold the reins
Down by Glen Wills Side nestles Shannon Vale
For three generations Fitzgerald cattle
Have grazed their mountain lease

Every hill and dale
But from his father's lease
Benny couldn't part
And as that closing date grew near
It broke poor Benny's heart
Yes their mountain huts are all deserted
And the breeding herds have all but disappeared
There's a shortage now of good baldy cattle
'Tis just as we all feared
For the closing of these mountain leases
Is plain selfishness and greed
There's tourists tramping on the creek flats
Where the cattle used to feed
But our mountain cattlemen
We know someday they'll be back
And the mountain tops once more will echo
To the bellowing of cattle
And the greenhide stock whips crack
Yes these mountain pioneers
In their saddles they ride tall
So I beg you fellow countrymen
Stand up and salute them all

'BURRADOO', KOETONG, VICTORIA

MG: Dad regularly attended the sheep and cattle sales in Wodonga. Twice a year he purchased a young pig. There was great excitement when the truck from the sale yards turned up. The driver would honk the horn and we'd run out. 'The pig's here, let's go and see the pig. What'll we call him?' We gave them all the original name of Porky and became extremely attached to them. We patted and stroked their bellies with sticks, and laughed at their antics in the mud. When you're nine or ten years old animals are much more fun than boys.

At every meal we ate some sort of meat, accompanied by vegetables.

Bacon and eggs for breakfast, assorted cold meats and salad for lunch, and beef, pork, lamb or chicken for dinner for as long as I can remember. We rarely ate fish. Occasionally someone would give us red-fin or Murray cod. We pleaded with Dad not to kill the pig. 'Can't he live? It's cruel, how can we kill him? He trusts us so much.' Dad felt terrible about it too, but money was scarce and he believed that he had to get on with the job of providing food for the family.

The morning of the pig kill I'd wake up with a terrible sense of despair and entreat Dad, on behalf of Porky, for a last minute reprieve. Dad's response was predictable. 'In a couple of days you'll be eating the crackling on delicious pork chops, and you'll have completely forgotten about Porky.'

Dad was usually assisted in this grisly task by Gordon 'Jet' Jackson, the head gardener at the Mental Hospital. Jet supplied our family with a sugar bag of veg from the looney bin for years. Dad would joke with Jet. 'Where did all those beautiful vegetables come from?' Jet would reply, 'Dunno Allan, they must have fallen off the back of a truck.' Jet and his wife Dot had three daughters of their own and they fostered four aboriginal children.

As the morning wore on they decided to get on with the pig kill before Jet had one too many beers. 'Come on Jet if you have another bottle you'll shoot me instead of the pig,' Dad would say as they walked over to the pig's sty. Animals always sense danger, and the doomed pig would start to whimper. At this point I would run inside with my fingers stuffed into my ears trying not to hear the fatal shot.

While Dad pinned the pig against the fence Jet or Bruce would shoot it in the head. Within seconds the poor pig would be on the ground soaked in its' own blood. In the meantime Mum and Jet's wife Dot would have filled an old tin bath in the backyard with boiling water. The pig was dropped in and soaked for a while before they removed its bristles with a wire brush.

A couple of hours later the gleaming pink carcase would be thrown onto a table and each family would carve up their side of our former pet. Our portion was stacked into the freezer which unfortunately was in my bedroom.

BRUCE GEE: Some of the pigs we had thought they were dogs because they were their only role models. They even used to chase the cattle with the dogs. Believe me until you've seen a pig snapping at a cow's heels you haven't lived. The trouble was, sooner or later they had to go into the freezer.

In my early 20s I came back from Melbourne to the farm for a weekend to find Lew and Dad lined up to kill a pig. It was really sad because the pig was looking at us like a human being, knowing something was up. The most humane way to kill a pig is to shoot it in the head. Dad said, 'It's time to kill the pig.' I went to the house and brought back the .22 rifle and loaded it. The pig was up against the fence and I was taking aim when Dad interjected. 'No, no you won't hit it from there.' He grabbed the gun off me, blind as a bat of course, walked over and put the muzzle about an inch from the pig's head and shot it in the end of the nose. You've never heard a scream like it. The pig went berserk. In the meantime, Dad was fumbling and trying to re-load the gun. The poor pig was running around like a maniac, and there was blood everywhere. Dad as usual was panicking, as he did in moments of stress, and screamed out, 'Give me another bullet, give me another bullet!' I wrenched the gun off him, slammed in a round and dropped the pig from 20 feet.

~

MG: I helped my father kill many animals, mainly on Friday afternoons. It is a gruesome aspect of farm life, but we had to eat. Dad killed sheep just on dusk because it was still light enough to see to get the animals into the yards, but the cooler air kept the flies away, especially in summer. 'Round em up, round em up, steady on, stay back boy,' my father commanded the yelping dogs as we watched the mob of sheep jostling against each other, eyes and nostrils flared with fear.

'Pick one out lovey. A fat juicy one. Hurry up before it gets dark,' Dad would say to me smiling with those watery blue eyes. We'd drag a protesting sheep across the yard and hoist it up onto the wooden floor of the shearing shed. No talk, and the dogs lay low and didn't bark. Dad would throw it on its' back and prop it up between his legs. The neck would be shoved hard against his thigh, then he'd pull up the chin and slash the sheep's throat with a razor sharp knife.

For an instant the sheep would go into shock, and then have one last kick as the blood flooded out of the wound. 'Killing's a terrible thing. Poor old sheepie.' Dad then hacked into the stomach, fanning open the rib cage, and pulled out the liver, heart and kidneys which he handed to me to put into the bucket. The tongue got the chop next, which he'd toss to the dogs. 'Here boy, here's your supper.'

Dad and I agreed that the dogs were worse than the flies when we killed. They darted and snapped at the fresh meat, and Dad would roar at them, 'Get to buggery, there'll be plenty for you later.' I was always amazed that with his almost total blindness my father cut his way around the sheep like a surgeon. 'Your Uncle Lew taught me how to kill a sheep. I've done lots of killing. Killed lots of Japs too.' Dad was a bit of a stirrer, and when strangers asked him what he did he relished in telling them, 'I'm a killer, a hired assassin, that's what I was trained to do.'

MG: A popular pastime in late spring and early summer was for groups of yahoos, as my parents called them, to grab the old man's rifle and go snake hunting. They seemed to see this as a curious rite of passage. It has always baffled me why many Australian's fear Africa for its' snakes, when nine out of the ten deadliest snakes in the world live here. North-Eastern Victoria is literally crawling with them. Browns, blacks, and the occasional tiger snake showed up in Wooragee.

A favourite schoolfriend of mine, David McIntyre from the booming metropolis of Back Creek, nestled in the picturesque Kiewa River Valley told me he frequently killed half a dozen tiger snakes during the two mile walk to the school bus stop. 'There's usually one waiting on the front step of our house, and several along the road. They're everywhere. My shoulder's sore from whacking them.' David's sister Robyn, a gifted artist, was a close friend of ours.

My uncle Lew was bitten by a black snake one afternoon when he was collecting eggs. I'll never forget his laconic response. 'I felt pretty crook for a couple of days. Bloody thing bit me hand when I reached into the nest. Nothin' to worry about though. I had a cuppa and a lie down when I got home. There's no point seeing the doctor. He wouldn't know what to do with a snake bite if one bit him on the bum.'

But the snake story which remains the most vivid for me, was when my mother took on a big brown one hot summer's day. We always knew at Wooragee which days were going to be real scorchers because of the stillness when you woke up. Not a breath of wind, and no birdsong except perhaps the plaintive caw of a crow. The dogs were already listless on the verandah, moving only to snap at a blowfly. Baking heat sizzled the garden, and we waited inside dreading any news of a bushfire, or that the water pump half a mile away at the creek had broken down. Dad, 'It would be just our luck today if that rotten pump breaks down. The last thing I feel like doing is getting that thing going today. One spark from a cigarette butt and the whole place would go up.'

In a vain attempt to keep a few patches of the lawn green, Christine and I regularly rotated the sprinklers, darting in and out of the spray in our bathers. One of our favourite games was to pretend that the lawn was a gigantic blue swimming pool complete with a diving board at the deep end, and a toddler's pool. We would lie on the lawn on our stomachs and have swimming races and fantasise that we had a kiosk which sold ice-cream, chips and Fanta.

This particular summer's day Dad was travelling in outback Queensland buying cattle, so there was only Christine, my mother and I at home. Bruce was away at school in Wangaratta. Mum was hanging washing on the clothes line at the back of the house, when she suddenly screamed at us, 'Get inside, go now, inside quickly!' We yelled from 'the pool' out front, 'What's wrong, why do we have to go inside?' 'Don't argue with me. Just this once, for God's sake do as you're told. Go inside and shut the door.'

Christine and I were perplexed as to why she sounded so angry. We rushed to the kitchen window and soon saw what all the fuss was about. Near the water tap was a large brown snake rearing up as my mother circled, never taking her eyes off it. She cried, 'Get back you bastard, get back, get back,' over and over, waiting for the moment to crack its' back with the length of fencing wire she wielded like a whip.

Even the two dogs got into the act, darting towards the snake, growling and snarling, until called back by my mother's firm commands, 'Red, stay back boy, go back'. The last thing she wanted was a tangle of dogs and snake. Many a fine farm dog dies from being bitten on the nose.

This harrowing confrontation seemed to go on for ages, and we cheered Mum on from the safety of the kitchen window. 'Be careful Mum, be careful. Get 'im, get 'im. Watch him.' The snake played her like a fish, and more than once when it reared I thought she would be struck. Thwack. Thwack. 'I've got you. I've got you, you bastard I've got you.' Suddenly it was all over. Even the dogs yelped for joy. We ran out to hug Mum who was red-faced, and soaked with sweat from the heat and strain of her duel with the snake.

When Dad arrived back from his trip, and asked for all the news, Mum casually told him, 'Things have been fairly quiet, but yesterday I killed a six foot brown snake.' Dad was shocked but very proud of her, as we were.

～～

MG: I know now that my father had Post Traumatic Stress Disorder. As a child one picks up tidbits of information, usually from eavesdropping. My mother told me a few things, but mostly they were fairly private about Dad's problems from the War. I knew that they had consulted people at Veterans' Affairs, and Dad had told me that he was assessed by a psychiatrist. I think they told him that things would be pretty difficult for a while.

The farm had a very stabilising influence on him, and my mother's love and care was a great comfort and almost certainly extended his life. Having a family gave him something to live for, but he was still plagued with anxiety. He took a variety of tranquillisers and sedatives, including Mogadon for at least twenty years, and also Amytal and Serepax.

When he tried to go off the sleeping tablets he had terrible night-mares. He consulted a sleep specialist who told him he could never go off them, although we eventually rid him of that dependency. When he first went off Mogadon cold turkey he had terrible withdrawal symptoms including hallucinations and claimed he was seeing snakes, and little men coming out of the walls.

AUNTIE MARGE SCHUBERT: Reg's manic depression first appeared when he was in his 20s. There's quite a bit of it in the Brewer family. Bert and Reg were both treated for manic depression at Mayday Hills Hospital, Beechworth. Years ago people didn't talk about mental illness, it was a subject which was 'put in the cupboard'. Poor dear Reg suffered the most, and I don't know how his wife Kath managed with seven children to look after. She is incredibly hard working, an amazing woman.

I think Dad's brother Richard may have suffered from it as well. He was married and had two sons and two daughters, including a set of fraternal twins. The other children were Ella and Randall. He died on May 5, 1919 aged 41 — of influenza — and is buried in the Albury Cemetery (1919 was the year of the world-wide flu epidemic which killed 20 million people). I remember his wife Sarah (Jarvis). She lived in Albury and wore little gold earrings.

Eulogy: Reginald Bernard Brewer

Reginald Bernard Brewer was born at Leneva on December 2, 1921, the son of the late Arthur Randall Brewer and Clara May Brewer. He was the fifth child in a family of nine being Arthur, Marjorie, Bert, Frank, Reg, Gwen, Mary, Kath and Ted.

As a young boy he grew up in Leneva and went to the Leneva West State School. On leaving school, he worked hard on the family farm.

Reg was a great lover of cards, such as crib, euchre and 500. He was the Captain of the Leneva Table Tennis team, and played in the Albury Association for many years with a lot of success.

Reg married Kathleen Schneider, and they lived for a time at 'Pinedale' until they built their home, 'Green Valley'. They had seven children. Lawrence, Kenneth, Regina, Patricia, Bernice and the twins Donald and Wendy-Lee.

He belonged to the Leneva Bushfire Brigade, and joined in all community work in the district. He was a caring man, and if anyone was in trouble would be the first to offer to help. Reg was a battler all his life. He battled fires and droughts to scratch out a living on the farm.

JUNE 24, 1995

~~~~

MG: For most Australians, Christmas is at odds with the snowy scenes depicted on Northern Hemisphere greeting cards. Christmas Day at 'Lyndale' was invariably a scorcher and the morning was a flurry of attending church, unwrapping gifts and tumult in the kitchen. Without fail, Peg and Bill McGuinness arrived at about 11am with a jar of fresh cream from their dairy and we'd all sit in the lounge-room munching peanuts and having a festive drink. By about 2pm Mum would become a bit flustered as the roast duck started to sizzle in the oven. 'I wish they'd go,' she'd mutter in the kitchen as Dad poured Peg and Bill another beer. One year after enthusiastically farewelling the McGuinness' we came inside to find Tootsie the cat gorging on the duck. We never sat down for Christmas lunch until about 3pm, then we'd retire to bed to sleep off the heat and gluttony.

Mum's Christmas Cake

1 cup sultanas

2 cups raisins

1 cup currants

1 cup mixed dried fruit

½ cup (125ml) well-drained unsweetened pineapple pieces

½ cup pitted dates

1 ½ teaspoon mixed spice

2 teaspoons nutmeg

½ cup (125ml) brandy

2 ½ cups (625ml) fresh orange or unsweetened pineapple juice

juice ½ lemon

3 egg whites, stiffly beaten

3 ½ cups wholemeal self-raising flour, sifted

1. Preheat oven to 190°C (375°F).
2. Place fruit, spices, brandy, orange and lemon juices in a saucepan. Slowly bring to the boil. Reduce heat, cover and simmer for 5 minutes. Allow to cool.
3. Fold in egg whites and stir in flour.
4. Pour mixture into a 22 cm square or round non-stick tin, lined with baking paper. Cover top of cake with foil and bake for 1 hour. Remove foil and bake for a further 30 minutes. Allow to cool in tin. In warmer weather, store in the refrigerator.

My father survived three heart attacks in his 50s and and after quitting smoking and adopting a Pritikin style low-fat, low carbonhydrate diet his health was excellent, but sadly prostate cancer claimed him.

In 1993, the year after my father died, I published a compilation of quotes by people about their fathers titled *Memories Of My Father*. I wrote then:

In October my father Allan Howard Gee would have been 73 years old.

This handsome, rough diamond, farmer, Navy and POW man played a pivotal role in my life. I loved his incredible sense of humour, tenacity, irreverant nature, intense loyalty to his family, respect for wild creatures, and compassion for others. His many words of wisdom included, 'To err is human, to forgive is divine.' Dad's generosity was overwhelming, not just in material help, but in time, advice, encouragement, and unconditional love.

He emerged from World War II aged 26, beaten but not broken. This big-hearted man clung to his dream of having his own property and living off the land as he had as a young boy in his beloved Silver Creek. I have never met anyone with such an unshakeable survival spirit, so when he decided with my mother Kath, to make a go of running a sheep and cattle farm at Wooragee their dream was realised.

The English author Martin Amis says in his memoir 'Experience', published in 2000. 'Mothers, fathers, aren't supposed to change, any more than they are supposed to leave, or die. They must not do that.'

Extract of Eulogy for Kath (Gee) Davies
who passed away on November 9, 1999

Kath grew up in Leneva, Victoria into a generation where devotion to husband and family was everything. She also embraced a changing world and was a fervent believer in women being well educated, confident and economically independent. Mum excelled at school and revealed her astute business acumen when she helped run 'Lyndale' for almost 30 years. She never strayed from her entrenched values of devotion to the family, and was sustained by her Christian faith. But we remember her for her passion for life and for sometimes, more than we were comfortable with, putting others before herself. Forever after we will raise a glass (almost certainly the Perth reunion commemorative glasses) to you and Dad and quote our favourite family toast, 'Happy days and nights'. Amen.

Age shall not weary them
Nor the years condemn,
At the going down of the sun
And in the morning
We will remember them

LAWRENCE BINYON

BIBLIOGRAPHY

References

Bradley, Ken. *Hellfire Pass Memorial Thailand-Burma Railway*. Sixth edition, updated by Rod Beattie, Australian-Thai Chamber of Commerce, 1998.

Chalker, Jack. *Burma Railway Artist*. Penguin, London, 1994.

Gibbney, H.J. *Eurobodalla: History of the Moruya District*. Library of Australian History, Sydney, 1989.

Harvey, Roy C.A. *Background to Beechworth*. Beechworth and District Progress Association, 1952.

Holmes, L.F. *The Ship's Bugler*. Naval Historical Review. September 1974.

Jones, Howard C. *A Baranduda History*. 1992.

McGaffin, Roy. *Leneva State School Centenary 1875-1975*.

McKie, Ronald. *Proud Echo*. Angus & Robertson, 1953.

Packer, Pat R. *A History of St Francis Bethanga*. 1992.

Payne, Alan. *H.M.A.S. Perth*. The Naval Historical Society of Australia, 1978.

Philipp, June. *The Making of a Mining Community: Bethanga, Victoria 1875-1885*. Latrobe University, Melbourne, April 1977.

Philipp, June. *Early Days in Bethanga and Springfield*. Latrobe University, Melbourne.

Rivett, Rohan. *Behind Bamboo*. Angus & Robertson, Sydney, 1946.

Roberts, Rowland G. *Age Shall Not Weary Them*. Patterson's Printing Press Ltd, Perth.

Shennan, M. Rosalyn. *Silver Threads and Golden Needles – The Early History of Silver Creek, Beechworth*. First edition, 1985.

Whitecross, R.H. *Slaves Of The Son Of Heaven*. Dymock's Book Arcade Ltd, Sydney, 1953.

Whiting, Brendan. *Ship of Courage*. Allen & Unwin, Sydney, 1994.

Additional sources and recommended reading

Bancroft, A. and Roberts, R.G. *The Mikado's Guests*. Perth.

Blair, Joan and Clay Jr. *Return from the River Kwai*. Simon and Schuster, New York, 1979.

Burchell, David. *The Bells of Sunda Strait*. Rigby, London, 1971.

Cassells, Vic. *For Those In Peril*. Kangaroo Press, Sydney, 1995.

Cassells, Vic. *Shipmates*. Paradise Point, Queensland, 1998.

Clarke, Hugh V. *A Life For Every Sleeper*. Allen & Unwin, Sydney, 1986.

Gill, G. Hermon. *Royal Australian Navy 1939-1942, Volume I*. Australian War Memorial, Canberra, 1957.

Jones, T.M. and Idriess, Ion L. *The Silent Service – Action Stories of the Anzac Navy*. Angus & Robertson, Sydney, 1944.

Nelson, Hank. *Prisoners of War*. ABC Enterprises, Sydney, 1985.

Parkin, Ray. *Wartime Trilogy*. Melbourne University Press, Melbourne, 1999.

Wall, Don. *Heroes At Sea*. Published by D. Wall, Mona Vale, NSW, 1991.